Italian and Itali.

Stanislao G. Pugliese
Hofstra University
Series Editor

This publishing initiative seeks to bring the latest scholarship in Italian and Italian American history, literature, cinema, and cultural studies to a large audience of specialists, general readers, and students. I&IAS will feature works on modern Italy (Renaissance to the present) and Italian American culture and society by established scholars as well as new voices in the academy. This endeavor will help to shape the evolving fields of Italian and Italian American Studies by re-emphasizing the connection between the two. The following editorial board consists of esteemed senior scholars who act as advisors to the series editor.

The Legacy of the Italian Resistance

Philip Cooke

Nov '23

To Ian,

The Resistance Continues!

Phil

palgrave
macmillan

First published in hardcover in 2011 by PALGRAVE MACMILLAN® in the United States - a division of St. Martin's Press LLC, 175 Fifth Avenue, New York, NY 10010.

Where this book is distributed in the UK, Europe and the rest of the world, this is by Palgrave Macmillan, a division of Macmillan Publishers Limited, registered in England, company number 785998, of Houndmills, Basingstoke, Hampshire RG21 6XS.

Palgrave Macmillan is the global academic imprint of the above companies and has companies and representatives throughout the world.

Palgrave® and Macmillan® are registered trademarks in the United States, the United Kingdom, Europe and other countries.

ISBN: 978-1-137-33125-0

The Library of Congress has cataloged the hardcover edition as follows:

Cooke, Philip E., 1965–
    The legacy of the Italian Resistance / by Philip Cooke.
        p. cm. – (Italian & Italian American studies series)
    Includes bibliographical references.
    ISBN 978-0-230-11410-4 (hardback)
    1. World War, 1939–1945—Underground movements—Italy—Public opinion.
2. World War, 1939–1945—Underground movements—Italy—Historiography. 3. Anti-fascist movements—Italy—History—20th century. 4. Politics and culture—Italy. 5. Popular culture—Italy. 6. Memory—Social aspects—Italy. 7. Public opinion—Italy. 8. Italy—Politics and government—1945–1976. 9. Italy—Politics and government—1976–1994. 10. Italy—Politics and government—1994– I. Title.

D802.I8C589 2011
    940.53'45—dc22   2011000522

A catalogue record of the book is available from the British Library.

This book is printed on paper suitable for recycling and made from fully managed and sustained forest sources. Logging, pulping and manufacturing processes are expected to conform to the environmental regulations of the country of origin.

Design by Scribe Inc.

First PALGRAVE MACMILLAN paperback edition: May 2013

10 9 8 7 6 5 4 3 2 1

For Elena and Danny

"Tell me, Daddy. What is the use of history?"

—Marc Bloch, *The Historian's Craft*

Contents

Illustrations

Acknowledgments

This book has been a very long time in preparation, and during the course of my research I have accumulated many debts that I hope, in the main, to have repaid. I would like to thank those organizations whose financial generosity has been crucial in facilitating the research and allowing me the time to write it up: above all the Arts and Humanities Research Council whose Research Leave Scheme enabled me to dedicate a sustained period of time to the project during the 2008–2009 academic year. Other grants over the years from the British Academy, the Carnegie Trust for the Universities of Scotland, the Royal Society of Edinburgh and the University of Strathclyde have allowed me to build up a vast bank of materials. I was very fortunate to have been given Visiting Fellow status at the University of Pisa in the first half of 2009. During his own leave of absence, Paolo Pezzino gave me access to his office as well as strict instructions to write, to use the excellent library of the history department, and the splendid facility that is the library of the Scuola Normale Superiore. I am particularly grateful to him and to his colleagues at Pisa, especially Luca Baldissara, for the congenial company and the ideal working facilities. Likewise my colleagues at Strathclyde, Joe Farrell and Andrew Wilkin, as well as Jon Usher at Edinburgh, have been enormously supportive of my work, especially when times have been hard. I must also mention libraries in Italy and the UK that have been invaluable: above all the Biblioteca Nazionale Centrale in Florence, whose staff have been unfailingly helpful to me over the years, the National Library of Scotland (NLS) and the libraries of the Universities of Strathclyde, Glasgow, and Edinburgh. At the NLS, Chris Taylor has been especially helpful, expanding an already extensive Italian collection that will, I hope, continue to serve scholars in the years to come. I have been fortunate to have been assisted by the staff of a number of Resistance Institutes in Italy, particularly in Florence, and at Reggio Emilia. But I would also like to record my gratitude to the staff of the National Institute in Milan, where my research into the Resistance began over 20 years ago. I would also like to thank those many friends, in Milan (Cathy Roblin), Florence (Karen McLachlan), Arezzo (Luca Calugi), and London (Robert Mather) who have generously provided accommodation and, of course, sustenance on my many visits. Anna Teicher has also kindly made her flat in the Oltrarno available to me more times than I can remember. Many colleagues have given up precious time to read draft chapters of this book. I hope to have forgotten no one, but I am most grateful to Stephen Gundle, David Ellwood, Mark Thompson, Robert Gordon, Guido Bonsaver, Jonathan Dunnage, Alan Morris, Maud Bracke, John Foot, and Roberto Bigazzi for their comments, most of which I have taken on board.

The late Tom Behan also read and commented on a chapter in his usual trenchant fashion. Tim Palmer also shared with me the fruits of his editing experience, and Marcel O'Connor provided technical assistance and advice with the cover image. I would also like to thank Giovanni Focardi, Paolo Mencarelli, and Gianluca Fantoni for their assistance and advice, as well as the many partisans, especially the late Angiolo Gracci, I have had the privilege to meet and speak with. I hope I have done none of them, particularly those who are no longer here to read the book, a disservice. Lastly, I must record again my thanks to Jenny Dalrymple for her infinite patience and support. The book is dedicated to our children, Elena and Danny.

Introduction

In April 2002, Silvio Berlusconi, the president of the Italian Council of Ministers, made an official visit to Bulgaria. This was Berlusconi's second term in office, after the short-lived experience of 1994.[1] At a press conference in Sofia that marked the conclusion of his visit, he first addressed a series of questions about the significance of his sojourn for relations between the two countries. He said nothing in any way provocative. But he then launched a vehement, but by no means unexpected attack, on three major figures in the Italian media: Enzo Biagi, the highly respected veteran journalist; Michele Santoro, the presenter and talk show host; and Daniele Luttazzi, the comedian. These three individuals were, in Berlusconi's view, the arch representatives of that section of the Italian media, specifically the state-run broadcasting company RAI, who had been on a mission to get him ever since he entered politics. And he intended to do something about it. They were, so Berlusconi maintained, guilty of making a "criminal" use of television and it was time that the new management of RAI put a stop to it. Did this mean, he was asked by astonished journalists, that the three men he had mentioned would have to leave RAI? "If they change" was Berlusconi's reply, "but since they won't change . . ." He ended by promising that once the senior appointments to the RAI board had been made (the government, incidentally, decides this) state television would become once again "not partial, but objective, and not influenced by the parties as it was during the military occupation by the Left."[2]

The "Bulgarian *diktat*," as it has become known, was by no means the first, and certainly not the last, of Berlusconi's clashes with the media. The three men he impugned reacted in different ways, but I would like to concentrate on Santoro's response. Santoro began his journalistic career with various newspapers, including the communist daily *L'Unità*, before moving to radio, and then television, where he developed his own provocative style, mixing interviews with *reportages*. In 2001 Santoro devoted special attention on his show *Il raggio verde* to the claim that the Berlusconi family had links with the *mafioso* Vittorio Mangano. It was this issue, above all, which had provoked outrage in the Forza Italia! camp. Santoro's response to the *diktat* was initially to indulge in some light sparring about RAI's contractual obligations toward him and then prepare for a "special edition" of the Friday night transmission *Sciuscià*. Before the program started, he received a telephone call from Agostino Saccà, the director of RAI, asking him which politicians would be present at the discussion. Santoro responded in his own inimitable fashion, telling Saccà that he already knew full well that no one from Forza Italia would be present, as media regulations in fact required. Saccà warned him that, if this happened, there was a risk that the program would be removed from the schedule. Santoro ignored him.[3] The show began with a handheld camera focused directly on Santoro's face. Unusually, there was no introductory music. Then Santoro began to sing, without the help of accompaniment. "Bella ciao," the song he sang, hopelessly out of tune, walking around the stage with long pauses between words, was the most famous song to have emerged from the Italian Resistance movement in the Second World War.[4] Although sung by many Italians, in many different contexts, including school trips and talent shows, the song has always been associated with the political Left and with the Resistance movement.[5] In more recent times it was sung at the G8 protests in Genoa in 2001 and, with the words changed, was used to insult the Minister of Education and her unpopular reforms in 2004.

A few months later a decision was taken, unsurprisingly, to end Santoro's contract with RAI, which eventually led to a case being brought for unfair dismissal, which the presenter won in 2005. But it is not this, nor Berlusconi's continued fraught relationship with the Italian media that interests us here. What is most intriguing about this notorious episode is Santoro's use of a song about the Resistance movement in Italy as a means of staging a protest against the undemocratic methods of Berlusconi. By April 2002, nearly 57 years had elapsed since the liberation of Italy from the Germans and the Fascists, yet the Resistance still clearly had, to borrow a phrase from Henry Rousso, the French historian of the memory of Vichy, an "astonishing presentness."[6] Furthermore, this was not the first time that the "memory" of the Resistance, a term that needs to be used with great care, had been used to protest against the media mogul turned politician. In 1994, when Berlusconi first came to power following a period of unprecedented turmoil in Italian political life, the April 25 "festival of the Liberation" turned into a massive demonstration against the new government, made up of a coalition that included Gianfranco Fini's right-wing *Alleanza nazionale* (National Alliance; AN), a party whose history could be directly traced back to Fascism. Indeed, since the April 25, 1994, demonstration the Resistance tradition and Berlusconi have been seen as almost irreconcilably antithetical, and this may well explain one of the reasons for Santoro's choice of song. It was only on April 25, 2009, that Berlusconi finally attended state celebrations of what is one of Italy's national days and then for reasons of political expediency. We might contrast this antagonistic stance with that of Berlusconi's French contemporary, Nicolas Sarkozy, whose inauguration in 2007 was, at one point, accompanied by the strains of "Le chant du partisan," sung by a mass military choir. At the same event the last letter of Guy Moquet, a communist partisan, was read in public and, later that year, Sarkozy decreed that the letter be read out in all French secondary schools. There is, it goes without saying, still much contemporary discussion about France's past, as the work of Rousso and Francois Furet have demonstrated (and the same could, of course, be said for Germany, Spain, and other countries that experienced violent conflicts in the twentieth century).[7] But in Italy the Resistance movement seems to occupy a special place in contemporary discussions and polemics.

It would, however, be an exaggeration and a gross simplification to see a simple causal connection with a Resistance "revival" in Italy and the mere presence of Silvio Berlusconi, even though the link between the political situation and historical debate is of the utmost importance. There are many more factors at play and, indeed, to use the term "revival" risks misrepresenting a complex and multifaceted problem. For some commentators, rather than a revival of memory, it is more accurate to speak of its "erasure," as Giorgio Bocca, the distinguished journalist and former partisan, has bitterly suggested.[8] Even one of the great Resistance heroes, Giaime Pintor, an intellectual who was blown up trying to cross enemy lines and whose "last letter" was one of the sacred texts of postwar Italy, has been portrayed as a tarnished individual, with a questionable attitude to Nazism.[9] For another authoritative voice April 25 is now a "no man's land."[10] But why does the debate appear so intense now? Who have been the protagonists of the debate, and where has it been played out? What is the relationship between history and politics in Italy, and what is the role of culture, as represented by the song "Bella ciao"?

This book is an attempt to answer these questions and others, and so make a contribution to our knowledge of the long-term impact, or legacy, of the Italian Resistance from 1945 to the present day. I take, as far as possible, a holistic approach that bridges the gap between historical and cultural analysis. What *The Legacy of the Italian Resistance* therefore tries to do is to investigate and unravel a double helix: the relationship, that is, between Italian politics and what I broadly term the culture of the Italian Resistance. The two strands are bound together and, it is hoped, that by looking at them as part of the DNA of modern Italy it might be possible to come to an understanding of what makes for such a complex and, one must add, divided nation. Culture here is understood as encompassing historiography, literary texts, films, monuments, and other media, including, as we have seen in the Berlusconi-Santoro clash, songs. As will become evident, I have given more emphasis to some of these cultural elements, particularly historiography, than to others. This is quite deliberate and related to what Gianpasquale Santomassimo describes as the "close connection between politics and historiography which is the result of long traditions of civic commitment operating in the twentieth century."[11] And as Rousso, writing about France, has observed, "historians and their books are a primary vector of memory."[12] As a consequence of this emphasis, tthere are some elements that have received less discussion than they no doubt merit: I am aware that some aspects of the visual culture of the Resistance, notably photographic images, documentary films, and paintings, do not occupy much space in the book. The same goes for Resistance museums, where there have been a great many interesting developments in recent years.[13] And, while tempted, I have not gone into the issue of street names, which have provoked much intense discussion. In the case of documentaries, it is worth stating that there already exist some very authoritative studies, as well as an outstanding "documentary about documentaries" entitled *25 aprile: La memoria inquieta*, the result of a collaboration between the academic, Giovanni De Luna, and the filmmaker Guido Chiesa.[14]

The book proposes

1. to investigate the various ways that the Resistance movement in Italy has impacted Italian politics, society, and culture over the period from 1945 to the present day;

2. to examine the means of transmission of the Resistance legacy via a range of different "vectors" (Rousso's term). Vectors include partisan associations, political parties, key individuals (e.g., Pietro Secchia, Piero Calamandrei, Paolo Emilio Taviani, Ferruccio Parri), journals, and a range of media (historiography, films, literary texts, memoirs, and so on);

3. to explore the ways in which the Italian State has (or has not) attempted to create a national Resistance memory and how this has conflicted with the regional and highly "localized" nature of the Italian experience;

4. to investigate the issue of the Italian Communist party's supposed "hegemony" of the Resistance by looking at the way the PCI and other political parties have themselves used, abused, or manipulated the Resistance legacy over the long term;

5. to create a way of understanding this impact that draws together, and reflects critically upon, the now large corpus of research on the interaction of history and culture and the "public use" of history.

In its initial design, the book was structured around different genres. However, as the research and writing evolved, it became increasingly apparent that separating genres was undesirable—the distinctions between genres are almost always blurred and the "texts" under scrutiny can only be understood by constant reference to the historical and political context. For these reasons I follow a chronological approach, with chapters dedicated to a series of periods that closely follow the main articulations of the history of the Italian Republic.

The five research questions outlined were determined by the nature of the political and historical debate in Italy over the last two decades and, more importantly, reflect and respond to the work of a large number of scholars who have made invaluable contributions to the secondary literature on the subject of the long-term impact of the Resistance. There have been very successful examinations of the place of the Resistance in political debate, notably in the work of Santomassimo and Filippo Focardi, who themselves build upon the results of earlier work carried out by Guido Crainz and others.[15] Massimo Storchi, an expert in postwar violence in Emilia Romagna, has also written convincingly of the role of postwar violence in the "struggle for memory."[16] The topic of the April 25 celebrations has also received extensive analysis, particularly by Cristina Cenci and, more recently, Roberto Chiarini.[17] While Resistance culture has received a lot of attention, with many books on films and literary texts, there has never really been a systematic attempt to place these texts in the broader historiographical and political framework in which they were produced and so give an idea of the role, and indeed the successes and failures, of Resistance culture over the *longue durée*. It is not difficult to find an explanation for this absence—there is a lot of material out there, and it is far simpler to concentrate on single periods, as Giovanni Falaschi did in his seminal study of the armed Resistance in literary texts, or on single texts, as exemplified by Lucia Re's work on Calvino's *Il sentiero dei nidi di ragno* and my own study of Fenoglio's *Il partigiano Johnny*.[18] But there are significant exceptions to this rule, such as Adriano Ballone's wide-ranging discussion in the Laterza *Luoghi della memoria* series, and Stephen Gundle's suggestive examination of the role of culture in the failure of the Resistance movement to create a postwar "civic religion."[19] While accepting that the nature of the Resistance and its political use in postwar Italy were partly to blame, Gundle argued that the "overwhelming emphasis" on these aspects had "obscured the fact that the Resistance tradition is made up of symbols, rituals, commemorations, monuments, images and cultural artifacts."[20] In an approach comparable to Gundle's, Luisa Passerini has shown how several literary texts published in the 1990s revealed different "Resistance memories," and placed "the recent past in a wider and more complex perspective; a perspective in which we no longer see ourselves and our adversaries as unambiguous and monolithic entities."[21]

On the other side of the divide, Francesco Germinario has published a study of the memory of Mussolini's *Repubblica sociale italiana* (Italian Social Republic; RSI) that concentrates on extreme Right historiography and memoirs over the long term.[22] Germinario's emphasis on memory points to another area that has received a lot of attention over the past decade or so, with Giovanni Contini's *La memoria divisa*, on the massacre of civilians at Civitella in Tuscany, and John Foot's book *Italy's Divided Memory*, which devotes a chapter to the Resistance, notable landmarks.[23] By building on the work of my predecessors, I hope this book will help to carry the debate forward.

One thing the book, quite emphatically, does not propose to do is to write or rewrite the history of the Resistance movement, an operation fraught with dangers and difficulties of all sorts, as 66 years of historiography have demonstrated. Unlike Rousso, I did not start out with the idea of writing a book about the Resistance only to discover that the corpse was still too warm to dissect. But it is useful to sketch out briefly some of the key aspects of the movement not least because, as Storchi has commented, "the memory of the Resistance is strongly influenced by the structural weaknesses of the Italian Resistance itself."[24] As this book will also try to show, the memory of the Resistance is influenced by structural weaknesses in postwar Italy as well as in its institutions and its political parties. In essence, then, the book deals with the interaction of two complex and flawed structures. It is little wonder that there have been so many points of fracture in the Resistance edifice over the years.

In straightforward chronological terms, the Italian Resistance movement began in September 1943 and finished at the end of April 1945.[25] Mussolini had been deposed in the early summer of 1943, to be replaced by Marshall Pietro Badoglio. After a period of uncertainty and complex negotiations, Badoglio announced on September 8 that Italy was no longer fighting with the Germans, who very promptly occupied as much of Italian territory as was militarily possible. At the same time, German troops rounded up as many Italian soldiers as they could capture and dispatched them to prison camps. Many of the soldiers who managed to escape capture made the decision to take to the hills and form what became the first partisan bands. It was at this point that many of "Mussolini's enemies," to use Charles Delzell's term, who had been forced underground or into exile, made the decision to act.[26] Members of the outlawed Communist party, the Socialist party (PSI), and adherents to the *Giustizia e Libertà* (GL) movement were very active in these early stages in terms of organization, recruitment, and strategy. Although it remains a controversial and contested issue, it was the case that the parties of the Left were the most active participants in the Resistance, although there was also significant partisan activity originating from the Christian Democratic Party (DC), as well as from individuals who claimed to have no political allegiance.

In organizational terms, the most important bodies were the Committees of National Liberation (the CLN). As the partisan war developed, other structures would be created, designed to coordinate, above all, the military side of partisan operations. The 20 months of the Resistance can be divided, according to Santo Peli, into five separate phases: (1) Beginnings (autumn-winter 1943–44); (2) January to June 1944; (3) June to December 1944; (4) December 1944 to February 1945 (winter crisis); and finally (5) spring 1945 (insurrection).[27] These five phases correspond to the major articulations of the Allied campaign as it progressed from the South to the North of Italy. By the time of the final phase, only the North of Italy above the Gothic line (north of Florence, but south of Bologna) remained to be liberated. During the entire period, partisans fought a civil war against the Fascists of the RSI, who remained loyal to Mussolini, as well as a war of liberation against the Germans.[28] They were helped, and also hindered in their task, by the Allies, whose attitude to the partisans was ambivalent, particularly after the Normandy landings of June 1944 shifted the focus of the war effort away from the southern Mediterranean.

Throughout the Resistance period there were extended and heated discussions between the various political parties, with the question of the monarchy and its continued existence, at the forefront. These discussions reached a new stage when, at the end of November 1944, the Partito d'Azione (Action Party; PDA), mindful of disquieting developments in the liberated center and South of Italy, sent an open letter to the other parties in the CLN that described their political program, for the present as well as for the future, in no uncertain terms: there would be no return to the pre-Fascist Liberal state but instead a new beginning with the CLN playing a key role in government.[29] The PDA letter sparked an exchange, the so-called debate of the "five letters," which saw the PDA, the PCI, the DC, the PSI, and the liberal Partito liberale italiano (PLI), all assuming different positions vis à vis the "institutional" question, as well as the role of the CLN in a post-Fascist Italy. For the PCI, the CLN's primary role was in the organization of the armed struggle and not in discussions about the new direction of the country after the war. The DC, on the other hand, stressed the need of a free role for the parties, with an expansion of the remit of the CLNs deemed unnecessary. The PSI spoke rather vaguely of a need of a congress of the provincial CLNs, while the PLI vigorously championed a return to the pre-Fascist state, monarchy and all.

The debate of the five letters also coincided with two other important developments, the first of which was the crisis of the first Bonomi government (that had succeeded Badoglio), eventually resolved by the withdrawal of the PSI, other socialist allies, and the PDA from the coalition. The second development was, if anything, of much more significance for the long-term political impact of the Resistance, and centered on the relationship between the Allies and the CLNAI (the CLN for Alta Italia—upper Italy), and more generally on the whole Allied attitude toward Italy. This is not the place for an in-depth discussion of Allied policy in Italy, a subject that continues to provoke much debate.[30] Suffice it to say that for a number of reasons connected with the geopolitics of Europe, a meeting was organized between representatives of the CLNAI and Sir Henry Maitland Wilson, educated at Eton and Sandhurst, and commander in chief of the Mediterranean forces. "Jumbo," as he was affectionately known, received Alfredo Pizzoni (politically independent), Ferruccio Parri (PDA), Gian Carlo Pajetta (PCI) and Edgardo Sogno (monarchist) with somewhat more warmth than they received in Naples and Rome from the Italian government led by Bonomi (who, it seems, refused to speak to them). Despite the pleasantries, however, "Jumbo" got them to sign a document on December 7, 1944, that represented, in Gambino's judgment, "nothing short of capitulation."[31] In exchange for 160 million lira a month and the promise of regular weapons drops to all partisan forces (including the communists), the CLNAI recognized the full authority of the Allies up to and after the Liberation. They also agreed to the appointment of General Raffaele Cadorna as commander of the military side of the Resistance operation (the Corpo volontari della libertà, CVL) and promised to ensure that, once the conflict was over, all the partisans would be rapidly demobbed and all weapons returned. Clearly this was not an agreement that would give the CLNAI much autonomy in the postwar, however much they would have wished or, indeed, dreamed of.

By early 1945 events moved quickly, extending to preparations for a general insurrection in the Northern industrial cities. This insurrection took place toward the end of April, with Milan rising up on April 25. Mussolini himself was captured and executed (by who, exactly, would become a subject of extended discussion), his body taken to the city of Milan and exposed to the vilification of the crowd in Piazzale Loreto. The square was chosen deliberately—in Dondi's words it was, for those who made the decision, both "necessary" and "inevitable"—as it was there in August 1944 that 15 anti-Fascists had been executed.[32] Mussolini was one of the many victims of a settling of accounts that saw many thousands (the number would be much debated after the war) of Fascists perish in acts of summary justice. With the war over, the partisans of all political persuasions looked forward in anticipation to living in the new democratic Italy that they had helped to create. It was at this point that the military side of the Resistance campaign stopped and the never-ending legacy, which is the subject of this book, began.

I

1945–1948

The CLNs will have to become the keystone of the new Italian democracy.[1]

From Piazzale Loreto to the Parri Government

On April 30, 1945, the day after the bodies of Mussolini and his lover Claretta Petacci, as well of those of several Fascist *gerarchi* were exposed to public execration in Piazzale Loreto, the Milanese newspapers published a statement by the CLNAI, the National Liberation Committee for Northern Italy, which assumed full responsibility for the executions. The "governing body" of the Resistance forces in the North, made up of senior figures from the six anti-Fascist parties, declared that "the execution of Mussolini and his associates, which we ordered, is the necessary conclusion of an historical phase which leaves our country covered in material and moral ruins." A necessary conclusion, then, but the CLNAI also went on to underline that these "understandable excesses" needed to come to an end: "in the new age which opens up to the free people of Italy such excesses must not be repeated." The CLNAI, the statement finished, would play a major role in the reestablishment of freedom and democracy "now that the insurrectionary struggle has finished."[2]

The post-Liberation CLNAI wasted no time in addressing the problem of the way forward for Italy, quickly elaborating a discussion document in early May that contained five key points they felt needed to be addressed by the Bonomi government in Rome. These five points were (1) the widening of the purge to the economic sector; (2) the clarification of the relationship between the prefects and the regional and provincial CLNs; (3) the relaunch of the economy involving the efforts of all Italians but excluding those who had profited from Fascism and the German occupation; (4) agrarian reform; and (5) the introduction of an outward looking foreign policy.[3] Once this vigorous and potentially revolutionary program had been released to the press, the CLNAI asked the Allies for permission, which was granted, to send a deputation to Rome. This deputation included the socialist president of the committee, Rodolfo Morandi, who had replaced Pizzoni, as well as his fellow socialist Sandro Pertini, the actionist Leo Valiani, the communist Emilio Sereni, the Christian Democrat Achille Marazza, and the liberal Giustino Arpesani. On May 7, they met first with Bonomi and then with the Central Committee of National Liberation (the CCLN). The meeting, for which the minutes survive, began at 4:30 in the afternoon with a rather distracting discussion about whether representatives of the Republican party should be allowed to be present and, once beyond this stage, whether they would be allowed to speak.[4]

When the socialist Morandi finally got to speak, he claimed that the purpose of the CLNAI's mission was not to seek the resignation of the Bonomi government but rather to "save" and "ensure" the unity of the parties. In the North, the CLNs had, he maintained, brought in a new "system of political and civil administration." He and his colleagues were not in Rome, however, to request a "Northern government," but they hoped that the energy that had been expended in the North would flow into a new national government and inform its decisions, in the interest of the whole nation. The North was not, he reassured his listeners, setting itself in opposition to the South, despite the fact that the struggle for liberation had been longer there.

On the basis of the minutes of this meeting, it is difficult to estimate exactly how diplomatic Morandi was as he spoke, but it is clear enough that, whatever the language employed, the Northern representatives had come down to Rome to knock a few heads together and to give out free lessons in how things should be done, particularly in terms of how the CLNs worked. They were not, Morandi continued, in a significant passage:

> just committees for keeping contacts between the parties, but something organic, and it is through the liberation committees of each town, each district, factory and business that the entire political activity of the country has taken shape. The CLNs have acted in a constructive way . . . This situation differentiates the North from the South . . . Recognizing the value of the CLNs in Upper Italy means ensuring for the whole Nation the fruits of what was an extraordinarily profound struggle, it means responding to a demand which must be satisfied; it means also not disappointing that expectation of renewal which is so marked amongst the masses in the North.

Morandi was followed by the socialist Sandro Pertini, who emphasized the unity of the CLNAI, leaving unsaid the very clear message that, conversely, the central committee was, in his view, divided. But thereafter he shot from the hip as he had always done and would continue to do throughout his long life. The compromises of the various governments since the fall of Fascism in July 1943 had not been satisfactory, and the "worker masses" were not "satisfied." The CLN had been deprived of authority by some representatives of the government, but the CCLN also had its own share of blame in this process—"it's shuffled off its responsibilities" (*si è autoesautorato*)—was the damning expression he chose to describe its actions, or rather, lack of them. Valiani and Arpesani then had their say, adopting a less confrontational tone. On behalf of the Christian Democrats, Marazza then began by thanking Arpesani for throwing some water on the fire and reassured listeners that the relationship between the CLN and the prefects was intended to be one of "close collaboration," rather than of dependence. Marazza gave a good indication of the temperature of the meeting when he remarked that the institutional question could not be discussed "as undiplomatically as it has in this meeting." The communist Sereni rounded off the CLNAI contributions. The liberal

Cattani then spoke on behalf of the CCLN and reassured the visitors from the North of their understanding. He also responded to Pertini, denying that there had been any "shuffling off of responsibility" from within the CCLN. An anodyne press release was then drawn up by Morandi and approved by all those present. The meeting finished at 7:45, having lasted some three and a quarter hours.

Despite the language of the official minutes, it is clear that this was more of a confrontation than a meeting. The representatives of the CLNAI, above all the Socialists, were clearly unhappy about the way things had been handled in Rome. They wanted changes and they wanted them quickly. And they did, despite claims to the contrary, want the South to adopt a Northern template involving the primacy of the CLNs. It was clear from this meeting, therefore, that the nature of the campaign in Italy would have a lasting effect on Italy's postwar development. The Resistance had, above all, been a Northern phenomenon. There it had lasted longer and had therefore become more deeply embedded. What the CLNAI representatives hoped to achieve was to create a more deeply felt Resistance spirit in the center and the South. The Resistance would, in this way, assume national proportions in the postwar. There would be other ways of "spreading" the Resistance message throughout the peninsula, but at this stage the priority of the CLNAI was the political realm and the vehicle was the CLNs. In the event this would not be a successful strategy—the CLNs were only ever going to survive until the election of the constituent assembly made them redundant (as happened, in fact, in June 1946). More importantly, perhaps, the CLNAI representatives also seemed to have forgotten who was really in charge in Italy in 1945—the Allies, who had already decided to put the CLNs "out of the game" in 1944.[5] And the Allies did not want Italy to move any further than in a circle back to the pre-Fascist liberal state, monarchy and all. The CLNs were extraordinarily valuable during the Resistance period, but the expectation and desire that they would carry the Resistance forward failed to recognize the reality of Italy's immediate postwar situation, as well as the parties' ambivalence toward them.[6] Catholics and communists were busy, to use Ventrone's terms "constructing Italian democracy," but the CLNs were not part of the building materials.[7] There were exceptions, and in Florence and Tuscany, for example, the CTLN (Tuscan Committee) had a more enduring legacy in administrative and political terms. This was mainly because the CTLN could operate its progressive social and economic plans, albeit with restrictions, from the liberation of Florence in the summer of 1944 up until it was phased out, and partly because of the success of its newspaper *La nazione del popolo*.[8] But this level of impact was not uniform across the country, where other local CLNs were outmaneuvered and nullified.[9]

By early May, the Allies were firmly establishing their hold over Northern Italy. In exchange for one thousand lire and a merit certificate partisans handed in their weapons, usually at the end of official parades at which they were publicly thanked for their efforts. Not everyone, of course, was happy to do this, and the Allies soon issued an ultimatum that decreed that all weapons had to be handed in by June 7. In each town, Allied officers met with representatives of the CLN and quickly made it clear who would be making the decisions. The power of the CLNs was thus reduced, as Gambino comments, "drastically."[10]

The Christian Democrats initiated the process of jettisoning Bonomi who, in December 1944, had agreed to resign as soon as the Liberation was complete, by suggesting that a new government was needed to reestablish law and order. The socialist leader Pietro Nenni then made a speech in Rome at which he announced his intention to stand as head of government. Nenni's diaries pick up developments the following day with a meeting at Palazzo Chigi of the six leaders of the parties that made up the CLN "hexarchy." Standing in for party leader De Gasperi, the Christian Democrat Scelba opposed Nenni's candidature as President of the Council of Ministers (*presidente del consiglio*) and, so Nenni claimed, suggested Ferruccio Parri instead. Parri was the leader of the PDA and had occupied a major role in the Resistance, meeting frequently with senior Allied officers, and occupying the post of deputy military leader of the CVL.[11] That Scelba put forward the name of Parri at this stage does, however, seem unlikely, and other accounts of these complex negotiations suggest that the Christian Democrat was far less specific.

Meanwhile in Rome the prevarication over a new government continued and the CLNAI in Milan showed increasing signs of impatience. Morandi delivered a radio message to the North in which he reassured listeners that he and his colleagues had, in their mission to Rome, done all they could to represent "the impact of the revolutionary experience which took place in the North."[12] Three days later, in a motion for the constitution of a new government, the CLNAI reminded the political parties of their responsibilities and asked that the new government be appointed by the CCLN, that it should fully integrate and assimilate CLNAI legislation (particularly in terms of a rapid, severe, and tenacious purge) and that the "valorous volunteers for liberty" should be incorporated into the police and armed forces.[13]

In an attempt to move things forward, a meeting was then organized for May 24 in Milan between representatives of the six CLN parties and the CLNAI. At this meeting the name of Nenni was given further discussion but, so it seems, was only weakly supported by the communists. Another document was drawn up illustrating the five key points on which all present at the meeting had agreed.[14] The document did little more than restate the need for the rapid formation of a new government, an interim *consulta nazionale*, elections for a constituent assembly, economic reconstruction and, finally, a vigorous program of purging (*epurazione*). But by this stage the liberals, and their leader Cattani, were feeling distinctly uneasy about the way things were going: not only was there a strong chance that a socialist would soon be in power but also at a local level the CLNs, a direct emanation of the Resistance spirit, seemed to be preparing themselves for what we would nowadays describe as an executive role. Following a meeting of the liberal party's central committee, Cattani asked the other parties for "clarification" about the function and composition of the CLNs. Furthermore, he expressed his and his party's concerns that the capillary extension of the CLNs could lead to a "collective authoritarianism, and a kind of six-fold totalitarianism."[15] The response to this letter was a document dated June 1, which certainly attenuated the scope of the CLNs and, according to Gambino, "practically marks the end of the CLNs as organs of political power."[16] There is an element of exaggeration in Gambino's judgment. But it is worth noting that the objections by the liberals and the ensuing qualifications about the role of the CLNs suggest that their fate had already been largely sealed long before they were wound down in 1946 and, more importantly, *several weeks* before the actionist Parri would form his government. In other words, while the eventual appointment of Parri appeared to suggest that Italy had a Resistance prime minister, the process of negotiation that led to his apotheosis had severely diluted the radical potential for growth and change that the CLNs clearly possessed.

The CLNAI were fully aware of the latest developments created by the liberals and promptly issued a statement that argued the need for the government to be established along the lines that had been *previously* agreed.[17] Morandi followed this up the next day with a radio message that constituted an ultimatum to Bonomi as well as a cry of protest to the political parties in Rome. The CLNs, Morandi thundered, had not organized "the gigantic effort of the Resistance" and taken on the "terrible responsibility of the insurrection" to then have to contemplate "this spectacle."[18] The spectacle was not just being created by Bonomi, who held tenaciously on to power, but also by the representatives of the political parties whose machinations were delaying the changes for which, according to the CLNAI, the Resistance movement had fought.

Eventually, the spectacle did come to an end, nearly two months after the Liberation. The DC suggested their own candidate, De Gasperi, but this idea was blocked by the Socialists in an act of retaliation for the DC refusal to endorse Nenni. Bonomi tendered his resignation, perhaps hoping that the acting king, Umberto of Savoy, would refuse to accept it. The CLNAI then sent another delegation to Rome, led by Morandi, and it was at this point that Parri's name was put forward by two members of the delegation—the communists Ugolini and Meneghetti. But in reality, the Parri solution did not have its origins from within the CLNAI, as it might appear, but was the result of earlier discussions between the actionist Valiani and the communist Longo who were keen to break the deadlock. In addition, Valiani hoped that with Parri at the head of government the PDA would extend its electoral base, beating off the challenges represented by the traditional parties that had emerged years before the Resistance movement started.[19] But not everyone in the PDA saw it in the same way as Valiani, with Ugo La Malfa seeing Parri's unexpected appointment as a potential danger to the fortunes of the party. In the end, La Malfa's fears proved to be extraordinarily prescient.

With "Maurizio" as head of government, it seemed on the face of it that the Resistance had taken its place at the top of the tree, and it is clear that this was how this appointment was widely interpreted. But this is a superficial reading, which does not account for the tortuous and very significant process I have described in the preceding paragraphs. Parri was a compromise, an ad hoc response to a difficult situation.[20] He was only proposed after the liberals had got their concessions limiting the CLNs. If he represented the Resistance it was now a force that had lost its teeth. Parri did not, therefore, owe his job to the vigorous Resistance wind that blew in the North, but to the stale and fetid air that lingered in the corridors of Rome. And how long he would last before the party leaders in the capital decided who would really run the country was a moot point.

During his short term of office, which began on June 21, Parri, as well as the press sympathetic to the PDA, made every effort to depict the head of government as someone who broke the mold of Italian politics.[21] The strategy was to present him as the antithesis of Mussolini and of liberal politicians. For Piero Calamandrei, who had founded the journal *Il ponte* in 1945, he was "something more than a hero: an honest man." In order to appear a man of the people, Parri tried to make a virtue out of the fact that he was a very ineffective public speaker, but that he was keen to communicate. To this end he established a weekly press conference. He was also careful to stress his role as a partisan, frequently referring to himself in the third person as "Maurizio." It was Parri who presided over the funeral of the Resistance hero Duccio Galimberti in September 1945. At an early meeting with the socialist leader Nenni, Parri even defined himself as "the 'average partisan', above the parties."[22] This approach was also radically different from that of his counterpart De Gaulle, the symbolic head of the French Resistance, who made a point of relaunching the French language in his grandiloquent speeches. De Gaulle's contribution to French politics was, it goes without saying, rather more long-lasting than Parri's.

One of the first acts of Parri's government was the establishment of a Ministry of Post-War Assistance, which was initially headed by the Sardinian, Emilio Lussu (a member of the PDA) and two undersecretaries: Mario Ferrara (PLI) and Enrico Berardinone (PCI). The ministry was the "first attempt by liberated Italy to respond to the problems of the post-war" and had a wide remit to provide assistance to a variety of categories: soldiers interned in Germany, civilians who had become refugees, demobilized partisans, as well as the families of soldiers and partisans who had been killed in the war.[23] It also enlisted the assistance of a wide variety of associations including the national partisan association, the ANPI, which will be further discussed later.

One of the most pressing issues to which Parri dedicated many hours of attention was that of the timing of elections in Italy. Should local, administrative elections come first (as the Allies maintained) or should the national elections take precedence? This might seem an issue of no great import, but it was, in fact, a crucial factor in the eventual waning of the Resistance spirit. Only a few days after Parri himself came to power, the British electorate had voted for change in the shape of Attlee's Labour Party, which promised the establishment of the welfare state, the nationalization of industry and a host of other reforms. A few months later France voted for a national assembly with the communist and socialist parties polling just over 50 percent of the votes cast. In these two countries early elections appeared to favor the Left. In Italy it was, predictably, the socialists who were keener than any for early elections. In a story that may be apocryphal, but is still worth recounting, Pertini implored Bonomi in early May to call national elections, but was met with the objection that there was not enough wood available to make the necessary number of ballot boxes. In Parri's own party there were differing approaches to the question, with one current arguing that the longer national elections were delayed, the more chance the PDA had of establishing itself as a party of government with the electorate. Parri himself appeared entirely unsure of what decision to take, at first advocating the long position espoused by La Malfa, only then to change his mind. He then came under increasing pressure from Washington to hold the administrative elections first. Eventually the possibility of a constituent assembly in place by November 1945 was shelved and elections were timetabled for June 1946.

The Parri government fell in late November, after only six months of existence, as a consequence of the liberal withdrawal from the coalition in protest at the direction of the *epurazione* process.[24] The DC, in turn, resigned from government arguing, mendaciously, that it was necessary to preserve unity. In protest, Parri held a press conference in the presence of the CLN, but it was an empty and meaningless gesture. The actionist leader was soon replaced by De Gasperi as the head of government, who kept his post as foreign minister.

The "Resistance factor" in the Parri government was more symbolic than real. As such, the defenestration of Parri was not quite tantamount to "the removal of the Resistance spirit from the heart of power," as Gundle has put it, but it was nevertheless a severe blow for Parri himself.[25] Far more damaging, however, was the damage that it caused the PDA as a whole. By the time the party met for its conference in early February it was in free fall, a "party without a future." [26] Parri and La Malfa left the PDA and eventually joined the Republicans, leaving behind a rump of individuals with largely socialist proclivities. But following a miserable showing in the 1946 elections (where the PDA won a paltry 1.5 percent of the vote and only seven seats in the constituent assembly) the party would eventually dissolve. The actionist diaspora would take many individuals to the PSI and to other political formations. One example among many is that of Aldo Garosci, veteran of the Spanish Civil War and a leading figure in the Roman Resistance. Garosci joined the PSI after the collapse of the PDA and would go on to write the *Storia dei fuorusciti*, the standard history of clandestine anti-Fascism.[27] Some very talented actionists, such as Ragghianti, former president of the Tuscan CLN, and Valiani, would withdraw from political life altogether (although Valiani appeared in Carlo Levi's *L'orologio* in the shape of the character Andrea Valente). The consequences of this painful process were highly significant for the question of the legacy of the Resistance. The PDA really owed its existence to the Resistance and it was in this period that it had flourished. In terms of its contribution to the organization of the movement it was only second to the PCI. The PDA had the potential to take the Resistance message and spirit alive and kicking to the very heart of postwar political life. The death of the party would shift attention away from the potential "presentness" of the Resistance as a political force, to an emphasis, among former members, on memory and on nostalgia for past glories.

Postwar Violence

At the very same meeting in early May at which Scelba opposed the candidature of Nenni, the DC representative also expressed grave concerns about partisan retribution in the North of the country where, he claimed, "around 800 people have been shot in Reggio Emilia and there are more people dead there than in the entire French Revolution."[28] Scelba's turn of phrase, as reported by the socialist Nenni, was colorful, but it certainly suggested that there were problems to confront, in addition to the selection of a new prime minister. What was the true extent of postwar killings? What were the causes of the violence and how and when was it brought under control?

The killings in Reggio Emilia highlighted by Scelba were not isolated but part of a "problem that affected not only the region of Emilia but all of northern Italy," with Fascists of all types, from the bottom to the top of the regime's hierarchy, facing possible summary execution.[29] Soon, however, the initial phase of "insurrectionary violence" began to fade, only to be replaced by other, more organized forms of retribution. During this second wave of killings, a common feature was the technique of lifting already incarcerated Fascists from prison and then executing them *en masse*. At Cesena, for example, on May 5, 1945, 17 individuals were killed by partisans after a group of Polish soldiers, representing the Allied forces, presented themselves at the police headquarters asking for the prisoners to be handed over to them, so that they could be transferred to another prison at Forlí. But Fabio Ricci, who had overall responsibility for the punishment of Fascists in the area, refused to comply with this request and, once the local partisans heard of this attempted transfer, they took the law into their own hands. On this occasion, and others, it seems that the catalyst for the executions was the fear that the Fascists would be released and that justice would not be done.

There were also other short-term factors that contributed to the wave of post-Liberation executions. Thirteen Fascists were killed by partisans in the prison at Carpi on the night of June 14–15, in retaliation for the 16 civilians who were killed on August 6, 1944, in the main square of the town. A similar revenge pattern applies to the killings in the Veneto town of Schio, when the news arrived that the 14 *scledensi* who had been deported to Mauthausen had all perished. This news seems to have catalyzed the local partisans who, under the leadership of Gino Piva, decided to break into the prison at Schio on the night of July 6, 1945, and execute 54 Fascists, including 13 women.[30] As the jails became more secure, the partisans invented more and more ingenious methods. A busload of Fascist prisoners left Brescia on May 14 with 43 people on board. The "ghost bus" (*corriere fantasma*), as it was later known, was stopped by partisan police at Concordia, near Modena, and an indeterminate number of prisoners (estimates range from between 8 and 16 victims) were forced to alight from the bus and were shot.

If it is possible to explain the prison and other similar killings in the context of reprisals and the associated fear that official justice would not be done, it becomes more problematic to apply such categories to certain other forms of postwar executions. In some cases, long-standing local factors, but also class elements, apply. A case in point is the execution of the seven Govoni siblings (the "*sette fratelli Govoni*"), namely Augusto, Dino, Emo, Giuseppe, Ida, Marino, and Primo Govoni on the night of May 11, 1945, at a peasant house near Argelato.[31] Eleven others were killed in the same venue at the hands of partisans from the Paoli brigade and the seventh *Gruppi di azione patriottica* (GAP) formation, which had been based in Bologna. The most detailed reconstruction of the demise of the Govoni, by the neo-Fascist father and son team of Giorgio and Paolo Pisanò, suggests that the original plan was to arrest only Dino and Marino (who had adhered to the RSI) but, out of fear that the surviving relatives would reveal the partisans' identity, they decided to kill them all.[32] Conversely, Sauro Onofri, a historian from the political Left, attributes the killings of the five Govoni who were not members of the RSI to "personal motives which were never clarified."[33]

A complex range of motives also seems to be behind the killings of the Manzoni Counts on the evening of July 7, 1945, at Giovecca, near Ravenna. The Countess Beatrice Manzoni, a servant, her sons Giacomo, Luigi, and Reginaldo, and a dog, were killed. The episode echoes an earlier uprising against the Manzoni in 1914, and it can thus perhaps be seen as a class killing *tout court*.[34]

As the summer of 1945 came to an end, so the number of killings continued to diminish, but they were not over, particularly in and around the city of Reggio. On August 31, 1945, Arnaldo Vischi, an industrialist and the vice director of the "Reggiane" factory complex, was stopped by three men as he drove to his home at Correggio. He was shot and his body was thrown into a canal. Vischi was not a Fascist and had indeed provided help for the local CLN. The motives for his murder were, and are still, unclear.[35] However, Vischi's killer was soon identified as the partisan Nello Riccò, and he was arrested by individuals working for the Reggio *questura*. In a bizarre twist, Riccò was then handed over to local partisans and promptly disappeared. Two other partisans who had an unspecified role in the killing of Vischi, Adelmo Cipolli and Mario Giberti, also disappeared in June 1947.

By this stage, therefore, partisans were involved in a killing that cannot easily be explained by the insurrectionary context. Furthermore, the partisans themselves had decided that the time had come to gain control over the elements that had carried out the killing. What had led to this bloody situation? How can we explain the fact that in 1946 there were four further murders in the *reggiano* "where the victims were no longer Fascists or co-operators with the Nazis, but in some cases anti-Fascists or persons with no political experience"?[36] On the one hand there are those who would attribute the murder of Vischi to individual hotheads who were unable to adapt to postwar conditions. This is the essence of the declaration by the former partisan Ervè Farioli in his explanation of the death of Vischi:

> When it came to Vischi . . . we found ourselves in a tight spot, in some difficulty, because on the one hand we knew—and we know—who carried out the hit—and he was a very fine partisan, even if he was a hot head, a real hot head, who then couldn't adapt to the process of democratization . . . The armed struggle meant that a few comrades lost their ability to transform themselves. Because you don't know what effect killing someone can have on you, you don't know what the psychological repercussions can produce, you leave but you don't know where you are going. And a few comrades, we lost them in that manner. They end up losing the plot, they see nothing else but the armed solution.[37]

But ascribing these killings to individuals, or even groups of individuals, unable to cope with the psychological impact of the return to legality, does not seem entirely adequate. For many years an alternative argument circulated that held great sway in a number of camps and that has also resurfaced in recent debates. This argument hinges on the idea that the communist party in the immediate postwar

period espoused a kind of double strategy. In public, the party adhered to a democratic strategic model; in private it encouraged the Resistance forces to continue
the task left unfinished at the end of the war. The PCI was therefore guilty of a kind
of duplicity (*doppiezza*). This particular argument was heavily promoted by those
forces who sought to undermine the PCI in the Cold War period and enjoyed a
revival during the late 1960s among the revolutionary Left. And in recent debates,
which have followed the demise of the PCI, the question of the party's would-be
preference for the barricades has been a favorite topic. But whether supported
by the Right or the Left, and whether articulated by writers and journalists of all
political hues, the *doppiezza* theory is not convincing.[38] Above all the PCI leader,
Palmiro Togliatti did not foster, approve of, or encourage such a strategy. It was
Togliatti who visited Reggio Emilia in September 1946 to order communist leaders, behind closed doors, to get a grip of the situation. Nonetheless, this does not
exclude that at local levels there were individuals who either believed that Togliatti
told them to behave legally, while really wanting them to prepare for armed insurrection, or (more likely) simply chose to ignore the party's official line in "the last
desperate attempts to change the political situation."[39]

This would seem to have been the case at Reggio Emilia, where the secretary of
the local communist party federation, Amedeo Nizzoli, ignored the party's instructions to come to order: "these things happened here because Nizzoli was our party
secretary . . . he used to say 'this is our policy, we must do this', but behind the scenes
he didn't behave that way. And I tell you this from personal experience." [40] Nizzoli
himself had announced to a fellow partisan what he intended when he returned to
Reggio once the war was over: "When Nizzoli was up in the hills we spoke frequently
of what would happen after. And he told me that there would be a good old clear
out . . . as soon as we got back down. And I told him that the party didn't say that,
and he went a bit serious and he laughed a bit as well." [41]

The problem, however, with all of these interpretations is that they are predicated
on the idea that these acts of violence were the product of a "sudden explosion,"
an instantaneous response to the end of the war when certain individuals (or the
PCI) simply lost control. If, on the other hand, these killings are seen as the result
of long-term deep structures it is possible, at least, to understand the reasons why
they occurred. This is the persuasive argument put forward by Crainz, who dates the
origins of the postwar violence to the rise of Fascism, which was particularly violent
in Emilia Romagna.[42] If we add to this long history of violence the escalation toward
the end of the war (between April 15 and 24, 105 partisans and 65 civilians were
killed in Reggio Emilia and the surrounding area) then we begin to get some idea as
to the reasons for the very extensive killings.[43] This is not to say that what happened
in Italy in the postwar period is in some way "pardonable." Indeed, it is questionable
whether historians are qualified to make such ethical judgments. But what can be
done is to try to make such events historically comprehensible.

The PCI and the Resistance

While the PDA's first postwar congress in February 1946 proved to be a swan song, the PCI's big event, which took place a month earlier, was a rather different affair. The fifth congress of the PCI began in Rome on December 29, 1945, and finished on January 6, 1946, and gave the party the opportunity to map out its future and also survey the recent past. Togliatti was able to inform delegates that party membership totaled 1,700,000. As a future party leader Alessandro Natta would write in the 1970s, this growth amounted to "historical approval of the existence and function of the PCI in the long battle against Fascism *and in particular during the struggle for Liberation.*"[44] Party delegates received a long self-congratulatory report on the PCI's contribution to the Resistance as well as an imposing selection of documents to digest.[45] These materials present a clear picture of the PCI's self-evaluation of its, the communist partisans and, above all, Togliatti's role in the Resistance.

For the PCI the cornerstone of the party's Resistance edifice was the so-called *svolta di Salerno* and the associated politics of national unity that became, in the words of Flores and Gallerano, the "official strategic reference point for the party."[46] When Togliatti returned from exile in 1944, he landed in Naples and soon after made what was for many (including senior members of his own party), a surprise announcement. In the interests of the war effort, the PCI was prepared to shelve the institutional question and cooperate fully with all the anti-Fascist parties and the government in the South. In this way, Togliatti very successfully established the PCI's democratic credentials. This was not a party of barricades and Molotov cocktails, but one of the ballot box. This democratic line would become the PCI's mantra during and after the war, after the other parties had abandoned all ideas of cooperation. The partisans, on the other hand, had used violence as a means to an end during the war (indeed, in many cases, after it) and it would not be easy for them to adapt to the different circumstances of postwar Italy. There was then, potentially, a conflict between the partisans and the party's approach and methods.

In addition to the democratic line that originated in the *svolta di Salerno* the PCI also insisted on a policy of action as opposed to playing the waiting game, known pejoratively as *attesismo* or *attendismo*. The PCI's instructions were not to wait out for the war to end but to fight, even if the consequences were severe (such as reprisals on civilians and partisans, or the execution of partisans). Particularly in the postwar, the insistence on the PCI's refusal to *attendere* would become part of its rhetoric. However, the battle against *attesismo* required the use of violence. The PCI, therefore, set itself up for problems ahead. The party had to show that it was capable of being part of a modern democracy (otherwise it risked being outlawed), but the very nature of the Resistance movement raised uncomfortable specters. If it turned up with a blood-soaked democratic ticket there was a risk that it would be refused entry. It was for this reason that, for the PCI leadership, those members accused of postwar violence represented a massive problem. The PCI reacted in different ways, at first denying that these acts had been carried out by its own comrades, then falling into silence and then, in a significant development, organizing an escape route into Yugoslavia and later Czechoslovakia where some former partisans would live for years in exile.[47] This strategy took the heat off in some ways, but it did not solve the problem and only created the impression that the PCI had something to hide. Opposition parties were not slow to spot these weaknesses and there was, as Sarah Morgan has argued, "a marked tendency on the part of the right and the centre-right to bring up these episodes as a means of attacking the PCI."[48]

By the end of 1945, therefore, the PCI's interpretation of the Resistance was already firmly established—the success of the movement was down to Togliatti and the strategy of unity. There were, of course, mythical elements in their discourse, but all wars generate myths and the PCI was not the only political party in Italy. Furthermore, while the PCI produced a *public* Resistance discourse, in private, senior elements in Togliatti's "New Party" also had some reservations, particularly when it came to the actions of rank-and-file partisans. These reservations are evident from the minutes of the meeting of the party's leaders from early April 1946 at which Pietro Secchia reported on the party's performance at the recent administrative elections. There had been problems with weak federations, as had been the case for Lombardy, but also, and more damagingly, these federations shared certain characteristics: "the leadership of these organizations was a bit sectarian, there prevailed 'partisan' working methods, not sufficiently democratic, broad, of the new type."[49] This *settarismo* was characterized by a tendency to stick with partisan ways: wearing red scarves and red stars, employing the clenched-fist salute, rather than being party-oriented. At the same meeting, Togliatti himself pronounced on the problem of the "new" party line and how it was not wholeheartedly espoused by some sections of the faithful. For their significance in understanding the attitude of the PCI top brass toward the Resistance, less than a year before the movement had ended, it is worth quoting Togliatti's comments at length:

> I believe, however, that there are many comrades who deep down are either not in agreement or do not understand what a politics of unity means; they believe it's just a trick, or they carry forward the party line but give it such a slant that, in propaganda, at meetings, in all external manifestations, the unitary element disappears and those people we should attract with our words are pushed away, because they think that we desire to overwhelm them . . . the party is becoming isolated and in elections all it can manage to do is a politics of class against class. *The tardy elimination of the residues of the partisan experience in some Northern provinces, the ostentation of the partisan movement, as a class element, the tone of certain songs, these are all things which look small but which, added together, make the party look much different from what we would really want it to be.*[50]

Mauro Scoccimarro, a senior veteran member of the party, even went on to reflect how the Resistance had become a liability in some areas: "A thing that has struck me in these last months and which has a symptomatic value is the fact that the partisan struggle, which for us should have been an element of prestige and which we should have claimed as one of our most outstanding merits, in many places we have had to hide it away."[51] In the specific case of Udine, DC propaganda ("which has put the party in an embarrassing position") had been so efficient as to lead to the decision to withdraw the local partisan leader from the PCI list.[52] In the period immediately before the election for the constituent assembly, it was clear that the Resistance presented something of a political problem for the PCI. This problem would not go away and would condition the communist memory of the Resistance throughout the history of the party. Indeed, it would be the PCI's successor, the PDS, which in 1990 would have to face the most serious consequences of the contradictions between the violent reality of the Resistance movement and the postwar politics of the party most closely associated with it.

The Togliatti Amnesty

In June 1946, Italians went to the polling stations to vote for the constituent assembly, which would be responsible for drawing up Italy's new constitution, and to take part in a referendum that would decide whether the country should maintain its monarchy or become a republic. By a lesser margin than had been expected, the Italian people voted for a republic. In the past it had been customary, upon the coronation of a new king of Italy, to mark such an important event with an act of clemency. The constituent assembly decided that it was appropriate to do something similar and Togliatti, the leader of the PCI, was charged with the responsibility of drafting the relevant document.

What has been described as the "Togliatti amnesty" was eventually presented to the assembly on June 22, 1946. According to Togliatti himself, it went through at least two earlier drafts before the final text was approved.[53] Discussions centered on the desire of the Christian Democrats to free as many Fascists as possible, as compared to the PCI's wish to do the opposite. As with the drafting of the constitution, which would go on to be the most important task of the newly elected constituent assembly, the text of the amnesty was the result of significant compromise between the PCI and the DC.[54]

The 16 clauses of the amnesty were preceded by a declaration from Togliatti himself. After an explanation of the guiding principles of the document, Togliatti went on to discuss individual clauses. When he moved to the discussion of political crimes (*reati politici*) he showed his trump card. Included in this category were a select group of individuals responsible for acts "in violation of the penal code, after the Liberation." Togliatti established a chronological limit to this partisan amnesty (July 31, 1945), explaining that it was not felt appropriate to punish crimes that were committed "because of the *force of momentum* within the anti-Fascist insurrectionary movement."[55]

The inclusion of an act of clemency toward partisans in a document almost entirely dedicated to the crimes of Fascism is surprising. This situation came about because of the different desires of the PCI and the DC for the amnesty. With the DC looking for an extensive amnesty toward the Fascists, Togliatti used the issue of the partisans as part of the bargaining process. With DC demands for a wide amnesty, this was a good opportunity to deal, once and for all, with the problem of insurrectionary and postinsurrectionary violence. However, the fact that the postwar killings were *decriminalized* in an act of amnesty was to be of some importance for the future of the partisan movement. What the amnesty does for the partisans is to pardon them for an act that is considered a crime but that needs to be understood as a product of the physical forces of the Resistance coming to a halt after 20 months of activity. For Togliatti, by July 31, 1945, the Resistance should have come to a complete standstill, but there is no explanation as to why this particular date was chosen. By generously including both Fascists and partisans in his amnesty document, Togliatti was trying to show that he, the leader of the PCI, was a statesman capable of showing largesse when it was necessary for the rebuilding of the nation.

Togliatti then went on to gloss article three of the amnesty: "Amnesty for other political crimes," which deals with Fascist crimes. The article itself provided an amnesty for those crimes that had previously been punishable under the earlier Decree Laws of July 27, 1944, and of April 22, 1945. However, the amnesty did not apply to acts that had been committed by high ranking officials, involved excessive cruelty, or were committed for material gain. This clause has been on the receiving end of much criticism from various quarters, with attention being paid to the phrase "particularly cruel tortures" (*sevizie particolarmente efferate*). The jurist, Achille Battaglia, later discussed the implications of the phrase, which led the courts to reach some highly questionable decisions. Battaglia demonstrated how the Court of Cassation argued that only cases when the "pain and torments created exceeded all limits of human suffering, and demonstrate in he who provoked them not only cruelty, but out and out barbarity and an objective ferocity" would not qualify for amnesty. This meant that a whole range of supposedly lesser *sevizie* were eligible for amnesty, including sexual torture and rape. Thankfully, Battaglia confined to footnotes those examples of *sevizie* that were not amnestied.[56]

The judges at the Court of Cassation therefore interpreted this clause of the amnesty in an unpredictable fashion, showing considerable latitude toward Fascist crimes. This generosity of spirit did not, however, apply to the partisans. In a significant development, the Italian judiciary began to interpret countless episodes of partisan activities, not as necessary acts or even as "political crimes," but as potential common crimes (*reati comuni*). Paradoxically, once the amnesty was promulgated, the judiciary began to investigate partisan crimes with much greater vigor than had hitherto been the case. Countless arrests followed that normally did not lead to prosecution, but which meant that the partisans in question could spend difficult months in jail waiting to be freed. Because of the nature of Italian law at the time, which did not prescribe a maximum period at the end of which an individual had to be charged or released, it was likely that those arrested could spend an indeterminate time in jail before being freed. In the most extreme case, one unfortunate individual, Alfredo Barbieri, spent four years and seven months in "preventive detention" before a court finally pronounced him not guilty of the crime of which he was accused.

The situation that this and other partisans found themselves in was then further exacerbated by a judgment of the Court of Cassation from December 1946 that argued that robbery was excluded from the April 1945 Decree Law "even if the offence was committed to allow the individual to continue living in the *maquis* in order to avoid the Germans." By the end of 1946 the reasons for the partisans' activities had been set to one side, and their actions were solely interpreted in the light of civil law. This was, therefore, a key year for the development of what was to become known as the "trial of the Resistance," with the June amnesty representing a turning point. The extent and nature of the problem of partisan arrests in 1946 can be gauged by the decision of the constituent assembly to issue a decree to limit the phenomenon, which was introduced by the PCI deputy Fausto Gullo. The decree itself seems to have come about because Togliatti and Gullo had circulated memos to the offices of the prosecutors instructing them not to proceed against partisans, but these memos had fallen on deaf ears. Gullo's decree was clearly well intentioned, but it had little effect. The arrests continued, leading to what Storchi has called a process of "forced self-absolvement" whereby "in the minds of the partisans every act of violence was right as well as politically and morally justified."[57] Storchi's comments on the "collateral effects" of these arrests and trials are, as ever, dead on, but it is also possible to extend his analysis a little further. The trials of partisans represent a significant chapter in the history of the Italian judicial system. Trials continued throughout the 1950s and, even in recent years, there have been a number of high-profile cases involving former partisans. The overall effect of this has been that the Resistance movement has been, in part at least, not judged by historians, but by judges, who use fundamentally different criteria and methods of analysis. The judge has to pronounce if an individual is guilty as charged. The historian's task is not to condemn, but to explain. Yet the fact that there has been an almost never-ending "judicial appropriation" of history has meant that much of the debate about the Resistance has been framed in stark terms—it is either condemned to imprisonment and disgrace or free to go to bask in the glory of absolution. All too frequently, historians, or individuals who pretend to such status, have failed to see the distinction between the judge and the historian, and written as though they were in court. As Storchi, in the conclusion to his book on the killing of partisans by other partisans, has rightly observed, it is not the task of the historian to "put on the clothes of an investigator or, even worse, a judge."[58] This may well be one of the reasons why discussions of the Resistance have been so polarized—both then and now.

The ANPI

The history of the ANPI, the largest of the Italian partisan organizations, began in Rome in June 1944 after the liberation of the capital and was the result of a decision taken by the CLN. The executive was composed of a number of key Resistance figures, the most important figure being Carlo Salinari, one of the leading Roman *gappisti* and a protagonist of the attack on the German troops in Via Rasella, which led to the Fosse Ardeatine massacre. The early activities of the Rome ANPI were dominated by the need to furnish assistance to demobilized partisans, for which a "Casa del Partigiano," offering board and lodging, was established in a former school in Via Savoia. The following year another partisan association was set up in Milan. The secretary of this northern association was the communist Arrigo Boldrini, a partisan leader from Ravenna who had been decorated by the allies for his leadership.[59] Other key members of the Milan executive included Cino Moscatelli, one of the leaders of the *garibaldini* in Lombardy and Enrico Martini Mauri, a former soldier and leader of "autonomous" partisan groupings in Piedmont.

These two distinct associations were a product of the nature of the Italian campaign, with Italy split in two by the Gothic line. Once the war was over and the whole of Italy free from German occupation, it became a matter of urgency to unite the two associations, separated geographically but not as yet politically, into one entity. This was achieved at a meeting at the end of June 1945. In its early stages the main role of the association, which had sections throughout the country, was to provide assistance, advice, and solidarity for expartisans. The ANPI expanded rapidly—by 1946 it had 2,732 different sections throughout Italy and 237,678 members. By September of the following year, the first national conference of the ANPI was held in the city of Florence. The choice of Florence was quite deliberate: the Tuscan capital was the first city for which the partisans could claim to have had a direct involvement in its liberation—Rome had not been freed as a result of the combination of Allied forces and the partisans. Already, then, one of the key issues inherent in the Resistance movement itself was beginning to emerge and to shape the way that the movement would impact postwar Italy. The Resistance was not a homogenous movement evenly spread throughout the country. It had been concentrated in the North of the country, not because the South was more or less organized or more or less willing to participate, but because the nature of the campaign meant that it was in the North that the Resistance lasted longest.

At the September 1946 conference the ANPI took a significant decision that would go on to define the place of the organization throughout the history of the Italian Republic. The organization, it was decided, would aim to go far beyond the remit of a simple veterans' association. Instead, the ANPI, it was hoped, would have a political role, shaping policy and giving former partisans a voice in the decision-making process. The problem associated with this decision was, however, quite obvious. If the ANPI was to have a political role, what were its politics? The association had its origins in the politics of national unity, which had been such a key characteristic of the war period. But by the end of 1946 the war was in the past as was, more importantly, the politics of compromise. The ideological plurality of the ANPI may have been a sign of strength when the association was founded, but it would represent a real problem as the political situation in Italy evolved and the different parties jockeyed for position in advance of the 1948 elections.

During 1947, the tensions that characterized the political situation in Italy had an obvious and inevitable impact on the association that, however, continued to expand numerically recruiting another forty thousand odd members during the course of the year. In early December the ANPI held its first national congress at the Teatro Italia in Rome. The choice of the Teatro Italia and the city of Rome were not, it goes without saying, random. The ANPI wished to demonstrate that it was a national organization that was, in turn, the product of a national movement. To reinforce this message the ANPI published a one-off number of a journal entitled *Il Tricolore*. The editorial of the paper, entitled "La difesa della Resistenza" (the defense of the Resistance) was penned by the actionist Dante Livio Bianco. In this way the association hoped to demonstrate its political pluralism. However, cracks were already appearing in the edifice and most of the discussions at the congress focused on how best the association could be configured so as to represent the diverse political views of its membership. By the end of the congress, at which Boldrini was elected president of the association, it seemed that the way forward would be to have a federal ANPI.

In mid-February 1948, a meeting of the ANPI executive committee was held. Representatives of Christian Democrat, Liberal, and autonomous partisans announced that they were leaving the association and less than a month later they would form the FIVL (Italian Federation of Volunteers of Liberty—*Federazione italiana volontari della libertà*), at a meeting held in Milan.[60] By this time the ANPI was in free fall. The association condemned the split and ascribed it to a political campaign which, from April 25, 1945, had attempted to "divide the partisan forces."[61] However, there was worse to come when another section of the membership, headed by Ferruccio Parri, went on to leave the association. Parri himself wrote a manifesto explaining the decision and the motives behind it. The new association, which would be named the *Federazione italiana delle associazioni partigiane* (FIAP) in 1949, was to be in reality and in appearance "independent from any party and any political interest." It would not become an instrument of anticommunist battles, Parri stressed. Nevertheless, the decision to leave ANPI had been provoked by the fact that "the supreme interests of the Nation" were "at stake." Parri finished the document in uncompromising terms, stating that those who criticized him and his associates for breaking partisan unity in favor of the forces of reaction needed to realize that it was the PCI's monopolistic strategy that had provoked the "forces of reaction" in the first place.

These were harsh words, and they demonstrate quite clearly that the splitting of the partisan world into three different groupings was an extremely bitter affair. The split came about for obvious contingent reasons; the Cold War polarized politics in Italy in an extraordinarily potent fashion. But the most important aspect of the split is not the split itself and its origins, but its long-term impact on the memory of the Resistance. The partisan associations were the primary carrier of the message of the Resistance and whatever they did, whatever initiatives they organized, it was impossible to get away from the simple fact that the postwar representatives of the movement were forever divided.

Partisan Unrest

In July 1946, the CLN were, as expected, dissolved. And as we have seen, the Togliatti amnesty was announced at the same time. These, and other events, were not well received by the partisan community and signs of unrest began to appear. The *Corriere della Sera* carries reports of strange activities in the hills throughout 1946 and 1947, but it was the "rebellion" of Santa Libera in August 1946 that really made the news. Large numbers of partisans from this small village near Asti in Piedmont dug out their weapons and returned to the hills, refusing to come down. Some sections of the press, according to Secchia, spoke of an "ex-partisan insurrection" and of the need for a "drastic state intervention."[62] The PCI took this very seriously indeed and sent Secchia and Davide Lajolo to persuade them of the futility of their gesture.[63] The rebels did indeed see sense, and after a week of protest returned home, but it was a sign of things to come.

The Santa Libera episode also raises an issue that has become a subject of much discussion in recent years. Did a secret army of communist partisans exist that would be ready to seize power when the order was issued? If such an army existed, who ran it? Was there, as Scelba claimed on several occasions, a dangerous Soviet-inspired "plan K"?[64] According to the prefects' reports from the period, there existed a well organized and heavily armed communist stay-behind operation.[65] This operation, so the argument goes, answered to none other than Secchia, the leader of the revolutionary wing of the party. All the communists were waiting for was the order to rise up. But the idea of a large secret army of this nature is, at the very least, an exaggeration. Of course the prefects report the existence of partisans in the hills—no doubt there were many nostalgic individuals who took themselves off to relive past glories.[66] But to interpret these cases as evidence of a massive and well-oiled operation is to willfully misrepresent the reality of the situation. By the same token, even though the Christian Democrat Taviani admitted in his memoirs that there were "white partisans" who had, under the leadership of Enrico Mattei and Enrico Martini Mauri, retained weapons in a kind of early version of Gladio, the argument that there were large-scale operations of such partisans is equally unconvincing.[67]

But there was a lot of unrest among partisans, as the Santa Libera episode shows. The following year in Milan, another similar episode would occur that would demonstrate the extent of the anger among the partisan community. Ettore Troilo was the leader of one of the larger communist partisan formations to operate in Lombardy, known as the Maiella brigade. After the war, no doubt to the satisfaction of the Milanese partisans, he was appointed prefect. This was most unusual—many prefects who had been in place during Fascism just kept their posts. By November 1947 the minister of the interior, Scelba, was making declarations about the potential communist threat that bordered on the obsessive. At the DC congress in Naples he described his fears of "difficult days" ahead: "I fear that the Left will be tempted to have recourse to violence. But we will use the power of the State against any attempt to call into question the freedom of our country."[68] Troilo's status as a "political" prefect of Milan was clearly in jeopardy. Duly, a few minutes before midnight on November 27, ANSA sent out a press release informing the papers that Troilo had been replaced by a "dottor Ciotola." By the time Troilo himself became aware of his career move, several thousand demonstrators had already reached the prefecture. Following the customary strike declaration, the communist firebrand Giancarlo Pajetta led a large group of partisans into the building. The occupation had begun. Legend has it that Pajetta, the *ragazzo rosso* as he was affectionately known, telephoned first Scelba at the Viminale and then the PCI headquarters in Rome to inform his leader that the party held the prefecture. Togliatti, so the story goes, replied ironically "and what do you intend to do with it?" and would regularly ask Pajetta at meetings over the years to come "how many prefectures does the party hold?" After some lengthy negotiations between Pajetta and the Christian Democrat Marazza (an individual with good Resistance credentials) the situation soon calmed down with Troilo obliged to accept his fate. The partisans went home, weapons and all. It is hard to see the "Troilo war" episode, as some have done, as evidence of an Italy on the verge of a civil war, or as another revolutionary moment that the PCI missed out on.[69] It was, and Pajetta was well aware, a symbolic protest. It was not the storming of the Winter Palace.

The "Troilo war" episode, and much else besides, reveals that the leader of the PCI had, at best, an ambivalent attitude toward the partisans. But it would be wrong to single out Togliatti for criticism. In many ways Pajetta deserves censure for taking an approach to the question of partisan discontent that was destined to fail and therefore leave them even more frustrated. What the PCI should have done was to channel the anger into something more creative, as would happen later with the influential movement of the "partisans for peace."[70] But in the meantime, the partisans were still seething about the way things had gone in Italy.

The extent of the disquiet can be gauged by looking at a special edition of *Il ponte* published at the end of 1947 titled *1947. Crisi della Resistenza*. Piero Calamandrei's piece on the "Clandestine Restoration" fully captures the tone, arguing that the Resistance crisis was not restricted to Italy but could be detected by other countries conditioned by the Cold War climate. Vittorio Foa suggested, rightly, that the Resistance crisis had its origins in the days before the liberation. Picking up on several of Calamandrei's points, Roberto Battaglia, Carlo Galante Garrone, and Paolo Barile all examined aspects of the legal situation in Italy, while Domenico Peretti Griva, Giovanni Ravagli, and Mario Bracci analyzed issues connected to the purge and the Togliatti amnesty. But matters would only get worse.

On April 18, 1948, the DC won a crushing victory in the elections. A week later, the celebrations for April 25 took place. While the prefects decreed measures to curb the demonstrations, the ANPI, rather disconcertingly, actually helped to contain the protests by sending a telegram to all its provincial offices instructing that everything should take place indoors. At the executive committee meeting, which took place on April 22, there had even been a suggestion put forward to make sure that in case of trouble there should be reliable ANPI representatives on the spot to calm things down. On the one hand this can be seen as an admirable example of restraint, or on the other it could be interpreted as a supine and craven acceptance of the PCI line, which demanded the maintenance of the democratic line, above all else.

The "*Attentato a* Togliatti"

If the partisans stayed indoors on April 25, the same did not occur on July 14, 1948. On that day Togliatti walked out of the parliament building at Montecitorio to be met by a Sicilian, Antonio Pallante, who shot him several times. Before he lost consciousness, Togliatti reputedly issued an instruction to keep calm.[71] But although the protests did eventually die down and Togliatti survived, there were many individuals who did not keep calm, including a large number of partisans. A general strike was called and large scale protests broke out in a number of cities.[72] Scelba, the minister of the interior, no doubt convinced that the "K plan" was in full swing, requested telegrams from his prefects to update him about the situation on the ground.[73] From Genoa the prefect Antonucci replied, saying the workers had all left their posts and were making their way toward the center of the city. In addition to the workers, there were also "numerous communist partisans and large groups of armed thugs" who had taken possession of vehicles, ordered the shops to shut, and set up road blocks. Police officers and members of the armed forces had been disarmed and ten *carabinieri* dragged off to the headquarters of the ANPI and the PCI. Weapons had been placed at strategic points, on the roofs of Via XX Settembre, in Piazza De Ferrari, and at the fish market. The prefect concluded his missive by stating that he had the "distinct sensation" that the parties did not control the situation. From Turin the troubling news arrived that the FIAT director Valletta was a prisoner in one of his own factories.[74] However, Valletta would later declare that he had not been kidnapped but had made the decision to stay in order to defuse the situation.[75] In Florence and Arezzo, as well as in Emilia Romagna, the situation was reported to be under control, with the parties of the "extreme left" doing their best to calm the situation.[76] At Abbadia San Salvatore, near Siena, the situation had deteriorated—the prefect, Zacchi, reported that one junior officer had been shot, another was "dying," and a third was "in a grave condition."[77] Overall, the impression that the prefects' reports give is one of a spontaneous uprising. The idea of a preordained plan, backed up by some sort of PCI- led military organization, is hard to accept, even though some of the prefects suggested this[78] Nevertheless, it was an interpretation of events that Scelba both endorsed and later spread, once he had fired the prefect of Genoa.[79] We do not know how he reacted to the news that the prefect of Savona offered an ice cream, politely declined, to the local secretaries of the PCI, the PSI, and the CGIL once the situation had calmed down.

The *attentato a Togliatti* was a crucial event in postwar Italian history. It showed that there were still some elements within the PCI who, when sufficiently provoked, were still prepared to take to the streets. It also showed that if a "K plan" did exist, it was nothing but a fantasy and that the PCI leadership, above all, did not have revolutionary ambitions. But these interpretations are made with the considerable benefit of hindsight. In the short-term, the *attentato* was artfully used by the DC to suggest that the PCI did have members, including of course partisans, who represented a danger to Italian society. No one seemed particularly concerned (with the exception of Moscow) that the leader of the PCI had been shot in broad daylight on a public street in Rome. Following the *attentato a Togliatti* there were widespread arrests and subsequent trials as well an increase in the arrests of partisans accused of crimes that took place during or after the war. The extent of the state persecution of the Resistance at this juncture in history has, probably, been over emphasized. But there is no doubt that for the communist partisans themselves these were very dark and dramatic days indeed.

Resistance Culture

With the liberation of Italy in April 1945, the way was now open for a potential rebirth in Italian culture following 20 years of Fascism and two years of Resistance. The debate among Italy's intellectuals, largely played out in cultural journals, was intense, and in many ways reflected the wider discussions that were taking place within, and between, the political parties.[80] Should there be a return to a pre-Fascist culture (an approach that echoed Croce's view of Fascism as a parenthesis)? Or should Italian culture look both forward and outward—to America and, of course, to the Soviet Union? There was much discussion about rupture and continuity in Italian letters, but one element that was oddly missing from the debate was a critical reflection on the culture of the Resistance period itself. The Italian Resistance had not produced a wealth of literary texts during the actual period of the struggle, in contrast to France, but there had been a lot of activity elsewhere, above all in terms of the partisan press, or *stampa partigiana*.[81] As Laura Conti's huge bibliography of the clandestine newspapers shows, this was a widespread phenomenon.[82] Not every partisan band had its own newspaper, or indeed single sheet of news, but it is clear that great importance was attached to the business of written communication at all levels: between the CLN and the partisans, between the political parties and the partisans, between the partisans themselves, between the partisans and the local population, and even between the partisans and the soldiers of the RSI. The *stampa partigiana* was, in Tarizzo's words, "crucial for the initiation of a dialogue," as well as the more traditional task of maintaining an "esprit de corps."[83] The *stampa partigiana* typically contained news, both national and local, accounts of partisan actions, obituaries of the fallen and occasionally literary pieces including poems and short stories. According to Falaschi, the poems were "not interesting," but the short stories were.[84] The *stampa partigiana* was, of course, many things, but its main task was to persuade its readers of the validity of the cause for which they were fighting, so that when sacrifices were made, they were not seen as useless and unproductive. The concept of the nation was at the core of the partisan press, with frequent reference to past glories, above all the Risorgimento, used as a means of justifying and explaining the aspirations of the Resistance, seen as a "second Risorgimento."[85] This rhetorical dimension led to the use and abuse of "classical style rhetorical forms, as well as expressions which derive from nationalistic, barracks-style, language."[86] What happens in the *stampa partigiana* in the period 1943–1945 is the establishment of the rhetorical paradigms, in terms of form and content, which would then characterize some postwar representations of the period. Above all, the parallel between the Risorgimento and the Resistance would become a constant feature of postwar rhetoric. There is, in other words, a "carry forward" effect that sees the topoi and language used in one period, for a particular purpose (that of encouraging morale and a sense of group identity), percolating into another period, when the Resistance was effectively over, but other battles were taking place. Not all writers, of course, slavishly adopted the prevailing discourse, but it would prove very difficult to break free of the vines of rhetoric that had been planted, quite legitimately, during the period of armed Resistance, and which were themselves, as Falaschi has suggested, a hangover from the excesses of Fascism.[87]

Memoirs

In terms of sheer quantity, by far the most popular genre of postwar Resistance culture was the memoir. This is a very flexible term that covers a wide range of works with sometimes very different ambitions—from the account of the deeds of a single individual, alive or dead (such as Bolis's *Il mio granello di sabbia* or Giuliana Gadola Beltrami's *Il capitano*) to a narrative of the deeds of a single partisan formation or division (Gracco, *Brigata Sinigaglia*; Giorgio Bocca, *Partigiani della montagna*).[88] Memoirs were published by small publishing houses, with restricted print runs and were intended for local audiences. Their publication was prompted by a very real need—to consecrate in printed form the oral narratives that circulated widely during and after the war. Many of the memoir writers explicitly stated in their prefaces that they were not writers of fictions, but simply telling the truth without any artistic intervention. In a sense, the memoir writers set themselves up as different from novelists; their works were not "high culture." In Falaschi's words, "the memoirs can be considered as a theoretically primitive form of anti-novel."[89] Quite naturally, the authors of these memoirs tended to privilege successes over failures, the good over the bad. There was, then, the process of carrying forward a certain type of discourse that I mentioned earlier. Equally, though, Italy was going through a difficult and complex rebuilding process after the war. Narratives of war experiences that exalted heroism and sacrifice, as well as unity and solidarity, all coincided with a wider narrative of collective rebirth. This was particularly the case so long as all the CLN parties were still cooperating, at least in public, with each other. When De Gasperi ejected the Left in 1947, memoirs from a communist perspective then also served a precise political function—they demonstrated that the *garibaldini* had fought for the good of the nation that was then being jeopardized by the machinations of the Christian Democrats. For the former actionists, the political dimension of the memoir would also be important, but added to this was the feeling of nostalgia.

Even, therefore, with works published very soon after the events of 1943–1945, there is an additional context (the immediate postwar years) that conditions the tone and content of these texts. One example among many is Valiani's book, *Tutte le strade conducono a Roma*, which is the first extended articulation of the thesis of a "betrayed Resistance."[90] Rather surprisingly, however, given the tone of other actionist works published after Valiani's, Togliatti and the PCI is largely spared criticism for the *svolta di Salerno*, seen by many orphans of the PDA as an act of appalling betrayal, the introduction of original sin that would then tragically compromise the revolutionary spirit of the Resistance.

Tutte le strade conducono a Roma is one of a triad of memoir style books that are widely considered to be the most important discussions of the Resistance to be published in the immediate postwar period. The second of these is Longo's *Un popolo alla macchia*, first published in April 1947, and the third is Raffaele Cadorna's *La riscossa*.[91] The latter is an attempt, from the perspective of a military man, to valorize the role of Italy's conventional forces in the war. Cadorna had himself been made military head of the partisan forces as commander-in-chief of the CVL. His appointment, championed by the Allies, was never a popular one with the more politicized elements among the partisan forces, and as time went on, Cadorna would increasingly become a magnet for polemic. In *La riscossa*, however, the polemic is largely contained. While Cadorna pushed the case for the professional armed forces, Luigi Longo's *Un popolo alla macchia* championed that of the "army of the people." The book is the classic statement of the PCI's take on the Resistance, interpreted as a widespread movement involving the entire *popolo*, encompassing both the working class and the peasants (whose contribution, incidentally, was questioned by Valiani). At the vanguard were, of course, the partisans of the Garibaldi formations with the PCI leadership at the top of the hierarchy. As the PCI's most experienced military figure, and formerly second in command of the CVL, Longo was uniquely qualified to make the case. But Longo was also, and above all else, a *politician* who, in 1947, was trying to make a case for his party to participate in the rebuilding of postwar Italy. It is, therefore, remarkable that Longo's book should be repeatedly accused of political bias. One wonders quite what could be expected of the deputy leader of the communist party in 1947 or, more likely, his ghost writer.[92] The Italian communists were quite capable of criticizing themselves, as the widespread practice of *autocritica* demonstrates, but this did not extend to accounts of the Resistance movement intended for widespread consumption in advance of the 1948 elections.

Literary Texts

Literary texts, as Passerini has written, "throw bridges between history and memory while reminding us of the significance of both."[93] In 1949, Italo Calvino, for whom "the Resistance experience was decisive for his human and artistic maturation," and who would go on to become one of Italy's most important twentieth century writers, published a survey of the literature of the Resistance in the journal *Movimento di Liberazione in Italia*.[94] The journal was published by the "National institute for the study of the movement for the Liberation of Italy," which had been set up by Ferruccio Parri to function as a center for research and documentation.[95] Calvino had himself participated in the Resistance and had published a novel (*Il sentiero dei nidi di ragno*) and a number of short stories on the topic.[96] As a reader for the Einaudi publishing house, he had also been obliged to read and make recommendations about potential publications to his immediate superiors, notably Elio Vittorini. He was, then, uniquely qualified to discuss Resistance literature and his article offers an invaluable insight into his thinking at the time, and the results of around three years of publishing activity. It also serves as a useful way into a major topic of this book.

Calvino began by admitting that, while Italian literature had been enriched as a consequence of the Resistance there was still no work that could make the claim "I represent the Resistance." By the Resistance, Calvino meant not simply the movement in the global sense, but also its spirit. Indeed, Calvino suggested there was no work that as yet captured the Resistance at a local, or even on a group level. Instead what writers who were already known figures by the time of the Resistance had achieved was to document their position as "individual intellectuals before the struggle." The Resistance was not then, a protagonist of these books, but the intellectual was. It is clear that the works that Calvino most had in mind (and that he discusses in more detail later) were Pavese's *La casa in collina* and Vittorini's *Uomini e no*.[97]

Uomini e no was published in July 1945, shortly after the war finished, and staked a claim to being the first Resistance novel published in Italy. Vittorini was himself an intellectual of great distinction and a man with a mission to, apparently single-handedly, revolutionize Italian letters. The vehicles he used were *Uomini e no*, as well as the journal he founded, *Il politecnico*. Vittorini had also joined the PCI, but he enjoyed a very uneasy relationship with the party, with its cultural policy, and with Togliatti in particular. The spat between the two, the end of *Il politecnico*, and Vittorini's break with the PCI, have been the subject of much discussion over the years. Indeed, after Togliatti's death, there was an attempt to rehabilitate Vittorini in the pages of *Rinascita*. But is it possible to rehabilitate *Uomini e no*? The book is set in Milan and has as its protagonist the intellectual Enne 2. The partisan name refers both to an aspect of the topography of Milan (*naviglio 2* means canal number 2) but also reflects the character's tortured quest for identity (two n's also stands for *niente nome* or the man with no name).. The most famous scene in the book portrays a hapless mendicant fed to an SS officer's dogs. The scene is, of course, reminiscent of the tale told by the atheist Ivan Karamazov when explaining to his brother why he rejects not God, but God's world, a world in which landowners feed children to dogs. But while Dostoyevsky had all the necessary credentials for dealing with the big questions in *The Brothers Karamazov*, Vittorini did not possess the same qualities and in the end he did not achieve the results he was striving for. To be fair to the writer, he does make a genuine effort to address the moral issues in a complex non-Manichean way; the book is not just about "men" and "non-men". *Uomini e no* is experimental on the technical level too, containing several italicized passages in which the narrator enters into a dialogue with his characters that stretches the geographical and temporal framework of the novel. But experimental though they may have been, the passages concerned only really provoke perplexity in the reader.

Calvino then went on to say that no "epic" or "choral" work on the Resistance had, as yet, been written. In this context he mentioned Nino Berrini's *Il villaggio messo a fuoco*, a work that was, in fact, originally conceived as the first part of a trilogy that would have, in its author's stated plan, gone on to narrate the story of the whole Resistance movement in Piedmont. Berrini was better known as a dramatist, and had once penned a play about the Provencal troubadour Rimbaud de Vacqueyras. And in the great tradition of the epic poets of the past, Berrini's trilogy remained unfinished at his death, stopping at the end of the first volume with the description of the burning of Boves that provided him with his title.[98]

Berrini's unfinished trilogy was emblematic of the failure of Italian literature to create a national epic out of the Resistance. Years later, Fenoglio would fill this gap in the shape of the much needed *Il partigiano Johnny*. But what Italian writers (including Fenoglio) would be very successful at was in the writing of short stories, which constituted for Calvino "an interesting phenomenon of 'literature for the masses', of the type Italy has not known . . . since the period of the chivalric poems and of classic short stories."[99] The episodic nature of the struggle seems to have lent itself to the short narrative form and some of the best examples of Resistance writing belong to this genre. One potential explanation for their popularity was the fact that the *stampa partigiana* frequently hosted short stories, and so there was a ready-made market for this type of fiction in the immediate postwar. Furthermore, and perhaps more importantly, short stories could easily be incorporated into newspapers and journals as happened with some of the stories written by Calvino and Marcello Venturi. Indeed, as Calvino commented, the phenomenon was not just limited to the left-wing press but could also be found in weekly partisan magazines and in Vittorini's *Il politecnico*. In the 1950s, further attempts were made to support the genre by the institution of literary prizes such as the Premio Prato, which led to the publication of a series of very popular collections in the 1950s.[100] Short stories also lend themselves to anthologies, as the popularity of Gabriele Pedullà's recent selection demonstrates.[101] The Resistance short story therefore occupies an important place in the development of postwar Italian literature.

Calvino also discussed poetry, making the observation that only in the figure of Alfonso Gatto, some of whose poems circulated clandestinely during the Resistance, did Italian letters have anything to rival the impressive achievements of the French. In the postwar, Gatto's poems were collected in *Il capo sulla neve*, published in 1947, but as Calvino commented there seemed to be a scarcity of such works. He hoped, perhaps, that there would be subsequent collections that would fill an evident gap. He would be disappointed. Writing some years later, the critic Gian Carlo Ferretti made the stark comment that the question as to whether Italy's poets had "sung the Resistance" produced an essentially negative response.[102] Italian poetry, with one or two rare exceptions such as the dialect poetry of Egidio Meneghetti, failed to meet the challenge that the Resistance presented.[103]

Rather modestly, Calvino did not discuss his own works, but I would argue that the comments he made in his piece (which went on to discuss novels set during Fascism and depictions of German prison camps) are very revealing about the choices he made in *Il sentiero dei nidi di ragno*, which he mostly composed in December 1946. Calvino's novel would have a famous preface attached to it in the 1960s, but in many ways it is this article, with its identification of the presence of the intellectual and the absence of the epic, which is the real preface to the book. *Il sentiero* very deliberately moves away from the depiction of the intellectual, and so distances itself from *Uomini e no*, by employing a child protagonist, Pin. The use of Pin as the organizing center of the book worked well enough, until Calvino wanted to introduce a lengthy "intellectual" discussion about the diverse motives for joining the Resistance, and was obliged, in a much quoted passage, to shift the focus of the narrative to the ruminations of the medical student Kim about the march of history. It is evident then that Calvino was good at identifying problems, but did not necessarily find the solution to all of them. The choice of a child protagonist would also seem to militate against any possible "epic" aspirations on Calvino's part, but as the authoritative critic Martin McLaughlin has argued, there is much evidence to suggest that *Il sentiero dei nidi di ragno* was designed as a small-scale epic: the twelve chapters of the novel mirror the twelve books of the *Aeneid* and "epic leitmotifs are attached to the characters."[104] Critics have also identified the presence of fairy tale elements, references to the classics (Ariosto, Ovid, Stevenson) and to *film noir*. There is a lot happening in *Il sentiero*, arguably too much, and it is evident that Calvino himself was troubled by the final outcome—he only sanctioned a second edition in 1954, and the preface to the 1964 edition is filled with doubts and almost a sense of self-loathing. Calvino also made significant changes to the 1954 and 1964 versions, removing some of the more extreme elements of the original (notably sex and violence).[105] Despite the problems of the book it does, however, have many qualities. In particular, the rather brutal description of the partisan band, with its echoes of Stevenson's rum crew from *Treasure Island*, suggested that card-carrying communists were capable of writing about the Resistance in a questioning fashion. In all the debate about the would-be communist hegemony of the Resistance myth there has been surprisingly little discussion about Calvino's rejection of "orthodoxy" in *Il sentiero*.

Films

In very much the same way that there was a high concentration of written texts on the Resistance in the period 1945–1948, there was also a large number of films produced in these three crucial years. [106] If anything, it was films—not literary texts, memoirs, or the publications of historians (communist or otherwise)—that did the most to shape ordinary Italians' conception of the Resistance as a united movement of almost the entire population. As was the case with France, films had a "decisive impact on the formation of a common, if not a collective memory."[107] But for films to have an impact, they needed to appeal to the viewing public. As Wagstaff has commented "they were part of the cinema market, competing with American and Italian films which offered the pleasures of narrative, entertainment, pathos, humor and music."[108] This is an important aspect of the phenomenon of Resistance films that the majority of critics have not really grasped, but which is essential if we wish to understand their importance. Before moving on to discuss the very famous films of Rossellini, it is worth mentioning a few cases that are less well known but are, in many cases, more interesting and revealing in terms of the popular dimension of Resistance cinema.

Giorni di gloria, first shown in cinemas in October 1945 (a few weeks after *Roma, città aperta*), is the first important "documentary" film about the Resistance, the result of a collaboration between Luchino Visconti, Marcello Pagliero, Giuseppe De Santis and Mario Serandrei.[109] The film is a loose montage, but there are three discernible narrative threads: the trial of the *questore* of Rome for his involvement in the Fosse Ardeatine massacre, the Fosse Ardeatine themselves—with image after image of the corpses of the 335 victims—and lastly, the "days of glory" of partisan activities and the liberation of the North in April 1945. It was Visconti who was in charge of the filming of the Caruso trial in September 1945. The first witness for the prosecution was Donato Carretta, the former director of the Regina Coeli prison, who had gone some way to redeeming himself by preventing retreating German soldiers from taking captives with them "by successfully arguing that many prisoners were ill and could not bear the rough journey."[110] But Carretta was lynched by the crowd when they mistakenly believed Caruso was about to be absolved. These images were shot as the events unfolded, but in the subsequent editing process a lot was removed. De Santis, one of the film's directors, has revealed that only a short excerpt (a "*pezzettino*") from the lynching footage was used in the final cut: "Perhaps we were wrong, but it was both a political and a poetic decision. This was an isolated episode—the Italian people were completely different. We wanted to show another Italy, the Italy of the Resistance, the Italy that had rolled up its sleeves." De Santis and his colleagues had to make choices when they put the film together, and they opted to show the Italy of the Resistance in a positive way. It was for this reason that, again according to De Santis, they turned down the offer from the Americans of the shots of Mussolini and Petacci lying on the ground at Piazzale Loreto as the crowd kicked and spat at them.[111] It is very easy today to hold De Santis and his colleagues up as an example of dishonesty, but it is necessary to remember that the war had only just finished. Their "censorship" needs to be understood in the context in which the film was made. As the French film critic Sorlin has written, "Film is not a photograph of reality, it has to conform on the one hand to the experiences and the memories of the viewers, on the other to those models and ideas that are *admitted in the country in which the film is produced*."[112] Quite apart from these difficult choices the filmmakers also had to face a practical problem when it came to showing partisans in action—there was, for understandable reasons, a shortage of such material. To get around this problem, former partisans "reenacted" episodes of guerrilla warfare. Nobody cared, apart from the odd reviewer, who spotted the difference between the documentary footage and the "reconstructed" material.

Rome, which is at the center of *Giorni di gloria*, was also the setting for *Due lettere anonime*, released in November 1945. Gina, the film's protagonist who collaborated with the partisans, was played by Clara Calamai, one of Italy's most famous actresses, made famous for her sensational performance in Visconti's *Ossessione*. The film gave a very effective portrayal of occupied Rome, but also had a large dose of dramatic elements—a love triangle, betrayal, and an apparent "crime of passion" committed by Gina when she murders her treacherous lover. The film was also designed to provoke a sense of injustice in its viewers—at the end of the film, Gina stays in prison while others were released. One outraged reviewer commented that in the North, Gina would have been released in triumph, whereas in Rome it was evident that the "wind from the North" did not blow. *Giorni di gloria* demonstrates that, for all their political content, the directors and producers of Resistance films were well aware that they needed to respond to the needs of the box office. And in Italy, melodrama sold.

While *Giorni di gloria* had many melodramatic qualities, there was no actual singing. But there were a number of important Resistance films that unashamedly placed songs and singing at the center of their plots. Of these, two stand out. *O sole mio* provided a starring role for none other than opera singer Tito Gobbi who played, most improbably, an Italo-American singer who worked for the Special Forces and was parachuted into the Neapolitan countryside in September 1943. His mission, to provide the Neapolitan Resistance with military assistance in the shape of coded messages sung over the radio, succeeds (although there are some obstacles on the way in the shape of a female spy who realizes her errors toward the end). No doubt to the great satisfaction of the audience, the character played by Gobbi also gets to marry the earthy Neapolitan woman who had helped him during his mission. In contrast, Carmine Gallone's *Avanti a lui tremava tutta Roma* (1946) had not just an opera singer, but an opera, as its core element. Again set in Rome, as were so many other films, the opera in question is *Tosca* (the eponymous heroine is played by Anna Magnani). The film also featured Tito Gobbi again, but on this occasion, he was the villain Scarpia. Though larded with obvious historical parallels to the Risorgimento, and a plot that borders on the surreal, the film was a big success. This was in part down to Gallone's involvement, and the presence of Magnani and the tenor Gino Sinimberghi as the heroes. But it was also evident that Gallone had hit on a winning formula that allowed him to turn recent history into a spectacular piece of entertainment.

A number of other films of the period give special attention to the role of religion and the Catholic Church during the Resistance. Of these, the most important are Blasetti's *Un giorno nella vita* and Vergano's *Il sole sorge ancora* (both from 1946). *Un giorno nella vita* is set in a convent where a group of partisans seek shelter from the German troops. The sisters try to avoid any contact with them, but as the film progresses, both the partisans and the nuns develop a mutual understanding, with one of the sisters taking the decision to abandon her calling and join the partisans. *Il sole sorge ancora* is the most overt cinematic articulation of the idea of the Resistance as a class war, with the factory workers' eventual victory over the Germans and the bourgeoisie symbolized by an enormous, thrusting, factory chimney at the end of the film. But this victory is only attained by the cooperation of the communist partisans and the Church, a synergy most evident in the film's most memorable scene: a partisan and a priest are executed by the Germans and when they fall, lifeless, to the ground, their bodies intertwine to form the shape of the cross. This "splendid and famous sequence" has as its soundtrack the chorus of the peasants who respond to the priest's prayers during his Calvary.[113]

The place of religion brings us to Rossellini, whose *Roma città aperta* and *Paisà* enjoy a privileged status in the history of world cinema. Three key scenes in *Roma città aperta*, the death of Pina, the torture of the Manfredi and the execution of Don Pietro have entered, as Gundle rightly observes, the "collective imagination," both in Italy and abroad.[114] They are also films that are surrounded by and obscured by their own myths—notably the use of amateur actors, real locations, unscripted dialogue, and other characteristics of neorealism. However, as David Forgacs has demonstrated, and as a generation of my own students has been repeatedly told, the neorealist label is far from productive when it comes to understanding these complex texts.[115] Both films are highly wrought and technically complex works of creative artifice that say as much, and possibly more, about the postwar interpretation of the Resistance as they do about the actual events of the period. *Roma città aperta* and *Paisà* are both heavily characterized by the discourses of nationalism and unity. The war is explicitly portrayed as a war of Liberation from the Germans (Fascists make only fleeting appearances) in which Italians of all social classes, political persuasions, and religious beliefs participated. Considered together, both films seem to cover almost the entire chronological span of the Resistance, from the Allied landings in Sicily in the summer of 1943 to early spring 1945. While *Roma città aperta* is confined to the capital, *Paisà* ranges over the length and breadth of the peninsula: Sicily, Naples, Florence, and the Po delta. Italy, so it seems, finds itself again in the experiences of the war and *Roma, città aperta* and *Paisà* are a complete portrayal of this process. This is certainly the impression the films wish to convey, and they do it extraordinarily successfully. However, a closer look at the films, of the type carried out by Forgacs, reveals there are many missing elements: for example, the deportation of the Jews and the massacre of the Fosse Ardeatine are absent from *Roma*, while the famous ending of *Paisà* ("Two months later, the war was over") means there is no discussion of the death of Mussolini and the postwar killings of Fascists. The reasons for these absences are not difficult to find: while Italy was trying to rebuild itself in the postwar, there were some subjects that needed to be highlighted and others that were better obscured. This is not to single out Rossellini for criticism—he was working in a specific political and cultural context that meant that choices were made, consciously or unconsciously, so that the Resistance movement was portrayed in a favorable light. In the immediate postwar period, above all prior to the 1947 ejection of the PCI from the government coalition, it was in the interests of the nation to present a particularly positive vision of the Resistance. Ideology, therefore, was more powerful than art. And, it is hardly necessary to add, this process was not confined to Italy, but can be detected in the culture of all those countries who participated in the Second World War and who sought to reframe the immediate past to deal with the exigencies of the present.

2

1948–1955

By the summer of 1948 the Resistance "wind from the North" had been reduced to little more than a gentle breeze.[1] Ferruccio Parri ("Maurizio"), one of the most potent political embodiments of the movement, had seen his postwar government collapse in acrimonious circumstances in December 1945. His own party (the PDA) had performed disastrously in the 1946 elections and then folded definitively in 1947. The DC, a party whose Resistance credentials were open to question, had won a crushing victory in the April 1948 elections over the communist PCI, whose leader had then hovered between life and death following Pallante's crazed attack on him outside Montecitorio. Meanwhile, the partisan association, the ANPI, had split along party lines: communist partisans remained in the ANPI, Christian Democrats, Liberals, and politically autonomous veterans formed the FIVL, while actionists, social democrats, and Republicans would go on to form the FIAP in early 1949. Many partisans were under arrest and faced trial, while the so-called "Togliatti amnesty" facilitated the liberation from prison of innumerable Fascists and former adherents of the RSI. The Resistance movement, with its apparent aspirations for a profound renewal in Italian politics and society, was close to total eclipse—the battle that began in September 1943 had been, according to Ginsborg's pessimistic assessment, "decisively lost."[2] Piero Calamandrei, the distinguished jurist, actionist, and university professor put it in different terms: Italy had moved from *resistenza* to *desistenza* (resistance to nonexistence). The anti-Fascist constitution was the only surviving vestige of the Resistance spirit.

There are, of course, some elements of exaggeration in this summary, but it certainly accurately reflects the "intense disappointment" of the former partisans themselves, then and now.[3] During the period 1948–1955, the process of erasure of the Resistance legacy was, however, arrested and there is a clear sense that certain elements of the movement, above all former actionists, attempted to retrench in what were tumultuous years for the Republic—during this time Italy controversially joined NATO (April 4, 1949), and there were elections for the second legislature in June 1953, elections that were contested according to a controversial new electoral law, the *legge maggioritaria* (majority law) or, as some defined it, the *legge truffa* (swindle law).[4] The years 1953–1955 also saw the tenth anniversary of the movement, an anniversary that inevitably reopened discussions and, indeed, led to a cautious reassessment of the Resistance by none other than the Christian Democrats.

In Defense of "Maurizio"

The arrest and trials of communist partisans that had been a feature of the immediate postwar period were given added impetus following the attack on Togliatti's
life. In 1949, over 3,500 partisans were arrested in the province of Modena, most
of whom were subsequently released after months in prison. Most damaging for
the PCI—which never really managed to elaborate a coherent strategy vis à vis the
postwar killings and other episodes of violence—one of its own deputies, Francesco Moranino, was investigated and charged with ordering illegal killings during
the Resistance period. He would go on to lose his parliamentary immunity and
flee to Czechoslovakia in order to avoid arrest. In effect, these episodes were little
short of show trials, a potent demonstration to the nation that the Italian state was
capable of confronting the blemishes of the past and putting its house in order.
But in the light of the recent revelations concerning the "cupboard of shame"—
the deliberate archiving of judicial material relating to Nazi war crimes in Italy and
the associated agreement between Italy and Germany to cover up the war crimes
of both nations—it becomes evident that the "trial of the Resistance" was, at best,
a case of transitional justice gone wrong, and at worst a shameful example of the
politicization of the judicial process.[5] The trials were, therefore, more a reflection
of the vexed context of the Cold War rather than an example of the impartiality
and ineffable search for truth of the Italian judicial system. It is also worth adding
in passing that trials of partisans did not take place anywhere else in Europe, or at
least not on anything like the scale they did in Italy.[6]

It was not, however, only communist partisans who were involved in trials in
this period. Ferruccio Parri himself was the subject of a sustained media attack
in the pages of *Il Merlo giallo*, the paper owned and run by Alberto Giannini, the
founder of the Partito dell'Uomo Qualunque (the Party of the Average Man).[7]
In an article published in 1948, Giannini argued that Parri owed his life to the
generosity of Mussolini, who had negotiated his release after the PDA leader was
captured by the SS in early 1945. Initially, Parri published a short article in December 1948 saying that he had no intention of stooping to the level of the individuals who sought to criticize him.[8] Giannini, either miscalculating the situation, or
perhaps deliberately wishing to provoke a fight, then published a further article
with the title "Parri won't take us to court," the result of which was that Parri did
exactly that. At the initial trial, Giannini was given a fairly stiff sentence, but in its
judgment the court recognized that the motives behind his actions were essentially
well founded. Parri's lawyers, led by Achille Battaglia, contested the court's decision, as did Giannini. At the trial held at the Court of Appeal, Parri's team of lawyers was swelled by the presence of Calamandrei, an indication of how seriously
the whole affair was considered. Again, Giannini was found guilty, condemned
to 14 months of imprisonment and ordered to pay damages and legal expenses.
This decision was later upheld by the Court of Cassation in 1951. Calamandrei
generously donated his legal fees of fifty thousand lire to the Turin-based journal
Resistenza, insisting that the donation remained anonymous.[9]

The *Merlo Giallo* case was not the end of Ferruccio Parri's judicial vicissitudes. On May 17, 1953, the *Meridiano d'Italia* published an article, written by the

neo-Fascists Ugo Franzolin and Franco Maria Servello proclaiming, "The sensa-tionalproof of Maurizio's double dealings." Reliable documents now showed pre-cisely, it was argued, the character of the "men of the Resistance" who had raised themselves up on a pedestal of "blood and mud." The most important of these men was, of course, Ferruccio Parri himself: "the man who was, to Italy's shame, the president of the council of ministers . . . the man who represented the 'wind from the North', and who was the highest expression of the Italy of that period, the Italy of massacres, killings and robberies."[10] On this occasion Parri did not hesitate, and in late October 1953, a defamation trial began in Milan against *Il Meridiano d'Italia* and the two journalists whose defense lawyers quickly managed to argue for a change of venue to Rome. This move bought the accused time and, for legal-technical reasons, the trial was subsequently halted and the accused amnestied.

The collapse of the trial galvanized diverse sections of the Resistance com-munity into action. On February 28, 1954, a demonstration in Milan was held in support of Parri. Parri himself called for a big gathering of Resistance forces before the year was out. But the climax to what was clearly a well-orchestrated event was the speech, delivered at the Lyric Theatre, by Calamandrei, entitled "past and future of the Resistance."[11] Calamandrei's chosen title was a reference to a let-ter Parri wrote to the Fascist judges who had condemned him to ten months of prison and five years of confinement in Ustica many years before. In 1927, Parri had written that Fascism would be defeated by "a second people's Risorgimento— not a Risorgimento led by the vanguard—which alone will link past and future."[12] Calamandrei's title not only represents an act of deference to Parri, who was seated in the audience and who would have instantly recognized the quotation, but also foregrounded a set of interpretations of the Resistance that were central to the actionist tradition: the Resistance movement was a movement of the people, and not of an elite; the Resistance movement was a continuation of the Risorgimento, but with the vital addition of the contribution of the masses; Fascism was a paren-thesis and a historical aberration.

In the course of his long speech, Calamandrei ranged over a number of issues: the spirit of the Resistance, its subsequent betrayal, and the sacrifices of so many. The celebrations of the tenth anniversary of the Resistance were not, he stressed, an act of homage by the quick to the dead. In an inversion straight from the man-ual of classical rhetoric, it was instead the dead who were calling on the people who were still alive to testify, as if in court, as to what the achievements of the last decade had been. The dead surfaced again, indeed the dead *spoke*, about a third of the way through the speech when Calamandrei quoted from the *Lettere di con-dannati a morte della Resistenza italiana*, a text published in 1952 (on which more later), and which contained the final written testimonies of partisans and anti-Fascists prior to their execution. What was so significant about the letters, Cala-mandrei claimed, was that whichever party and whichever faith the condemned belonged to, they always expressed belief in an "idea." Thus the actionist Duccio Galimberti, executed near Cuneo, wrote, "I have acted for an idea and to bring about good: for this reason I am calm and you too should be so." And Guglielmo "Willy" Jervis etched into the cover of a Bible found close to the site of his execu-tion the words: "Don't cry for me. Don't call me a poor man. I'm dying for having served an idea." Calamandrei's strategy of calling the dead of the Resistance into the Lyric Theatre in Milan may strike the modern reader as forced and excessively rhetorical. But that misses the point. The language and rhetorical strategies that Calamandrei employed were part of a set of shared codes that his audience both expected and anticipated. There was, in other words, a common language, a kind of Resistance *koiné*, which circulated at the time. And Calamandrei was, without a doubt, the master practitioner of it. He finally brought his panegyric to Parri and the Resistance to a close by highlighting the "deepest human virtues of the Resistance" such as religious commitment (broadly interpreted), a coherence of thought and action, sincerity and seriousness in life—virtues that the young people who had died in the Resistance handed down for the future. Virtues that, Calamandrei concluded, were symbolized in the "serenity without illusions," in the "pained smile," in the "peaceful and reasoned courage" of his interlocutor and dedicatee, Maurizio.[13]

Spurred on by his supporters, Parri then took out a civil case against *Il Meridiano d'Italia* and the two neo-Fascist journalists, which he won in April 1955. The judgment at this trial was later confirmed at an appeal on January 20, 1956.[14] What, then, was the overall significance of the Parri libel trials, for Parri himself and for the Resistance movement in general? In the case of the first trial, against the *Merlo Giallo*, the defeat of Giannini came at a cost to Parri's authority. He did not win a seat in the 1953 elections and the negative publicity the trial generated could not have helped. In the 1958 elections, after the *Meridiano d'Italia* trial, Parri was elected to the senate. There were, of course, other factors in the resuscitation of Parri's political career, but the two trials that took place at the beginning and middle of the 1950s reveal a shift in Parri's fortunes and, as his most recent biographer has argued, a conscious decision on his part to "cultivate . . . his image as the voice of anti-Fascism and the Resistance."[15] On a wider level they indicate a change in the fortunes of the actionist side of the Resistance movement that found in Parri a figure around which it could organize its activities. At the opposite end of the spectrum, for the neo-Fascists and the *Meridiano d'Italia*, the attack on Parri proved to be a miscalculation. No doubt they hoped that by disgracing Parri they would further undermine the Resistance edifice. As Carli Ballola has commented, the target of the attack was not so much Parri, "but the Resistance *in toto*."[16] But the end result was quite emphatically not the end of the Resistance tradition. If anything, the Resistance movement (and Parri) emerged refreshed from the episode.

Calamandrei, *Il ponte*, and the Orphans of the PDA

The vigorous defense of the former leader of the PDA suggests that, while the party may have collapsed, the actionist *tradition* was alive and well. Paradoxically, the end of the party as a political entity provided the spark that ignited certain keepers of the actionist flame. These individuals, Calamandrei, Giorgio Agosti, Leo Valiani, Aldo Garosci, and the Galante Garrone brothers, to name but a few, formed a substantial group, "a sort of moral community,"[17] of high-caliber intellectuals who were primarily based in two cities, Turin and Florence. The key actionist figure in the period, and mediator, along the Florence-Turin axis, of a staggering amount of political and cultural activity, mostly channeled through *Il ponte*, was the Florentine Calamandrei, staunch defender of Parri.[18]

The first issue of *Il ponte* was published in 1945 by the Florentine publishing house Le Monnier. Le Monnier quickly severed ties with *Il ponte*, arguing that the political plurality that had characterized the journal at its inception had given way to a strictly actionist viewpoint. From 1946 onward, the journal was published by La Nuova Italia and Calamandrei relied on the collaboration of his two faithful pupils: Tristano Codignola and Enzo Enriques Agnoletti. *Il ponte* primarily published articles on contemporary political matters and on recent history. It also published literary texts, including stories by Calvino and Carlo Cassola, as well as translations from a variety of languages. There was also a substantial reviews section, a discussion section and an often amusing rubric containing polemical observations on contemporary Italy. As the journal developed, it published a series of monographic issues that frequently attested to its international interests; for example, the July and August 1954 edition was dedicated to the Dutch Resistance. But *Il ponte* dedicated most space to more strictly national, as well as local, issues (the Liberation of Florence, the tenth anniversary of the Resistance, the commemoration of the actionist partisan Dante Livio Bianco). This is not the place to write, or rewrite, a history of a journal that has rightly received a considerable amount of scholarly attention in recent years.[19] Nonetheless, it is worthwhile devoting some attention to the journal's treatment of the Resistance, which I will do by concentrating on the two-year period running from June 1953 (defeat of the *legge truffa*) to the tenth anniversary in 1955.

By 1953, the first legislature of republican Italy was coming to the end of its five-year term. With elections approaching, the DC decided to introduce a bill that would alter the very strict rules of proportional representation that were enshrined in the constitution. The *legge maggioritaria* (majority law), or *legge truffa* (swindle law) as it was almost universally known, was designed to offer 65 percent of the seats in the chamber of deputies to any party, or group of parties in formal agreement with each other, that obtained 50 percent plus one of the votes.[20] The law passed through the Chamber of Deputies with great difficulty, and was then rushed through the Senate in controversial circumstances, which are still unclear today. Whatever was the case, the *legge truffa* led to the formation of two small political groupings who split from the Social Democrats and the Liberals (who supported the legislation) and who formed *Unità popolare* (Popular Unity) and *Alleanza democratica nazionale* (Democratic National Alliance) respectively.[21] *Unità popolare* put forward three candidates in the election: Calamandrei (who stood for the electoral college of Turin), Parri, and Codignola. These three fought a campaign based on the defense of the values of the Resistance and the constitution, depicted as an organic development of the armed struggle. In the Turin journal *Resistenza*, Parri explained that the movement was not the product of a restricted personal protest but had "precise and concrete political objectives."[22] The PCI campaign did not lay any emphasis on the Resistance and was much more broad-based, focusing on contemporary discussions.[23] The DC, on the other hand, maintained a line they had used to great effect in the 1948 elections: that of attacking the extremes at the red and black poles of the political spectrum.

Although they were only small operations, the effect of *Unità popolare* and *Alleanza democratica nazionale* was to accumulate enough votes to prevent the application of the *legge maggioritaria*. But it was a close affair—the DC and the parties in its grouping won 49.8 percent of the votes and missed out on the big prize by some 54,000 votes. *Unità popolare* and *Alleanza democratica nazionale* crucially accumulated 1 percent of the votes cast and so could lay claim to having been responsible for the prevention of a "swindle" that, they claimed, brought back memories of the Fascist Acerbo electoral law. Calamandrei's letters offer a number of insights into the physical demands of the 1953 election and reveal that he was highly skeptical that any of the *Unità Popolare* candidates would actually be elected. This turned out to be true, but for Calamandrei, the defeat of the swindle law was a victory for the Resistance. And Calamandrei ensured that readers of *Il ponte* were left in no doubt about the significance of this victory. His article in the June 1953 issue of *Il ponte*, polemically titled "The Resistance has resisted," began with gloating observations on the electoral collapse of the DC, and the failure of what he described as the "referendum" on the majority law. The DC, he claimed, had made many tactical mistakes over the years, but they could all be reduced to one, overarching failure, that of having "betrayed the spirit of democratic co-operation left by the Resistance."[24] The sacrifice of the partisans and their commitment to the regeneration of the political struggle enshrined in the CLN, had been, so Calamandrei continued, offended by the DC over the previous five years. Widening his analysis, Calamandrei touched on the baleful polarizing effects of the 1948 elections and of the Cold War. But the Cold War, and the opposing positions assumed by the major political parties who had fought together in the Second World War, did not excuse the DC for having "repudiated with horror" the Resistance in a kind of "crusade against the heretics."[25] Calamandrei's scathing article ended with the observation that, although the DC should not be excluded from power for all its faults, the party should see the 1953 elections as a wake-up call that would make them return to their first principles.

The celebrations, however, did not last long before they were overshadowed by a crushing loss for the Resistance, the actionists, and Calamandrei personally. On a stunning day in mid-June, Dante Livio Bianco, the former *giellista* partisan, collaborator of *Il ponte*, and close personal friend of Calamandrei, went on a routine mountaineering expedition. Bianco knew the mountains well, but on Sunday, July 12, 1953, he lost his footing near the summit of Saint Robert and fell to his death. His body was recovered the following afternoon by two of his fellow partisans. Parri placed on the corpse three red carnations, gathered from the monument to Duccio Galimberti, another actionist. At the seventh sitting of the newly elected chamber of deputies (July 23), Antonio Giolitti made a speech commemorating Livio Bianco. Deputies from various political parties voiced their approval of Giolitti's words, but all DC deputies, including the speaker Giovanni Gronchi, maintained, as De Luna has commented, an "obstinate silence" as they listened on insouciantly.[26]

Two days after the funeral, Calamandrei wrote to Giorgio Agosti in Turin. He had, so he wrote, returned from Valdieri (where the funeral took place), "bewildered and devastated." His wife Ada had taken to her bed at their coastal retreat at Poveromo. *Il ponte* was ready to go to press and he had managed to add two pages about Livio Bianco. On one page there would be a photo of him and his brother from the time when they were partisans; on the other, some carefully chosen words. But, Calamandrei revealed, the grief he felt meant he was unable to write about him calmly. He had written, however, a kind of epigraph that could be published opposite the photo. But he was unsure as to whether this might appear "jarring" so soon after his death. An alternative would be simply to print the death notice that had been published by the partisans from Cuneo and publish the epigraph in the special commemoration issue that came out in April 1954. Agosti, who was one of the editors of a 1954 Einaudi edition of Livio Bianco's partisan diary and other related writings,[27] was asked to decide and send a telegram to the offices of *Il ponte* indicating either "I choose Cuneo" or "I choose the epigraph." [28] He chose the epigraph, which begins with the striking image of Livio Bianco, a few meters from the summit, spurring his climbing partners on to finish the mission they had set out to accomplish: "at all costs we must climb to the top."[29] The need, not just to climb the mountain, but to take the Resistance movement to its conclusion is clearly established in this first stanza, which also evokes the Ulysses episode in Dante's *Inferno*, where the charismatic hero encourages his men to seek knowledge beyond the pillars of Hercules. In the second and central stanza, Calamandrei reemploys the same rhetorical topos he had used in the speech he dedicated to Parri. From the "black mountain," 10 years after they had first assembled, the shades of the partisans in eternal lookout recognized their leader, and waved their scarves and sang once more as he continued his climb to the top, desiring to remain young among the others who had themselves died young. In the third and final stanza, Calamandrei moves away from a third person description of the fatal climb to invite his readers, the *Il ponte* community, to suspend their grief and look up to the top of the mountain in search of Livio Bianco, here addressed as "*tu*" (in other words, as if he were still alive). The epigraph moves toward its end with a request to Livio Bianco to give a sign if he sees any hesitation. The line from the first sentence "*a tutti i costi bisogna salire*" (at all costs we must climb to the top) is then repeated, creating a sense of circularity and closure, as does the final couplet: "*anche se questo è morire*" (even if this means death). These final words, with the poetic construction of "*è*" plus an infinitive functioning as a noun, also consciously echo the most famous lines of the fifteenth century Spanish poet Jorge Manrique's *Coplas a la muerte de su padre,* where life is compared to a river flowing into the sea: "*que es el morir.*"

This highly crafted and extraordinarily recondite epigraph, with its references to the classics of Italian and Spanish literature, was one of a number that Calamandrei wrote in the 1950s to commemorate various individuals and events. Unlike the work dedicated to Livio Bianco, which appeared only on paper, many of Calamandrei's epigraphs were, quite literally (and therefore faithful to the Greek etymology of the word), inscribed in stone. Put another way, in Calamandrei's epigraphs the stones are made to speak. The number of them, and the importance they had in the development of the language of the Resistance, means they occupy a category of their own, which lies at the intersection of poetry and monuments. Calamandrei's epigraphs can be found throughout the city of Florence—on the wall of the Rosselli brothers' house in Via Giusti, on their tombstone at the Trespiano cemetery, at the "Villa Triste" on the Via Bolognese where the Banda Carità tortured their victims, as well as on the Palazzo Vecchio itself. They can also be found on, or in, municipal buildings at Mantua, Campegine, and Cuneo, as well as at the church at Madonna del Colletto, where the *giellisti* Duccio Galimberti and Livio Bianco, formed the first partisan bands in September 1943. By far the most famous, and the one that gave the Resistance movement one of its longest-lasting phrases, *"ORA E SEMPRE RESISTENZA"* (now and forever Resistance), is the "Monument to Kesselring" in Cuneo. The occasion that inspired the epigraph (see Figure 2.1) was the release from jail, in the autumn of 1952 of Kesselring, the German officer in charge of military operations in Italy during the war. Kesselring returned to Germany where he was given a hero's welcome and, during the last eight years of his life, became an object of worship. Upon his return, Kesselring declared that he had no regrets about his period in charge of the German campaign in Italy, and went so far as to suggest that Italy should erect a monument to him in gratitude. In the first stanza of the epigraph Calamandrei replied directly to Kesselring (in the informal *"tu"* form, which was not characteristic of this extraordinarily polite man) and said that his wish would be granted but that Italians would choose the stone from which it would be crafted. The second stanza then contains a series of descriptions of what the monument will *not* be made of:

NON COI SASSI AFFUMICATI
DEI BORGHI INERMI STRAZIATI DAL TUO STERMINIO
NON COLLA TERRA DEI CIMITERI
DOVE I NOSTRI COMPAGNI GIOVINETTI
RIPOSANO IN SERENITÀ
NON COLLA NEVE INVIOLATA DELLE MONTAGNE
CHE PER DUE INVERNI TI SFIDARONO
NON COLLA PRIMAVERA DI QUESTE VALLI
CHE TI VIDE FUGGIRE

[Not with the smoking stones
Of the innocent villages laid waste by your massacres
Not with the earth from the cemeteries
Where our young comrades
Rest in peace
Not with the untouched mountain snow
Which for two winters challenged you
Not with the spring of these valleys
Which watched you flee]

As the stanza proceeds, with the emphatic repetition of *"Non,"* so the material for the monument moves from the tangible to the metaphoric. This poetic elision continues into the third and final stanza where, in one lengthy and spiraling sentence, Calamandrei promises that the silence of the tortured and the pact of the free men who came together to oppose the shame and terror of the world, will be waiting for Kesselring who, if he returns to Italy, will find the quick and the dead, gathered around a monument that is called *"Ora e sempre Resistenza."* The epigraph to Kesselring is therefore characterized by the same kind of rhetorical inversion that Calamandrei had already employed elsewhere. But in this epigraph the inversion topos runs through both the content and the form of the text, leading to a cumulative

Figure 2.1. Piero Calamandrei's epigraph—a 1990s version at S. Anna di Stazzema (Tuscany).

effect that means that the last line, "*Ora e sempre Resistenza*," issues forth from the stone in an extraordinary exclamatory charge.

In the period under examination, therefore, Calamandrei and his circle can be seen to have devoted themselves to a wide range of activities, but it is possible to discern three connected themes: (1) the promotion of the memory of the *Giustizia e Libertà* (GL; Justice and Liberty) movement, most potently symbolized by Carlo and Nello Rosselli, the Florentine brothers assassinated in France in the 1930s; (2) the promotion and defense of the Resistance movement of 1943–1945 and specifically of the role of the GL partisans and actionist leaders; (3) the defense of the figure of Ferruccio Parri, who was throughout on the receiving end of a series of attacks from various quarters. Calamandrei, in particular, used the heavy weapons at his disposal, above all his skills as a writer and speaker, to reinforce the actionist paradigm. Yet, if we move forward to today, it is evident that the actionist view of, and defense of the Resistance, has not endured. This is certainly the view of the distinguished journalist and former *giellista* partisan Giorgio Bocca, whose most recent contributions to the Resistance debate are characterized by barely disguised disgust at the betrayal of the movement. Where did things go wrong? For Giovanni De Luna, part of the blame lies with the historians who have failed to give the attention due to the GL movement, and to the PDA itself. Certainly De Luna, author of a distinguished history of the PDA, is not at fault here. But to attribute the blame to the fact that the communist side of the Resistance has benefitted from excessive scholarly treatment misses the point. The actionist paradigm faltered for a number of reasons related to the particular characteristics of the PDA and its followers. The PDA was a party made up of intellectuals who sought, but failed, to get their message to the masses. Their electoral failure is ample evidence of this. But this failure was not, as has been frequently argued, wholly a result of factions within the party. Whatever message the PDA had, they did not have the means at their disposal to get it across effectively to the broader populace. Parri, it was widely commented, could not speak to save his life. He had extremely limited oratorical skills. Calamandrei, on the other hand, had these skills by the spadeful. But his language operates at such a level that it requires a level of decoding and interpretation beyond the capacities of all but the most highly educated. This is not to dismiss Calamandrei's contribution, but it needs to be understood that his style of writing and speaking belonged to an era that is now long past. The carefully crafted classical rhetoric of his epigraphs may have suited certain audiences in the 1950s, but they now strike us as excessive and posturing. Furthermore, they had an effect that no doubt would have appalled Calamandrei—they established a kind of linguistic paradigm that many subsequently tried to copy, feeling that the only suitable language of commemoration was the language of Calamandrei. To give him his due, Calamandrei excelled at what he did. But his many imitators, whose style can be traced in countless speeches and monuments, can be compared to the worst Petrarchists, who tried to emulate their master but ended up turning him into a cliché.

A further problem connected with the actionist tradition was also identified by Giorgio Agosti in his diary. In October 1954 he attended a "melancholy" meeting in Turin of the GL association. There were only seven individuals, including

Agosti, in a "squalid venue." As far as Agosti was concerned, *giellismo* was coming to its end; it didn't attract new, young elements. It was simply a tired veterans' association that, 10 years after the Liberation, offered a space to partisans who had not sorted out their lives and considered it "a substitute for coffee."[30] There are elements of self-indulgence here. But Agosti was not just wallowing in his own misery. The comment about the impossibility of renewal, because of the inaccessibility of the movement to successive generations, is significant and highlights one of the problems the Resistance movement in general never really resolved: how to pass the message of the Resistance on to young dynamic elements who would keep it alive and maintain, as the years passed, its radical charge.

The actionist approach also had another effect that may have proved costly in the long-term fortunes of the Resistance. By focusing on the three areas described, which belonged to three stages in the history of the actionist tradition, Calamandrei and his associates emphasized what they saw as the substantial continuity of their movement from anti-Fascism to the Resistance and from then to the *dopoguerra*. A single line that "linked the different anti-Fascist generations" was thus created and had the effect of homogenizing what were in reality separate and delineated phases of the history of twentieth-century Italy.[31] The reasons for this emphasis on a single thread are not hard to find: continuity suggests coherence, long-term commitment, and organization. But the uniqueness of the Resistance period was sacrificed in this process.

Novels, Short Stories, and Other Forms of Culture

The Resistance novels of Calvino, Vittorini, and Pavese were all published in the intense period of 1945–1948. The years 1948–1955 did not have the same levels of literary activity, but nevertheless saw the publication of some key works, most notably Renata Viganò's 1949 novel *L'Agnese va a morire*, Beppe Fenoglio's collection of stories, *I ventitré giorni della città di Alba*, and Carlo Cassola's *Fausto e Anna* (both 1952).

Renata Viganò had been a partisan *staffetta* and after the war became a correspondent for *L'Unità*. Her husband was the partisan leader Antonio Meluschi, who also published works of fiction as well as editing the journal *L'indicatore partigiano*. Meluschi was one of the many former partisans to be arrested after the *attentato a Togliatti*, the subject of one of Viganò's short stories.[32] When Viganò sent her typescript to Einaudi, it fell into the hands of the writer Natalia Ginzburg, who read it with great enthusiasm—publication of the book was, in her view, "a must." Ginzburg continued to show interest in Viganò and her work and it was she who wrote to the author in October 1949 to tell her that the first edition had sold out.[33] The book, a straightforward "popular epic" according to the critic Manacorda, tells the simple story of the sacrifice of a peasant woman whose husband, Palita, is taken away by the Germans.[34] Agnese, a name with obvious symbolic resonances, decides to help the partisans and shares their hardships with them. She learns that her husband did not survive the journey to Germany, and she herself is killed at the end of the story by a German officer she had earlier, so she thought, bludgeoned to death. In keeping with a tradition that goes back to *Roma, città aperta*, the German soldiers are depicted as dehumanized beasts. The Allies, in turn, fare little better and are shown as being responsible for hampering the efforts of the partisans. General Alexander's message to the partisans to dig in for the winter comes in for some particularly harsh criticism. More than any other text, literary or otherwise, *L'Agnese va a morire* provides access to the communist interpretation of a Resistance betrayed *during the war* by its partners in the struggle against the Germans and the Fascists. But it does have some more innovative elements—*L'Agnese va a morire* is one of the few Resistance texts that gives thorough treatment to the relationship between the partisans and nature, particularly in a number of what the critic Gatt-Rutter defines as "major set-pieces."[35] There is extensive use of pathetic fallacy to reflect the dark moods of the partisans, but the book also gives the impression that, at times, there was a third enemy (or a fourth if we include the Allies) in the shape of the forces of nature that impede the progress of the partisans. *L'Agnese va a morire* has stood the test of time for a variety of reasons. For the PCI, the book was the nearest thing to an Italian version of Maxim Gorky's *The Mother* and quickly established itself as required reading for all party members, particularly women. Later, Einaudi published a schools edition. A film version was made in the 1970s, which the Catholic critic Paoluzi recommended in the mid-1950s and, to cap it all, in what was an otherwise sweeping condemnation of virtually all communist culture, Alberto Asor Rosa praised it in his *Scrittori e popolo*. The book was also an international success and was translated into Hungarian, Polish, Czech, Spanish (published in Argentina), Russian, and Chinese. Above all, the reason for the enduring success of *L'Agnese va a morire* lies in its powerful, no-nonsense assertion that the Resistance was not an exclusively male phenomenon. In 1955, Viganò would go on to add further weight to this view by publishing a volume of biographical sketches of women who had participated in the Resistance.[36]

Viganò's text seems to have progressed very smoothly through the editorial process following Ginzburg's initial acceptance. The same cannot be said for the collection of seven short stories that Beppe Fenoglio submitted to the same publisher in 1949, with the title *Racconti della guerra civile*. By the time the stories came out in 1952, one had been dropped, the title had changed several times and another six, non-Resistance, stories had been added to the collection. For this, we have to thank Elio Vittorini, who made the major editorial decisions at the time. Leaving aside for the moment the changes to the design of the volume, it is the change in the title, on which Vittorini was most insistent, which is most to be condemned. Arguably, had the expression *guerra civile* been kept, we may not have had to wait until the early 1990s and the publication of Pavone's *Una guerra civile*, for there to have been some consensus about the nature of the war fought in Italy from 1943 to 1945. The six Resistance stories that were published begin with "*I ventitré giorni della citta di Alba*," an ironic account of the short-lived partisan occupation of Alba, and finish with "*Un altro muro*," a grim story of the execution of partisans. Significantly, no German soldiers appear in any of the stories, a clear indication that the struggle was between Italians. The enemies are, without exception, the Fascists of the RSI. The collection is also endowed with a chronological and temporal unity. The four stories that follow the title story all occur after the Alba episode and take place in different sections of the Langhe. In the last story ("*Un altro muro*") we come full circle and are back in Alba. When they were first published, they were greeted with some hostility in the communist press.[37] This hostility, however, needs to be understood in the context of the climate of the early 1950s.

If PCI critical reaction to Fenoglio was hostile, it was as nothing compared to the response to Cassola's *Fausto e Anna*, also published by Einaudi in 1952.[38] The novel charts the tortured relationship between Anna and the autobiographical protagonist Fausto, who joins a group of partisans when things do not work out between them. It is almost as if the political choice is a response to inner turmoil, rather than the product of a "commitment" to an ideal. Fausto becomes increasingly uneasy about the partisans' recourse to the summary execution of German prisoners. Their moral universe is dominated by vengeance and is unfavorably compared with that of an Allied soldier whose phrase "I am an honorable soldier" haunts Fausto in the last section. In Cassola's highly pessimistic worldview it is not history, as such, that interests him, but the isolated individual within history, and his, or her, existential torments are the subject of his narrative.[39] The book was published in the Einaudi series *I gettoni*, edited by Vittorini, and it was the entire series that the communist critic Giuliano Manacorda savaged in the pages of *Rinascita*, devoting special attention, however, to *Fausto e Anna*. Fausto, Manacorda observed, viewed the partisans with disdain, and they were depicted as nothing but "a bunch of cowards and assassins." As for anti-Fascist unity, this hardly seemed to exist, and was indeed compromised throughout the book by the communist presence. The *gettoni*, Manacorda concluded, were not all to be condemned, but they had hosted a lot of bad stuff, notably Calvino's *Il visconte dimezzato* and, in a clear swipe at Cassola, the "tritest regurgitations of a widespread antipartisan propaganda."[40] Cassola soon replied, accusing Manacorda of failing to make a necessary distinction between literature and propaganda, at which point Togliatti himself was moved to intervene in a *postilla*.[41] There was, it is clear, a certain amount of posturing on both sides, but the encounter again demonstrates the extraordinarily politicized nature of cultural discussion in Italy at the time. Whether or not Cassola was interested in the historical phenomenon of the Resistance, or in the futility of the search for happiness through love (as critics have argued), was not particularly relevant. To be fair, neither Cassola nor Manacorda should be condemned for their actions. They were simply part of a much wider political and historical conjuncture that conditioned the Resistance debate at the time.

These three works by Cassola, Viganò, and Fenoglio belong to the canon of Resistance writing and make frequent appearances on undergraduate courses in Italian studies, but another publication of 1952 has become, it is no exaggeration to say, the "sacred text" of the Resistance. The *Lettere di condannati a morte della Resistenza italiana* is a collection of the last letters of partisans, anti-Fascists, and other "resisters" prior to execution. This text, edited by Giovanni Pirelli and Piero Malvezzi, first appeared in 1951 when, as an unpublished typescript, it won a prize, the *Premio Venezia della Resistenza*.[42] Einaudi published the first edition in 1952. The *Lettere* were nothing short of a publishing sensation and the first two editions rapidly sold out. A third edition soon followed, containing further letters, many of which had been brought to the attention of the editors in the intervening period. Since then, the *Lettere* have been republished on countless occasions and in many different formats. Five of the *Lettere* were used by the composer Vittorio Fellegara for an orchestral piece involving a choir and "reciting voices."[43] At least one, if not more, versions of the *lettere* have been released on vinyl.[44] The neo-Fascists countered, in 1960, with their own edition of the *Lettere di caduti della Repubblica Sociale Italiana*, an example of the kind of tit for tat strategy that has consistently characterized the postwar battle for memory. The *Lettere* led to a sequel, in the form of the well-known collection of letters of the European Resistance with a preface by Thomas Mann that was published in 1954. This volume has also had a life of its own—inspiring one of Luigi Nono's most famous works, the *Canto sospeso*, as well as the monument to the European Resistance at Como where extracts from the letters appear on huge slabs at the center of the work.

The most important characteristic of the *Lettere* is their adaptability. They have been used to create other cultural forms, such as the musical pieces and monuments mentioned previously. But they have also been used, most frequently, in schools on or before the April 25 celebrations and commemorations. Above all, from 1960 onward the reading by a teacher or, frequently, a former partisan, of a few of the letters became one of the required rites in schools throughout Italy. It is difficult to find an educated Italian who does not recall such events, sometimes with fond nostalgia, sometimes, it must be said, with distaste. Furthermore, the *Lettere* contain testaments that are underpinned by a very broad ideological span. This political plurality has meant, and still means, that the *Lettere* contain something for everyone (with the exception of neo-Fascists) and so have been one of the few Resistance texts around which there exists some form of consensus. Gundle suggests that the "volume gave rise to a view of the Resistance as a moral revolt against Nazi paganism and totalitarianism."[45] Pietro Scoppola, the doyen of historians of Christian Democracy, identifies the Catholic discovery of the Resistance with this publication.[46] In addition to its multicolored political spectrum, the volume also possesses one key *uniting* factor: whatever their beliefs, the last letters suggest, as Calamandrei himself emphasized, that all the deaths were for an "idea"—whether that idea be communist, socialist, actionist, or Catholic. In other words, there were no apolitical deaths in 1943–1945—at the moment of ultimate sacrifice, the condemned individual thought not of himself (or herself), or of his family (particularly his mother), but of the country. It is, of course, open to debate whether all the individuals who were executed during the Resistance devoted their last thought to Italy. But this misses the point. The *Lettere*, eloquently described by Gatt-Rutter as one of Italian culture's "least literary" but "most austere monuments" proposed a very powerful image of a Resistance *ars moriendi*, which has had a lasting hold on the Italian imagination.[47]

Roberto Battaglia's *Storia della resistenza italiana*

In April 1950, a conference on "The Resistance and Italian Culture" was held in Venice. The initiative was originally the idea of the *azionista* intellectual, Franco Antonicelli. The conference document sought to remind the "people without memory" that republican Italy had been built on the sacrifice of the partisans and the army of Liberation and asked all the democratic forces of Italian culture and politics to defend and promote the values of the Resistance.[48] Along with Antonicelli, the conference organizers included the communist Roberto Battaglia and the *azionista* Joyce Lussu and Ignazio Silone. The conference was well attended by individuals from across the political spectrum, including Calvino.

During the course of the conference, Roberto Battaglia gave a speech on the history and historiography of the Resistance. Calvino liked what he heard and, in a letter to Battaglia, encouraged him to write a short, accessible history of the Resistance for Einaudi's series, the Piccola Biblioteca Scientifico-Letteraria. Calvino hoped the book would be suitable for intellectuals and workers, as well as for the young.[49] Three years later, in April 1953, Einaudi published a volume that went considerably beyond Battaglia's original brief and only really appealed to the first category identified by Calvino. At some 621 pages, including maps, photographs and a sizeable bibliographical appendix, the *Storia della Resistenza italiana* is a mighty volume.[50] Ever since its first publication, followed by a second amended edition later in 1953, an abridged version published in 1955,[51] and a substantial update published posthumously in 1964, Battaglia's history has provoked both hostility and admiration. Whatever its merits, the book occupies a key space in Italian Resistance historiography. Up until the publication of Pavone's *Una guerra civile*, some 40 years later, Battaglia's *Storia*, whether you liked it or loathed it, was the master text of Resistance historiography.

Roberto Battaglia was originally an art historian, with several important publications to his name, who adhered to the GL movement, and fought with *giellisti* partisans in Umbria.[52] The declassification of Special Operations Executive (SOE) documents has revealed that Battaglia was recruited by Lt. Col. Salvadori of the British Secret Services in June 1944 and worked as an allied liaison officer to a Major Oldham. Along with various letters asking, with some frustration, for payment for services rendered, there is a brief appraisal of Battaglia written by an anonymous British officer, AM 203, in 1945. Battaglia, his appraiser writes, was a "first-class man who has proved that in addition to being a man of letters he is a fighter and a man of action." He was "warmly recommended for re-employment" and, in a highly revealing comment on Allied attitudes to the future of Italy, AM 203 suggested that "if ever anyone were needed for service against a communist Italy, subject would probably be as willing to fight communism as he was fascism, himself being a true democrat and a lover of freedom at heart."[53] We can only imagine how AM 203 would have reacted to Battaglia's publications of the 1950s. Naturally, there is no reference to his relations with the SOE in his memoir, *Un uomo, un partigiano*, published in 1945 when he was an active member of the PDA.[54]

In the immediate postwar period Battaglia went on to be involved in the process of securing official recognition for partisans and published an article on the subject in the special number of *Il ponte* dedicated to the crisis of the Resistance.[55] Following the collapse of the PDA he became a member of the PCI in 1948. In 1949 he published his first article in *Rinascita* on the DC's attack on the Resistance.[56] By the time he was writing his *Storia*, his views vis à vis communism had therefore changed considerably.

The first edition of Battaglia's *Storia* was published in April 1953 and comprises 17 chapters. The book proposes and reinforces a familiar teleological reading of the Resistance seen as a process which, despite setbacks of many sorts, concluded in the successful uprisings of April 1945, at which point the weapons were laid down. Throughout the grand narrative of the *Storia*, Battaglia gives pride of place to the Communist Party, seen as the prime organizer of the movement. The PDA is also assigned a major role in the unfolding story. Both the communists and the actionists are seen as opposers of the forces of *attesismo,* the waiting game that was played by more moderate forces, notably the DC. A further protagonist are the masses—the workers whose strikes were instrumental in bringing down Mussolini and the peasants who supported the partisans. The Resistance movement is also seen as a straight continuation of the Risorgimento, an interpretation Battaglia had strongly criticized in the earlier *Un uomo, un partigiano.*

The publication of Battaglia's history was met with near jubilation in the pages of the ANPI journal *Patria indipendente.* In the main, the ANPI journal published positive responses, including an interview with Carlo Levi who emphasized, yet again, the links between the Resistance and the Risorgimento. And it was on the question of this historical parallel with which Togliatti himself began his review in *Rinascita,* his only significant written engagement with the Resistance during the 1950s.[57] Togliatti was in total agreement with the comparison and his review of the book was positive, although there were some sections in the book he found "jumbled" and "confusing."[58] However, not everyone greeted Battaglia's history in such a glowing way.[59] The former actionist Enzo Enriques Agnoletti dedicated a long and perceptive review to the work, which was published in *Il ponte.* Agnoletti began with a detailed defense of the Allies, unjustly lambasted, in his view, throughout the *Storia.* Agnoletti also pointed to, and was the only reviewer to write with sensitivity on, the "doubling" that ran through the book. The author Battaglia, once an actionist, was now, Agnoletti observed, a committed communist and was, in a sense, in dialogue with himself, with his past choices, with his noncommunist and even anticommunist self of the war period—the interior debate "of the new man with the former man runs throughout the narrative."[60] Agnoletti also criticized Battaglia for using mostly secondary sources, rather than archive materials, but the review also saw many positive aspects in the book. Despite the book's unilateralism, the Resistance was "there" as were the problems of the movement. There was, too, a sense of a national struggle and of its connection with the international context.

Agnoletti's review saw both good and bad in Battaglia's book and ascribed the bad to the former actionist's change in political allegiance. If we use this approach, then we can begin to understand the nature of Battaglia's book. It is, clearly, the product of a man trying to come to terms with his two selves—or three if we add

Roberto Battaglia the art historian. Equally, the *Storia* is a product of its times and of the intense nature of political debate. Perhaps Luigi Longo did stand over Battaglia and offer corrections, as Vittorio Foa once suggested, although I suspect this is a tall tale. But this doesn't mean that it is a work that should be dismissed as a "party book." All texts are ideologically conditioned and a reading that understands and accounts for, rather than rejects, this dimension leads to infinitely richer results. By looking at this text from its twin ideological perspectives, readers can find out a lot about the Resistance and, perhaps in equal measure, they can gain invaluable insights into the nature of the Resistance debate in the 1950s.

Resistance Historiography after Battaglia

Battaglia's *Storia* was not the only contribution to the Resistance historiography of the period, although it had the most impact.[61] The following year, the two key figures in the PCI organization of the Resistance, Longo and Secchia, weighed in with their own books, published by Riuniti in the same series: the "library of the working class movement." Secchia's *I comunisti e l'insurrezione* and Longo's *Sulla via dell'insurrezione nazionale* both argue for the primacy of the PCI in the organization of the final key moment of the Resistance, the insurrection in the big industrial cities of Turin, Genoa, and Milan at the end of April 1945.[62] The Secchia volume contains articles published in *L'Unità* and *La nostra lotta*. The publication of contemporary documents was seen as particularly valuable to the Resistance debate as they offered, so it was thought, privileged access to how things really were during the time of the movement and were not sullied by memory or interpretation. Whether or not this was really the case is another matter, and the Secchia volume, which includes sections on the mobilization of the party and the masses, on armed struggle and mass struggle and on the party as the "motor force" behind the insurrection, demonstrates how careful selection and presentation can be used to give a particular slant to a complex phenomenon. In addition to the works by the PCI's big guns, Riuniti also published Mario De Micheli's *7a GAP*.[63] Unencumbered by footnotes or any reference to sources, the book tells in a simple, direct manner the story of the Bolognese *gappisti*. Clearly designed for consumption by a communist readership, the book provides a familiar epic tale of heroism and sacrifice. Of course the book didn't tell the "truth." But that wasn't the issue. It was 1954, the PCI had won six million votes in the 1953 elections and wished to build on this success. If this meant engaging in the "political use of history," no one within the PCI would have any qualms.

The PCI was certainly not alone in 1954—the "orphans" of the PDA published two significant works in that year. The first, entitled *Una lotta nel suo corso*, is a collection of letters and documents relating to the activities of the PDA from 1943 to 1945.[64] Most of the letters were sent by or to Carlo Ludovico Ragghianti, the *actionist* who became president of the Tuscan Committee of National Liberation (CTLN). The letters are framed by a preface written by Ferruccio Parri, which attempts to show how the approach of the PDA could have had relevance in the context of the current political debate. Parri suggested that people who did not campaign for a class revolution or for the preservation of the status quo of the classes (i.e., the communist and Christian Democratic positions respectively), might find in the letters a valuable lesson in how to use a process of "democratic evolution" in order to bring about the "unfinished Liberation."[65] Parri's preface, therefore, blames the failure of the actionist paradigm on the politics of the two parties who went on to dominate postwar political life. But, paradoxically, the documents in the book seem to offer a different explanation. Many of the letters reveal tensions within the PDA that were destined to surface disastrously immediately after the war. For example, when Leo Valiani, the leading representative of the party within the CLN, writes to Ragghianti and others that the PDA, the communists, and the socialists have formed a tacit voting agreement, the response from the Tuscan CTLN is one of outright condemnation. There were also problems created by the nature of the relationship and the process of articulation between the forerunners of the party, the *Giustizia e libertà* movement, and the PDA. These problems are discussed frankly in a break in the narrative of the documents that the editors insert as an *intermezzo* (intermission). We learn that when the long-term, anti-Fascist Aldo Garosci returned to Italy from exile, his desire was that the new party would be absorbed into the GL movement and not the other way round.

The second actionist book of 1954, *Disegno della liberazione italiana*, is a collection of articles and documents, written by Ragghianti himself.[66] Ragghianti had been a leading figure in the Tuscan liberation. In Parri's government he was an undersecretary for culture. At the Rome congress of February 1946, Ragghianti teamed up with Valiani in a failed attempt to stop the party from splitting. As with *Una lotta nel suo corso*, the *Disegno* also contains much discussion on the reasons for the failure of "actionism." But in this book, although there are some references to internal debates, this side of the history of the PDA is largely obscured. The Parri government, when the problems really came out into the open, is given only three brief pages.[67] Instead, the focus for Ragghianti's explanation of the actionists' failure is the communist party. In the first *saggio*, dedicated to the history of the CLN, Ragghianti underlines how the PDA was, from its inception, firmly against the Badoglio government. The PDA, above all else, felt that Italy needed to go forward without its monarchy and the Badoglio government was just an extension of that institution. The *svolta di Salerno* is, therefore, portrayed as not only an act of betrayal by Togliatti and the communist party but also as the original sin that led to all the problems that Italy and the PDA suffered after the war. Without the *svolta di Salerno*, he continued, Italy would have gotten rid of the monarchy without the need for a referendum; without the *svolta*, the Parri government would have survived; without the *svolta*, there would have been no Togliatti amnesty and admission of the Lateran pacts into the Republican Constitution. The PDA, nevertheless, could claim one significant success had stemmed from their efforts: they had stopped the Resistance from having a communist outcome.[68] There is much bitterness in this first article and the rest of the book seems to reflect a deliberate decision to move toward more congenial subject matter such as the early life of the PDA and the clandestine periodical *La Libertà*.

Ragghianti also had a hand in persuading Massimo Salvadori to turn into a book a series of articles on the Resistance that had originally been designed for an

Italo-American audience. Salvadori had worked for the British Special Forces during the war, was a "liberal anti-Fascist," and a member of GL, and it is therefore not surprising that the book is broadly actionist in its outlook. But there are also some significant departures from "actionist orthodoxy" that make the book worthy of comment. Salvadori argues that, despite one or two episodes at ground level, there was substantial unity among the differing political parties. This unity was only broken after the war was over and was a result of wrangling between the parties of the constitutional arc. Such an interpretation is at variance with the standard actionist model that saw the unity of the movement broken by the *svolta di Salerno* in March 1944. Salvadori would thus seem to lean toward a typically communist viewpoint, except that he attaches no blame to the Allies (as the communists did), emphatically not guilty of any "Machiavellian plans" to scupper the revolutionary spirit of the Resistance.[69] Salvadori shows some considerable understanding of the political situation during the Resistance, stressing throughout the high degree of politicization of the movement. Salvadori also had some important comments on who was the major organizing force: "In first place in the organisation of the clandestine army were the PDA and the Communist Party (indeed the latter more than the former)."[70] Salvadori's work, therefore, has some striking similarities with that of the man he recruited into the partisan movement, Roberto Battaglia. But firmly based in the United States, and an advisor to NATO, Salvadori was emphatically not a communist.

Difficult Years for the ANPI

The ANPI held its second congress in Venice in March 1949. The event was dominated by the split in the association that was clearly painful and difficult to manage. This period saw the birth of one of the central pillars of ANPI's rhetorical strategy—the unity of the Resistance. The insistence on the united nature of the movement served to suggest that the split into factions was not a result of preexisting tensions but a direct consequence of the Cold War climate. The separation into ANPI, FIAP, and FIVL was not a reflection of the nature of the Resistance itself, an organically compact movement, but an artificial accident of history. In this way the ANPI was able to maintain a dialogue with those partisans who went over to FIAP, in the hope that they could at least maintain open channels of communication. Boldrini, the ANPI president himself hoped, despite the fact that the historical situation was not good, that his association and FIAP could stay "in contact and not at odds with each other."[71]

The emphasis on unity was a survival strategy, an effective one at that, and it allowed the association to portray itself as democratic. Others thought differently, such as the *Meridiano d'Italia*, which gave a different interpretation of the association's acronym, calling it the "*Associazione nazionale pericolosi impazziti*" (National association of dangerous crackpots). Furthermore, the paper argued that the association should be disbanded since, following all the resignations, it had become the "paramilitary organisation of the Communist Party." The association was an "authentic arsenal of arms and weapons of war . . . working for the foreigner . . .

it rebels against established authority, shoots at the police, kills *carabinieri*, creates the terrorist environment in which the Bolshevik fifth column can seize the power the public vote has denied it."[72] The ANPI survived but, as a result, the *disunity* of the Resistance became a taboo subject.

In addition to the strategy of unity, the ANPI also attempted to reinforce its position by supporting initiatives on aspects of the Resistance that were not easily attacked or susceptible to politicization. March 1950, for example, saw the first conference on "Women in the Resistance." Its organizers were the actionist Ada Gobetti and the communist Carla Capponi, working together in a display of female solidarity. In Naples the following month, there was a conference dealing with the "partisan combattants abroad," at which both Boldrini and Parri were present. The Italian Resistance outside Italy became one of the ANPI's favored areas, and event followed event throughout the 1950s. On numerous occasions these events were associated with the patriotic theme of bringing back to their homeland the sons of Italy who had fallen abroad. Thus in December 1950, the bodies of Italian partisans who had fallen in Albania were returned to their native Bari. Likewise, in 1952, the ANPI supported the campaign to bring back five *carabinieri* who had fallen in Czechoslovakia and were eventually returned to Tarvisio. With Czechoslovakia and Albania as two established communist states, the ANPI was able to show that, when it came to the supreme sacrifice, it was not politics that counted but *pietas*.

Noble sentiments, however, did not apply when Yugoslavia was the object of discussion. In February 1951, the ANPI made the decision to expel two of its members, Aldo Cucchi and Valdo Magnani, from its ranks. Magnani had fought alongside Tito's partisans in Yugoslavia, whereas Cucchi had been a leading figure in the Resistance in Emilia Romagna. The PCI's position with regards to Tito's Yugoslavia led them both openly to criticize the party, for which crime they were duly expelled. The ANPI national executive followed suit, branding them "traitors of the Resistance" to be held up "to the contempt of the partisans and the people of Italy." Even Cecchini, the official historian of the ANPI, who argues throughout his two-volume history of the association that the PCI and ANPI were separate entities, was forced to admit that the expulsion "perhaps marks the moment in which the lack of autonomy was at its height."[73] Despite the "Magnacucchi" affair, expulsions from ANPI in the 1950s were relatively rare and the number of members grew steadily, to the extent that it could legitimately be considered a mass movement: at the end of 1948, the ANPI had some 199,000 members, by the end of 1949, this number had risen to 220,000 and by April 1951 the association could boast a membership in excess of three hundred thousand.

In March 1952, the first issue of the ANPI journal *Patria indipendente* was published. Initially, it was issued fortnightly and its editorial committee comprised Emilio Lussu, Leonida Repaci, and Giovanni Serbandini. Fausto Vighi had overall responsibility. The title was chosen by Antonello Trombadori and is a clear reference to the Risorgimento and emphasizes the interpretation of the period 1943–1945 as a war of liberation from the Germans. *Patria* went on sale on Sunday, an important day for the distribution of the PCI organ *L'Unità*. *Patria* could thus be sold and distributed alongside *L'Unità* and therefore occupied an important position, subordinate of course to *L'Unità*, but also as an adjunct to it, acting as a focus for former partisans to maintain an important part of their political identity. Some of the larger ANPI sections, such as Bologna and Milan, also had their own papers, printed less frequently but serving a local purpose.

At the end of June 1952, ANPI held its third national congress in Rome. The conference slogan was "For the honor and independence of the nation." The dominant themes of the congress were the campaign for peace, the opposition to German rearmament, the opposition to the entry of Turkey and Greece into NATO, the opposition to Yugoslavia, profound disquiet over the reemergence of Fascism and, lastly, a commitment to unity between the forces of the Resistance. The political document approved at the congress underlined this last point. Only with a concerted campaign would it be possible to keep alive the "the ideal flame of the First and Second Risorgimento."

The conference also called for greater cooperation between intellectuals and the forces of the Resistance. As far as art went, the communist artist Renato Guttuso had already risen to the challenge—his painting of *La battaglia di Ponte dell'Ammiraglio* (see Figure 2.2) depicted what looked like a key battle of the Risorgimento, with Garibaldi on horseback at the top right of the painting. Closer inspection reveals that his followers are none other than a range of communist

Figure 2.2. Renato Guttuso. *La battaglia di Ponte dell'Ammiraglio.*

Resistance heroes: Pajetta, Longo, Trombadori, and even Vittorini are all there in an astonishing pictorial rendition of the second Risorgimento topos.[74]

Other intellectuals made efforts to reach out to the younger generations in a series of Resistance stories for boys and girls, published between 1953 to 1955, four of which were illustrated.[75] The authors—Renato Giorgi, Ada Gobetti, Guido Petter, Giuseppe Mani, Luisa Sturani, and Gabriella Parca—all had Resistance credentials but little experience of writing children's stories. The results were mixed, as is demonstrated by two of the books published in 1953. Gabriella Parca's *Il piccolo ribelle* tells the story of a 14-year-old boy, Marco, who decides to join the partisans after German soldiers try unsuccessfully to burn his house down. The story is told in a simple, direct fashion. There are no references to politics, although the picture on the front cover shows a partisan with a red scarf. There is, perhaps predictably, a certain amount of second Risorgimento rhetoric that, rather improbably, issues from the mouth of Marco: "It doesn't matter if I'm only 14 years old . . . I must fight too . . . That's what boys did during the Risorgimento, that's what every Italian boy should do today."[76] But, apart from the occasional lapse, the book is fast moving, contains plenty of action and excitement, and would probably have gone down reasonably well with a teenage boy in the 1950s.

Rather less successful is Luisa Sturani's *Una storia vera*. In her preface, the author tells us that the story we are about to read is based on the heroism of the youngest Italian awarded a Gold Medal of the Resistance, Franco Centro, who was executed in the square in Castiolo d'Alba in February 1945. Centro was a partisan *staffetta* who assisted the 99th Garibaldi brigade. This is promising subject matter, but in the hands of Sturani, the story is too static. The first two pages are descriptive, unlike *Il piccolo ribelle* where the action starts immediately. There are a number of political speeches that issue from the mouth of the partisan leader "Lince," but they are crude and awkward and seem misplaced: "the partisans died to build the first brick of that great building which is called a free socialist Italy."[77] After his capture and torture he is taken off for execution where he asks for his partisan star to be given back to him before he is shot. He duly pins it to his chest, unbuttons his shirt and shouts defiantly: "Shoot at my chest. Long live Italy."[78] Of course, this is a work of fiction and Sturani was perfectly at liberty to write the ending of the story as she saw fit. But it is difficult to imagine a young reader, then or now, being particularly convinced by this kind of stuff. Children had moved on from the time of De Amicis' *Cuore*.

1955: The *Decennale*

Almost a year before the tenth anniversary celebrations began, Pietro Secchia gave a polemical speech in parliament criticizing the government for focusing their efforts on the Liberation of Rome.[79] His speech was more an attack on the Scelba government—part of the political joust—than anything else, but it had an element of truth in it. The Italian State did "Romanize" the memory of the Resistance in the 1950s (and beyond), concentrating on the massacre of the Fosse Ardeatine that was heavily pushed as a useful symbol of the martyrdom of the whole of Italy. But the state did not control everything, even if some of its senior representatives might have liked to, and if the government was not willing to organize the celebrations in the way Secchia wanted it, there were plenty of other people around to step in and organize the party. The celebrations for the tenth anniversary of the Resistance began as early as January 26 in Milan, when Calamandrei delivered his "Speech to the Young on the Constitution born of the Resistance." Later that year, Laterza would publish Calamandrei's *Uomini e città della Resistenza*, a collection containing his speeches and epigraphs. The Milan speech in defense of Parri served as the introduction to the volume. In March, an appeal was signed by Pertini, Pajetta, Achille Battaglia, and others for a National Resistance conference. But it was in April when most events of this type took place. In the middle of the month a conference on the relationship between the CVL and the CLN was held in Turin. Even Cadorna, the president of the FIVL who had long refused to lend his name to such initiatives, sent a message of adherence. At the conference there was an appeal to introduce the teaching of the Resistance in Italian schools, to introduce legal recognition of the CVL, and to declare an amnesty for all those partisans found guilty and imprisoned for common crimes during or after the war. Other conferences took place around the country, including the third conference on the "Resistance abroad" and the first conference of the Gold Medals of the Resistance.

In the political arena, Ferruccio Parri was put forward as the Left's candidate for the president of Italy. Although he did not win, the fact that he was put forward suggests that "Maurizio" was well and truly back. The year 1955 was, understandably, a bumper year for publications with works from across the political spectrum including, for the first time, a contribution from the Christian Democrats in the shape of a special number of the journal *Civitas*. The journal's editor, Paolo Emilio Taviani, began with a discussion of "the meaning of the Resistance." Other contributions included Achille Marazza's piece on Christian Democracy as a "political force of the Resistance," a discussion of the organization of partisan warfare by Cadorna, and Ettore Passerin D'Entreves' article on the Risorgimento and the Resistance. As if to show that this was not just a one off, *Civitas* went on to publish an article by Alfredo Pizzoni in its June edition that discussed the tenth anniversary.[80] Pizzoni himself was one of the speakers on the platform in Milan on April 25, along with Cardinal Montini and Taviani (there were no communist or socialist speakers).[81]

The Catholic interest in the Resistance also extended to literature, particularly poetry. In 1955, Aristide Marchetti and Guido Tassinari, both Catholic partisans who had fought with Beltrami and Di Dio's "Fiamme Verdi," edited an anthology of European Resistance writing.[82] Opening with a preface by the Christian Democrat Gronchi, the work contains stories by Calvino and Fenoglio and passages from Pavese and Vittorini, but the Italian material is mainly poetry: Quasimodo, Saba, Solmi, Fortini, Gatto. Resistance poetry, dominated by the lyric and most frequently characterized by a mood of spiritual reflection, therefore offered Catholic readers an apolitical diet of suffering and sacrifice. Resistance poetry would continue to be the culture of preference of the Catholics for many years to come. By the mid-1950s, therefore, the impact of the *Lettere di condannati a morte della Resistenza italiana* had provoked a rediscovery of the movement from the Catholic world that, from that time onward, was very keen to show that it had made its own valid contribution and had its own particular ethical interpretation of the

Resistance.[83] The PCI was, therefore, emphatically not alone in claiming its place in Italy's recent history, a fact that sits uncomfortably with the argument that it "hegemonized" the Resistance.

In this context, the PCI took the opportunity to publish a number of Resistance related works, including a special issue of *Rinascita* that repeated the usual themes: the strikes of March 1943, the struggle for unity, the Northern insurrection of April. The authors were the same as ever: Longo, Pajetta, Secchia, Massola, but there was one innovation of note. In a section on partisan democracy in the "freed zones," Gisella Floreanini wrote about the experiences of a woman in the government of Ossola.[84] Roberto Battaglia's history was published in an abridged version designed to attract a less sophisticated readership. For this project Battaglia was assisted by Giuseppe Garritano, a communist intellectual, journalist, and translator. Together they reduced Battaglia's imposing *magnum opus* to a third of its original size and produced a volume that is still in print today.[85] Another communist journalist, Renato Nicolai, published what is one of the first "book-interviews," ostensibly an account given to him by Papà Cervi of the life of his family and the death of his seven sons. The book, which in the words of Pajetta was "alive," has run to many editions and ranks along with the *Lettere di condannati* and Pintor's "last letter" as one of the most widely read Resistance texts.[86] Pintor's letter would also appear in a 1955 anthology, *La Resistenza al fascismo*.[87] The editors, Fausto Vighi and Maurizio Milan, were both former *garibaldini*; Vighi was the editor of *Patria indipendente*, and Milan had published a Resistance novel the previous year that told the story of the fourth Garibaldi assault brigade.[88] They chose largely communist texts for their collection, but there were a number of actionist and socialist pieces, as well as an extract from Cadorna. In effect then, the anthology tried to do two things: show the leading role of the communists in the Resistance and underscore the unity of the movement.

From the socialist side, Renato Giorgi published *Marzabotto parla*, another highly successful book that used a rather unscholarly, even cavalier approach, to oral testimonies. But no one, least of all Giorgi, seemed to care. By 1991, no fewer than 14 editions of the book had been published.[89] Giorgi's book was but one of a number of Resistance titles published by the socialist Edizioni Avanti! in the mid-1950s, including Piero Caleffi's *Si fa presto a dire fame*, a book that dealt with the author's experience in a German labor camp and that was more widely read at the time than Primo Levi's *Se questo è un uomo*.[90] On the whole, though, the socialist party's cultural efforts were slanted toward the celebration of what was, for them, a heroic period—the years of unarmed anti-Fascism in the 1930s—rather than the Resistance period as such. The "Matteotti" Resistance formations would have to wait a long time until their contribution would be given the attention it deserved.

For the April 25 celebrations, the Italian state's publishing house, the Istituto Poligrafico dello Stato, published an imposing collection entitled *Il secondo risorgimento*.[91] Unlike the *Civitas* special issue, this volume would have been printed in significant numbers and was intended for widespread circulation. The volume was one of the initiatives of the committee of ministers responsible for organizing what was called the "celebration of the 10th anniversary of the Resistance and the return to democracy in Italy." Evidently, however, the return to democracy did not involve a contribution from the communists, who are absent from the volume, except in those moments when they come under attack. The book contains almost five hundred pages of text and is carefully organized to give the state's slant on a long historical process of which the Resistance was but one link in the chain, starting with the Risorgimento, and interrupted by the temporary break of Fascism. There are three contributions dealing with the Resistance period as such. The first of these is by a military figure, General Clemente Primieri, who was the commander of the Cremona division during the latter stages of the war. Primieri's 90 page contribution is a robust and trenchant defense of the armed forces from September 8 to the Liberation—his approach echoes a meeting of the Council of Ministers in early January that stressed that in the course of the celebrations it would be necessary to "exalt the role of the armed forces."[92] The piece finishes with long congratulatory quotations from Churchill and General Mark Clark about the performance of the Italian armed forces.

Raffaele Cadorna's account of the CVL is, mercifully, shorter and contains little that had not already been written in his 1947 *La riscossa*. It is, however, worth mentioning that Cadorna uses the taboo expression *guerra civile* on a number of occasions.[93] By far the most innovative part of Cadorna's discussion has, however, nothing to do with the Resistance, nor with the CVL. A whole section is dedicated to the virtually unknown theme of the Italian soldiers who were deported to Germany, the Internati Militari Italiani (IMI). Cadorna gives a devastating picture of the hunger and privations of the IMI and concluded that the whole episode was one of the noblest and most generous pages of the Italian Resistance.[94] Cadorna's identification of a group of Resisters among the imprisoned armed forces in Germany was, in many ways, ahead of its time, and anticipates a theme that began to receive adequate treatment some 40 years later.

The third piece on the political aspects of the Resistance was by Mario Bendiscioli, an important historian of the Reformation and the Counter-Reformation, who was also director of the archives of the National Resistance Institute in Milan. Bendiscioli's title is a little misleading as the piece does not discuss the politics of the Resistance formations but concentrates on the CLN, offering a survey of the different parties that adhered to the committee. The contribution is rather anodyne, if not evasive, and never really gets to grips with the issue. But in this way Bendiscioli delivered what was probably required of him.

In opposition to the Italian state's official volume, a group of (mainly) former actionists published *Dieci anni dopo* in 1955.[95] The work contains contributions from the likes of Calamandrei and Achille Battaglia, and is essentially an unrelenting statement of the actionist thesis of a betrayed Resistance. The book led to an editorial by Giorgio Amendola in *Rinascita* that laid the blame for the betrayal on foreign interference, rather than on any deficiencies of the Italian political parties, including the PCI.[96] As Santomassimo has pointed out, the target of Amendola's editorial was not just the Actionists but also the senior figures within his own party (Longo and Secchia) who promoted the idea of a betrayed Resistance.[97] The book, therefore, provoked an internal debate between the forces of the Resistance, rather than a confrontation with the State.

Conclusion: 1949–1955—Two Speeches in the Chamber of Deputies

On May 9, 1949, the PCI deputy, Umberto Calosso, together with a host of other signatories from all parties except the DC, asked in the Chamber of Deputies why the government had not, that year, promoted national celebrations for April 25. Was this failure due, the question continued, to Laodicean tepidity, or was it a sign of a perilous return, conscious or otherwise, to an atmosphere comparable to that of the years 1919–1920? The reference to the rise of Fascism was labored, but Calosso certainly had a point. April 25 had become, as Santomassimo later commented, "much more of a problem than a resource" for the Italian government.[98] It was, as Ballone concedes "an anniversary which divides."[99] In 1953, the socialist *L'Avanti!* reported that schools were told by the Ministry of Education that the national day was to celebrate the birth of Marconi. Calosso received a reply from Achille Marazza, who was an Undersecretary in the Ministry of the Interior and a former DC representative in the CLN—Marazza had attended the meeting in Milan, along with Cardinal Schuster, Sandro Pertini, and others, where Mussolini's fate was discussed. Marazza's reply indicated that, on the contrary, instructions had been given to relevant bodies to put out the flags, introduce a festive timetable, and pay state employees double wages. Unlike 1947 and 1948, however, the government had not called this a national holiday, which would have involved the small additional measure of illuminating public buildings, because the Senate had, in June 1948, approved a bill to limit their number. In this way, Marazza stated, the small number of national holidays, such as the June 2 celebrations, would acquire all the more significance. The downgrading of April 25 was not, therefore, an indication of tepidity but a sign of respect for the decisions of parliament and for the constitution. As he ended his answer, comments were heard from the extreme left of the chamber. In line with parliamentary procedure, the speaker asked Calosso whether he was satisfied with the reply. In a recondite reference to the book of the Apocalypse, Calosso cleverly maintained the "lukewarm" theme of his original question by declaring that he was neither "hot nor cold." He was pleased to have had a reply from Marazza, a former representative of the CLN, but he could not express satisfaction at the bureaucratic nature of the reply: whether or not municipal buildings had been lit up was not the reason he asked his question. He then proceeded to give a staunch defense of the Resistance movement. An article published in the center-Right newspaper *Il Mondo* had spoken of the Italian "civil war" and, faced with this reality, the paper had argued it was better not to shout about it. The same had initially been said about Garibaldi, Calosso suggested: at the battle of Calatafimi, Italians had killed Italians and so it was not celebrated. But then "*i nostri padri*" (our forefathers) suffused with national sentiment, had come along and said that it was time to celebrate the *Mille* and Calatafimi. Calosso continued his historical parallel, larding his speech with references to Lamartine and Nievo (Calosso was, incidentally, a university professor). But it was not all highbrow stuff: partisans were special individuals who would risk their lives to save a dog, an observation backed up with an anecdote from Calosso's own personal experience. After several requests from the speaker to finish, punctuated by increasing irritation from the center of the chamber, he concluded with an evocation of a mass held in the winter of 1944, which was attended by Christian Democrats, Communists, Socialists, and Liberals. It was this spirit that needed to be maintained, Calosso concluded ironically, in order to protect the priests from attack.

Calosso was a socialist who had been an important contributor to Radio Londra during the war. He briefly made national headlines when, in January 1952, he was twice attacked by a group of neo-Fascists who attempted to prevent him from giving a lecture at the University of Rome. In the Chamber of Deputies, De Gasperi expressed his sympathy, but also blamed the Left and denounced extremism from both Left and Right. Although we do not know if the events are linked, Calosso did not stand for reelection in 1953 and spent the last six years of his life pursuing his academic interests. Had he stood in 1953, he would no doubt have been happy to attend the afternoon sitting of Friday, April 22, 1955, where the speaker, the Christian Democrat and future president of the republic, Gronchi, made a speech in celebration of the Resistance that, though not exactly hot, was far from lukewarm.

Gronchi rose to his feet, accompanied by the members of the government, and observed that the tenth anniversary of the Resistance (and he used *this* particular term and not Liberation) had been celebrated in a solemn and austere fashion throughout the country. This said, it was necessary for the Chamber of Deputies, which included among its members many men who had shown their devotion to freedom and to the country, to associate itself with the Resistance. He then paid homage to those who, for the cause of liberty, "*fecero olocausto della loro vita*" (in other words, died). Gronchi finished his speech by once again referring to the sacrifice of the partisan martyrs, from whose dying lips could be heard three key words: liberty, justice, Italy. No doubt the likes of Calamandrei, Codignola, and Parri, all absent from the chamber, would have been delighted to hear such an obvious reference to the *giustizia e libertà* ideal. These three words, Gronchi concluded, did not just form a spiritual testament but a program for the moral and civil progress of the people of Italy. He sat down to "loud, general and prolonged applause." To cap it all, the Social Democrat deputy, Domenico Chiaramello, who represented the partisan hotspot of Cuneo, then asked to speak. In the name of the entire chamber he asked that Gronchi's noble speech, an "exaltation of what was the heroic Resistance of the Italian people" should be displayed throughout all the municipalities and villages of Italy. The proposal was approved by acclaim, and Gronchi added that it indicated that the will of the chamber was to operate within the path of the ideas of the Resistance. It was all too much for Domenico Leccisi, one of the neo-Fascists who had dug Mussolini out of his grave in 1946. To hostile response from the left and the center he tried to introduce discussion of another date (no doubt Mussolini's death) but was not allowed to. Instead he tried to commemorate the sacrifice of all the Italians who had died for their country: "The Resistance had its dead, and so did we." Further interruptions ensued, particularly when Leccisi referred to the "the so-called Liberation." It was time, Leccisi, concluded, to draw a veil of peace and love over such a painful phase in the history of Italy. He was ignored and the chamber moved swiftly on to the next item on the agenda: an amendment to a clause in a bill on taxation.

By the time of Gronchi's speech, a decade had passed since the end of the Resistance. As Gundle has written, throughout this period "the cult of the Resistance enjoyed only a weak and partial sponsorship from above . . . The Church, the DC and the state establishment recoiled in particular from any celebration of armed Resistance." There were signs, however, that some elements "from below" in the Catholic world were beginning to open up toward the Resistance. The publication of the *Lettere dei condannati* in the early 1950s was crucial here. The appearance of a work entitled "Christian democracy remains faithful to the ideals of the Resistance" would have been unthinkable in 1948 but by 1955 such a work was published in Rome.[100] Of course, the Catholics did not embrace the ideals of the *armed* Resistance, but neither did the PCI, for whose leadership the use of violence in the past conflicted with the strategy of the party in the present. It was no surprise that they latched on to the *partigiani della pace* (partisans for peace) campaign of the 1950s in order to give an irenic gloss to the Resistance. With so many of the "partisans for peace" being former partisans themselves, it was hoped that the word, and the concept, would become associated with nonviolence. If, as Gundle has argued, the "Resistance was appropriated by the Left and especially the PCI" in the period it was a very measured, and qualified, form of appropriation. [101] Only the actionists were in a position to champion unrestrainedly the movement without fear of political recriminations. But that was because the actionists had no political power and therefore no strategic imperative.

3

1955–1960

Gronchi's speech of April 1955 indicates a shift in the fortunes of the Resistance movement from the perspective of the Italian State and Christian Democracy, but its significance should not be overemphasized. Only a few days after he brought the house down with his rhetoric, he was elected president of the Republic, beating off competition that included Parri.[1] Crucially, he owed his election to votes from the Left who were doubtlessly influenced by his concession to the Resistance spirit. But Gronchi was an ambiguous, slippery figure, as would be clearly demonstrated during the Tambroni affair in 1960 (see chapter 4), when he and the Italian government moved, albeit briefly, toward the Right. In this chapter, I will look at the relatively short period running from the end of the tenth anniversary up to shortly before the dramatic events of June and July 1960. This is a period that has not attracted much attention from historians of the Resistance legacy but that nevertheless is characterized by a number of significant developments.[2]

ANPI, the PCI, and the 1958 Resistance "Gathering"

At the Milan "mobilization" of 1954, Ferruccio Parri issued a plea for a large-scale unitary "gathering" (*raduno*) of Resistance forces. This aspiration led to the establishment of a National Resistance Committee in February 1956, to which the ANPI adhered.[3] The committee contained an impressive list of members ranging, quite literally, from A to Z (from Franco Antonicelli to the Christian Democrat Adone Zoli). Despite the presence of Zoli, however, the Catholic partisan association, the FIVL, and its leader Cadorna refused to participate in the initiative. The initial activity of this committee was to organize Parri's gathering, which would eventually take place in 1958, after many and complex vicissitudes. In the meantime, however, the ANPI itself was busy organizing its fourth congress that was held in Milan in April 1956. On this occasion, the neo-Fascist *Meridiano d'Italia*, for whom the Resistance movement was always a target, commented that the congress had taken place in a near clandestine atmosphere. Nobody knew the congress was even taking place, the paper suggested, an indication that the country had "definitively shelved the Resistance 'phenomenon.'"[4] This was, the paper concluded, the fourth ANPI congress, but there was some doubt that there would be a fifth.

It is unlikely that the ANPI was much concerned by the feeble irony of the *Meridiano d'Italia*. More worrying were developments in the Soviet Union. Only a month earlier, delegates at the twentieth congress of the Soviet Communist Party had been shocked by Khrushchev's "secret speech" and its revelations about Stalin. The exact nature of the speech was unclear, but by March details were beginning to emerge and *L'Unità* released some heavily censored details. By the time of the ANPI congress Togliatti had given a report to the central committee of the party and there had been some discussion at a meeting of the national council with Giancarlo Pajetta and, above all, Giorgio Amendola, contributing to the debate. The ideological ferment reached its peak with the events in Hungary, followed by the Soviet invasion, in the autumn of 1956. These were torrid times and the confusion and disarray within the ranks of the ANPI is evident. Initially, in a "Greeting to the People of Hungary," the ANPI executive unequivocally expressed its support for the revolt, but when the Soviet tanks rolled in, there was no message of condemnation.

The ANPI, no doubt, looked forward expectantly to the PCI's crucial eighth congress, which took place in December that year. The eighth congress is significant, above all, for Togliatti's speech during which he gave full articulation to the strategy of the Italian road to socialism—a road in which there was no space for those who dreamed of revolution. This was, of course, the road that Togliatti had followed from the time of the *svolta di Salerno*, but never before had the democratic model been propounded with such force and vigor. Togliatti explicitly referred to the "duplicity" that had characterized some elements of the party. It was obvious to whom he was referring—to the partisans who preferred the rifle to the ballot box and, above all, to Pietro Secchia, the would-be leader of the "revolutionary wing" of the party. This characterization of Secchia was, and continues to be, a deliberate manipulation of the true nature of this complex figure, about whom there is still much to be discovered. But irrespective of Secchia's would-be dreams of the barricades it was certainly the case that partisans identified with him, and to an extent Longo (who had fought in Spain) rather than with the bureaucrat Togliatti. Secchia had been responsible for party organization for a number of years and had, so evidence suggests, made an unsuccessful attempt at taking over the party leadership in the early 1950s. When his right-hand man, the former partisan Giulio Seniga, disappeared with large quantities of the party coffers, in an apparent protest about the direction in which the party was heading, Togliatti seized his opportunity. Secchia was removed from his post, sent to organize the party in Lombardy, and replaced by Amendola at the helm of party organization. Amendola promptly embarked on a thorough and systematic operation around the various party federations, training those elements who still had an attachment to revolutionary methods and, where necessary, cutting away the more resistant branches. The years 1956 to 1960 were therefore characterized by antipartisan operations from within the PCI.

For the ANPI the organization of Parri's Resistance gathering must have represented a welcome distraction from these internal developments. In October 1957, another attempt was made to organize the event. On this occasion it was none other than Zoli, a member of the National Resistance Committee, who refused permission on the grounds of the threat to public order. Meanwhile, in his diary an apoplectic Giorgio Agosti ranted about Zoli's hypocrisy, and the irreconcilable nature of Christian Democracy and antifascism.[5] A date in early December was then set, but with very strict conditions: a maximum number of three thousand demonstrators was fixed, there was to be no march through the streets of Rome, and a visit to the Ardeatine Caves would only be permitted if the demonstrators went around the walls of the city to the massacre site. Even then, the police authorities in Rome managed to find a way of putting the event back—an outbreak of Asian flu led to cancellation for public health reasons. Eventually, the authorities caved in and granted the request for a gathering, but insisted that the event should start at the unlikely hour of 9:30 on the morning of Sunday, February 23, 1958. The day before, partisans began to arrive at Termini station from all over Italy, wearing tricolor scarves to emphasize that the following day's proceedings were to be a show of unity. During the afternoon, Papà Cervi arrived on the fast train from Bologna, along with some three hundred partisans from the city. The flag from Marzabotto was decorated with 1830 stars to commemorate each victim of the Nazi massacre, and Togliatti himself signed the article that appeared on the front page of *L'Unità* (alongside a Guttuso drawing of the "People's Insurrection") on the day of the demonstration. *L'Unità* described in detail how the event would unfold: at 9:30 the crowd that had assembled at the Arch of Constantine would process along the Via dei Fori Imperiali to Piazza Venezia. At the front, there would be the band of the grenadiers, followed by the flag of the CVL to which would be affixed a gold medal for military valor. This flag would be accompanied by five others from the Cremona, Folgore, Friuli, Legnano, and Mantua regiments. Behind these flags there would then be the *gonfaloni* of the cities decorated with the gold medal (such as Bologna, Marzabotto and Parma), the representatives of the Resistance, the surviving partisans who had been awarded gold medals, and behind them two thousand relatives of the fallen. At the back of the procession there would be *carabinieri* and mounted police. Once at Piazza Venezia the crowd would then begin to line up behind the six flags—one united rank of soldiers and partisans and three groups of participants. Once all were gathered, the CVL flag would be carried by ensigns to the tomb of the Unknown Soldier, deposited in the "Sacrarium of the Flags" from where civil, military, and Resistance representatives would be looking on. Adone Zoli, the DC prime minister, would read a message from the President of the Republic.

This, at least, was the plan, designed to portray a carefully managed image of the Resistance as a movement that united Italians from across the political spectrum, which involved both partisans and conventional forces fighting together and that, above all, saw innumerable citizens offering their blood as sacrificial cement for the new Republic. According to Agosti, however, things did not quite turn out as planned. He felt, he wrote, that he could not turn down the invitation to be one of the Resistance representatives, principally in deference to Parri. But he thought with melancholy of the "first class funeral of the Resistance" he would attend. Discussing the ceremony itself, he commented that Rome was as deserted at 9:30 a.m. on a Sunday as Turin is at 7:00 in the morning. He climbed the steps of "that ignoble piece of cinema studio which is the Altar of the Nation" and listened to Zoli's "hurried and garbled" speech that was interrupted by whistles.[6] Behind him was Cadorna, his face wooden and without expression, the world of the Resistance alien to him. The orchestration of the event was "dull and disconnected" and gave the impression that there was a desire to finish quickly. To the strains of Mameli's national anthem the flag of the CVL was carried up the steps of the monument, followed by the standards of the *comuni*. At the point that the flag was placed in its holder Nino De Totto, a deputy from the MSI, shouted "Long live the Italian Social Republic."[7] He was struck by "Rosci," presumably a partisan, and leapt on by others. The government wreath was then attacked by another young man from the extreme right, who was first given a sound beating then pushed down the steps. Agosti commented that the police were soft and inefficient and he left embittered.[8]

Despite Agosti's near cosmic pessimism, the Rome gathering was, however, an important milestone in the state's acceptance of the Resistance as part of its fabric. This was an event that took place in the capital, in the heart of the city that had seen Fascists march in triumph along the same route as the partisans now took. Rome itself was not a "Resistance city," and it had been the theater of one of the more controversial episodes of the period—the attack at Via Rasella and the reprisals at the Ardeatine Caves. By the mid- to late-1950s the massive monument complex at the Caves had been completed and inaugurated. Mirko's gates, together with the statues reminiscent of Michelangelo's slaves escaping from their marble casing, and finally the massive stone slab that protected the tombs of the victims, but that allowed a dim light to shine upon the fallen, constituted a national monument of conspicuous symbolic significance. When the partisans processed to the Ardeatine Caves later on in the day there was a tangible sense that the Resistance had finally taken its place in the long history of Rome.

Agosti also went on to attend the fifth ANPI national congress that was held at the Teatro Carignano in Turin in June 1959. The conference slogan, in foot high letters behind the speakers' platform, reminded delegates that the Resistance was the "continuation of the patriotic traditions of the Risorgimento" and the guarantor of the freedoms of the constitution. The risorgimento rhetoric was even more insistent than usual, as the conference was held during preparations for the celebrations of the one hundredth anniversary of the expedition of Garibaldi and his "thousand." Boldrini, the ANPI president, spoke of the Constitution, of youth and of the atomic bomb. A speech by Domenico Peretti Griva, the first honorary president of the Constitutional Court, catalogued the failings of the government to honor the text and spirit of the Constitution from 1948 onward. No doubt the leadership of the ANPI were happy with the way things went. But the actionist Agosti was not so keen. In his diary he wrote that the opening ceremony had "profoundly nauseated him" and railed against the customary speeches about Resistance unity, the communist orchestration of the event, characterized by the presence of partisan priests, heroes of the Soviet Union, "poor old papà Cervi" and, worst of all, the trumpet blowers from the various associations of war veterans and war-wounded.[9] By the afternoon he could take no more and left the building. His decision to leave was, so he felt, more than vindicated when he came across a friend who had also taken an early exit in protest at comments made about Pál Maléter, the Hungarian general who had been hanged, along with Imre Nagy, in a Budapest prison in June 1958.

In January 1960, the PCI held its ninth party congress. There were 934 delegates present at the congress and, of these, just slightly more than a third were formally described, in the official statistics, as "active partisans." Togliatti's speech, initially concerned with issues of *détente*, confirmed that the PCI recognized that Italy belonged to the West for reasons of history, geography, and culture. The party was, in other words, continuing to move away from the Soviet Union. As for internal party matters, Togliatti referred to some perplexities and hesitations following his speech at the previous congress. But a "more enhanced ideological commitment" had followed, together with a change in the composition of the local party leadership and the correction of "individual errors." Togliatti was keen to underline that the "stick" had not been used to resolve these problems. In the afternoon session of Tuesday, February 2, Giorgio Amendola, the man who did not "use the stick," rose to his feet to give his speech, aware that the party leader's comments implied criticism of his methods. Toward the end, Amendola stated that Togliatti was quite right to say that a political line could not be imposed with the stick. Frank discussion was the method required and, if a comrade was wrong, if he expressed dissent, then it was necessary to convince him and help him to find the "right road." However, if the dissent could not be dealt with there was no place for him in a "body of political leadership." There was, he continued, no space for reticence, silence, or "duplicity." Amendola then moved on to give a concrete example of a comrade who had been a friend from the time of their imprisonment under Fascism. "Giorgio," his friend had said, "I don't understand this strategy, but I don't want to get in the way." With discussion and fraternal help, Amendola continued, this comrade could be convinced that the "right road" was the one the party was now following, and it would take them to victory in Italy. Critical severity, therefore, against those who committed infringements, was what was required, together with fraternal aid. This was, Amendola continued, the nature of democracy in the party, the democracy of a revolutionary party, of revolutionary combatants who discuss things freely in order to better contribute to the fight. At the end of the speech the congress burst into the regulation applause and there was a brief pause. No doubt the chair of the afternoon session, Pietro Secchia, needed the time to recover from what he had heard. More than anyone Secchia knew what Amendola was talking about, and it was a vicious piece of conference organisation to have him preside over the very session in which the man who had taken his old job discussed the changes he had brought about. The significance of it all was not lost on the communist intellectual Luciano Barca, who found himself elected to the central committee after the conference:

> From Liguria to Emilia to Lombardy the "stick" belonged to Giorgio Amendola or, according to the region concerned, to one of the men Amendola entrusted to run things post Secchia. It's true that for his . . . correction of errors which had their origins in the past (and, above all in Emilia and Friuli Venezia Giulia, in the period immediately after the Liberation), Amendola had to break off some firmly attached encrustations (*incrostazioni profonde*), sideline comrades who had fought face to face with the Nazis . . . But it's equally true that, in some cases, the authoritarian methods used have struck down young comrades . . . and this can't be in any case the normal leadership style of a democratic party.[10]

Amendola was replaced as head of party organization by future leader Enrico Berlinguer after the conference. But by that stage his work was done. Togliatti had organized a clear out and got someone else to do the dirty work for him. Faced with the increasing unpopularity of Amendola's methods, which would have been damaging to his own authority, he then got rid of him as well. Clearly, Togliatti's long years in Moscow had taught him a thing or two.

In his lucid reflections on the 1960 party congress Barca also makes a reference to the PCI's commitment to safeguarding the values of the Resistance in the preamble to the new party statute. However, the extent to which this was a genuine commitment, or simply a sop to those who had suffered during Amendola's reign, is open to discussion. We get a more accurate reflection of the PCI leadership's attitude to the Resistance by looking at a text that is not mentioned in Barca's diary. On the eve of the conference, each delegate received a thick volume containing all the documents and directives issued by the leadership and central committee of the party between December 1956 and January 1960. In over five hundred pages of documents there are three brief and passing references to the Resistance. No special reference is made to April 25, but other anniversaries (May 1, the October Revolution, International Women's Day) are celebrated. Indeed, a document was released on April 25, 1958, but it discussed atomic weapons and contained no mention of the Resistance. When the Resistance is mentioned, it is the bigger central committee, and not the inner circle of the *direzione*, which issued an obituary honoring Concetto Marchesi, the "Resistance rector" of the University of Padua.[11] Marchesi, we learn, made the University of Padova "the centre of the Resistance in the city and in the entire region of the Veneto," but most attention is devoted to his contribution to ideological debate within the party and to his scholarship.[12] In the case of the writer Sibilla Aleramo, the dramatic experience of the war and the Resistance is mentioned in passing.[13] Such was the real nature of the PCI's "appropriation" of the Resistance only a little more than a decade after it had come to an end.

Ada Gobetti's *Diario partigiano* and the Emergence of the "Partigiana"

In 1954 the women's commission of the Turin ANPI published a book on Piedmontese women and their contribution to the Liberation.[14] This was the first publication to give serious consideration to the whole issue of women's participation in the Resistance, an issue that was destined to assume more and more importance as time passed, particularly in the 1970s. The book gave details of no less than 99 female partisans who had been killed, 185 women who had been deported, and 38 female civilian casualties. Despite enthusiastic reviews, particularly one by the historian Piero Pieri in *Il ponte*, which called for the book to be widely distributed, read, and commented on in Italian schools, the volume has largely been forgotten. The book, however, contained a preface by Ada Marchesini Gobetti, who would go on to write one of the key texts of the Resistance tradition, the *Diario partigiano*.[15] In 1955, Gobetti distributed to various friends a typescript of a book that was based on the diary she had kept during the war. Gobetti was the wife of Piero

Gobetti, the anti-Fascist intellectual who had died in Paris in 1926 as a consequence of a beating from Fascists. As well as being a key figure in the GL movement, she had been one of the protagonists of the Resistance in Piedmont. The
diary, which she originally wrote in French, was published by Einaudi in 1956 and
had an immediate impact, awakening Italians to questions of a gendered Resistance that had hitherto only been posed in the fictional work of Viganò. Quite why
Gobetti's diary should have proved so popular is a difficult question to answer.
Ada Gobetti was an individual of undoubted prestige and the continued interest in her late husband who was, along with Giacomo Matteotti, an anti-Fascist
martyr of impeccable credentials, would have done much to help promote the
book. Likewise, the context of the city of Turin itself, which did much to promote
Resistance memory in the 1950s (and beyond), would also have been a factor. But
most importantly, the 1950s see the first signs of the arrival of the "female subject"
in Italian society. When in the 1960s and beyond an authentic women's movement
developed, Gobetti became an important figure and her diary took on the dimensions of a key text, along with Aleramo's *Una donna*, within the history of Italian
women in the twentieth century.

One of the consequences of the success of Gobetti's diary was that it seems to
have given publishers, who in the 1950s (and beyond) were conspicuously mascu-
linist institutions, the confidence to publish other texts by women resisters, such
as the books by Lucilla Massone Muratti and Daria Banfi Malaguzzi.[16] Even the
Christian Democrat women's association got in on the act, publishing a collection
of documents on Lombardy.[17] But it wasn't just the publishing industry that was
showing a greater sensitivity toward the *partigiane*. In 1954 the Resistance Institute
for Venice assembled a commission of experts to decide on who should be given
the commission for a monument to the *partigiane* of the Veneto. The commission
was populated by heavyweight intellectuals such as the art historian Giulio Carlo
Argan and the architect Bruno Zevi (there were, of course, no women). The job
was offered to the sculptor and former partisan Leoncillo, who produced a work
in *majolica* that depicted a lone female partisan armed with a rifle. The monument
clearly references, and distances itself from, Mazzacurati's work dedicated to the
partigiano that had been inaugurated in the Piazzale della Pace in Parma in 1956
and that set the paradigm for sculptural representations of the male, communist
partisan. Leoncillo also adorned his sculpture with a red scarf, a decision that
immediately led to problems in a region known for its "white" political proclivities. He was asked to produce a version with a less politically charged scarf, which
he duly did. This time the scarf was brown. Carlo Scarpa produced a pedestal for
the work, with the inscription "Il Veneto alle sue partigiane," and the monument
was unveiled at the *giardini* in Venice in September 1957.[18]

Historiography

The tenth anniversary of 1955 had led to a glut of publications and also provided
the impetus for a series of works that came out in the period running from 1956
to 1959. In one significant development, Italy's national statistical agency (ISTAT)

finally published its detailed breakdown of fatalities during the period 1940–1945.[19] But those wishing to find out how many partisans had been killed would have been hugely disappointed. As the president of ISTAT rather glibly admitted in his preface, there was a lack of reliable information, which meant that partisans ended up in a category of "various, or otherwise not indicated." The ISTAT could surely have tried a little harder to gather concrete statistics, and this failure contributed to a significant information deficit. More importantly, it was also indicative of the state's lack of interest in the partisans in general.

One of the most important publications of the period was Franco Catalano's history of the CLNAI, one of the first works on the Resistance to make extensive use of archival documents. Catalano's detailed study underlined the central role of the CLNAI, particularly in terms of organization and finances but also revealed the ideological cracks that would widen once the Resistance period was over. Catalano's study is also noteworthy for its even-handed approach to the whole question of the CLNAI, avoiding much of the polemic that had characterized the treatment of this subject by individuals who had themselves been leading figures in the organization. Indeed, there is a sense that, in the mid-to-late 1950s, there is a gradual ideological attenuation in publications about the Resistance. Renato Carli Ballola's general *Storia della Resistenza* was published by the PSI's *Edizioni Avanti!* and the author was a member of the leadership of the party, but his history is not a party book in the sense that it does not express a "socialist view" of the Resistance.[20] There are, of course, moments when Carli Ballola cannot resist scoring points against the PCI and the DC, with the *svolta di Salerno*, above all, coming in for some coruscating criticism as a Soviet inspired means of gaining entry into Italy. No doubt Carli Ballola would have been intrigued to find this theme investigated in excruciating detail once the Soviet Archives were opened up in the 1990s.

Perhaps surprisingly, one of the most explicitly political books of the period was published by a leading Christian Democrat, Paolo Emilio Taviani. Taviani was, along with Enrico Mattei, the most important partisan in the DC and was unquestionably the leading DC minister with a partisan past, occupying the post of minister of defense from 1953 to 1958. In 1955, the journal he edited, *Civitas*, had published a special number dedicated to the Resistance, one of the first signs of a new approach to the movement from within certain ranks of the DC (see chapter 2). *Civitas* was a journal that only really circulated among the party's intellectual elite. The following year, in 1956, Taviani took an arguably bolder and more "populist" step by reissuing his history of the insurrection in Genoa that had been written in May 1945 and first been published in an early number of *Il ponte*.[21] Readers in the 1950s of Taviani's text, complete with an ample documentary appendix, would have felt distinctly shaken by the tone of the volume that, it is only a slight exaggeration to say, could easily have been written by the communist Pietro Secchia. The word "insurrection" was not part of the Christian Democrat lexicon in the 1950s (nor indeed in subsequent decades) and neither were some of the comments on the significance of the events in Genoa themselves. Taviani stated, in no uncertain terms, that the insurrection in Genoa, where a strong and organized invading army had been forced to surrender to "insurgents," was unique in the Second World War.[22] It was, he continued, the most significant event in the

Liberation of Northern Italy and was recognized as such by the Allies. The text is written in an objective third person and only once does Taviani use the first person in his account. This occurs when he discusses German attempts to broker a deal via the Church. Taviani was summoned by the bishop of Genoa to be told of this move, but he turned down the proposal there and then: "I told him straight away that the CLN would not entertain any deal with the Germans."[23] Maybe this was how Taviani had reacted in April 1945, but it was not the way Christian Democrat ministers interacted with senior figures in the Catholic Church in the mid-1950s. Indeed, the episode is uncannily reminiscent of Pertini's refusal to come to a deal with Mussolini in the presence of Cardinal Schuster in Milan in April 1945. In a sense, by republishing his 1945 account, Taviani was acting loud and proud about his past: *he* hadn't played the waiting game during the final stages of the war. This point is reinforced in the description of the CLN meeting, chaired by Taviani himself, of the night of April 23–24 where, *only after some hesitation* (from which quarter it is not specified, but not Taviani) the decision to attack was finally taken at 1:00 a.m., with the first shots being fired between 4:00 and 5:00 a.m. By 10:00 the following morning, the town hall, the telephone exchange, the police headquarters, and the prison at Marassi were, Taviani wrote, "in the hands of the people in revolt."[24] Later on that same day, a band of insurgents led by a certain Raffe, "an extravagant laborer from the Pré area," had cleared the old town of Germans. German threats to bombard the city were effectively dealt with by the CLN representative Secondo Pessi, who said they would all be tried as war criminals if they did such a thing. Pessi was a communist. With Meinhold's surrender, the insurrection at Genoa came to an end, the most brilliant "citizen insurrection" of the war that had led to the destruction and dispersal of two German divisions "by a people at arms and by the partisans."[25]

Taviani's brief history almost seems to be stretching the hand of friendship out to the communists in a kind of historic compromise *avant la lettre*. But order was restored fairly rapidly, as can be detected from a brief spat from the end of the decade involving the Christian Democrat Adone Zoli and the Communist Orazio Barbieri. Zoli's *Acqua limacciosa sotto "Ponti sull'Arno"* (muddy water under the "Bridges over the Arno") is a brief text, published in 1959, in the form of an extended letter to Ferruccio Parri, who had authored the preface of Orazio Barbieri's history of the Resistance in Florence, *Ponti sull'Arno*, published by the communist party's Editori Riuniti.[26] Zoli had been alerted to a review of Barbieri's text written by Carlo Francovich, which had been published in *Il ponte*.[27] In his review, Francovich had been highly critical of Barbieri's history, leaping to the defense of the Christian Democrat Zoli, about whom there were a series of negative, if not polemical, comments throughout the work. Zoli gave a point by point rebuttal to Barbieri's accusations and, once he had "cleared the waters," he went on to suggest why the Florentine communist had written his accusations: "Orazio Barbieri didn't want to attack the citizen Zoli, or the lawyer Zoli, but the Christian Democrat, the high-ranking Christian Democrat, Zoli."[28] What Zoli didn't say was that Barbieri's negative take on his Resistance activities was actually connected to wider issues. By the late 1950s, the whole question of the Catholic contribution to the Resistance had become an important issue, out of which the DC stood to make a certain amount of political capital. Barbieri's insinuations about Zoli's weakness were really a swipe at DC moves to (retrospectively) claim their slice of the Resistance cake.

Both Zoli and Taviani were high-ranking figures in the DC. As time went on Taviani, above all, would become the key figure in the transmission of Catholic Resistance memory. In the PCI, his opposite number was Pietro Secchia whose removal from high office galvanized him into being even more active in promoting and defending the Resistance movement. Two of his many speeches from the period were published as separate pamphlets. The first of these, on *La Resistenza davanti ai tribunali della storia*, was delivered in 1957 at Monte Amiata, the scene of violent disturbances following the *attentato a Togliatti*. The second was delivered to partisans at Biella and contained an intriguing departure from the norm— Secchia questioned the second Risorgimento topos.[29] In addition to these two speeches, Secchia also coauthored, with the Resistance leader Cino Moscatelli, an imposing history of the movement in the key zones of Biella, the Valsesia, and the Valdossola. In their preface the authors wrote that the book was a response to the "numerous Fascist publications" of recent years and to the "writings which heap calumny on the Resistance." They wished to tell the "new generations" about the acts of heroism of the communist partisans and they would do this simply and without rhetoric.[30] Usually, of course, claims in prefaces in Resistance books that what was to follow would be rhetoric-free were quite specious. Nonetheless, *Il Monte Rosa è sceso a Milano* is not characterized by overblown tales of heroism. There are the customary discussions of *attesismo* and criticisms of the maneuvers of the bourgeoisie. But the partisans who fought for the Catholic Resistance leader, Beltrami, are generally viewed positively. Beltrami himself maintained "the most cordial relations" with the *Garibaldi* formations and did his utmost to prevent tensions between the parties.

Toward the end of the decade, Claudio Pavone and Giampaolo Pansa, two figures who would go on to be at the center of Resistance debate in the 1990s and beyond, made their first significant appearances on the historiographical scene. Pansa attended a conference at the University of Genoa in May 1959 dedicated to Resistance historiography. Despite his comparative youth (he was in his early 20s) Pansa, so he later himself claimed in an interview, rose to his feet and asked to speak. Why, he asked provocatively, was no one willing to tackle the issue of the RSI? His question provoked an apoplectic response from a partisan who felt this represented a concession to Fascism. But the conference chair, none other than Ferruccio Parri, encouraged him to continue. At the end of the conference, so Pansa claimed, Parri wrote a check to help him in the course of his studies.[31] As for his studies, Pansa would, in the early summer of the same year, go on to discuss his degree thesis, a vast study of the Resistance in and around Alessandria, supervised by Guido Quazza at the University of Turin.

Pavone made his mark in a rather different way, in the form of a long and scholarly article published in the journal *Passato e presente*.[32] Pavone's piece on the "ideas of the Resistance" took as its starting point the commonplace of the Resistance as a Second Risorgimento. Rather than exposing the fatuous nature of the historical parallel, what Pavone did in his article was rather more interesting. By analyzing a vast array of sources from right across the political spectrum, Pavone demonstrated how the Risorgimento had been used over extended periods by different political forces in order to provide some ideological underpinning to their own operations. As Pavone convincingly showed, everyone from the Fascists, through to the Christian Democrats, the PCI, and the PDA, had, at different times, appropriated the Risorgimento as and when it was expedient. In the case of the communists, Pavone showed how Togliatti had, in the 1930s, shifted from condemnation to praise when the political wind changed direction. Pavone's piece provoked responses in *Passato e presente* from various individuals, including Battaglia.[33] But what everyone seemed to miss was that Pavone's article demonstrated, in an extraordinarily detailed fashion, how Italy's recent history was not fixed and objective but subject to the constant mutation and manipulation caused by contingent political exigencies. In other words, Pavone's article is one of the first by an Italian historian to recognize the existence of a phenomenon which, only in the 1980s would be termed, the "public use of history."

Literary Texts and Films

In the previous chapter, we saw how DC interest in the Resistance expressed itself in the cultural arena by way of the 1955 anthology edited by Marchetti and Tassinari. The following year, a young Catholic journalist, Angelo Paoluzi, published what is probably the first attempt to offer a serious survey of Resistance literature. Paoluzi's study is not well known, but it is nevertheless worthy of attention, particularly as the author went on to become a major figure in Catholic journalism, becoming the editor of the daily *Avvenire* in 1979. Paoluzi's study begins by highlighting the wide impact of the Resistance—a phenomenon that affected all social classes. The response of Italian writers had been to emphasize two aspects of the period: namely the "civic commitment" and the "religious character, in the broad sense" of the "Resistance struggle."[34] Paoluzi found evidence for what might at first seem a strange thesis from a variety of sources: Thomas Mann's preface to the *Lettere di condannati a morte della resistenza europea*, Raffaele Pettazoni's *Italia religiosa*, and Calamandrei's speech at Milan in defense of Ferruccio Parri. Paoluzi then proceeded to attack the way "myths" had been made about the Resistance, referring evidently to the communist party, but without saying as much. In line with other critics, Paoluzi made a distinction between works published during the Resistance ("literature of the Resistance") and those published after the fact ("literature on the Resistance") and commented that Italy had no equivalents of Eluard, Aragon, Malraux, or Vercors. He did not offer any explanation as to why this conspicuous gap existed. As was commonplace, Paoluzi indulged in spurious comparisons with Italy's nineteenth-century past, agreeing wholeheartedly with the suggestion that the partisan struggle was the final battle in the Unification of Italy. He then turned to a series of publications and authors that he identified as part of the "historical heritage of the nation": Pintor, Dante Livio Bianco's diary, *Una lotta nel suo corso*, and the *Lettere di condannati*.[35] Of these, Paoluzi was only wide of the mark in his judgment of the letters between actionists, which have definitively faded from memory. But the accuracy of Paoluzi's judgments is not the point. In this text we have a Catholic making observations that are only on the surface part of a literary-critical enterprise. In reality, and at a deeper level, Paoluzi is making very careful and precise choices and, by extension, recommendations about individual texts that could appeal to Catholic mentality in the 1950s. Of Pintor, for example, Paoluzi stated that his sacrifice highlights the Resistance as a "moral fact."[36] These were the same arguments that had been used by the communists—Pintor had the unusual distinction of being a hero for everyone except the neo-Fascists. Dante Livio Bianco's partisan diary is valorized for its objectivity—it doesn't undervalue the role of the communists as, Paoluzi jibes, the communists were then doing "with the formations of different political persuasions."[37] But it is the *Lettere di condannati* that most excited Paoluzi, who quoted long extracts from them. In his mini anthology, he includes a passage from the letter of the 19-year-old Giacomo Ulivi who wrote with a "lucidity which can be found in all of them, young and old, Catholics and socialists, workers and managers."[38] Paoluzi does not, of course, single out communists, but the mention of workers and socialists was a fairly radical move by an individual of such orientations. Paoluzi goes on to make interesting comments on narrative fiction. In an uncanny echo of Togliatti's criticism of Vittorini's *Uomini e no*, he describes it as a "fervid" but, in part mistaken, book that owes too much to Faulkner and Dos Passos. He rates the work of Pavese highly but, in a moment of spectacular bad taste, he attributes his suicide to the betrayal of the man and the Resistance by the communist leadership.[39] Viganò's *L'Agnese va a morire* is described as having the most evident communist stamp of all the novels, but Paoluzi still rates it highly. In a sense, what Paoluzi seems to be doing is praising texts that were clearly part of left-wing culture, but in each case he is careful to suggest to his readers that he is far from being a closet communist. These were texts that could, therefore, be safely read by Catholics, as long as they were provided with adequate guidance. In a book that is ostensibly about literature, Paoluzi then turned to historiography. He could not, unsurprisingly, bring himself to praise Battaglia's history of the Resistance, which he described as an attempt to heap all the glory of the clandestine struggle onto the communists. Even worse was the abridged version of the book, destined to propagate tendentious interpretations among "easily led and ignorant readers."[40] We might wonder why in a work of literary criticism Paoluzi decided to talk about history books. The explanation is not hard to find—at the time there did not exist, nor indeed would there ever exist, a history of the Resistance written by a Catholic historian. To make up for this deficiency, Paoluzi is trying to encourage his readers to turn to literary texts instead. Of course, some of these come from the wrong side of the ideological fence, but that does not mean they should be discounted or discarded. In a way, he is suggesting that these books can be read "against the grain" and with profit by Catholic readers. In the final section of the book Paoluzi also has a swipe at Calamandrei and singles out his speeches about Lauro de Bosis and the Cervi brothers: "traditional style rhetoric has not spared the Resistance and the author shows us this."[41] Calamandrei would almost certainly have taken the trouble to write a carefully crafted reply to Paoluzi, but the Florentine jurist died in September 1956. He may, however, have been happy to see that, partly because of his efforts in Milan, Catholics were now discovering the Resistance and its values.

Paoluzi's study contains a bibliography that includes, as we would expect, works by Calvino. However, while the bibliography lists the Resistance short stories and *L'entrata in guerra*, there is no place for the novel *Il sentiero dei nidi di ragno*. Paoluzi must have been aware of this work, and the reasons for its apparent exclusion are mystifying. *Il sentiero* is an "ideological" book, but then so is Viganò's *L'Agnese va a morire*, which Paoluzi praises. One possible explanation is that Calvino's novel contains a certain amount of earthy language and a lot of sexual activity (albeit "off-stage'), perhaps suggesting that while the Catholic critic was ready to initiate a dialogue with the Left, he was not yet prepared for intercourse. Whatever is the case, by the mid-1950s Calvino himself had ostensibly moved away from the Resistance thematic toward new subjects and new approaches—the trilogy and the collection of Italian folk tales. Nevertheless, it is not quite accurate to say that he had completely abandoned the Resistance. In the special number of *Il ponte* dedicated to the tenth anniversary, he published the short story "Paese infido," which describes the hostile reaction of a once friendly village to a partisan called Tom.[42] The story is suffused with a profound sense of pessimism and resentment that can also be detected in the longest novel of the trilogy, *Il barone rampante*, published after Calvino's bitter split with the PCI after the events of 1956.[43] Few critics would label *Il barone rampante* as a Resistance novel, but the book does nonetheless contain more than a few obvious references to the period. For example, during the protagonist Cosimo's early years in the trees, he and other locals form groups to protect the forests from attack. The common enterprise of working together creates a sense of solidarity that disappears once the enemy is defeated. It is not at all fanciful to interpret these eighteenth-century groups as prototypes of the twentieth-century partisans. Similarly, the encounter between Cosimo and Prince Andrei at the end of the Napoleonic period, characterized by the Russian's bewildered discussion of the purpose of war, reflects the kind of disorientation expressed by many former partisans in the 1950s.

While *Il barone rampante* contains an indirect take on the Resistance, two works of the late 1950s were more explicitly about the period. The first of these was Rossellini's 1959 film *Il generale Della Rovere*, a film version of a book by Indro Montanelli that was inspired by his experiences in the San Vittore prison. The film's protagonist, played by Vittorio De Sica, is a con man who is employed by the Germans to impersonate the badoglian General Della Rovere and identify partisans in a Milanese jail. However, the con man gradually becomes aware of the noble characteristics of the prisoners and, at the end of the film, sacrifices himself for them. The film is interesting in the sense that it adds a fourth panel to the war triptych of the 1940s and generates much of its meaning via spectator knowledge of the earlier works. In order to make the comparisons between the films more explicit, Rossellini's promoters managed to suggest that it had been made on a low budget, but this would appear to be a marketing expedient rather than an accurate reflection of the actual costs. In *Roma città aperta*, alongside the figures of the priest and the communist partisan, Rossellini depicted the *romana*, Pina, whose *beau geste* in the central scene of the film became part of Italian collective memory of the war. *Il generale Della Rovere* takes things a stage further by suggesting that, during the Resistance, even petty criminals could be heroes. The film is clearly an attempt to suggest that everyone, and not just communist partisans, priests, and proletarian women, were capable of resisting. Even the choice of De Sica, whose performance in the film is exceptional, seems to be a direct reference to Aldo Fabrizi in *Roma, città aperta*—by the late 1950s, De Sica was better known in Italy as a comic rather than a serious actor. The film enjoyed a certain amount of critical success, notably at the Venice Film Festival, but it has never attracted the kind of critical attention of the earlier films. Ultimately, what the film offers is a very anesthetized depiction of the Resistance with politics supplanted by the central theme of moral awakening and sacrifice. Of the civil war, fascism, and the RSI there is nothing.

In stark contrast to the anodyne *Il generale Della Rovere*, another work of 1959 boldly got to grips with the violent reality of the Second World War in Italy. Luigi Squarzina's play, *La Romagnola*, was first performed at the Teatro Valle in Rome in February 1959 with a cast that included the 22-year-old Virna Lisi, who played the protagonist Cecilia, and Luca Ronconi. Squarzina described the play as a "kermesse;" in other words a peasant festival characterized by music, drunkenness, and sex. The play begins with a group of musicians strolling onto the stage and tuning up their instruments. The guitarist posts up the date of the first scene of the "kermesse." It is 1940 and, in addition to the musicians, the stage is occupied by an insouciant Gavanina (Ronconi) who looks on while Cecilia lies under a broken-down car that she is trying to fix. Cecilia, it transpires, runs a Fascist traveling library that distributes propaganda to the people of the *Romagna*. She is obliged to seek mechanical assistance from the peasant Michele and spends the night at a farm that is celebrating the harvest. It is hot, and Cecilia stirs the passions of a number of men—the peasant Michele, a local aristocrat and, finally, a fervent Fascist. Michele and Cecilia dance the tango together and kiss passionately, only to be observed by the count. To make matters even tenser, Domenica, a peasant fortune teller, appears and makes seemingly dire predictions about the fate of those present. Much occurs, however, before her predictions come true in April 1945. Michele and Cecilia become lovers and move to Bologna where he struggles to succeed as an artist, painting scenes of peasant life under Fascism. Unbeknown to Cecilia, the count arranges for Michele to be "discovered" by a Russian gallery owner. When he realizes the false nature of his success, Michele decides to respond to his call-up papers and ends up driving a senior officer in Sicily, with whom he inspects the deserted defensive positions on the island in the run-up to the Allied invasion in the summer of 1943. He returns to Bologna on the night of the Allied bombing of the city, and narrowly misses Cecilia, who accepts the count's offer of safety and becomes his lover. In the darkness, Gavanina is killed, and from this point on, the play becomes increasingly somber. The third and final part of the play is dedicated to the Resistance period and is characterized by extreme acts of violence. In a brief scene, Walter Reder makes an appearance, listening to music as the massacres at Marzabotto take place. Cecilia kills the count by striking him over the head with a poker. She then discovers that Michele has fallen for a *staffetta* and tells the Fascists where he is hiding. He is tortured, but before he is executed, he claims responsibility for the death of the count. Cecilia herself is tried and executed by the partisans, along with many others in episodes of summary justice.

All of Domenica's vaticinations, therefore, come true in the bloodbath of the final scenes of the play.

La Romagnola is a play that does not simply attempt to "mirror" the reality of the long period that it covers. It is not, by any stretch of the imagination, a realistic work. Instead it is a hybrid, as the word "kermesse" suggests, which borrows from a variety of styles, genres, and theatrical practices. The influence of Brecht is clear— from the use of music to the technique of having one of the actors addressing the audience directly. Equally it owes a debt to Greek tragedy as well as to Greek comedy—Squarzina directed both Aeschylus and Aristophanes. In line with Brecht, Squarzina's aim seems to have been to shake his audience out of its leaden torpor. Indeed, the play certainly succeeded in stirring up passions. On its first night, neo-Fascists blocked the roads around the theater. As the actors took to the stage, they were met with whistles as well as rotten eggs and vegetables. Nonetheless, they carried on. As one member of the audience later observed, there was a feeling that the theater had returned to its original function as an arena of "confrontation and the debate of opposing opinions."[44] In view of the innovative nature of Squarzina's play and, above all, for its astonishing civil war finale, it is a sad indictment of Italian theater that *La Romagnola* has never been reprised.[45]

The same year, 1959, also saw the publication of Fenoglio's *Primavera di bellezza*, an ironic title that refers to the second line of the Fascist song *"Giovinezza."*[46] Published by Garzanti, the book describes the intellectual formation of Johnny under the Fascist educational system, followed by officer training. The collapse of the army in Rome on September 8 is effectively described, but the book only dedicates a few pages to the Resistance: Johnny joins a partisan formation in 1943 but is killed by Germans in an early skirmish. Any readers familiar with the Resistance stories of *I ventitré giorni della città di Alba* would have been disappointed. They would not, however, have been aware that the decision to kill Johnny off at this early stage was really the result of Fenoglio's loss of confidence in a work of huge dimensions that would only be published posthumously in the late 1960s in the form of *Il partigiano Johnny*.

The period 1956–1960 sees, therefore, the PCI adopt what could be called a "duplicitous" approach to Resistance memory. Its publishing house, Riuniti, was never so active in promoting the Resistance, while at the level of party organization this was a time when partisan elements, above all Secchia, were subject to very strict controls. The DC, on the other hand, continued to show signs of an interest in a Catholic Resistance with intellectuals like Taviani and Paoluzi making an important contribution. But the DC was not yet ready for a full-scale promotion of the "white" Resistance and it lacked, so it seems, its own historians capable of engaging in battle. The actionists continued their activities, but their golden period was in the early 1950s.[47] Calamandrei himself died in September 1956 leaving behind a lasting legacy, particularly in the city of Florence, but also a void that the actionists struggled to fill. By the end of the 1950s, therefore, the Resistance movement was certainly a presence in Italian political and cultural life, but it had not been, to use a metaphor that became popular, released from the customshouse. Events in the Ligurian city of Genoa in the summer of 1960 would, however, provide the catalyst for the definitive release of the movement and its marketing to Italy as a whole.

4

From the Customshouse to the Pantheon: From the Pantheon to the Piazza

1960–1970

The events of June–July 1960 have very precise origins in the controversial elections of 1953. The failure of the *legge truffa* in those elections (see chapter 2) was a significant blow for the DC and a victory for the politics of the Resistance. But it had long-term consequences as well that were equally, if not more, important. It meant that, in order to maintain its position of power, the DC would have to seek new alliances.[1] Where these new alliances would be found was, however, unclear. On the one hand, the DC could approach the PSI, which continued to distance itself from the PCI (particularly after 1956), on the other hand the neo-Fascist MSI also offered possibilities. Either route, however, presented difficulties to a party that was divided by various currents, both Left and Right. Objections to the PSI would inevitably come from the Catholic Church, while the MSI was seen by many as unacceptably compromised by its historical and ideological roots in the RSI. In practice, the various factions within the DC played out a complex strategy of cultivating both the Left and the Right, waiting to see which way the wind might blow. Gronchi's election to the presidency was a case in point and was the result of votes from the Left but also from the Right. In the case of the right-wing votes, it was the DC politician Fernando Tambroni who brokered the deal with the MSI and who was rewarded for his efforts with the prestigious post of Minister of the Interior. [2] And it was to Tambroni that Gronchi turned in 1960 in an attempt to tackle a crisis that had all but paralyzed the Italian political system since the 1958 elections. The "Tambroni affair" that thereby ensued would lead to fatalities, some of the worst excesses of state power to be seen in postwar Italy, the emergence of a "New Resistance" and, eventually, the first center-Left coalitions.[3] The DC was not, however, alone in jockeying for position. All parties, including the PCI, were in flux with the Resistance and its memory inevitably bound up with the shifting ideologies of the period.

The Tambroni Affair

By the time Gronchi invited Tambroni to form a government (March 1960), there had been a series of short-lived coalitions led by senior DC figures such as Amintore Fanfani, Zoli, and Antonio Segni. When the liberals withdrew their support from Segni, this meant that his majority depended on MSI support, a situation he could not entertain. Tambroni, on the other hand, was apparently happy for his coalition to be shored up by the MSI, and when he presented his government to the chamber of deputies his speech offered no concessions to the PSI and was thus seen as an invitation to the MSI to support him. In the vote that followed, this is precisely what happened with the MSI votes playing a decisive role. After a faltering start, which saw Tambroni respond to DC orders on high to resign, Gronchi asked him to make another attempt along the same lines. This government, which proved to be rather long-lasting, provoked considerable alarm and the journalist Vittorio Gorresio spoke for many when he wrote in his diary, "Just great, it's the 15th anniversary of the Liberation and we are celebrating it with the return of the Fascists to power."[4]

The Tambroni government represented a very significant development in Italian politics. Since its formation, the MSI had been a marginalized party, living in the ghetto of Italian politics and under the almost constant threat of enforced extinction. But by April 1960 it was playing a decisive role in the formation of a government. The party, so it seemed, could now potentially look forward to a future that it could only have dreamed of a few years before. In order to better understand where the party was going, the MSI leadership decided to organize a conference. These events were normally held in what might be termed "safe locations" in the south of the country, but for its conference scheduled for the end of June the MSI decided on Genoa as a venue. Genoa was a city with a strong anti-Fascist identity built on the very solid foundations of the insurrection of April 1945, the same insurrection about which the Christian Democrat Paolo Emilio Taviani had written with such eloquence and passion only a few years before. Genoa was not then just a stronghold of the communist Resistance, it was one of the symbols of the much-vaunted unity of the movement.

News of the MSI congress appears to have reached anti-Fascist ears by early June 1960. In order to celebrate the Festival of the Republic on June 2, there had been for many years a gathering of partisans and anti-Fascists at Pannesi, a location just outside the city, where one of the earliest partisan formations was based. In 1960, the meeting was addressed by the veteran communist Terracini, and it was there that the decision was taken to mobilize forces. Meetings were held of former members of the Ligurian CLN, of the ANPI of Genoa, and of a host of other organizations, including the trade unions. In view of the tumultuous events that were to follow, there has been a tendency to interpret June and July 1960 as the moment when the forces of the Resistance and the unions suddenly awoke after a long period of torpor. But this is a rather inaccurate picture. As I have tried to demonstrate in the previous chapter, the Resistance was still a strong presence in the late 1950s. In Genoa itself, the prefect stated in his reports to the ministry of the interior that both the ANPI and the trade unions were both active in 1959 and, quite possibly, for some time before that. What was special about 1960 was, as the historian Salvatore Vento has noted, that the ANPI, the trade unions, and a number of other forces came *together* in a way that had not previously occurred.[5]

Before the MSI conference of June 30, however, there was much to be done. On June 10, the Federal Resistance Council of Liguria issued a memorandum that summed up the feelings about the putative MSI event in no uncertain terms. From the graves of the Turchino and the "blood-soaked ground of the Benedicta" the cry that was heard was "Genoa still burns" (Genova brucia ancora!)." The document thus deliberately evoked the memory of the Resistance as a means of fighting the MSI. This use of the Resistance as rhetorical weapon became even more insistent in a speech given by Sandro Pertini at a mass demonstration on June 28. Pertini began his speech by addressing the "People, partisans and workers, Genoese of all social classes." The authorities in Rome, Pertini continued, were anxious to discover who it was who were organizing these demonstrations of anti-Fascism. Pointing to the partisan flags present at the demonstration as well as to the hills behind Genoa, Pertini indicated where they would find the answer to their question—the organizers were the men shot at the Turchino, the Benedicta, the Olivella, and at Cravasco, the men and women tortured at the student halls of residence where "the terrible cries of the victims" and the "sadistic laughter of the torturers" could still be heard.[6] In Pertini's rhetoric, the dead had risen from their graves to haunt the resurgent supporters of the MSI. This was stirring stuff, performed by a master of his art, and the crowd was soon in ecstasy. As his speech continued, Pertini spoke passionately of the values of the Resistance, and of its victories and achievements, all threatened by the return of the MSI. But, Pertini ended to thunderous applause, they would be stopped "whatever the cost" (costi quel che costi).

In the end, the MSI were, indeed, prevented from holding their conference when a demonstration of June 30 erupted into violence. The ANPI president himself, Giorgio Gimelli, toured round Genoa with the *questore* of the city helping to restore calm, but there were casualties, particularly among the forces of law and order. Significantly, there were no deaths in Genoa (as would occur a few days later in Reggio Emilia) and no shots were fired, although a number of witnesses have testified to the presence of weapons in Genoa that day. [7]

The demonstrations in Genoa spread to other cities in Italy, prompting talk of a "New Resistance" from the pen of Carlo Levi in the pages of *ABC*.[8] In Reggio Emilia on July 7, a large crowd of demonstrators, including young men dressed in striped t-shirts, gathered in the main square and sang partisan songs. The festival atmosphere was shattered when the police began to fire on the crowd killing five men—Lauro Ferioli, Marino Serri, Ovidio Franchi, Emilio Reverberi, and Afro Tondelli—aged between 19 and 40 years of age. The relatives of the victims of this appalling crime have since waited in vain for the perpetrators to be brought to justice.

The events at Reggio and elsewhere illustrated graphically that the costs of a DC-MSI alliance were too high to be seriously contemplated and Tambroni was forced to resign. The road was now therefore open for the DC to cooperate with the PSI, but the first center-Left government was formed by Aldo Moro as late as

December 1963, with the participation of the DC, the PSI, the Social Democrats, and the Republicans. The agonized making and maintenance of the center-Left was accompanied by a process by which the Resistance and antifascism, whose return in 1960 was seen as the catalyst for political change and renewal, was relaunched and endowed with the national, official, legitimacy that it had lacked in the past. Most significantly, this was a widespread, almost cross-party legitimacy, with Christian Democrats and Catholics in general rediscovering their contribution to the movement. Piero Malvestiti, one of the founders of Christian Democracy was the quickest off the mark from within the party, publishing a curious, and forgotten, analysis of the Resistance.[9] However, the process of legitimization was neither linear nor straightforward—the PCI were not after all in the coalition (and neither were the neo-Fascists), and there was debate within the party about the center-Left. This debate would reach boiling point at the eleventh congress of the PCI, the first after the death of Togliatti in 1964, which saw a very public airing of a major split between the so-called Left and Right of the party, embodied by Pietro Ingrao on the Left, and Amendola on the Right.[10] The debate about the memory of the Resistance thus continued both between and, in the case of the PCI, within the party. Furthermore, the 1960s saw the emergence of a new generation whose relationship to authority, to the past, and to the PCI, was characterized by no little tension. As Forgacs has written, the movements of the 1960s were a "historical watershed" in which "accounts of the past handed down to . . . young people by their parents were also challenged."[11] Above all, with the rise of the student movement in the mid-to-late 1960s, the various state and party models of the Resistance were subject to searching questioning, if not outright attack.

The Resistance in the Pantheon

It is not hard to find indications of a new relationship between the Italian state and the Resistance after June and July 1960, but it is important to measure the quality and not the quantity of this evidence. On April 25, 1961, RAI, the state television channel, broadcast the first ever documentary on the Resistance to be seen on the screens of Italy. *Documenti della Resistenza* was a significant event and its importance was not lost on the PCI, which requested it be shown in Italian schools. It even met with the approval of an establishment paper, the *Corriere della Sera*. Praise for the documentary was not, however, unconditional, with the socialist *Avanti!* commenting that the program did not give enough attention to the Left, and the actionist *Resistenza* arguing that it was too slanted toward the innocent victims of the period, rather than the "conscious combatants."[12] Furthermore, it would be wrong to see this, and other pieces of evidence, such as the documentary broadcast the following year on *Pagine della Resistenza Europea*, as signs of unconditional acceptance of the Resistance at the RAI. In 1961, RAI refused to broadcast a documentary on the Marzabotto massacre that had been made by the director Di Gianni and invited the Catholic director Siro Marcellini to make a different version.

In addition to a new media interest in the Resistance, there were other public demonstrations of a change in attitudes. In October 1961, sixty thousand partisans processed through the streets of Turin in order to celebrate the one hundredth anniversary of Italian unity. This historical coincidence (one hundredth anniversary of the Unification combined with the rediscovery of the Resistance) led to a renewed interest in the articulation of the second Risorgimento parallel, as a number of publications from the period demonstrate.[13] However, there was a problem with the parallel as the Catholic Giuseppe Rossini pointed out: the Unification was not a welcome development for Catholics, especially the Papacy, and there was a risk that they would not find a space in the nation-building exercises of the 1960s.[14] Unlike the Parri-inspired gathering of the late 1950s, the 1961 march encountered no difficulties in getting the necessary permissions—this was a state-run show. At the head of the procession were various Resistance figures, including Longo, Parri, Pertini, Audisio, Lombardi, and the Republican La Malfa. The Christian Democrats were represented by Catholic partisan leader and charismatic symbol of the economic miracle, Enrico Mattei. By the following October, he was dead—the victim of a plane crash whose causes still remain a mystery. The premature death of Mattei was of some significance in that it checked the development of "white" Resistance memory. Mattei was a dynamic and popular figure who would surely have played a starring role in the 1960s as the quintessential representative of the Catholic Resistance. The void he left was not adequately filled: Taviani was an intellectual and, although a senior Christian Democrat minister in a succession of governments, he did not have the necessary scope (and indeed skills) to spread the message of the Catholic Resistance to the broader populace.[15] As we have already seen, another DC intellectual, Malvestiti, published a study of the Resistance but this had little impact beyond a restricted circle of readers. Other works were published by Catholics such as Sergio Cotta and Mario Bendiscioli, but again these were learned academic works that only really appealed to a restricted audience.[16] The Catholic publishing house, Edizioni Cinque Lune, tried to address the problem, publishing a series of 16 short biographies of "*cattolici nella Resistenza*," including one of Mattei.[17] The Catholics did then have their heroes in the shape of Mattei and the likes of Primo Visentin from the Veneto, where white Resistance memory was particularly strong, Giancarlo Puecher from Lombardy, and Don Aldo Mei from Tuscany. Puecher has been the subject of several books, Visentin is commemorated by a statue dedicated to him at Padua University (see Figure 4.1) and Don Aldo Mei's last letters were published in the *Lettere di condannati a morte*. He remains a revered figure in Lucca with a square and a school named after him. But they never rivaled communist heroes like the Cervi brothers or the actionists' Duccio Galimberti.[18]

In 1963, the celebrations for the twentieth anniversary began in earnest. This is in contrast to the tenth anniversary when commemorations and celebrations were only really confined, at least at state level, to the Liberation period of 1945. By sheer coincidence, the 1963 elections were held on April 28, and the PCI chose to make a connection in its electoral propaganda describing a vote in its favor as "a Liberation vote." The party emphasized the contribution of the masses, giving particular attention to the commemoration of the strikes of March 1943. The totemic date of September 8, 1943, was, for the first time, officially commemorated with the Socialist leader, Pietro Nenni, giving a speech titled "The Baptism of the

Figure 4.1. Arturo Martini. Monument to Palinuro/Masaccio (Primo Visentin), Palazzo Bo, University of Padua.

Resistance."[19] The choice of Nenni was no accident—only three months later the first center-Left government was formed by Aldo Moro, made up of a four-party coalition involving the DC, the PSI, the Social Democrats, and the Republicans. The year 1963 also saw the first official commemoration of the popular insurrection in Naples, with a speech on this occasion given by the Christian Democrat, Giovanni Leone. In 1964, the strikes of March 1944 were commemorated in parliament and later in the month it was Moro's turn to get in on the act with a speech commemorating the victims of the Fosse Ardeatine.[20] Events in Rome during the war continued to be at the center of attention, with the June liberation of the capital celebrated in both the Senate and the chamber of deputies.

All these developments were wholeheartedly embraced by the ANPI, which held its sixth congress in Rome in February 1964. This was also the association's first congress after the Tambroni affair and, as a consequence of the Resistance movement's recently found official favor (which extended to financial assistance to all three partisan associations), there were messages of support from, and indeed the presence of, a number of governmental officials.[21] Excombatant associations from outside Italy were also well represented with delegates from Great Britain, Spain, Portugal, France, Yugoslavia, the Federal Republic of Germany, the USSR, several Eastern European countries and, finally, Israel. From the world of Italian culture the most significant presence was that of Gillo Pontecorvo, who had played an important role in *Il sole sorge ancora* and who would go on to make a film about the Algerian resistance (*La battaglia di Algeri*) in 1966, which many viewers interpreted allegorically as a film about the Italian movement. Boldrini's speech reflected a new optimism in the capacities of the organization to intervene in the debate about the social and political problems of the times. But, predictably, the theme of unity was still given pride of place: "United we can be an important part of democracy, divided we have dispersed our forces. And the country needs us: we want to serve Italy."[22] The message of unity was also supported in communications from Argenton of the FIAP and from Enrico Martini Mauri of the FIVL. [23] It was noticeable, however, that the leader of the FIVL, Cadorna, did not send a message of support and would continue to adopt the same polemical line he had espoused throughout the 1950s.[24]

Not everyone was happy with the center-Left, with its spin on the Resistance and the "rivers of empty rhetoric" that flowed through the period.[25] The first issue of *Quaderni piacentini* (April 1962), one of the journals that would most contribute to the vigorous political and theoretical debate of the 1960s, contained an unsigned editorial, attributable to its founder Piergiorgio Bellocchio, which criticized the turn of events in no uncertain terms. That year's April 25 had, the editorial commented, taken *Quaderni piacentini* by surprise. It had been commemorated by "establishment newspapers," on radio and television, in flags, processions, marching bands, and in speeches. After 17 years in quarantine, the Resistance had finally passed its examinations and was allowed to proceed to the next year of study. It was now worthy of all the other wars of the Italian people: 1848, 1859, 1866, 1896, 1911, 1935, and 1940. This was, the editorial ironically observed, a fine result for the resisters, moved and almost incredulous in the face of these developments. The Resistance no longer created fear, was dead, and so "Long Live the Resistance."

"No," *Quaderni piacentini*, wrote three times in succession. They didn't want the Resistance to be commemorated with monuments dedicated to the fallen of all wars, inaugurated by bishops, prefects, and assorted military figures. Silence was better. The real meaning of the Resistance was "revolution" and "renewal," the editorial concluded polemically.[26] The editorial was read by a young Luisa Passerini who would later write that she (and many others of her generation) had "agreed passionately" with its sentiments.[27]

Quaderni piacentini was by no means a lone voice. A far more mainstream journal, the Florentine *Belfagor*, published an epistolary exchange between the veteran anti-Fascist Augusto Monti and Enrico Sturani in May 1963, which took a critical view of the representation of both the Resistance and Fascism. What struck Sturani was the way that, in books, conference papers, films, and so on, the ideological side of history had been diluted, and even the people who had fought in the Resistance seemed to have forgotten about the political aspects of the struggle. This neutral approach to history risked, Sturani concluded, giving space to a certain type of fascism. In his reply, Monti extended the nature of the debate to the second Risorgimento topos. This approach had been damaging for the Resistance, he suggested, because the Unification had itself been the object of serious criticism. With the Unification called into question, so the Resistance was itself open to attack. The overall effect was that it was now seen, not as a revolutionary movement, but as a retrograde historical phenomenon that had "restored" Italy to its pre-Fascist state. It would have been far better to keep the Resistance within its true historical limits, Monti continued, and in that way the real significance of the movement would have been understood. Indeed, he noted ironically, he had tried on several occasions to publish an article arguing this case, but it had always been turned down.[28]

The debate continued when the following year Pietro Secchia contributed to, or deliberately provoked, a polemical exchange about the "beatification of the Resistance," which began with a letter in the *Rivista storica del socialismo*, but then transferred to the pages of *Rinascita*. Secchia's original letter decried the endless procession of Resistance celebrations insofar as they were designed to legitimate the center-Left government and not the Resistance itself. The letter was augmented by comments by the "new left" editors of the journal Luigi Cortesi and Stefano Merli, who traced the origins of the "falsification" of the Resistance to the very heart of the PCI, and to the long-term "national unitary policy" of the party. It was high time, they argued, to bring an end to the "cult" of the Resistance and bring back to the full light of day the original "proletarian surge" that characterized the two years of what they significantly termed the "civil war." The PCI reply in *Rinascita* was authored by the historian Aurelio Lepre, and took issue with the myth of the "betrayed Resistance" that, so he suggested, Secchia, Cortesi, and Merli, had all fallen for. Secchia himself replied first by saying that no one, least of all himself, viewed the political debate about Italy's future that took place during the Resistance as being solely about opposing models of proletarian revolution versus constitutional democracy. Rather, Secchia argued, the aspirations of the partisans were for effective democracy. In turn, Cortesi criticized Lepre for suggesting that they had fallen for a mythical version of the Resistance—the class elements of the movement were a reality, and not a myth, he suggested. Furthermore, he continued, this was only one element of their original adjunct to Secchia's letter. The wider issue of the damage done by the strategy of unity, which had played into the hands of the forces of the false bourgeois democracy embodied by the DC-PSI pact, had not been addressed by Lepre.[29]

These discussions highlight that there were significant divisions among the Left about the way the issue of the Resistance was being addressed. It could be argued that they are a reflection of changes within the PCI, with the likes of Amendola making calls for more dialectic within the party and the later emergence of the "Ingrao faction." But most importantly, they point to what is the single most important characteristic of the 1960s—the appearance of a generational cleavage. Cortesi and Merli were in their early 30s at the time, while Sturani was in his early 20s. Young communists were asking searching questions of the PCI and the party struggled to find an adequate response. But it was, nevertheless, aware of the problem and in 1965 made an attempt to reach out to the young via cultural representations of the Resistance. The *Rinascita* issue of April 24, 1965, contained a special number of its monthly supplement *Il Contemporaneo* specifically aimed at the young that, along with a series of testimonies, published an anthology of Resistance poems by Alfonso Gatto, Umberto Saba, and many others, illustrated by drawings by the likes of Giacomo Manzù and Carlo Levi. What was striking about Gatto's verse was that much of what he published was newly written in the 1960s. His 1966 collection *La storia delle vittime* thus contains verses composed during and immediately after the war, as well as in the period 1962–1965.[30] There can be no more telling example of the "Tambroni effect" on Italian culture. The *Rinascita* supplement also contained another, even more surprising development, the publication of numerous articles from *Il politecnico* and an interview with its hitherto ostracized and vilified (by Togliatti) editor, Elio Vittorini. *Rinascita's* resurrection of Vittorini, made possible by the death of Togliatti, would seem to imply a tardy recognition within some sections of the PCI cultural machine that the writer had a valid contribution to make to the resurrection of left-wing literary culture. Whether or not Vittorini's approach would have brought about cultural renewal was, however, irrelevant. Almost 20 years had passed since the *Politecnico* debate, and this attempt to relaunch him to a new generation of readers must have created nothing but bewilderment.

While the nature of Resistance celebrations in the early 1960s were the subject of animated discussion among the Left, nothing that was said did anything to alter preparations for the official events of 1965. By this time, a new president had been elected in the shape of the Social Democrat leader, Giuseppe Saragat, an election that gave further impetus to the processes described earlier. Saragat was elected in late December 1964, after no less than 21 separate ballots. After the twentieth ballot, Saragat showed he was prepared to come toward the PCI, who then voted for him, by publicly requesting the support of all democratic and anti-Fascist parties. Support for anti-Fascism was thus seen as a necessary value in order to obtain the presidency.

The twentieth anniversary celebrations of 1965 were organized, for the first time, by a national committee, as compared to 1955 when a restricted group of members of parliament was given the task. This committee was chaired by Prime

Minister Aldo Moro and members included the communists Longo, Terracini, Scoccimarro, and Boldrini. On April 25, speeches were made by leading members of all political parties—the socialist Nenni, who was deputy prime minister, delivered the speech in Milan. But the celebrations were far from over. In early May the "Nuovo canzoniere italiano" group put on a show in Milan entitled "Bella ciao." The show, the work of Roberto Leydi and Filippo Crivelli, had caused controversy at the previous year's Spoleto Festival when Michele Straniero had performed the antimilitary song, "Cursed be Gorizia" (Gorizia tu sia maledetta). On this occasion, the offending song was not performed. "Bella ciao" most certainly was, and by the mid-1960s it had become the most popular Resistance song by far—according to a letter to *L'Unità* published in 1965, the song, in a version performed by Yves Montand, had even reached Siberia. Indeed, the 1960s were a golden period for Resistance songs and a series of artistic collaborations, notably the Turin-based "Cantacronache" group, founded by Straniero, Fausto Amodei, and others, did much to popularize them. Calvino himself collaborated with the group and his 1959 song "Oltre il ponte" became an integral part of popular and protest culture. The same levels of success and impact applied to Fausto Amodei's "Per i morti di Reggio Emilia," which commemorated the dead of July 1960 by comparing them to fallen partisans. Significantly, it was a publishing house directly linked to the PSI that recognized the political potential of the Resistance song. The socialists began by publishing an anthology in 1960, before moving to recordings.[31] By 1965, the "Dischi del Sole," part of the Edizioni del Gallo enterprise, had released no less than 10 records of *Canti della Resistenza italiana*, compiled by the likes of Straniero, Leydi, and Cesare Bermani. Straniero also collaborated with Sergio Liberovici on a three-record anthology of *I canti della Resistenza europea*, which contained 46 songs from 16 different countries, all in their original languages. Even the popular star Milva got in on the act, releasing a series of anti-Fascist songs and putting on a show at the *Piccolo* theater in Milan, directed by Strehler, titled *Canti e poesie della libertà*. The championing of the Resistance song was not the only contribution the socialist publishing house made to the relaunch of the Resistance during the 1960s—Edizioni del Gallo collected no less than ten different books into a special multivolume collection totaling 2,410 pages, including Nenni's *Spagna*, Egidio Meneghetti's dialect poems *La partigiana nuda*, and Giuliana Gadola Beltrami's memoir of her husband *Il capitano*, first published in 1945.[32] Despite these efforts, the PSI did not, in the 1960s (nor subsequently) make as much of their contribution to the Resistance as one might have expected. It is, for example, striking that the socialist historian Gaetano Arfé should have presented a paper at a major conference in 1968 on the political parties during the Resistance, but then, for reasons that are not clear, failed to send a version for publication in what would become a key volume in Resistance historiography.[33] For the PSI there was a historical continuum beginning with the opposition to the rise of Fascism, to clandestine anti-Fascism, to the Resistance, but the last link in this chain was given less attention than the first two.[34]

On May 5, the chamber of deputies did not sing "Bella ciao," which would have been asking too much, but it did celebrate the twentieth anniversary, subsequently publishing the texts of the various laudatory speeches that were made.[35] On May

9, what was termed the "national partisan gathering" in Milan, was shown live on state television's RAI1 channel. For the occasion, Saragat delivered a long speech in praise of the partisans and the Resistance movement, emphasizing their role in the creation of the Italian Republic.[36] On the same day, a concert was broadcast on RAI3 that contained works by Schonberg, Symphony no. 4 by Mario Zafred, and the "Funeral Concert for Duccio Galimberti" by Giorgio Federico Ghedini. Not to be outdone, RAI2 showed a documentary on women in the Resistance—destined to be one of the big themes of the 1960s (and 1970s)—directed by the, as then little-known, Liliana Cavani.[37] Although the documentary presented the Resistance as a second Risorgimento, the interviews had, as Crainz and Gallerano have commented, a "notable vivacity" and testified to a "widespread female protagonism."[38] The partisans were not, however, happy with the television coverage and a deputation of gold-medalists went to RAI headquarters hoping to meet the director of programs, Ettore Bernabei. He did not show up.[39]

The twentieth anniversary celebrations were, therefore, a national multimedia event involving a wide variety of genres and styles of celebration—from speeches in parliament and in Piazza Duomo in Milan, to music both popular and classical. They would also have involved school children in events throughout the peninsula, and it is to the question of the Resistance and its place in the Italian educational system to which we will now turn.

The Resistance in the Schools and Universities

Every year, the Minister of Education has issued all schools with a directive to commemorate April 25, but how and whether head teachers responded was another matter entirely. As research on a school at Greve in Chianti has shown, strenuous efforts were made, particularly by showing Resistance films, to take the issue seriously, but Greve (as indeed was most of Tuscany) was a communist stronghold, and it is not surprising that teachers promoted the Resistance in the days leading up to the *festa nazionale*.[40] In the 1950s, furthermore, history teaching had stopped at the First World War and, despite various pleas for change in the 1950s, nothing concrete had ever happened.[41] The Resistance, therefore, was simply not on the curriculum. One of the first indications of a wider change in attitudes, post-Tambroni, was the decision in 1960 by Giacinto Bosco, the Minister of Education in Fanfani's government, to extend the teaching of Italian history beyond 1918. Teachers were now able to proceed up to the constitution and Italy's place in the new Europe. However, a ministry directive is one thing; the reality of what happened in Italian schools is another. Many Italian teachers were hostile, for a variety of reasons, to the idea of teaching contemporary history. Quite apart from this obstacle, which would prove very difficult to break down, there was also a shortage of suitable materials and, where materials did exist, such as the anthologies put together by Armando Saitta, Roberto Battaglia, and Raffaele Ramat, it was not always clear what to do with them.[42]

The picture that emerges about the teaching of the Resistance, and of the place of contemporary history in general is, therefore, mixed. An investigation, carried out by a young man from Voghera, Claudio Bertoluzzi, and published by *Il ponte* in 1965, involving the analysis of questionnaires completed by over a thousand secondary school children in the North of Italy, seemed to confirm the worst fears. The children revealed worrying levels of ignorance, as well as hostility to anti-Fascism and the Resistance, producing apocalyptic comments in the pages of the Florentine journal. Bertoluzzi himself concluded the detailed documentation by referring to a "clean break" between the anti-Fascist generation and his own. [43] The problems were not, however, restricted to primary and secondary education. In the universities, too, the situation was not positive. While it was, of course, possible to study history in Italian universities, it is striking that it was only in the 1960s that serious proposals were made to establish history as a self-standing degree-level course.[44]

Historiography

The late 1950s and early 1960s saw a whole series of public lectures, as well as conferences, dedicated to the recent history of Italy.[45] These were genuine and praiseworthy efforts to render the past more easily accessible to a public who, so it was thought, would be more likely to listen to a historian than read about history. Among the many initiatives there was a cycle of lectures on "Thirty Years of Italian History" at Trieste that included a contribution by a Catholic professor of the philosophy of law at the city's university, Sergio Cotta.[46] Cotta had already published a number of short bibliographical articles in MLI in the 1950s and would go on to write more extended studies in the 1970s and 1990s,[47] but his 1962 speech, published as a pamphlet in the same year, contains many interesting, challenging, and revealing observations about the nature of debate at the time. Cotta began by squarely addressing the various ways the Resistance had been interpreted over the years. The initial celebratory phase had been more "passionate and vibrant" than "lucid and penetrating," but, Cotta conceded, this was entirely comprehensible. Once the celebrations were over there had then been a "more defined intention" to create out of the Resistance and its ideals the "political discourse of the new democratic era which was opening up for Italy." [48] With the subsequent exclusion of the communists from power, Cotta suggested that it was entirely comprehensible that the PCI should have latched onto the period and transformed it into a golden age of unity that had been betrayed. But comprehensible though this may have been, it had led to a distortion of the real nature of the movement. In a striking passage Cotta maintained that the Resistance was "Like all vast popular movements . . . a combination of different ideas and strategies, frequently in contrast with one another, united by a common faith in certain very general values . . . so, by denying the Resistance that dialectic which is characteristic of all human experiences which are truly alive, and separating right from the start, with a clean cut, what is alive from what is dead, *means killing it off entirely.*"[49]

The "death" of the Resistance was, therefore, one of the consequences of the topos of "unity," a concept that flew in the face of the fact that the Second World War was, above all, an ideological conflict. Worse still was the second Risorgimento topos that had the effect of diluting the Resistance by locating it in a single process starting with the unification. There is much persuasive material in Cotta's pamphlet that very effectively captures the problems created by the "public use" of Resistance history. But it could have gone further. Cotta was right to see the emphasis on unity as damaging, but to ascribe it to the PCI alone only gives a partial picture. By the early 1960s, the PCI were far from alone when it came to banging this particular drum. All parties that could claim some participation in the Resistance were falling over themselves to emphasize the united nature of the movement and indeed, its connections with the Risorgimento. As a consequence, the Resistance did not just die; it was embalmed.

Whereas Cotta spoke of, but did not actually demonstrate partisan conflict, Giorgio Bocca did, but in an indirect way. Bocca, a GL partisan, had published a memoir immediately after the war but then, like many others, had not actually published on the Resistance for a long period. This changed in the 1960s with two publications: a short history of the partisan republic of Ossola published in 1963 and a long general history of the movement that came out in 1966.[50] The book on Ossola was one of several publications of the period that traced the history of the various partisan "republics," such as the Christian Democrat Ermanno Gorrieri's account of Montefiorino and Anna Bravo's analysis of the Alto Monferrato.[51] The reasons for the popularity of books of this type are straightforward—they show how individuals of diverse political creeds can work together at a micro level, encouraging readers to consider how at the macro level in the early 1960s similar compromises and successes were being achieved in the center-Left governments.[52] Or so it was hoped.

Bocca's 1966 general history is, obviously, far more wide-ranging than the short account of Ossola. Throughout the book, Bocca presents a broadly "actionist" viewpoint, criticizing the communist betrayal of the CLN at the *svolta di Salerno*, a topic that continued to provoke debate (and still does today).[53] Bocca also gives some details about difficulties between formations, but also repeats the tired second Risorgimento parallel that characterized the Ossola volume.[54] Bocca's book also demonstrated an important quality that would characterize all of his many subsequent writings on the Resistance—he could write in a clear and accessible way and carry a story from beginning to end, a quality noted by the communist Paolo Spriano in his review of the book.[55] This may seem a rather obvious point, but it was one that was clearly lost on the many individuals who wrote on the Resistance both before and after Bocca. It is probably this, rather than what Bocca had to say about the formations, which made this book so popular among young readers in the late 1960s.

Bocca's was not the only general history of the period. Roberto Battaglia's *Storia* was republished in 1964, with substantial changes and additions as compared to the two 1952 versions.[56] A lot of the material from the original early chapters was also removed, but the interpretative framework of the book remained the same. Battaglia's belief in the Resistance as a second Risorgimento also remained constant, as was evidenced by a collection of essays published posthumously and entitled *Risorgimento e Resistenza*.[57] Along with these general histories and other republications (including new editions of Longo's *Un popolo alla macchia* and

Carli Ballola's survey, published with a new title) the 1960s were also characterized by a large number of regional or city histories, such as Carlo Francovich's study of Florence, Enzo Piscitelli's of Rome, and Guerrino Franzini's book on Reggio Emilia and the surrounding area.[58] What these, and many other books published over a long period clearly demonstrated was the essentially regional, if not fragmented, nature of the Resistance movement. The Resistance in the Veneto, for example, was a very different phenomenon from the Resistance in Tuscany. This may seem a banal point, but the need to understand the Resistance at a local level first helps to explain why we had to wait until the early 1990s for a book, Pavone's *Una guerra civile*, which finally gave shape and coherence to a range of diverse regional experiences.

The regional histories made extensive use of individual memoirs. It is not surprising that the 1960s saw the republication of many of these memoirs, such as those written by Battaglia, Chiodi, Lazagna, and Martini Mauri.[59] But there were also some new memoirs published that testified to the range of Resistance experiences, such as the account published by the politically autonomous Icilio Ronchi della Rocca.[60] The most notable work, however, of this new current of *memorialistica*, was the diary of the Jewish partisan Emanuele Artom, which became something of a cult text in his native city of Turin and would, eventually, provide Pavone with a key source for his analysis.[61]

As Pietro Secchia sat through his successor Giorgio Amendola's speech at the PCI congress in early 1960, he no doubt meditated on what would be the best way forward for him. As a senior figure in the PCI, he was finished, but as the principal vector of communist partisan memory, he had only just begun. The 1960s are Secchia's golden publishing period, starting with the 1962 book *La Resistenza e gli alleati*, followed in 1963 by *Aldo dice 26 X uno*, in 1965 by the *Storia della Resistenza italiana*, and culminating in the late 1960s with the vast, multiauthored, multivolume enterprise that was the *Enciclopedia dell'antifascismo e della Resistenza*.[62] During this period he was also frequently invited to give speeches, inaugurate monuments, and participate in all sorts of Resistance commemorations as he commented in his reply to Lepre in *Rinascita*.[63]

The 1962 volume on the vexed question on the relationship between the Allies and the Resistance is a collection of documents that presents the issue from the perspective of the Italian side. This was the first of Secchia's collaborations with Filippo Frassati, who during the Resistance period fought with "apolitical" partisans in Ossola, but who converted to communism subsequently. This collection would only have had a fairly limited readership, whereas *Aldo dice 26 X uno*, is probably Secchia's most conscious attempt to reach out to a mass audience. In a series of rapid and concise chapters, Secchia moves from the popular insurrection in Naples in 1943, to Florence in 1944, and then to the uprisings in the North in April 1945. At a time when the question of spontaneity versus organization was a hot topic within the PCI, Secchia's discussion of Naples would have struck a chord with the young, "spontaneous" demonstrators of 1960 and 1962. The message was clear: the barricades were only likely to produce results in the context of a long-term strategy. Secchia also highlighted the common purpose of the PCI, the PDA, and the PSI during the course of the insurrections, as compared to the vacillations of the DC and the liberals. Secchia also addressed the question of the second Risorgimento, one of the central girders of the Resistance memory edifice. Building on his 1959 speech, Secchia stated that a straightforward parallel was not accurate. The Risorgimento had not seen the masses operate as protagonists, but the Resistance had. Although apparently breaking with the tired rhetoric of the second Risorgimento, there is actually a great deal of orthodoxy in what Secchia writes. On one hand, his comments go straight back to Longo's concept of a "popolo alla macchia." On the other, they incorporate Gramsci's analysis on the failure of the Risorgimento actively to involve the masses in the process of the historical renewal of Italy.

While *Aldo dice 26 X uno* is concise and lively, the 1965 publication (another collaboration with Frassati) is quite the opposite. The *Storia della Resistenza italiana*, in two volumes, breaks through the thousand-page barrier. Both Secchia and Frassati acknowledged in their preface that there had been a tendency for communist discussions of the Resistance to contain inflated claims. What would follow therefore was not a heroic narrative, but it was still an epic tale, an aspect emphasized by the imposing dimensions of the volumes.

If the thousand pages of the 1965 *Storia* seemed excessive, they were nothing compared to the mammoth dimensions of the encyclopedia, for which Secchia wrote many of the entries. A new publishing house, La Pietra, was set up to publish the volumes, the first of which appeared in 1968, the second in 1971, the third in 1976 and, after many travails (including a new publisher), the sixth and final volume in 1986. As with all works on the Resistance, the encyclopedia is as much about the times in which it was conceived as it is about the historical events it reconstructs. By the mid-1960s, a compelling alternative to the almost universal cliché of the Resistance as a second Risorgimento was beginning to emerge.[64] The Vietnam war, and other battles against imperialism, American or otherwise, were seen as forms of Resistance and offered a new spin on the 1943–1945 period, which was thereby rendered, it was hoped, contemporary and relevant. This interpretation is most evident in the special April 1965 issue of the PCI ideological journal *Critica marxista*, whose editorial, attributable to Longo, referred to "striking analogies between what the Americans are doing in Vietnam and what the Nazis did in Europe."[65] The issue itself contained articles and documents that sought to give greater clarity to (but also defend, in the case of Emilio Sereni's piece) the PCI's ideological position during the Resistance period, as well a polemical review by Frassati on Catholic Resistance historiography, followed by three contributions on Vietnam. *Critica marxista* was edited by Alessandro Natta and Luigi Longo, then party leader, and it is clear that this particular historical parallel came from the top, from a PCI leader who had fought in the Spanish Civil War and had been one of the military leaders of the Resistance. It is unlikely that Togliatti would have permitted such an analogy had he been alive. Secchia's encyclopedia reflected this shift in emphasis by giving full coverage to Resistance movements throughout the world. But while the encyclopedia gave space to this new interpretation it was also characterized by its insistence on the familiar theme of unity that was very effectively emphasized by Secchia's decision to secure contributions from across the political spectrum with the exception, naturally enough, of the neo-Fascists.[66]

The Tambroni affair represented a defeat for the MSI, but it also had a galvanizing effect for the extreme Right in publishing terms. Throughout the 1950s, there had been a steady stream of memoirs describing the individual experiences of RSI veterans, but in the early 1960s the publishing patterns changed. Among the many developments, one of the most important was the decision to try to provide an RSI alternative to the highly successful last *Lettere di condannati a morte* (see chapter 2). Duly, in 1960 the National Association for the Fallen of RSI, based in Milan, published the *Lettere di caduti della Repubblica Sociale Italiana*, with an introduction by Don Angelo Scarpellini, who had been largely responsible for collecting the materials.[67] Don Scarpellini's introduction stressed the patriotic nature of the adherents to the RSI, but gave particular emphasis to martyrdom, an aspect that is carried over in the introductory matter to each letter. Officers, Scarpellini claimed, were pleased to hear that for the purposes of execution they would be tied to a pole "like a cross" and recalled "Jesus Christ, not showing the horror or the repugnance which might have been expected."[68] In a similar vein, a Sienese member of the RSI demonstrated affinities with Saint Catherine of Siena by asking to be shot in front of the cathedral at Alba. On the face of it, this is all dignified stuff, but Don Scarpellini reveals just what kind of country the soldiers of the RSI were really fighting for when he quotes from the last letter of Giorgio Monti: "The dead should be avenged. Italy needs us young people so that the negroes, in the service of England, do not contaminate the sacred soil."[69]

The National Association for the Fallen of the RSI published many other works, but the most important and prolific contributor to neo-Fascist memory, a "central figure in neo-Fascist historiography," was the journalist Giorgio Pisanò, an RSI veteran himself, who had been an officer in the Decima Mas.[70] Pisanò began to write for the *Meridiano d'Italia* in 1948 and then, in the 1950s, moved to the popular weekly *Oggi*, edited by Edilio Rusconi. Rusconi then went on to found his own publishing house that published an array of magazines, including the flagship *Gente*. Immediately after, and in a clear response to the Tambroni affair, Rusconi invited Pisanò to gather and publish material, particularly visual material, relating to the Resistance. This material was initially published in a series of photo reportages in *Gente* in 1960. Pisanò then followed this up with a "text only" version in the shape of the book *Sangue, chiama sangue* (blood begets blood), and then in the form of text and images in the three volume *Storia della guerra civile*, published in 1965.[71] All of these publications (and more would follow) essentially propose and repropose the same arguments about the Resistance and the partisans in a conscious effort to, in Germinario's term, "denationalize the Resistance"—in other words separate the Resistance effort (above all the communist Resistance effort) from the process of nation-building.[72] The partisans were, Pisanò maintained, characterized by their extreme levels of violence that was used to one end—the establishment of a Stalinist dictatorship. This violence occurred during the war, but also and most significantly, in the immediate postwar period in the notorious "triangle of death" when the revolution was at is closest. The partisans were also chiefly responsible for the Nazi massacres that had taken place during the summer of 1944. This is particularly the thesis of *Sangue chiama sangue*, which focuses on the killings at the Fosse Ardeatine, at Sant'Anna di Stazzema, and at Marzabotto that were all a product, Pisanò argues, of partisan tactics—the more deaths there were, the more chances the communists would have of seizing power. The attack on the Resistance was also a clear attempt to justify and legitimize the operations of the soldiers of the RSI, caught up in a bloody civil war while maintaining unswerving loyalty to their country, under threat from communist takeover. In addition to lambasting the partisans throughout all these publications, Pisanò also got stuck into the Allied soldiers, notably black American soldiers, who were accused of all sorts of crimes, above all sexual violence. Pisanò's vision of the "depravity" of the Resistance and its allies is, of course, not one that has found universal favor. But whatever we may think of his ideas, and however questionable and repellent they may be, it is worth saying that Pisanò had, and still has today, an audience who are sympathetic to them. Above all, his ideas have found a source of legitimization in the recent works of Giampaolo Pansa, like Pisanò a journalist, but who, in the 1960s (and beyond) had quite different ideas.

Pansa's interests in the Resistance began with his 1950s *tesi di laurea*, which was eventually published in 1967. Before this monograph came out, however, he published two other works that would have lasting impact. The first of these was a brief pamphlet, *Viva l'Italia libera*, probably one of Pansa's most popular works before the mass sales of the last decade. [73] In addition to the 1964 first edition, there were also subsequent editions published in 1976, 1986, 1995, and 2004. The volume was initially published to commemorate the twentieth anniversary of the executions of eight of the most senior members of the Piedmontese CLN. *Viva l'Italia libera* would have represented something of a relief for Pansa, who was working on the revisions to his thesis and on an annotated bibliography of the Resistance in Piedmont, which was published in 1965 to coincide with the twentieth anniversary. The bibliography is an astonishing work of scholarship, containing Pansa's detailed descriptions of 1984 items that had been published in a variety of sources, including 151 different periodicals, on the Piedmontese Resistance from 1945 to 1963. According to his own version of events, Pansa worked long into the night in order to complete his bibliography and there is no reason to doubt him. The volume is for specialists only, and has been a vital reference tool for the many scholars and students who have worked on this key area of the Resistance movement.[74]

Pansa's 1967 monograph, *Guerra partigiana tra Genova e il Po*, is a work that combined those skills of scholar and writer that were already clearly in evidence in the publications I have just discussed.[75] In *Guerra partigiana* Pansa employs a wide range of source texts from archival documents to an impressive array of secondary materials. He also interviewed a number of former partisans at a time when oral history did not exist as a discipline in Italy, nor indeed elsewhere. Despite its considerable length, *Guerra partigiana* is not a difficult read and is characterized by a clear structure and logical progression from one section to the next. At a time when Italian academic writing was vitiated by a range of stylistic crimes, it is a breath of fresh air. The book is also noteworthy for the way that it refuses to sidestep the tactical errors made by the partisans, particularly in the early stages of the conflict. It also does not shy away from discussing in detail the frequently difficult relations between partisan formations of different political persuasions. But the book also has a great sense of *pietas*, notably in the chapters that discuss the wholesale slaughter of partisans at the Benedicta and the Turchino. Pansa is clearly, of course, sympathetic to the partisans and the reader gets the feeling that he is on their side throughout. But he is not prepared to indulge in a sanctification of the Resistance movement in Piedmont. *Guerra partigiana* is not a "revisionist" work, but it certainly suggests that some rethinking had been done.

Cinema

The early 1960s saw an explosion of films with war and Resistance themes, including Florestano Vancini's *La lunga notte del '43* (1960), an adaptation of a short story by Giorgio Bassani, and the film version of Cassola's novel *La ragazza di Bube* (1963), which had been an enormous popular success when it first came out in 1960.[76] Cassola's treatment of the Resistance had stirred controversy in the past, but the 1960 novel actually said very little about the Resistance period, concentrating instead on the postwar difficulties encountered by a former communist partisan, Bube, a character based on the "true story" of Renato Ciandri, and his real life *ragazza*, Nada Giorgi.[77] The film, which presents very few variations on the novel, featured a young Claudia Cardinale playing the dedicated Mara, next to Bube played by George Chakiris, fresh from his success in *West Side Story*. The film also featured a memorable soundtrack and title song that, curiously, is still a popular number in Japan. Irrespective of the merits or otherwise of the film, *La ragazza di Bube* clearly illustrates that the Resistance had real box office potential. Cardinale and Chakiris both had star quality, in truth Chakiris less than Cardinale, and the film is an effective vehicle for their undoubted good looks, enhanced in Cardinale's case by the clothes she wears, which owe their design features to the 1960s, rather than the immediate postwar. *La ragazza di Bube* had an undoubted impact, but the two most interesting films of the period were, for a variety of different reasons, Dino Risi's *Una vita difficile* (1961) and Nanni Loy's *Le quattro giornate di Napoli* (1962).

Una vita difficile starred one of Italy's greatest comic actors, Alberto Sordi, famous, among other roles, for his depiction of a young Roman man obsessed with all things American in *Un americano a Roma*. The trailer and prerelease publicity for the film, characterized by a smiling Sordi strutting about the beach resort of Viareggio, suggested to audiences that they were in for another comic *tour de force*. No doubt they would have been initially perplexed by what they saw. The film opens in Stygian gloom, as a narrow rowing boat deposits a man by a lakeside in Northern Italy, a possible reference to the final scene of *Paisà*, which opens in a very similar way. The bearded man (Silvio), played by Sordi, is a partisan who also writes the local Resistance bulletin. Narrowly avoiding capture, Silvio seeks shelter in a guest house only to be captured by a German soldier who takes him outside to shoot him. Silvio's life is fortuitously saved when Elena, the daughter of the owner of the guesthouse, dispatches the German with a blow from an iron. With this moment of slapstick, no doubt viewers thought that normal service had been restored. Instead, the film brilliantly exploits the countercasting of Sordi to offer what becomes, far from a comedy, a bitter satire of a quarter of a century of postwar Italian history starting with the Resistance and ending in the Italy of the economic miracle, symbolized by the excesses of Viareggio and the arrogant Mercedes-driving *lucchese* who takes Elena from Silvio. The film does, of course, contain some justly famous comic scenes, notably the dinner at the monarchists on the night the 1946 referendum result comes out, but overall *Una vita difficile* is a bleak indictment of the failure of postwar Italy to match up with the hopes of the Resistance. In the wrong hands, the result could easily have been excessively rhetorical, but the film contains enough self-irony to prevent this from happening. Silvio is not portrayed as a Resistance hero, but as a man of flesh and blood who chooses to leave his comrades for the winter comforts that Elena, and her bed, provide.

Risi would briefly return to the "betrayed" Resistance theme in 1963 in *I mostri*, a film made up of short scenes and sketches about Roman life in the 1960s. In one episode, titled *Scenda l'oblio*, a character played by Ugo Tognazzi is sitting in a cinema with his wife. On the fictional cinema screen there are images of German soldiers killing civilians, who are lined up against a wall. The scene provokes only one comment from the Tognazzi character—the tiles used on the top layer of the wall are exactly the type he wants for their garden. As with *Una vita difficile* this is a very effective piece of satire, reminding viewers that it is all very well making films with a Resistance subject, but the impact of that subject depends on the way the audience interprets it. In *I mostri*, Risi encourages his viewers to look not just at the faults of Italian politicians but at themselves.[78]

We do not know whether Nanni Loy saw *Una vita difficile* while he was making *Le quattro giornate di Napoli*. He would have certainly been aware of it, not least because the actress he chose to represent one of the Neapolitan women who populate his film was Lea Massari, who played Elena in *Una vita difficile*. But Lea Massari is where the comparisons stop, for *Le quattro giornate di Napoli* is a completely different film with completely different aims and methods. Loy chose his subject matter for explicit national-patriotic reasons, linked to post-Tambroni Resistance discourse, as he had already done with his earlier film *Un giorno da leoni* (1961). The rebellion at Naples, as we have seen in previous chapters, was significant because it suggested that the movement of 1943–1945 was not just limited to the center and North of Italy, but also extended to the South and, indeed, had its origins there. By valorizing the *Quattro giornate*, the South was also part of a national process that began in the autumn of 1943 and from there spread, by example, to the center and North of the peninsula. Furthermore, the expression "*Quattro giornate*" linked back to the famous "*Cinque giornate*" of the Risorgimento, when the Milanese had risen up against the Austrians.

Given the subject matter and the historical conjuncture, it would be unrealistic to have expected Loy to produce anything but the type of film he made. As Brunetta has commented, the film appears to have been made as if it belonged to a "canonical genre" with "rules to be respected."[79] *Le quattro giornate di Napoli* is, from the outset, a rousing celebration of the four days, of the people of Naples, of the soldiers and sailors, and, above all, of the street urchins of the city. The message is clear throughout, and Loy makes his point relentlessly, no more so than in the scene that shows the first act of armed rebellion by the Neapolitans. The Germans are repelled, but there are casualties, who are loaded onto the roof of a car, draped in the Italian flag (plus the Savoy crest) and paraded around the city for the edification of the populace.

At the same time as *Le quattro giornate* shows a glowing portrait of the people of Naples, it also presents a diabolical vision of the German soldiers who, with one possible exception, are faceless, merciless, killing machines. Although the Christian Democrat Giovanni Leone suggested the film be shown to all Italian school children and reviews in *Rinascita* were glowing, not everyone was happy with the representation of the Germans, nor with the film in general, and criticism was fierce in West Germany.[80] But these negative reactions really reveal that Loy had succeeded in his task as a filmmaker. He was, after all, neither a diplomat nor a historian. The depiction of the Germans implies that the film is, in many ways, a *Roma, città aperta* for the 1960s, and there is no doubt that Loy exploits viewer knowledge of Rossellini's work to create meaning in his own film. This is particularly the case when it comes to the scenes depicting the heroism of the *scugnizzi*. In *Roma, città aperta*, one of the film's more marked departures from historical truth was the band of child partisans run by the cripple, Romoletto. In the case of Naples, on the other hand, there was real evidence of child participation in the *quattro giornate*, ably demonstrated by the young Gennaro Capuozzi who was awarded a posthumous gold medal for his contribution to the Resistance for (according to his citation) throwing hand grenades from a machine-gun emplacement before being struck down by an enemy shell. Loy places the story of Capuozzi at the heart of the film's narrative and takes things even further than the medal citation. In the film, Capuozzi picks up a hand grenade that has been dropped by a stricken insurgent and runs fearlessly toward a German tank, managing to hurl it at the enemy before being cut down in a hail of gunfire. *Le quattro giornate* also featured one of Italy's star actors, Gian Maria Volonté, playing an officer who had lost his hand to frost bite during the Russian campaign.

Volonté also appeared in another Resistance film later on in the 1960s, Gianni Puccini's *I sette fratelli Cervi* (1967). The film is heavily dependent on Renato Nicolai's book and interview with Papà Cervi, but also contains significant differences—notably in the attention devoted to Aldo Cervi (played by Volonté). By placing Aldo at the center of the film's narrative, Puccini also emphasizes aspects of his character that would have appealed to some elements of his audience: Aldo is an impetuous nonconformist who refuses to comply with the disciplined approach of the PCI, and he lives "in sin" with the mother of his children in the Cervi *fattoria*. The film therefore consciously seeks to update the Cervi story to the heady climate of the 1960s, no more so than in the final execution scene that sees one of the brothers raising a clenched fist in a moment of defiance before death.[81]

Literary Texts

The films of the 1960s were characterized by a large dose of the celebratory, but in *Una vita difficile* it was evident that other approaches were possible. Some of the literary texts of the period took this approach further, such as Luigi Meneghello's

I piccoli maestri, which employed irony and self-deprecation as a distancing device.[82] Nevertheless, there were still many literary works that maintained the established orthodoxies, such as Ubaldo Bertoli's *La quarantasettesima* and Franco Antonicelli's play *Festa grande d'aprile*.[83] But it was the posthumously published works of Beppe Fenoglio, *Una questione privata* and *Il partigiano Johnny* both of which had similarities with Meneghello's narrative, which represented the most important works of the 1960s.[84] *Una questione privata*, which Calvino viewed as the crowning achievement of Resistance literature, has as its protagonist an intellectual, Milton, whose contribution to the Resistance is conditioned by his obsessive search for the truth about his lover, Fulvia, and her relationship with his best friend, Giorgio. For Fenoglio, it is not the issue of the depiction of the Resistance *per se* that interests him, but the interaction between the intellectual and the movement. A private matter, the love triangle, is thus played out against the wider backdrop of the Resistance period. The backdrop, itself, is however far from a gray frieze. In particular, the descriptions of the power of nature, a force that takes on increasingly threatening and dark characteristics, highlighted an aspect of the Resistance period that was present in the memoirs (as well as in *L'Agnese va a morire*) but never assumed the same levels of drama as it did in Fenoglio's works.

Alongside the literary texts intended for an adult audience, which have received a lot of attention from critics, there were also a conspicuous number of books aimed at a younger market that have attracted very little comment. In the mid-1960s the N. Milano publishing house released no fewer than 10 books in two years in its *Giovane Resistenza* series.[85] The publisher was a former partisan and the books had originally been part of a competition that published the best 10 of 105 submitted typescripts. The jury was chaired by the president of the Court of Cassation and readers were invited to fill in a post card in order to choose the best work of the ten published stories. The results of this decalogue of children's books were mixed, but there is a sense that the authors were genuinely making an effort to make the Resistance rather more appealing to the young by trying to make the stories vigorous and exciting. There was much heroism, but also a move away from the sacrificial model of the 1950s—one child is blinded in an explosion, but he recovers his sight by the end of the book.

The "Giovane Resistenza" series was not unique and met with competition from the Paravia publishing house whose "La bancarella" series contained works on the Unification, the First World War, and the Resistance. One of these was penned by Luisa Sturani and on this occasion the result, *I partigiani del ciar*, was considerably more successful than her 1953 book *Una storia vera* (discussed in chapter 2).[86] Other publishers attempted to combine didactic material with narrative, as was the case with Luigi Ugolini's *Quei giorni*, but the supporting apparatus is more a distraction than an aid.[87]

The problems encountered by children's writers are best illustrated by a brief discussion of two other books from the same period, Carlo Picchio's *Scarola* and Ermanno Libenzi's *Ragazzi della Resistenza*.[88] *Scarola: romanzo per ragazzi* was first published in 1965 and was eventually translated into English in the 1970s. The hero is a young Roman boy who loses his mother and sister during an Allied bombing raid and joins the Resistance. He is clearly an updated version of

Romoletto from *Roma, città aperta* and helps coordinate a successful attack on a German train depot (an obvious reference to the film) and is eventually reunited with his soldier father at the end of the story. The novel is highly effective in portraying fear and also, in a significant development, depicts the human side of the German occupier. But the final pages of the novel, with Scarola seeing Naples and the ruins of Cassino are contrived, and the decision to make Scarola's father into a carpenter who makes a cradle for a newborn child means that the book ends with some heavy-handed symbolism. Libenzi's *Ragazzi della Resistenza*, on the other hand, fits in squarely with the martyrological paradigm of the 1950s. After a turgid historical introduction by Franco Antonicelli, which would no doubt have encouraged many a young reader to hurl the book away in frustration, the book proceeds to offer its readers 11 biographies of young Resistance heroes—10 boys and a girl—who come from the deep South (Naples, Capua), to the far North (the Trentino). The description of the death of Ercole Chiolerio captures the tone: "He died without bitterness, his soul at peace, in the hope that his sacrifice would contribute to giving a better future to all men."[89] Libenzi's intentions were no doubt genuine and deeply felt, but the book is redolent not only of the 1950s but also of the nineteenth century—the age of Collodi and De Amicis. Libenzi's moral tales ended with an appendix that contained the motivations for the various medals awarded to the young heroes of the book. It is unlikely, however, that the young readers of the 1960s would have ever reached this point.

Monuments

The 1960s were also an important period for the building of monuments. In a move that would have not gone down well with the neo-Fascists, the Milanese authorities gave permission for a monument to be built in Piazzale Loreto. Naturally, it was the victims of the killings of 1944, and not Mussolini and the *gerarchi* who were commemorated. The Piazzale Loreto monument is located in a traffic island next to one of the many roads that converge at what is now a very busy interchange. It consists of a stone plinth that supports a bronze slab. On one side of the slab the names of the victims, who fell "in the name of liberty" are inscribed above a bas-relief; on the other side there is a naked life-size figure, reminiscent of Christ, but without any visible sign of a cross. It is an oddly confusing monument in many ways. It is, for example, unclear which is intended to be the real front. Looking from Piazzale Loreto itself the viewer sees the names of the victims and is invited to contemplate their sacrifice. But the quasi-religious significance of their deaths is then relegated to the reverse of the work, which bears the figure of the naked man and is the largest sculptural feature of the monument that, read in this way, seems to have been added as an afterthought or as a compromise gesture to ecclesiastical authorities. Notwithstanding these issues, it is important to underline the fact that the monument in Piazzale Loreto went on to assume over the years significant symbolic valences. For many years the marches that took place on April 25, and many other demonstrations for that matter, would pass by the monument before proceeding along Corso Buenos Aires and from there to Piazza Duomo via Porta Vittoria. The monument to Piazzale Loreto was thus a vital "memory node," reminding the demonstrators that Mussolini and the *gerarchi* were brought, in April 1945, to that specific square, for a specific reason.

The following year the remains of 782 of the victims of the Marzabotto massacre were given a resting place in the shape of a sacrarium. Monuments were also built in Tuscany at San Sepolcro and Massa Marittima. The Risiera di San Sabba, which the Germans had used to imprison soldiers and other Italians prior to deportation (if they survived the experience), became a national monument in 1965 and, subsequently, there was an architectural competition for a project to turn it into a museum, which was opened in 1975. The sheer scale of the Risiera di San Sabba project reflects a move toward the creation of more complex and ambitious sites of memory, such as the Resistance park opened in the city of Ancona in 1965. The project involved the landscaping of a hillside in an already existing park at Borgo Rodi. Visitors enter the monument through a set of gates and then proceed up a narrow stairway that opens up into a series of small squares or terraces. On the way up, they pass by 16 marble plaques, each of which contains a text written by Franco Antonicelli, which narrate the course of the Resistance from 1922 to 1945. At the top of the final terrace there is a bronze sculpture by Pericle Fazzini that soars into the sky above the epigraph: "The Republic which emerged from the Resistance bathes in the glory of its origins." This is a rather ham-fisted finale to the Ancona monument experience, but the attempt to involve the spectator in a dynamic process of memory creation, achieved through the active construction of Antonicelli's marble text, anticipates some of the developments of the 1970s.

The more radical, innovative, and above all secular approach to monument design, characterized by the Resistance park at Ancona, is also reflected in three monuments from the late 1960s: in Venice, Cuneo (Figure 4.2), and Udine (Figure 4.3). The Venice monument, of a dead *partigiana* lying in the water, replaced the earlier (destroyed) monument to the *partigiane* and was inaugurated in 1969. The monument in Cuneo, on the other hand, was a more abstract affair, with its diverse and dynamic elements suggesting the powerful forces of the Resistance at the moment they were unleashed.

But it is the last, and most abstract of these monuments, that I will discuss in detail. The original idea for a monument in the city of Udine, one of the cities awarded a gold medal for its contribution to the movement, can be traced back to a proposal presented to the city council by the mayor, Giacomo Centazzo, in April 1958.[90] The council approved the idea and issued a document describing why the monument was needed, where it should be placed, how much it would cost, and who would pay for it. The initiative was supported by various associations and its aim was to realize a monument to the Resistance that would have two functions, to "glorify the high moral values of all the Friulian people who during the struggle for Liberation gave their all to recapture lost liberties" and to "remember to our successors the virtues of our people in their demands for the profoundest motives of civil and democratic life." The location for the monument, for a variety of reasons, but above all, for its proximity to the city's ossuary, was to be the center of Piazzale XXVI Luglio, essentially a roundabout where several of the city's main streets converge. The costs were not to exceed 25 million lire and a national competition would take place in order to decide who would be given the task. All competitors would

Figure 4.2.   Umberto Mastroianni. Monument to the Resistance. Cuneo.

be required to commemorate and honor "with dignity . . . the highest values of the Resistance" and at the same time create a piece of architecture that would accord "prestige and decorum" to one of the most important squares of the city.

A year later, the town council appointed a committee of judges made up of the mayor and various councilors, several sculptors, an art historian and two Resistance representatives: Fermo Solari and Fausto Barbina. The committee examined some 33 different projects, and by the end of the first day of deliberations a clear favorite had emerged, entry number 17, entitled *Forra* (gorge), a joint submission involving the architects Gino Valle and Federico Marconi and the sculptor Dino Basaldella. The project principally involved two different, but related, architectural elements. The main feature was four imposing concrete walls joined together to form a rectangle and suspended in space by three columns. On one of the inner walls there would appear a lengthy extract from Calamandrei's speech at the Lyric Theatre in Milan in 1954, beginning with the famous line "When I consider this mysterious and miraculous movement of the people." In front of this rectangle, before the unsupported front wall, there would be a semicircular fountain, located below ground level. The lowered fountain, and the suspended concrete form, would create a visual space allowing the spectator to look "through" the monument to the streets beyond it. Basaldella's sculpture, an abstract winged figure, placed inside the rectangle, but at eye-level, would also be clearly visible from outside the monument. Francesco Tentori, one of the architects on the panel, was struck by the "purity" of the design and felt that this would give the monument a "classical quality" and a "simplicity" that would make it an enduring work of art. Tentori saw the similarities between the concept and the Fosse Ardeatine monument and felt that this was a firm guarantee of its success. Tentori was spot on—the monument clearly references the Fosse Ardeatine construction and Dino Basaldella was the brother of Mirko Basaldella, who had designed the famous gates. Tentori approved of the fountain and the statue and of the way the square would be lowered to accommodate the monument. Above all, the project found favor in Tentori's report because of its organic integration with the other features of the square. There were, however, concerns as to whether the large concrete block would fit in with the spatial proportions of the square, and it was agreed that the judges would go the following day to examine this question. The engineer in charge of public works, Giorgio Paulon, gave a positive opinion and with only one dissenting voice (that of the art historian Renzo Biasion) the decision was taken to go ahead with the *Forra* project. The final written decision of the judging panel praised the "expressivity without rhetoric" of the work, but also referred obliquely to one of the difficulties of commemorating the Resistance in Friuli. The combination of Calamandrei's text and the sculpture would "in a lyrical and serene way," capture the "spiritual message of the Resistance, its prospects and hopes, rather than the painful and brutal sequence of events of the war." These "events of the war" included the Porzus killings, when in early 1945 Catholic partisans were killed by communists for reasons that are still not clear today (see chapter 8). But it was clear that a monument celebrating the Resistance would, of necessity, steer clear of this painful episode.

Figure 4.3.   Gino Valle. Monument to the Resistance. Udine.

Quite apart from the difficult issue of the Porzus killings the monument would, however, take some time to be realized. For reasons that are not clear, following the results of the initial competition, there was a five-year gap before matters really got underway. In 1963, the architect Valle built a mock-up of the concrete rectangle out of tubes and jute sacking. The plan was to see how the monument would fit into the space in the square and give the authorities in Udine an idea of what to expect. However, the model for the monument appears to have attracted strong negative reactions from the local *udinesi*, who did not approve of the project for both aesthetic and political reasons. The mayor of the city, the former partisan Bruno Cadetto, had his work cut out to convince the people of Udine of the worth of the project. In order to get the town council behind him, Valle gave a presentation to the city council in which he explained some of the ideas that lay behind the design of the monument. The restricted nature of the square itself meant that it was not possible to construct a monument that could only be viewed externally, he explained. What was needed was a monument that had both internal and external aspects. The different elements of the monument had specific symbolic functions: the *forra* represented the open wound, the pain, which had led to the Resistance, while the fountain, which attenuates the noise of the traffic, creates an "atmosphere of meditation." The water was, of course, a natural element and the interaction between the monument and nature would be emphasized by the planting of climbers that would grow up the sides of the concrete walls. The design was also a conscious attempt to maintain a link with the already existing ossuary, and at the same time, do something different. Finally, Valle explained, the concrete quadrilateral, represented "the objective values of the Resistance, the choices that were made."

Valle made several alterations to his concept before it was finally unveiled on April 25, 1969, at an opening ceremony that was itself a carefully choreographed event. At 8:15 in the morning archbishop Giuseppe Zaffonato celebrated a Mass in the ossuary that was dedicated to the fallen of the war of Liberation and all other wars. Zaffonato underlined, in the presence of the president of the region and the mayor of Udine, the high moral values of the all those who had been killed. At 10:30, Mariano Rumor, the president of the council of ministers, arrived to be met by various officials, including Colonel Tucari, the commander of the *carabinieri* in Udine. By this time, the partisans were already arriving at the assembly point on Piazza I Maggio, the *garibaldini* in their red scarves and the *osovani* in green. The bands played, the crowds sang, and the sun shone. The victims of the German deportations were first commemorated, and then the crowds marched to the monument along a carefully chosen route passing through Piazza Libertà and Via Cavour. Along with the flags of the partisans were those of numerous other associations, including the Italian army, and all the flags of the cities that had been awarded a gold medal for contributions to the Resistance. There were, however, some elements who hoped to spoil the party: in Piazzale XXVI Luglio the marching partisans were greeted by a group of young protestors, pejoratively labeled as *cinesi* ("Chinese," i.e., Maoists) in the official publication that came out the following year, who shouted and waved signs, but we are told, did not provoke any serious incidents and were, in any case, not from Udine. The mayor, Cadetto, began the speeches by reading out a message of support from Giuseppe Saragat in which the president of Italy paid homage to the 3,463 *friulani* who had been killed during the struggle for the liberty of the nation. He then thanked Rumor and the senior representatives of the two partisan associations, Boldrini of the ANPI, and Aurelio Ferrando from the FIVL, for their attendance. Cadetto then gave a brief history of the long process behind the building of the monument (which had cost 120 million lire in total, five times the original limit), including references to the forces who had opposed it, and who suggested instead the construction of a school or some other building with a more obvious social function. Others had gone so far as to suggest that the Resistance should not be remembered but forgotten. All of these objections were, however, overridden by the necessity to commemorate the Resistance and, above all, the 3,463 fallen of Friuli who were discussed in detail during the course of the speech. Boldrini was next, and he began his oration by listing his addressees: Rumor, the president of the region, the mayor, the representatives of both chambers, the citizens of Udine, the partisans and then, finally and pointedly, the "young." He discussed in the usual terms the struggle that had seen communists and Catholics, socialists and republicans, men from the PDA and the liberal party, as well as soldiers and officers fighting together as one. The sacrifices of the people of Udine were part of Italy's common martyrology that included the fallen in the labor camps, the soldiers of Lero and Cefalonia, and the soldiers who advanced from the South when they responded to the call to arms of a new Italy. Toward the end of the speech Boldrini turned to the question of youth who looked on with "critical eyes." Addressing Rumor himself, Boldrini conceded that they all had been young once and in the heat of the struggle they had looked for rapid shortcuts to construct Italy. But rapid solutions had not been possible—instead Italy had been made by democratic methods, notably by way of the constitution. No doubt Boldrini's comments were well intentioned, but there is nothing more infuriating than being told by someone of advancing years that it is easy to make mistakes when you are young. Old people can make mistakes too, and the senior representative of the Resistance in Italy might have done better to recognize this.

Ferrando, the national secretary of the FIAP, spoke after Boldrini. His speech contained little of note, except for the list of the martyred that began with the names of *osovani* killed by Fascists, but ended with the names of Bolla and Enea, killed by the communists. This was not exactly explicit stuff, but the reference to Porzus was clear enough. Then came Rumor, who gave what must have seemed like an interminable speech, before walking around the monument, visiting the ossuary and the local DC headquarters before getting back on his plane at 2:30. The event ended with a dancing display performed in regional costume, which was greeted with enthusiastic applause from the crowd.

The monument in Udine continues today to offer a focal point for commemoration ceremonies. But the monument itself now seems under threat from various forces—the buildings around it have increased in height and the original fears about the relationship between the monument and its surroundings seem to have been proven correct. Furthermore, the climbing plants that were designed to interact with the monument now seem to have overtaken it, suggesting that the forces of nature and time are more powerful than the Resistance that the quadrilateral represents.

From Paolo Rossi to the "Contested Resistance"

On April 27, 1966, a student of architecture at Rome university, Paolo Rossi, was attacked by neo-Fascists while distributing political leaflets. The attack took place on the steps of the law school, a discipline known to attract right-wing sympathizers, then and now. Rossi suffered serious head injuries in the fight, fell into a coma and died shortly afterward. The incident provoked a wave of protests, targeted at the rector of the university, Ugo Papi, who was accused of an excessively tolerant attitude to the Right. In the chamber of deputies, Tristano Codignola halted proceedings to announce the death, and the Minister of the Interior, the former partisan Taviani, made a speech in which he noted the tragic coincidence of the events in Rome with the anniversary of the Liberation. In his memoirs, Taviani reflected that this was the first time the communists applauded a speech by the Minister of the Interior.[91] Significantly, the individual who was invited to address protestors at the university the following day was the one-time "Resistance prime minister," and symbol of the wind from the North, Ferruccio Parri. In his speech, greeted by shouts of "*Resistenza*," Parri called for the resignation of the rector and also said to the young crowd: "The Resistance continues with you." This was a moment of extraordinary significance—the high watermark in the relationship between the Resistance and the postwar generation had been reached and the older generation of anti-Fascists understood this.[92] Parri himself would never be so popular. He was the living embodiment of anti-Fascism having, albeit unsuccessfully, introduced a bill in July 1960 to outlaw the MSI. In 1967, he would gain further plaudits by being one of the most vigorous denouncers of the antidemocratic practices of the Italian secret services that would come to light in the wake of the SIFAR (Armed Forces Information Services) scandal and the emergence of details concerning the failed "Piano Solo" in 1964.[93] In 1968, he was again siding with the students, calling a press conference on the eve of May Day where, it was claimed, the police in Rome had not only beaten but also tortured a young protester.[94]

By the late 1960s, the situation would change, with the young adopting a far more questioning and antagonistic relationship to their Resistance forebears. As the protest cycles of the 1960s got into full swing, many anti-Fascists, but not Parri himself who became an "itinerant icon" in the period, were no longer seen in such a positive light.[95] The Resistance, so the young had been remorselessly told throughout the early 1960s, had led to the birth of the new Italy. But by the mid- to late-1960s, if not earlier, that new Italy was looking distinctly rotten. The much vaunted center-Left governments, which were the most tangible manifestation of the kind of political cooperation that had supposedly characterized the Resistance period, had been a disappointment. In turn the PCI, who had championed the strategy of unity during the Resistance, found itself accused of compromises that had undermined the revolutionary potential of the movement. Furthermore, the educational system was in a mess and students demanded change. In early 1968 Ferruccio Parri's journal *L'Astrolabio*, which he had founded in 1963,[96] sent a correspondent to Palazzo Campana in Turin, then occupied by students, to report on the latest developments. The article begins on the afternoon of February 15, where around 50 students belonging to the "agitation committee" were awaiting the arrival of Franco Venturi, one of Italy's foremost authorities on the Enlightenment and on Russian populism, as well as a former actionist partisan who had coedited Dante Livio Bianco's diary in the mid-1950s and was a regular contributor to the Turin-based journal *Resistenza*.[97] The students would only allow Venturi's lesson to go ahead if it took on the format of a debate, rather than a lecture performed *ex catedra*. Venturi refused, and within a few minutes the lecture hall was filled with the sounds of his increasingly irate calls for order: "I request silence . . . I will not have a discussion with a crowd . . . when the lesson has started no more talking . . . I will grant you one freedom: that of allowing you to use your right foot and then your left to leave."[98] Soon he was banging his fists and shouting, and the students left the room.

Together with the daily agitation bulletin the students had also started to produce dossiers about their professors. What struck the journalist was that the professors who were subject to the most vitriolic attack were the ones with an anti-Fascist past: Venturi, but also Aldo Garosci, the author of the standard text on anti-Fascists in exile, and Guido Quazza, the doyen of Resistance historians.[99] Why was such bile reserved for the "the profs. decked out in their Resistance coat-of-arms?" The answer, so it seemed, lay in the way these professors refused to see the profound aspirations for freedom in these protests, interpreting them only as an attack on their power and prestige. History had moved on since April 25, 1945, but the old anti-Fascists did not always understand.

The old anti-Fascists did not, however, just bang their desks in frustration. Giorgio Amendola, for example, whose status within the PCI was becoming increasingly important after the death of Togliatti, collected his various articles on the Resistance in a volume whose preface specifically located the reasons for its publication within the climate of "Resistance contestation."[100] Some, such as the political philosopher Norberto Bobbio and Quazza himself tried to enter into a dialogue with the students. Both Bobbio and Quazza published important articles in the Turin-based journal *Resistenza*. In Quazza's piece, published in September 1968, the historian rightly identified the reasons for the protests against the Resistance—the new Italy "born directly from the Resistance" had failed, and so, therefore, had the partisans.[101] But, as Quazza acutely argued, it was not exclusively the former partisans who were subject to criticism, but more the model of the unitary "tricolor" Resistance that was being targeted. With the publication of influential texts such as Renzo Del Carria's *Proletari senza rivoluzione* fanning the flames of the idea of the betrayed Resistance, the unitary model would soon be challenged by the classist paradigm of the "red Resistance" and would provide the late 1960s and 1970s with what Ganapini has described as one of its "most popular and significant" slogans: "the Resistance was red, not tricolor."[102]

The young people who shouted out "*La Resistenza è stata rossa e non tricolore*" looked for their inspiration to those partisans who most closely fit the revolutionary model. Secchia was, of course, one of them, as was his close associate Giovanni Pesce who, in 1967, published a text of totemic significance, *Senza tregua*. Pesce had been a volunteer in Spain and then gone on to be one of the leaders of the Milanese *gap* organizations. After the *attentato* on Togliatti, Pesce became the head of PCI security, in the newly formed "commission for vigilance."[103] He first published his partisan diary *Soldati senza uniforme* in 1950, followed in 1955 by his account of his adventures in Spain, *Un garibaldino in Spagna*. Neither of these books had any great impact, but *Senza tregua*, which is a revision of *Soldati senza uniforme*, most certainly did. Published by Feltrinelli, the first edition rapidly sold out and a second followed. The book depicted healthy cooperation between workers and partisans and so fitted very neatly with the "workerist" climate of the period. But by far the most famous aspect of the book is the unforgettable description of the heroism of the *gappista* Dante Di Nanni, cornered by Fascists and Germans in a flat in Turin. Single-handedly Di Nanni held off the enemy for some considerable length of time, hurling improvised grenades made from dynamite at the armored cars below until, with his last cartridge used against a Fascist, he threw himself from the terrace down onto the street below.[104] Whether or not Pesce's description reflected the reality of the moment did not matter—this was meat and drink to young, politically committed, activists who had been fed a diet of what Parri memorably called the "the Resistance shrink-wrapped by Andreotti."[105] *Senza tregua* also became a decisive book for many who chose the path of "armed struggle" in the 1970s, such as Enrico Baglioni (a future leader of Prima Linea), who described it as a sort of "formative novel" for him and other militants.[106] When Pesce dedicated the book to his daughter and to the young who were invited to "continue the Resistance" he most certainly did not intend them to take his advice literally, but this was what happened.[107] After the publication of *Senza tregua*, Pesce was always first on the guest list for events held by the extraparliamentary Left, above all in his power-base of Milan.

During the 1960s, the legitimacy of the Resistance came at a heavy price. It was firstly given clearance to leave the customshouse (*sdoganato*), where it had been languishing since 1945, and then allowed to travel to the Pantheon where its "national character" was highlighted.[108] The Pantheon is, it goes without saying, reserved for the dead. The student movement then sought to resurrect the Resistance and restore the revolutionary charge they believed it had originally possessed. What, as Santomassimo has commented, was "crushed" in this process was the Resistance of ordinary Italians.[109] But when a neo-Fascist bomb went off in the center of Milan in December 1969, the reinterpretation of the Resistance would move to an entirely new, and even more charged, phase.

5

1970–1978

The bomb in Piazza Fontana in December 1969 marked the beginning of a long period of violence and subversion in Italy that would culminate in the kidnapping and murder of Aldo Moro in 1978 and the Bologna railway station bombing in 1980.[1] One of the most obscure events of the whole period saw, in early December 1970, Prince Junio Valerio Borghese, the former head of the crack submarine corps the X Mas, attempting a military coup. Borghese, along with some supporters, occupied the Ministry of the Interior for a brief period. The coup never really got off the ground, but it was a warning that the Italian state could, potentially, be destabilized, as would happen in Chile in 1973. The Borghese coup also graphically demonstrated that the past, in the shape of one of the most important figures in the RSI of 1943–1945, still acted on, and was active in, the Italian present. In view of this context it is not in the least surprising that the Resistance movement was the subject of much attention in the period, particularly in 1975, with the celebrations for the thirtieth anniversary of the movement.

Songs, Monuments, Historiography

In the 1970s, Resistance songs enjoyed a huge popularity, as is reflected in the album *Il vento fischia ancora* released by "Duo di Piadena" in 1972. The record contains, with one exception, Resistance songs, and begins and ends with the famous song "Fischia il vento." Two years later, Piazza della Signoria in Florence witnessed what was probably the largest ever public performance of "Bella ciao," involving a thousand massed bands, totaling ten thousand musicians. The following year, the ANPI of Galluzzo and Scandicci, two small towns on the outskirts of Florence, set up a cultural center in an old *Casa del Popolo* and called it the *circolo* "Bella ciao." "New" songs of Resistance that had been written in the 1960s were also a regular feature at demonstrations and elsewhere, such as Fausto Amodei's "Per i morti di Reggio Emilia," as well as Paolo Pietrangeli's "Contessa," which invited comrades to take to the squares with hammer and sickle and use them. If the wind blew in the past, it was now blowing stronger, the song continued, and anyone who denied this had thrown their red flag in a ditch and deserved to be spat upon. The Resistance was, most emphatically, back—relived, rethought, and reinterpreted—by the younger generations.

The 1970s were also a golden period for monuments. According to Galmozzi's research, monument construction was at its most intense in the years from 1969 to 1975 when "62 monuments were built and the highest annual average was reached in 1975 . . . with 23 works."[2] Emilia Romagna, unsurprisingly, led the way with monuments to the Bolognese *partigiane* in Villa Spada in the center of the city and to the *fucilati* of Sabbiuno di Paderno in the periphery. Both monuments actively involve the viewer in the creation of memory in a manner reminiscent of Umberto Eco's concept of the "open work."[3] In other words, each individual spectator assembles a text by piecing together diverse fragments to make up a whole that is always unique and unrepeatable. In this way, the monuments ceased to be static objects and were brought to life in their interactions with their spectators. The monument at Sabbiuno di Paderno (see Figure 5.1), created by a group of three sculptors, was inaugurated in 1973. It commemorates a hundred partisans killed over a number of days in December 1944. They were shot and their bodies cast down the side of the *calanque*, a geographical feature typical of the area. The visitor leaves the museum where the prisoners spent their last hours and proceeds along a walkway that is punctuated by stones bearing the names of the dead. The curved wall at the end of the walkway represents the place where the firing squad stood—at the bottom of the *calanque* there is a cross. There is an audio accompaniment as well (oral testimonies punctuated by the song "Oltre il ponte") making the monument a genuine multimedia experience. As with many Resistance monuments, it has frequently been attacked by neo-Fascists. Uniquely, however, the monument risks being destroyed by the even more powerful forces of nature—as

Figure 5.1. Letizia Gelli Mazzucato, Umberto Maccaferri, and Gian Paolo Mazzucato. Monument to the *fucilati* at Sabbiuno di Paderno.

the years have passed, the *calanque* has eroded and receded, threatening to reclaim the work.[4]

Though less of an "open work," the monument in Savona by Fabbri, which depicts a man breaking free from his bonds, is certainly dynamic. Conversely, Manzù's far more famous monument in Bergamo, from 1977, shows a partisan hanging upside down, while his mother looks on in desolation, her arms outstretched toward his lifeless corpse. It is a modern version of the "Pietà," but it seems to offer no hope of revival or resurrection, and indeed Gundle has written perceptively of the way the "utterly bleak and hopeless imagery of the work" freezes the viewers' responses.[5] A similar pessimism characterizes another sculpture in the North of Italy—Quinto Ghermandi's bronze in Brescia where the wings of liberty are paralyzed and unable to burst free into flight.

Not included in Galmozzi's list is a monument dedicated to Claudio Varalli and Giannino Zibecchi in the center of Milan. Varalli had been killed by neo-Fascists on April 16, 1975, whereas Zibecchi was killed by a *carabinieri* armored car that mounted the pavement at a demonstration the following day. The monument, cast in bronze, shows images of young demonstrators waving banners containing familiar 1970s slogans such as "you will pay dearly, you will pay for everything" (*pagherete caro, pagherete tutto*). At the top appear the smiling faces of Varalli and Zibecchi and the caption beneath them describes them as "fallen partisans of the new resistance" (see Figures 5.2 and 5.3). At the foot of the monument, in large letters, is inscribed the final line from Piero Calamandrei's epigraph: "*ORA E SEMPRE RESISTENZA,*" itself an unmissable slogan at any mass demonstration of the 1970s. When the monument was officially opened Varalli's friends wrote, "Comrade Claudio died a partisan and we remember and honor him as one."[6]

The period also saw intense publication activity, with the 1971 initiative of the communist publisher Editori Riuniti, which collected eight classic volumes in a boxed set collectively titled *Antifascismo e Resistenza*, amply illustrating the heady fervor of the times.[7] The Riuniti collection gave out positive signs of communist unity, but in 1973 a clash at the top of the party that had rumbled on since 1943 came to a head in a public manner with the publication of books by Longo and Amendola.[8] The latter's *Lettere a Milano* showed just how bitter the confrontation between the PCI leadership in Rome and Milan had been, and how the Togliattian line had caused great anxiety, even disbelief, among many. Amendola's explanations of his own subsequent realignment remain unconvincing, as indeed do those of his most recent biographer.[9] Whatever the case, Amendola's views on the Resistance continued to be challenging. From the 1950s onward, Amendola had maintained a line of strong criticism toward those who argued that the Resistance had been betrayed. In the 1970s his target was, predictably, Longo, who published a book entitled *Chi ha tradito la Resistenza.*[10] In his "Interview on anti-Fascism" with Piero Melograni, Amendola also explained why in recent years he had tried to push, particularly to the younger generations, a more limited interpretation of the Resistance phenomenon. It was not, he stated, a matter of "national unanimity," but rather a movement of a "minority."[11] Such arguments did not always go down well, he conceded, and he commented on how he had been whistled at during a speech in Turin when he questioned the idea that the Resistance was "only red" and added that Christian Democrats and Socialists had been part of

Figure 5.2 and Figure 5.3. Unknown artist. Monument to Zibecchi and Varalli (Milan).

the movement.[12] These views offer further evidence of different interpretations of the Resistance from within the very top levels of the PCI. Again, the idea of a PCI-manufactured monolithic Resistance myth does not really stand up to analysis.

There were also key publications in historiography, such as Guido Quazza's *Resistenza e storia d'Italia*,[13] which tried, at least in part, to link certain aspects of the Resistance with the themes of the 1970s, with the partisan formations seen as microcosms of "direct democracy." Quazza was, therefore, making an effort to respond to the questions raised by the student movement, including the role of the PCI, of which Quazza had always been critical. Quazza's book, now almost entirely forgotten, ranged over a number of themes (including violence) and suggested a broadening of the chronological span of research into the before and after of the Resistance. Quazza's book also contained other "research hypotheses," but few of these have been taken up.

While Quazza's book analyzed many issues, the British scholar David Ellwood concentrated on the vexed question of the relationship between the Allied forces and the Resistance and demonstrated, on the basis of profound archival research, that the notion that the Americans and the British had tried to control and circumscribe the movement was far from being a communist "myth."[14] Ellwood demonstrated that Allied policy toward the Resistance was conditioned by a mixture of strategic and political imperatives related to Italy's delicate position in the *future* map of Europe.

In the same way that Quazza's book reflected contemporary themes and issues, so many of the publications from the 1970s address the question of women. This was not, as earlier chapters have shown, an entirely new development, but there is no doubt that interest in gender issues reaches its height in the 1970s. Numerous conferences were held that gave many women their first real opportunity to speak of their own experiences.[15] The publication of *La Resistenza taciuta* in 1976, which contained the testimonies of a selection of Piedmontese women collected by the pioneering figures of Anna Maria Bruzzone and Rachele Farina, blazed a trial and is widely recognized as a key moment in the development of women's history in Italy.[16] Along the same lines, the lawyer and activist Bianca Guidetti Serra interviewed 48 women from Turin who had been active through the Resistance period and published transcripts of the interviews in her two-volume *Compagne*.[17] While, perhaps, Guidetti Serra's book lacked the kind of rigor in transcription that oral historians now require as a matter of course, *Compagne* was nevertheless a pioneering work that did a great deal to change the image of the Resistance from something that only the men did.[18]

As in previous periods, a number of literary texts were published as well as books on the Resistance intended for children and anthologies.[19] Of these, probably the most interesting publication, if only for its title, was the collection *La guerra civile in Italia*, a work that has since faded into almost complete obscurity.[20] The choice of title indicates very clearly that the idea that the "civil war" interpretation was totally silenced until the 1980s is not entirely accurate. The expression *guerra civile* is freely used by Antonio Pitamitz in his introduction, and the anthologized works, by Nuto Revelli, Davide Lajolo, Vittorini, Fenoglio, and Ubaldo Bertoli, but also from RSI texts such as Rimanelli's *Tiro al piccione* and

Mario Gandini's *La caduta di Varsavia*, all illustrate the violently fratricidal nature of the conflict. The reasons for the particular interpretation of the volume are made clear on the rear cover: "After more than thirty years from those dark days, these pages are a warning to the new generations not to fall into the horrors of a fratricidal war." The book was, therefore, not an attempt to rethink the Resistance, but a contingent response to the contemporary Italian situation. When the book was published, the second "fratricidal war" had not yet reached its peak, and worse was yet to come—an indication that culture was not as strong a weapon against violence as was so frequently believed.

The early 1970s also saw the deaths of two key Resistance figures, Pietro Secchia and Alcide Cervi, and their funerals offered ample opportunities for commemoration, as well as polemic.[21] At a different point of the political spectrum, this is a period in which expartisans of monarchist persuasions, the most famous of which being Edgardo Sogno, organized semiclandestine associations with a view to ridding Italy of communism.[22] The whole neo-Resistance process culminated in the election of a Resistance hero, Sandro Pertini, as president of the Republic in July 1978.

As we have seen, one of the central aspects of the Resistance in the 1970s was what might be termed the "generational problem." That is the way in which the message of the Resistance generation was perceived, reread, and recoded by successive generations who had not participated in the war itself, but who, in the 1970s were engaged in analogous battles and struggles. This takes us on to the highly controversial issue of the links between the Resistance and terrorism.

The Resistance and Terrorism

In November 1974, Renato Curcio, the historical leader of the Red Brigades wrote to his mother from his prison cell in Casale Monferrato (from which, incidentally, he escaped in early 1975):

> Dearest mother Yolanda, many years have past since the day when I went forwards towards life, and I have left you alone. I have worked, studied and fought . . . Distant memories have come back to me. Uncle Armando, who used to carry me on his shoulders. His clear, smiling eyes which looked forward to a society of free and equal men. And I loved him like a father. And I picked up his rifle which only death, brought by the murderous hand of the Nazifascists, had wrested from him . . .[23]

"Uncle Armando," the father figure to whom Curcio refers here, was his mother's brother. Curcio's real father, Renato Zampa, was absent from most of his early life and it is clear that Armando filled an important gap when he appeared after the September 8 armistice (at which time Curcio would have been nearly two years old). Armando joined a *garibaldina* brigade and fought in the Piedmontese hills. On April 25, 1945, he went along with his partisan comrades to Turin to celebrate the liberation, only to die in a Fascist ambush on the way back home. Though tempting, it is not my intention to get involved in psychological explanations for Curcio's activities in the 1970s. Nonetheless, the tantalizing reference to his partisan uncle and to his weapon, which Curcio "picked up," does clearly indicate a generational affinity.[24] As we shall see, this affinity is not restricted to Curcio but is also discernible in other *brigatisti*. In his autobiography (which I should add is not a particularly reliable source), Alberto Franceschini describes how he was given a Browning and a Luger by an ageing partisan: "It was not just a handing over of weapons: he was giving me his ideals, his youth and his strength which he had no more."[25] We have to remember that Franceschini's is a retrospective reconstruction (ghosted at that), and that the ideas that appear to belong to the partisan are more likely to have been artificially ascribed to him by Franceschini. Certainly more credible is Franceschini's account of the process that led to the adoption of the name "Red Brigades." He specifically states that the use of the term "Red Brigades" was a direct act of homage to the Resistance: "we were all in agreement that it had to connect us to the Resistance, to the partisan war."[26] Together with Curcio and Margherita Cagol, they had initially thought of "Brigate Garibaldi" (Garibaldi Brigades) but rejected it because of its Risorgimento associations. After various other combinations they finally decided on *Brigate Rosse (BR)*. This use of a Resistance-inspired *sigla* was not limited to the BR. In *La mappa perduta*,[27] a significant piece of research carried out under the direction of Curcio himself, we find a number of organizations whose names have clear Resistance origins. Among the "major organizations," *La mappa perduta* lists a number of other formations who used the word *brigate* as well as the GAP (Groups of Partisan Action), an organization to which we will return later. Under "minor formations" we find the "Proletarian Movement of Offensive Resistance" as well as two organizations who took their names from Resistance heroes: the "Proletarian Brigade—Erminio Ferretto," which operated in and around Mestre from 1972 to 1974 and the "Dante di Nanni assault brigade," active in Tuscany from 1976 to 1979. Erminio Ferretto is not a particularly significant figure.[28] Dante di Nanni, on the other hand, was one of the most famous of the Milanese *gappisti*, whose death was described in Giovanni Pesce's *Senza tregua* (see chapter 4). *Senza tregua* was also the title of an extreme-Left organization and its periodical, again Milan-based, which mutated into the terrorist organization "Prima Linea." *La mappa perduta* states that many other "microformations" used the name Dante di Nanni throughout the 1970s. Indeed, the enduring nature of this figure was confirmed to me on a visit to Brescia in 1997 when I spotted the graffiti "*Viva* Dante di Nanni" in large letters on a wall in the city center (see Figure 5.4). Other organizations used the word "Resistenza" as a "watch-word" or as a means of labeling. Hence the *Nuclei Comunisti* appealed for the construction of "Nuclei Clandestini di Resistenza" or "Nuclei di Resistenza Clandestini." This appropriation of Resistance memory was severely criticized by the partisan organizations and, above all, the PCI-dominated ANPI. In a document prepared for the April 25 celebrations of 1977 and titled "Towards a political turnaround," ANPI singled out the "incorrect evaluations" of those violent, criminal elements who had "assumed as a symbol the spirit of sacrifice and heroism of the Resistance, even going so far as usurping the names of its formations."[29] It is clear that the ANPI was concerned about the way the public perception of the Resistance was being affected by its misuse but that it struggled to defend itself adequately in this period.[30]

This use of the word "Resistenza" as a watch-word takes us into an area that is, arguably, far more revealing than the *sigle* that we have just looked at. Using again

Figure 5.4.   Long Live Dante Di Nanni. Brescia 1997.

the Red Brigades as our point of departure, a number of publications from the early phases of the history of the brigades make explicit references to the Resistance. In early 1971, Giorgio Curli, the "Fascist head-teacher" (*preside nero*) of the Istituto Secchi at Reggio Emilia, had his car attacked after he had suspended various left-wing students. The flyer that circulated around the school the next day (probably written by Franceschini) was signed "The New Resistance for Communism." During the same year *Sinistra Proletaria* (the "legal" arm of BR and to an extent its predecessor) published two editions of a journal titled *Nuova Resistenza* (April and May 1971). The editorial of the first issue of *Nuova Resistenza* is a key document for our understanding of this whole issue. Following a number of phrases full of "seasonal" metaphors: "on the earth of their counter-revolution grows the flower of the partisan struggle" or "the spring of a powerful resistance approaches," the editorial moved on to discuss what it understood by the term "resistance" in the light of the contemporary situation:

> In this spirit we have decided to use, as the title for our political journal, the watchword: NEW RESISTANCE.
>
> This indicates the new horizons which are opening to us, and at the same time the continuity with traditions of struggle which, though perverted by a revisionist or bourgeois leadership, did involve the best forces of our country.
>
> New Resistance does not then have the flavor of a nostalgic and apolitical relaunching of the Resistance thematic, and does not inherit from it the defensive strategies which characterized that struggle against the aberrant aspects of "democracy" and, furthermore, was unable to integrate into the critique of the armed movement the very structures of politics and production of the capitalist State.

New Resistance has, instead, for us the wholly youthful and offensive sense that this watch-word acquires in the context of the word-wide imperialist war which opposes, beyond all national frontiers, the armed counterrevolution to the revolutionary struggle of the proletarians, the peoples and the oppressed nations.

It's the Resistance of revolutionary China of President Mao.

It's the Resistance led by Vietnam and the revolutionary peoples of Indochina.

It is this revolutionary character, unitary and world-wide, because imperialist repression is itself compact and world-wide, which we understand in our use of the watch-word: New Resistance.[31]

Nuova Resistenza perceived a fatal flaw in the Resistance movement; that is, an inability to understand the nature of capitalism and its contradictions. The Resistance was thus seen as vitiated right from the start. It is interesting that the authors of the piece feel that the problem with the Resistance was what, in their view, it "was" in the period 1943–1945, and not how it had been represented in the postwar period, particularly in the rhetoric of the center-Left in the 1960s. As we shall see later, many young people do not "contest" the Resistance itself, but the nature of its transmission. There is, therefore, a highly complex process of rejection and appropriation based on different models and interpretations of the movement itself. Here it is useful to mention in passing the tripartite scheme of class war, civil war, and war of liberation formulated by Claudio Pavone in his 1991 book. It could be argued that in the 1970s, it is the Resistance as a class war that is the prevailing view among the younger generations. The other two wars are relegated or bracketed off.

The two numbers of *Nuova Resistenza* contain a number of articles that are signed BR and GAP, as well as a long document by the German RAF and an interview with one of the Tupamaros. It is clear, then, that the BR also felt part of an international context. The extract quoted earlier is from the book *Brigate Rosse. Che cosa hanno fatto, che cosa hanno detto, che cosa se ne è detto* authored by the *soccorso rosso* (Red Assistance) organization and published by Feltrinelli in 1976. Many of the members of *soccorso rosso* were themselves arrested because they were suspected of direct involvement with terrorist activities (e.g., Edoardo Arnaldi, Eduardo di Giovanni and, most famously, Giambattista Lazagna). The book sees a direct line between the BR and a series of Resistance predecessors who continued their partisan activities in post-Liberation Italy, such as the "Stella rossa" formation in Turin, the partisans who took part in the Schio killings in July 1945 and the members of the "Volante rossa" who were active in Milan in the late 1940s.[32] *Soccorso rosso*, therefore, traces the heritage of the BR back, not to a critique of a flawed Resistance model, as *Nuova Resistenza* does, but to specific segments of the partisan struggle who were considered by the PCI to be unacceptably heterodox. In essence then, the harking back to extra-PCI formations reflects the current positions of many 1970s organizations, terrorist or otherwise who positioned themselves to the Left of the PCI.

The importance of the Resistance is also confirmed by research into terrorism based on oral testimonies. In their introduction to their *Storie di lotta armata* Raimondo Catanzaro and Luigi Manconi see "the reference to the Resistance and the war of Liberation" as one of the elements that emerge from the biographies of the interviewees.[33] For example, in an interview conducted by Luisa Passerini, Alfredo Buonavita shows how his youth at Borgomanero was conditioned by the town's proximity to the key partisan area of the Valsesia, where the "legendary" Resistance leader, and subsequently PCI deputy, Cino Moscatelli had operated. Buonavita had spent long hours listening to the stories of expartisans and was a close friend of Moscatelli's daughter and referred to "this, let's call it moral, continuity," between the Resistance and the armed struggle of the 1970s.[34] When challenged by Passerini on this point, who reminded him he had issued a document denying the existence of a "neo-Resistance thread," Buonavita's response was to say that this was the case in terms of BR strategy but not with respect to the "formation of comrades."[35] Other terrorists interviewed for the volume *Vite sospese* provide yet more evidence of the role of the Resistance in their intellectual formation.[36]

It does seem clear that the Resistance played an important part, particularly in the early stages, in the development of red terrorism. But, it is necessary to add, there was not a causal link, as many have argued. I would now like to turn my attention to an organization that had close links with the BR in its early stages, the GAP, a very deliberate reference to the GAP of the Resistance.

The whole issue of the GAP has been inextricably linked with Giangiacomo Feltrinelli's death at Segrate, where his shattered body was found by an electricity pylon. Whether he was blown up in an accident, or the victim of a secret service plot, we will probably never know. What is clear is that the image of Feltrinelli has long suffered from tendentious and partial accounts that in the words of one of his most acute analysts has turned him into a "grotesque and pathetic character."[37] Fortunately, more serious work has been published on Feltrinelli of late, and we are in a much better position to understand the activities of this complex figure. Feltrinelli was one of many people who warned of an imminent right-wing coup in Italy. In his pamphlet titled *Persiste la minaccia di un colpo di stato in Italia* he argued that it was necessary to organize the Marxist-Leninist avant-guard and constitute "cells and committees of Resistance."[38] By this time Feltrinelli has begun to frequent a number of expartisans including Giovanni Pesce, Cino Moscatelli, and Giambattista Lazagna. Pesce, for example, had been particularly helpful to Feltrinelli when the millionaire had offered hospitality to Rudi Dutschke, one of the leaders of the student movement in Germany. Dutschke was recovering from gunshot wounds and Pesce provided him with a body guard during his stay in Feltrinelli's villa.[39] He was also in contact with Curcio and Franceschini. The former has famously described how Feltrinelli taught them about the importance of always keeping a "revolutionary rucksack" at the ready in case it became necessary to take to the hills. Among other things the rucksack had to contain salt (worth money in South America but very little in 1970s Italy) and some Havana cigars. Curcio and Franceschini considered Havana cigars too much of a luxury item, so they packed Toscanelli instead.[40] The GAP (Gruppi di Azione Partigiana), founded and financed by Feltrinelli, appeared on the scene between April and May 1970 and their chief activities involved illegal radio and television broadcasts (in this case interruptions).[41] Viewers would find the sound to their programs interrupted by the tune of the "Red Flag" followed by phrases such as: "Nixon is a Fascist, a killer and an arms trader; Fascist squadrism is supported by the police, the cara-binieri, the magistrates and the industrialists . . . against Fascist squadrism what is needed is partisan politics . . . and reprisals." The GAP thus used Resistance terminology in their pronouncements and Feltrinelli himself was, according to a statement from the 1979 GAP-BR trial, "influenced by the survival of myths of the Resistance which some of his comrades proposed uncritically . . . and which made him consider the nascent guerrilla warfare as the continuation, the 'second phase,' after thirty years of interruption, of the war of liberation."[42] But this does not mean the GAP were "above all made up of old ex-partisans" as the entry on them in one volume suggests and as many people still mistakenly believe.[43] At one of the GAP trials from the early 1970s, the only defendant who had anything to do with the Resistance was Giovanni Gibelli who wished he had been a partisan but wasn't.

One important figure who was arrested for his connections with the GAP and the BR was, however, an expartisan—Giambattista Lazagna. Lazagna's partisan memoir *Ponte rotto* was republished by Feltrinelli who had met him in one of his bookshops in Genoa, and quickly became a close friend. Feltrinelli allegedly pro-vided Lazagna with money through the so-called Robinson Crusoe account held in a Swiss bank. Lazagna was arrested on March 22, 1972, and detained for several months. The evidence against him was largely based on the testimony of Marco Pisetta, which it turned out had been "dictated" to him. Though never brought to trial, the authorities remained convinced that Lazagna was actively involved in ter-rorist activities, and he was arrested again in September 1974 (along with Curcio) in connection with an investigation into the BR—again the evidence against him was provided by an informer, on this occasion the colorfully named *Frate Mitra* (Father Machine-gun). Again he was freed after much protest, including a march from Turin to Fossano that included the participation of Dario Fo and Franca Rame. According to Philip Willan's account of Italian terrorism, the Italian secret services had planned to use Lazagna as part of their strategy following the BR kidnapping of Judge Mario Sossi in 1974. The secret services apparently intended to kidnap Lazagna themselves, force him to reveal the BR hideout, and then kill all and sundry (including, so it seems, Sossi).[44] Lazagna was again arrested in the late 1970s for his connections with Feltrinelli and acquitted.[45] There were, then, obvious connections between the GAP and the Resistance. There were, however, significant differences between the model of appropriation in their case and that of the BR. The GAP, and Feltrinelli, were more interested in a strategy of defense (against a right-wing coup) than in bringing about a revolution by violent means.

Youth

So far we have managed to reconstruct only a very partial picture of the atti-tudes of the youth of Italy in the 1970s toward the Resistance. Though obviously widespread, only a very small percentage of Italians joined the *partito armato*. What of those young people who were involved in the debates and discussions of the time but did not choose the path of the *lotta armata*? As we have seen, the late 1960s are marked by a vexed relationship between the student movement and the Resistance characterized by contestation on one hand and a hermeneutical rereading of the movement that emphasized its "red," rather than "tricolor," aspects. The slogan "La Resistenza è stata rossa e non tricolore" was still popular throughout 1970s and there is evidence that the hostility to the movement continued.[46] In an article in *L'Unità*, written on the occasion of the fiftieth anniversary of the Resistance, Francesca Archibugi stated that for her generation, which lived through a decade characterized by hard rock, heroin, and black nail varnish, the Resistance was an indigestible bore or *pizza*.[47] By the same token, it is not difficult to find evidence of anti-ANPI feeling among the younger generations. After the death in Florence in May 1975 of Rodolfo Boschi, who was protesting with others at a demonstration organized by the PCI, ANPI, and others, another demonstration was organized. At this demonstration, Orazio Barbieri, the Resistance representative, was only able to speak after "provocative attempts by extremist groups" were stopped.[48] In Florence, at least, the relationship between ANPI and some of the more extreme elements among the young of the 1970s clearly worsened. In April 1977, the ANPI, together with various other organizations gathered together to *stop* a left-wing demonstration:

> 23/04/77—on the occasion of a provocative demonstration by extremists, organized in Florence and starting with a rally at Piazza Santa Croce, the Committee for the Defense of Democracy met at Palazzo Vecchio, mobilized the democratic and anti-Fascist forces of Florence, isolated the hoodlums and the provocateurs, and ensured their initiative failed.[49]

This was by no means an isolated incident. In 1977 in Bologna, the ANPI organized a defense squad to protect the photographic monument in Piazza Nettuno in the city center. The protestors were horrified.

The extent of concerns among the ANPI can be measured by a speech made by Carlo Salinari at the eighth national congress of the association held in Florence in November 1976. For Salinari, the education system was to blame: it produced teachers who couldn't teach, doctors who couldn't cure their patients, engineers who didn't know how to build, philosophers with no philosophy, and sociologists without sociology. It was this that led to the disaffection of young people, drawing them into "utopian . . . dreams of revolution or to the artificial paradise of drugs" and gave them the "exciting taste for violence."[50] This was all very well, but Salinari, who was also a university professor, did not offer anything coherent to deal with the problems.

A conference held at Brescia in April 1970 also reveals a high level of dissatisfaction among young Italians toward the Resistance. The president of the Resistance Institute of Brescia began proceedings by claiming that the Resistance had "a lesson to transmit to the new generations who are so restless and inclined to protest, a lesson of responsibility and moral commitment."[51] After a series of speeches by the great and the good, a Giuseppe Finazzi was invited to speak (last) on behalf of the "young." Referring ironically to the "extremely erudite speech" by Enzo Petrini (a Leavisite plea for young people to improve themselves by reading Resistance novels), Finazzi said that he and his friends had "a strange reaction, almost of indifference and refusal."[52] He then went on to explain why, arguing that it was still possible to resist then, ethically and morally. Finazzi saw Resistance as rebellion and explained his views in uncompromising terms: "Today, refusing a passive, consumer system is rebellion, asking for the real value of things is rebellion, and asking for some basic changes is also rebellion. Being, in this world, honest and sincere is rebellion. These are our opinions. And the men in the schools should listen to us."[53] Similar sentiments, though expressed in less forceful terms, can be found in the essays submitted to a competition organized by the FIVL of Parma. The competition offered four study grants for essays on a series of topics such as, "What are, in your view, the principal ideas of the Resistance as enshrined in the Constitution of the Italian Republic?" But by far the most popular subject (two out of four of the national winners and five out of nine of the entries for Parma) was the following: "We often hear: 'The Resistance is not finished . . . the Resistance continues'; what interpretation should be given to these statements?" In her prize-winning answer, Maria Antonietta Uccelli argued that the question should throw out a "challenge to all post-war politics, to all of culture" to reconsider both Fascism and anti-Fascism: "Outside all of the weary watch-words. It's not easy, but it's the only condition which might permit us to speak and to write—this time without any trace of rhetoric—that the Resistance has not exhausted its moral resources and has known how to become something real and concrete, beyond all the meetings, all the parades, all the commemorations."[54]

6

1978–1989

A Resistance President

On July 8, 1978, Sandro Pertini was elected President of the Republic after an exhausting and tortuous process that required no fewer than sixteen ballots of the joint college of senators and deputies.[1] Pertini was, it is hardly necessary to recall, a veteran socialist, a protagonist in the flight of the socialist leader Turati from Italy to France, an anti-Fascist who had suffered exile and imprisonment (in Turi along with Gramsci), and one of the most important figures in the Resistance movement.[2] It was he who, along with Luigi Longo, Leo Valiani, and Emilio Sereni, all members of the Northern insurrection committee, signed Mussolini's death warrant. Throughout the 30 or so years that preceded his presidency he was the keeper of the flame of the Socialist party's memory of the Resistance as well as one of the key carriers of the Resistance message in general. Pertini preferred the power of the spoken word over the written, and despite frequent requests from leading exponents of the socialist Edizioni del Gallo, he never wrote his memoirs of his many experiences. But, on the other hand, his speech in Genoa in June 1960, which brought the dead back to the *piazze* of the city, constitutes, as we have seen in a previous chapter, one of the key moments of the revival of memory of the movement. As president of Italy, Pertini was no longer, at least officially, a Socialist, but he was still an anti-Fascist and a Resistance figure of the first order, and throughout his seven-year period of office, widely considered the most successful presidency in the history of the Republic, Pertini's past accompanied him wherever he went, and wherever the political situation in Italy took him.[3] Pertini's election thus represents the "highest moment of institutional recognition" of the memory of the Resistance, albeit more than 30 years after the events themselves.[4]

Pertini set the tone of his presidency with his inaugural address to the senate and the chamber of deputies that he gave on the morning after his election. Led in by the speaker, the communist Pietro Ingrao, Pertini was welcomed to thunderous applause from the members of both chambers who had risen to their feet. Once he had read out the presidential oath, followed by even more applause, Pertini began his speech in a solemn and measured tone. Pertini, as well as all who listened to him, was painfully aware that his predecessor, Leone, had sullied the dignity of the highest office of the Italian State. Hence, Pertini noted that his every action would have consequences for the state and the nation as a whole, and was careful to emphasize that he would loyally and scrupulously observe the letter of the Republican Constitution, a document to which he referred throughout. Pertini looked forward to the forthcoming elections to the European parliament and expressed the wish that Italy could have an international role as a peacemaker. In what became a much-quoted (and also frequently repeated sentence), he spoke of his desire to see the arsenals of war emptied and the grain stores of the poor replenished. But it was Italy's internal problems that most concerned him. For the sake of the nation it was, he continued, necessary to guarantee the fundamental values of justice and liberty, an unmistakable reference to the Rossellian dyad. Indeed, as the speech came toward its final third, Pertini laced his rhetoric with references to anti-Fascism and the Resistance. The Republic needed to be just and free from corruption, strong but humane: "That is how those people who fought for liberty after twenty years of struggle against Fascism and two years of a war of Liberation wished it to be." Violence, by which he meant terrorism, had to be combated: "We must give no quarter to this violence. We must firmly defend the Republic, whatever the cost to us as individuals." As the joint assembly applauded this sentence, some may even have noticed the intertextual reference to the great speech of June 1960, which ended with the exhortation to defeat the MSI "whatever the cost" (costi quel che costi). Judging the sentiments of his audience to perfection, Pertini then went on to pay homage to a politician he described as of great intelligence and vast culture, Aldo Moro, who would have been in Pertini's position had he not been "cruelly assassinated." The speech ended in traditional manner with a homage to his predecessors, including Leone now living in "bitter solitude." Pertini then added an apparently extemporary coda of great significance: "I cannot, as I come to a conclusion, fail to remember the patriots with whom I shared the experiences of the Special Tribunal, the risks of the anti-Fascist struggle and of the Resistance. I cannot fail to remember that my conscience as a free man was formed in the school of the workers' movement at Savona, and was then given greater vigor by looking at the luminous examples of Giacomo Matteotti, Giovanni Amendola and Piero Gobetti, of Carlo Rosselli, Don Minzoni and of Antonio Gramsci, my unforgettable comrade in prison."[5] Nothing like this had ever been before heard during a presidential inauguration. And it would certainly not happen again. The endorsement that Pertini received as he made his reference to Gramsci may not have been entirely unconditional, particularly from the DC ranks. But outside the chamber, the partisan community was quite simply ecstatic.

Sandro Pertini had been a member of ANPI since its inception and was a member of the honorary presidency of the association. He took the opportunity to address the association soon after his election and he emphasized, in no uncertain terms, how the former partisans could make a contribution to the battle against terrorism: "If the State gives way," Pertini told the partisans, "the Republic's days are numbered. We must defend this Republic which we ourselves conquered."[6] In March 1980, shortly after the antiterrorist laws had been passed, Pertini visited the region of Puglia in the south of Italy where he was greeted by workers as the "partisan president." At Turi, where he had been imprisoned, he had a quiet moment in Gramsci's cell where, according to his press officer Antonio Ghirelli, he embraced Gramsci's bed.[7] During the same tour of the South he made a speech in Brindisi condemning the terrorists who "usurp our names and emblems. 'Red Brigades', they say. I have met the real red brigades, and I was one of them during the war of Liberation." If necessary, he promised, he would descend the steps of the Quirinal palace to fight against them.[8]

In early 1980, the main target of Pertini's rhetoric was, therefore, the Red Brigades and Left-wing terrorism in general. Attention, however, shifted to the Right when neo-Fascist terrorists planted a bomb in one of the waiting rooms at Bologna railway station, killing 85 civilians and injuring two hundred. The Bologna bomb constituted one of the worst terrorist outrages of the twentieth century and led to understandable fury directed toward the Italian authorities who had been shown to be incapable, or even unwilling, to confront the worst excesses of the terrorists. Government representatives at the funerals of the victims of the Bologna massacre were received with some hostility but, in contrast, Pertini and the communist left-wing mayor of Bologna were applauded. There was also a large ANPI presence at the funeral.

By the middle of 1980, the campaign against the BR was in full swing. At its head was the *carabiniere* Carlo Alberto Dalla Chiesa who entrusted one of his senior officers, Enrico Galvaligi, with the task of looking after the high security prisons where many of the terrorists were held. Galvaligi managed to bring a prison riot, led by *brigatisti*, under control, but he was to pay for his actions. On New Year's Eve 1980 he was assassinated by the *brigatisti* Remo Pancelli and Pietro Vanzi. Galvaligi had been an active partisan fighting in the hills north of Varese, and his killing provoked particular dismay among former partisans. Pertini, along with representatives from a number of political parties as well as the partisan associations, was present at the funeral.

The memory of the Resistance was, therefore, strategically deployed during moments of public mourning connected to terrorist attacks. In the case of the Bologna killings, the links between the two periods were made even more specific by locating the memorial to the victims of the massacre in the central square of the city, next to the photographs of the Bolognese partisans who died in the struggle in 1943–1945. As an extension to this strategy of association Pertini also sought, quite literally, to promote the Resistance at the uppermost levels of the Italian state. When in January 1980 the former socialist leader and life senator Pietro Nenni died, there was a vacancy that needed to be filled. Pertini took the bold decision to appoint Leo Valiani, the former actionist and member of the *consulta* and the constituent assembly.[9] Apart from a very brief spell in Pannunzio's radical party in the mid-1950s, Valiani had been outside the political realm for a long time, working first for the Banca Commerciale Italiana and then as an editor for a publishing house, as well as dedicating his time to journalism (*Il ponte*, *Il Mondo*, *L'Espresso* and, from 1970 onward, the *Corriere della Sera*) and the writing of history. He was, as we saw in an earlier chapter, the main proponent of the "betrayed Resistance" topos, a theme to which he returned in his 1982 study of the Italy of De Gasperi.[10] His elevation by Pertini proved to be an extraordinarily felicitous

choice, galvanizing him into action after a long period of relative political torpor. From his position of great authority, as well as his proximity to Spadolini,
Valiani contributed to the debate on terrorism (arguing vociferously against the
dissociation laws promoted by the PSI), the economy as well as the Mafia, making a total of eleven speeches to senate up to September 1985. His *interventi* were
still characterized by a strong anti-Fascist stance and, as was the case with Pertini,
the values of anti-Fascism and the Resistance were a constant reference point. We
do not know the exact nature of Valiani's relationship with Pertini. Whatever the
case, it is clear that he was far from being the "president's man" in the senate and
was, of course, quite capable of expressing his own views. But his position as life
senator meant that the values that Pertini represented were also to be found at the
very heart of the upper chamber of Italian democracy. At a level that included, but
also went beyond the symbolic plane, the Resistance inhabited both the Quirinal
palace and *palazzo* Madama.[11]

For the April 25 celebrations in 1984, Pertini decided that he would make his
presence felt in his native Liguria and in the city of Genoa, one of the "gold medal
cities," honored thus for its successful insurrection. On April 24, Pertini's plane
arrived at the Cristoforo Colombo airport where he was met by the authorities
before heading to his birthplace of Stella San Giovanni. There he visited the family tomb and chatted with his friends about his childhood days, his family, and
his "gentle" character as a child. It was only afterward that he changed, Pertini
quipped. He then returned to Genoa where, to the surprise of reporters, he did
not go to "Rina," the *trattoria* in the port area of the city that had become his
traditional eating place over the years. Instead he was taken by the liberal minister Alfredo Biondi to "Cicchetti 1860," an ancient *trattoria* in the Quinto dis-
trict. There is no indication as to what Pertini consumed during his lunch. All
of these apparently banal details, no doubt supplied by the Quirinal press office,
served a very precise purpose in terms of the construction of the public image
of Pertini. He was, the message was clear, not just the primary representative of
the Italian state. He was an ordinary individual with a capacity for self irony who
liked a decent meal. Not just the president of all Italians, but an Italian himself. He
was, as the crowds loved to call him, simply "Sandro," a man who embodied both
modernity and tradition.[12] Later on in the day, however, Pertini would revert to
being a statesman. In the afternoon he processed, along with the authorities and
partisan associations from Piazza De Ferrari to Viale Brigate Partigiane where a
plaque was unveiled to commemorate the activities of the partisans in the sixth
zone of operations. The mayor Cerofolini gave a speech, followed by the *presidente
della camera*, the veteran communist Nilde Iotti. Iotti's speech concentrated on the
problems then faced by Italian democracy, on the need for reform, on the urgency
of cooperation between the trade unions and political parties. And finally, Iotti
intoned, for things to happen Italian workers, who were not afraid of something
new, had to pull together. The Resistance was absent from the speech, but this is
not an indication that the movement had been forgotten. Instead, the Resistance
was present in other, arguably more significant, ways: in the choice of the city of
Genoa itself, in the plaque, in the crowd full of partisans and, most importantly,
in the figure of Pertini.

The following day, Pertini was in Piedmont to commemorate the martyrs of the Benedicta—the same individuals he had so effectively evoked in his speech of June 1960. The choice of location was not arbitrary. The massacre took place on April 7, 1944, and it was a massacre of partisans alone. According to the *La Repubblica* journalist, again no doubt working from a press release, the partisans were killed in groups of five, after they had been ordered to dig their own graves. The Benedicta was, therefore, an appalling act around which there was no evident controversy. No partisans who had recklessly attacked German soldiers without fear of the consequences, no tactical errors, no innocent civilians caught up in the Resistance maelstrom. The Benedicta was emphatically not the Fosse Ardeatine. The crowds began to gather at the Benedicta memorial site at dawn on the day of the ceremony, hoping to catch a glimpse of Pertini, show their affection and, if possible, shake him by the hand. Pertini did not disappoint, approaching a crowd of partisans decked out in tricolor scarves. The crowd surged forward and the police struggled to keep the barriers in place. Pertini, undeterred, chatted away and shook the hands of the partisans. When he reached the memorial site he was met by a host of dignitaries including Cardinal Siri and Paolo Emilio Taviani. He descended the steps to the graves of the victims and then several loud trumpet blasts brought all those assembled to silence. The drapes covering two new plaques then fell to the ground to reveal carefully chosen inscriptions: "*Vollero un'Italia migliore*" (They fought for a better Italy) and "*Non dimentichiamoli mai*" (Let us never forget them). Speeches followed by Cardinal Siri, Taviani, and Boldrini, and the ceremony ended with thunderous applause for Pertini before he headed to Genoa to board the presidential DC9.

One of the more striking features of the presidential visit to Genoa and the Benedicta is the fact that Pertini did not make a speech. By then his spoken interventions were mainly limited to state occasions, such as visits from foreign heads of state or his end of year message to the people. Nonetheless, he rarely missed an opportunity to refer to the past—when Queen Elizabeth and Prince Philip came to Italy Pertini spoke of the British support for the Unification and Allied assistance during World War II. The more selective approach to speech making in the latter years of his presidency may or may not have been a conscious choice, but one of the effects of this was to concentrate public attention more on the image of Pertini, rather than what he said. Pertini had an extraordinary photographic presence and there are any number of striking images from the period that fully demonstrate one of the many facets of his charisma. Of course, not all of these pictures are redolent of the Resistance. Some of the more memorable pictures are, for example, of Pertini attending the World Cup Final in Spain in 1982, posing with the team, applauding the *azzurri* victory, or sitting opposite Enzo Bearzot on the DC9 with the trophy on the table. Most memorable of all is the photo of Pertini standing by the coffin of Enrico Berlinguer. The PCI leader had taken ill in June 1984 following a speech at Padua where he spoke of the Resistance figures Curiel, Meneghetti, and Marchesi.[13] Pertini brought the coffin back to Rome in the presidential plane and was photographed in profile, head bowed, grasping the side of the coffin firmly with both hands. To his right, the image of the hammer and sickle loom large, occupying the top half of the composition. But frequently pictures of Pertini did have a Resistance theme: at the funeral of the partisan leader Cino Moscatelli Pertini places a supporting hand on the shoulder of a grieving child; following a visit to the sacrarium at Marzabotto in 1979, Pertini is visibly moved and wipes away the tears with a white handkerchief.

A Socialist *Presidente del Consiglio*

When Pertini moved into the Quirinal palace in 1978, he left the headquarters of the PSI, at 476 Via Del Corso in Rome. Under the leadership of Bettino Craxi, others would follow, but for quite different reasons, related to his aggressive strategy to create a new party and to distance the PSI from the PCI.[14] In the summer of 1978, Craxi published an important statement of his political credo in the form of a lengthy article titled "*Il Vangelo socialista*" (the Socialist Gospel).[15] The article was partly a response to an interview that had appeared in *La Repubblica* where Berlinguer had reaffirmed the values of Leninism. Craxi's piece took as its inspiration the writings of the French political philosopher Proudhon as well as those of the founder of the anti-Fascist GL movement, Carlo Rosselli. From Rosselli, as well as from Bertrand Russell and G. D. H. Cole, Craxi argued "there comes a unique invitation to separate socialism from communism." A forensic dissection of Lenin's *What is to be done?* ensued, followed by a reference to Rosselli's definition of socialism as a "socializing and organizing form of Liberalism." This was erudite stuff (and certainly not written by Craxi) and provoked something of a stir, notably among veteran socialists who were none too happy with the spurious appropriation of Rosselli for the purposes of reinforcing Craxi's flimsy credentials as a man capable of profound thinking.

The names of Tristano "Pippo" Codignola and Enzo Enriques Agnoletti should, by now, be familiar. They were, as we saw in an earlier chapter, close collaborators of Piero Calamandrei and distinguished anti-Fascists, before, during, and after the Resistance period. After the experience of the 1953 elections and the *Unità popolare* movement, both went on to join Nenni's socialist party in 1957, with Codignola given responsibility for PSI educational policy, a particular passion of his, during the 1960s. It was Codignola who announced the death of Paolo Rossi to parliament, demanding that proceedings stop. By the late 1970s, however, both were becoming progressively more uncomfortable with the direction that the party was taking under Craxi. Codignola's views on Craxi's PSI were aired in an extraordinarily lucid and frank article published in *Il ponte*. Among the many cogent points about Craxi that were articulated, the one that stands out in the context of this study is the denunciation (Codignola's term) of Craxi's frequent use of Rosselli in his theoretical discussions. Acknowledging Rosselli's theoretical weaknesses, Codignola fumed that the "moral inspiration, of a Mazzinian/Salveminian type, which informs all his works, cannot be discerned in the political praxis of the current leadership of the party." [16] In another editorial published later that year, he repeated the point.[17] Codignola, it was clear, did not want the socialist leader to manipulate the thought and ideas of Rosselli for his own purposes—light-years separated the distinguished Florentine anti-Fascist and the Milanese politician, particularly in moral terms. As events of the 1990s showed, Codignola was a man of great prescience.

By early 1981, the situation had deteriorated further and, in a survey of the current position of both the PCI and the PSI, Codignola launched various criticisms at both Craxi and Berlinguer, but reserved his contempt for the socialist leader's own unique version of democratic centralism.[18] Matters came to a head when Codignola published an "Appeal to Socialists," imploring them to return to the moral values that had recently been so compromised under Craxi's reign. The net result was that Craxi ordered, in October 1981, the expulsion of Codignola as well as the signatories of the appeal, a long list that included a number of veterans including Enriques Agnoletti, Renato Ballardini, Michele Coiro, and Gianni Ferrara.[19] In this way, Craxi not only got rid of some awkward voices of dissent, but he also sent out a clear message that the values that these people represented, notably anti-Fascism and the Resistance, had no place in the modern PSI as he conceived it. As his reign as leader of the PSI continued, only to be terminated by the corruption scandals of the early 1990s, so Craxi mounted further strategic attacks on the Resistance.

The Reder Affair

Pertini's visit to Marzabotto took place at the end of 1979. As with all of Pertini's acts of homage to the Resistance it was by no means an arbitrary decision to visit the sacrarium that housed the remains of the largest Nazi massacre to take place on Italian soil.[20] Marzabotto had always been a controversial and sensitive affair and by the mid-1970s the debate was beginning to heat up again. By that time there were two German officers still in jail for crimes committed during the war: Herbert Kappler and Walter Reder, found guilty in postwar trials for the killings of the Fosse Ardeatine (Kappler) and Marzabotto (Reder). Over the years, both officers had presented various requests for release. In April 1967, for example, Reder wrote to the Mayor of Marzabotto asking to be pardoned. His main argument was that his mother was then very ill and she would wish to see her last surviving son before her death.[21] His appeal was turned down but was followed by others citing ill health and genuine remorse. All these requests proved unsuccessful until Kappler was granted "conditional liberty" by a military court in Rome in 1976. The decision provoked outrage and protestors covered the walls of the military hospital of Celio with graffiti describing Kappler as an "executioner." Shortly afterward the decision was overturned, but Kappler's lawyer, Cuttica, continued to present requests for release invoking humanitarian grounds as well as arguing that such a gesture would demonstrate that the Italian judicial process was not conditioned by politics or partiality of any sort. The usual delays held up the appeals until, in an astonishing development, Kappler escaped from jail. In one version of events, Kappler's *fuga* was the result of a bilateral agreement; in another it was Kappler's wife who lowered him out of his hospital room with a rope and then drove him to Germany. Whatever was the truth of the matter, there was outrage in Italy that such a thing should have occurred. Kappler's escape had obvious consequences for

Reder. It meant that more attention was focused on him, now the last remaining war criminal on Italian soil, and many Italians expressed the wish that he, at least, would stay in jail and pay the full price for his crimes. By mid-1980, however, the supreme military court in Bari recommended that Reder should be freed after a further five years in jail. Predictably, protests followed, the largest occurring at the end of September concluding with speeches by Boldrini, the mayor of Genoa, and his counterpart from a town in France that had suffered a Nazi massacre. A parliamentary debate ensued in November with attention being devoted, among other things, to a phrase of Reder's that described the Resistance as a series of "cowardly attacks carried out by armed civilians."[22] Not everyone, however, was against the idea of freeing Reder—the socialist Ugoberto Alfassio Grimaldi wrote to the party newspaper L'Avanti! saying that as a socialist he could not condone life imprisonment.

In the years leading up to 1985, various initiatives were organized by different organizations to commemorate the massacre of Marzabotto, as well as to restore some of the buildings that had been burnt to the ground more than 40 years before. The leading figures were the socialist Giorgio Ognibene and the archbishop of Bologna, Giacomo Biffi. Above all, Biffi and other church figures worked tirelessly to supplant the communist memory of the massacre with a Catholic model. To this end, the diocese of Bologna organized the construction of a Via Crucis linking Casaglia to San Martino (where many of the killings had taken place). All around the area there sprung up monument after monument depicting the crucifixion, suggesting that the victims were modern martyrs. Biffi outraged partisans at one ceremony when he referred to the dead of before and after 1945 as victims of opposed ideologies that were both "anti-Christian and therefore against humanity."

Marzabotto thus became a political, ideological, and religious battleground during the 1980s and, as the fateful day approached in 1985, the atmosphere became ever tenser. By this stage Craxi was, it could be argued, at the height of his powers. Not only was he a man of some arrogance, he was also shrewd and callous. This last of his many negative characteristics came to the fore when, following pressure from various quarters including ANPI, he decided to invite the people of Marzabotto to express their views on the matter of Reder's release, as they had done in the late 1960s. But there was a crucial difference between 1967 and 1985. On this second occasion, whatever the views of the relatives of the victims, Reder was going to be released. The vote was meaningless, but it could be turned to Craxi's advantage by provoking discussion and polemic. And this is exactly what happened. At a meeting held at Marzabotto at the end of 1984, 260 relatives quite predictably voted to keep Reder in jail. Of the four who declared themselves in favor of his release only one turned up in person to express her views—Lucia Sabbioni.[23] But while at Marzabotto there was, and always would be, an overwhelming majority against Reder, plenty of people felt it was time to release him. In an article in La Repubblica Giorgio Bocca, who was and still is held in very high respect in Italy, expressed his views in his customary no-nonsense style.[24] Bocca came out in favor of freeing Reder for various reasons but, above all, because his continued imprisonment reflected a long-term anti-Fascist intransigence that he felt the need to condemn. There were other enemies to be fought, Bocca argued.

The release of Reder thus took on much wider dimensions than anyone, with the possible exception of Craxi, could have imagined.

At the end of January 24, Reder was pardoned by Craxi and returned to Austria. He was met at the airport by Friedhelm Frischenschlager, the defense minister, who shook his hand and escorted him to officers' quarters. In Italy, representatives of the *pentapartito* were all squarely behind the socialist prime minister. The DC president Flaminio Piccoli stated that Craxi had done the "right thing," while the liberal Patuelli intoned that the decision demonstrated the superiority of Italian justice over and above totalitarianism and the barbarities of war. Martelli, second in command in the PSI, explained that there had been neither "pardon nor forgiveness," but rather "the application of an international convention between Italy and Austria." For the Republican Biasini it was a decision that should have been taken previously, while Reggiani, for the PSDI, made a distinction between punishment and vendetta.[25] The Left was, of course, outraged, and Ugo Pecchioli, a member of the PCI central committee, described the decision as a "troubling signal." Likewise, senior figures in the various veterans associations, such as Enzo Enriques Agnoletti and Gianfranco Maris, voiced their concerns, with the latter arguing that the event contributed to the attempt to "empty and flatten out the values of the Resistance and anti-Fascism." In Rome, a protest was organized against the decision, with speeches given by Cruicchi, the mayor of Marzabotto, Gigliozzo from the ANPI and Elio Toaff, the chief rabbi. One particularly outraged Roman, Roberta Sbardella (the daughter of a "Resistance martyr"), wrote to the mayor of Rome demanding that her father's remains be removed from the Verano cemetery. Sbardella explained the reasons for her request in no uncertain terms, identifying Craxi, "with the arrogance which characterizes him," as the villain of the affair.[26]

PCI and PSI

The Reder affair was clearly a key moment in the early 1980s battle for memory. Within the PCI the most critical voice was not that of the party's new leader Alessandro Natta, who had himself been one of the 600,000 soldiers deported to Germany in 1943, but Ugo Pecchioli. Pecchioli was a former Resistance leader in Piedmont and went on to be a member of the *direzione* of the party after the tenth congress in 1962. In the 1970s he was the PCI's unofficial Minister of the Interior, dealing with the problem of terrorism, and by the mid-1980s he was a leading PCI figure in the senate. The Reder affair as well as the fortieth anniversary of the Resistance provoked him into writing an article on the contemporary significance of the Resistance that was published in *Rinascita* in March 1985.[27] Pecchioli's article ranged over several topics and criticized the idea of the Resistance as part of a "civil war" because it placed Fascists and anti-Fascists on the same moral plane. But above all he was not happy with the way the Resistance was viewed as a historical phase that had finished: "the freeing of the Nazi criminal Reder has taken on the dimensions of a signal in this direction." Pecchioli contextualized these developments within political shifts—the decision by the government to use MSI votes, the new prime minister's announcement of the end of the "ghettoisation" of the

MSI and, even more worryingly, the emergence of a series of dubious practices to force legislation through parliament by bending the rules of modern democracy. He also criticized "a certain afascist historiography," by which he meant Renzo De Felice and his followers, for having propounded a "mitigated, justificatory vision of the twenty years of Fascism," which had itself been used by the mass media for the purposes of "simplified and disorientating disseminations."[28] He then moved back to discuss the significance of the Resistance and its contribution to the foundation of Italian democracy. Given the attempts to label the "patrimony of anti-Fascist values" as outdated and even an encumbrance, it was necessary to find a "firm response."

To find an article on Resistance and anti-Fascism in the pages of *Rinascita*, a journal founded in 1944 and, alongside *L'Unità*, the most important means of communication with the party faithful is not, on the face of it, much of a surprise. But, rather tellingly, Pecchioli's article is the first significant article on the topic of the Resistance to appear in *Rinascita* in the 1980s. In the five-year period running from 1980 to March 1985 there are only brief and passing references to the Resistance period in short commemorative pieces on Giorgio Amendola and Franco Calamandrei, two highly significant anti-Fascists. No mention at all is made of April 25. Luigi Longo's eightieth birthday was celebrated in a series of articles on the pages of the journal, but none of these made reference to his leadership role during the Resistance. Indeed, when the former party leader died later on that year, the obituary penned by Luciano Barca again ignored Longo's contribution during 1943–1945. This silence about the past in the pages of *Rinascita* did not go unobserved. In May 1980, one of the journal's readers, Carlo Ostellino from Turin, wrote a letter of protest. "Dear *Rinascita*," he began, "35 years before, after the announcement made by Radio Italia Libera, partisans of all political hues had begun to prepare for the insurrection. The general strike spread to all the cities of the North and *gappisti* and *sappisti* surrounded German positions. Meanwhile, clandestine presses," Ostellino continued, "printed thousands of flyers, leaflets and papers in order to mobilize the people of Italy into the final act of liberation. Many hundreds of patriots would die in the days to come. Dear comrades on the editorial team," Ostellino concluded, "I must confess to you that I am totally amazed that, in the issue of *Rinascita* of 25 April 1980, there isn't one word to remember these, I believe, not insignificant events in the history of our country."[29]

Pecchioli's article led to follow-up pieces by the historian Nicola Tranfaglia, who located the debate in the historiographical arena, and the socialists Francesco De Martino and Gaetano Arfé.[30] De Martino was the leader of the socialist party prior to Craxi, and Arfé was a former editor of *L'Avanti!*. The fact that they chose to contribute to the debate on the pages of the communist *Rinascita* is itself significant. Significant too were the responses they proposed. De Martino expressed concerns about the spread and legitimization of extreme Right ideas in Western Europe and, above all, in France. Meanwhile, Arfé agreed with Pecchioli's proposal to relaunch discussions about Fascism and anti-Fascism, but he warned against the tired formula of speeches given by the various different representatives of "the constitutional coalition" whose effect was to send everyone home as they were before. A wider cultural approach was required. Different methods were therefore needed, but the enemy too was different. It was, Arfé argued in a significant passage, difficult to persuade the post-Resistance generations that the main enemy was Almirante's MSI when important political figures, businessmen, and financiers had been shown to be involved in organizations such as P2 and in "shady deals." In other words, the enemy were no longer the assassins of Matteotti or Rosselli or the people who had condemned Gramsci to die in prison, but individuals who belonged to the here and now. Arfé did not go so far as to name names, but it is clear enough that among the "authoritative representatives of the political world" against whom it was necessary to fight in the context of a reinvented and reinvigorated anti-Fascist Resistance spirit, there figured the leader of his own party.

During the April 25 celebrations, Craxi played what was on the face of it, an orthodox role, attending ceremonies of commemoration. As *presidente del consiglio* he no doubt realized that it would be potentially damaging to be openly critical of the Resistance in the context of the fortieth anniversary celebrations. Instead, other leading socialists, either directly or indirectly taking their cue from Craxi, published critical articles in the *Corriere della Sera* and the socialist journal *Mondoperaio*. [31]

Lucio Colletti, the author of the *Corriere* piece, had been a member of the PCI until the Soviet invasion of Hungary. In the 1960s he was the editor of the journal *La sinistra*, but in the mid-1970s he abandoned Marxism. By the 1990s he had joined Forza Italia! and was a loyal party deputy and supporter of Berlusconi until his death in 2001.[32] In the early 1980s, when he published the *Corriere* article, his ever-shifting allegiances were, however, with the PSI, whose main political target at the time was the PCI. Colletti wasted no time getting down to business—the celebrations for the fortieth anniversary would celebrate anti-Fascist unity and the equation anti-Fascism equals democracy. But Colletti argued, in terms redolent of Ronald Reagan's rhetoric of the evil empire, the PCI were not democratic, as they were indissolubly associated with the Soviet Union. As evidence of this subjugation, Colletti quoted from Togliatti and Berlinguer (who had in 1978 argued that Lenin's theory of revolution still had some validity) and finished his piece with an attack on the PCI leader Natta. Along similar lines, Ruggero Guarini in *Mondoperaio* argued that the real value of anti-Fascism, which had entered a phase of crisis as shown by the ever more conventional celebrations of April 25, should be antitotalitarianism—a concept the PCI struggled with because of its basic political philosophy that meant that the party continued to be anti-American, and therefore antidemocratic. Of course both articles were part of the skirmishing that preceded the 1985 elections (and Colletti effectively admitted this in his opening paragraph), but it does clearly indicate that the PSI had worked out that one way of undermining the PCI's credentials was via an attack on the Resistance.[33]

It was in this charged context that the April 25 celebrations arrived. In 1985, Pertini stayed in Rome and, accompanied by the defense minister Spadolini, went to the *Vittoriano* and to the Fosse Ardeatine. The subject of the "civil war" was high on the agenda with a DC minister, Granelli, criticizing those historians who championed this concept, which exculpated the Fascists and put on the same level the persecuted and the persecutors. In Naples, De Martino echoed these thoughts, but also denied the link between the partisan movement and terrorism. In Milan, Aldo Aniasi called on Boldrini, Enriques Agnoletti, and Taviani to unite the three separate partisan organizations. Also in Milan, Tina Anselmi called on the assistance of the Resistance in the fight against corruption and P2.

Resistance Culture

The early 1980s saw the release of two films set in the Resistance period. The first, Orsini's *Uomini e no*, was a brave attempt to convert Vittorini's novel to the screen, but the results are not overly impressive. Vittorini's dialogues, which in the book have a defamiliarizing effect similar to that theorized by the Russian formalists, simply seem leaden when voiced by actors. Orsini uses a wide range of camera angles and lighting effects to recreate the troubled and disquieting atmosphere of Vittorini's Milan, but the techniques are forced and unconvincing.

Orsini was a friend and collaborator of the Taviani brothers who released *La notte di San Lorenzo* in 1982.[34] This is a film of quite a different order than *Uomini e no*. The Taviani brothers mark their decision to embark on a career in cinema following their first viewing of Rossellini's *Paisà*. Inspired by the style of Rossellini, they went on to make a documentary film, now apparently untraceable, about the town of San Miniato in Tuscany where, on July 22, 1944, some 58 villagers perished in a church when a bomb exploded. The identity of the perpetrators of this massacre is, however, a much-contested subject. Immediately after the event, those responsible were held to be the retreating German soldiers who gathered the victims in the church with the consent, for some connivance, of the local bishop Giubbi. Three different enquiries cleared the bishop, but attributed the blame squarely to the Germans. Given the extent of the Nazi massacres in Tuscany in World War Two, this was not an unexpected conclusion. No trial for the killings at San Miniato ever took place, and the relevant files were archived in the "cupboard of shame" by the *procuratore generale* Santacroce in 1960. In the 1950s, however, an alternative explanation was offered, which attributed the blame to an American bomb dropped in the course of the advance. The "friendly fire" thesis was later enthusiastically espoused by Paolo Paoletti and, following a further commission of enquiry, involving highly qualified historians, this has become the "official version."[35] Even then, the story of the massacre is not over. Two memorial plaques in San Miniato record two different versions of the events, a classic example, as John Foot has argued, of divided memory.[36] For his part, the historian Paolo Pezzino maintains that the evidence for both explanations is contradictory.

The Taviani brothers place the issue of the "massacre" at the narrative center of their film, but show that they were well aware that they were dealing with a subject with multiple interpretations. In the early 1980s, the prevailing interpretation was, however, that of a planned German reprisal for partisan activity in the area. In view of the instability of their subject the Taviani brothers opted to make a film that was not so much aware of the problems of interpretation, but made them one of its core features. Indeed, the theme of the subjective nature of history is insisted upon throughout *La notte di San Lorenzo* and is introduced in the opening credit sequence that acts as a frame. Through a window (a very literal "frame"), the audience looks out onto a night sky punctuated by shooting stars. It is an opening sequence that deliberately references the first episode of *Paisà*, when the ill-fated Joe from Jersey and his guide Carmela look out and see shooting stars in a Sicilian night from the summer of 1943. But, as a female voice tells us and a sleeping child, the shooting stars bring back memories of a night in 1944, another night of San

Lorenzo, from many years before. And it is the story of this night, when the narrator was a young girl, which she prepares to recount to the child and to the viewer. The opening sequence thus makes it quite clear that what we are about to see is not an event, or series of events, but a retrospective narrative of that event filtered through the memory of one participant individual who, we infer, picked up further information about the events as the years went by and individual memories became collective ones. To history, there is then added the dark glass of the present. But the film does not just show that the contemporary view can impinge on the past. In the past too, interpretation was a problematic affair. In an early scene, the villagers of a fictional San Martino (*not* San Miniato) are duped into believing that the American liberators are proceeding up the hill. They hear the sounds of a marching song, which gets progressively louder, and gather to welcome them. Overcome by the enthusiasm of the moment a young boy shouts "I see them," but, it turns out the music was a trick played on the populace by a local bourgeois aided by his gramophone and an improbably loud speaker. The complex interplay between diegetic and extradiegetic sound serves to foreground the confusion in both the villagers and the audience. It also highlights the role of how hopes, expectations, and desires, play a part in perceptions of reality. In this scene, the Americans do not arrive, but the emotions aroused in the audience are not far off the "real thing." Wish-fulfillment then makes a series of subsequent appearances in the film: when one of the villagers, of Sicilian origin, goes in search of the Allied soldiers she hopes will bring her news of home, only to be shot by Germans; when the villagers, unable to make sense of the explosions believe, albeit temporarily, that San Martino has not been blown up; and, finally, in the film's finest moment, when the narrator-protagonist transforms in her imagination the partisans into Homeric warriors whose lances finish off a Fascist in the grand style.

The battle scene in the wheat fields, of which this Homeric moment is but one brief feature, is remarkable for its civil war qualities, particularly so as the film predates the intense discussions of this subject from the mid-1980s onward. All the participants in the battle know each other and as Fascists, partisans, and civilians die in a grisly and violent hecatomb, the viewer is constantly reminded that this was not just a war between Italians but between people who had known each other from childhood. There is even an appearance by a *"ragazzo di Salò" avant la lettre* in the shape of a young boy whose father is the leader of the RSI squad. The boy is a fanatic and is captured along with his father at the end of the battle. He begs for his son to be spared, but sees him shot before him and takes his own life to end his appalling grief. The film ends with a cleansing storm to wash the violence away (water and washing are one of the film's symbolic constants) and the people of San Martino are able to look forward to a new life. The film returns to the present, with the narrator speculating on the veracity of her account. *La notte di San Lorenzo* is a very significant achievement, which has not only met with considerable critical acclaim but has been sensitively analyzed by a string of film scholars, particularly in the United States. Frustratingly, though, the film's insistence on the subjectivity of experience, on the problematic nature of memory, on myth and on perceptions, and on the flux of history seems to have escaped the attention of the vast majority of the Italian public as well as the nation's historians.

The 1980s saw little in terms of new literature dedicated to the Resistance at a time, paradoxically, when Italian writers renewed their interest in history and in the historical novel.[37] The communist publisher Riuniti did, however, publish a new book on the Resistance for young people in 1979, written by Ada Della Torre—a teacher and intellectual who was part of Primo Levi's circle in Turin (indeed, she was Levi's cousin).[38] In her preface Della Torre conceded that one of the big problems with writing for children had been the celebratory tone of her predecessors, which she tried to avoid. Della Torre also stressed the contemporary relevance of the Resistance. In a comment at the end of the book Gian Carlo Pajetta was, however, keen to stress that the similarities did not justify contemporary acts of violence. Riuniti also published an anthology edited by Giovanni Falaschi, but it contained no new works.[39] As for poetry, Vico Faggi, a well-known writer for the theater as well as a poet, published his collection *Corno alle Scale*, which contained a number of poems inspired by his experiences as a partisan in the Frignano region, but these Resistance lyrics had already been published in the late 1960s.[40] Faggi's poetry was steeped in the tradition of the Italian lyric— personal, reflective, poignant and, as a consequence, read only by a happy few.

A work of an entirely different nature and impact was Carlo Mazzantini's *A cercar la bella morte*. Mazzantini had been a soldier in the RSI's *Guardia nazionale repubblicana* (GNR), stationed in Piedmont, and the book is a reconstruction of these, sometimes extraordinarily violent and visceral, experiences. *A cercar la bella morte* was apparently composed over a number of years, during which time its author struggled to find a publisher until, finally, Mondadori was persuaded to take it on board. Whether or not this was because of the delicate "taboo" nature of the subject matter, as is claimed, or simply a reflection on the vagaries of the publishing system, is not a question that offers a simple answer. The fact that the book came out in the mid-1980s, at a time when the whole question of the RSI was being rethought, would fit in conveniently with the thesis that the book was a product of its context and so reflects the changing ideologies of Italy at the time. But I prefer to see the book more as a work that conditioned and influenced debate, rather than simply reflecting it.[41]

A cercar la bella morte is a literary work of some complexity. For the left-wing historian Bersellini, certainly not an RSI sympathizer the work was "sincere, well-written, intense."[42] And the authoritative English critic, Peter Hainsworth, even went so far as to refer to the text's "great sophistication and subtlety." [43] In view of some of the scenes in the book, particularly those that portray teenage masturbation, visits to brothels, and various other luridly described sex acts, Hainsworth is no doubt referring to the narrative techniques and myriad intertextual references in the work, rather than to its content. *A cercar la bella morte* is organized around a series of different, but related time frames. The first of these is, obviously enough, the period from 1943 to 1945. The second relates to the retrospective viewpoint of the narrator, telling the story from a distance. These two time frames are an integral part of any narrative that reconstructs an individual's past experiences. But to these Mazzantini, adds a third layer, which itself has numerous subdivisions. This third layer relates to the broad arc that runs from the time of the narrative to the time of the act of narrating and manifests itself in the text in the shape of the various encounters Carlo has with his comrades and their relatives in the intervening years. Occasionally, these encounters are chance ones, or with people he does not actually know, but who awaken a torrent of memories. On each encounter the individuals themselves tell, or retell stories, which themselves become part of the final narrative. The overall effect of these multiple time frames and multiple narrators is to create an extraordinary sense of density in which time and history coalesce in a manner much sought after by European writers of fiction, but which found its highest expression in Proust's *À la recherche du temps perdu* (among other things the title of Mazzantini's book is a clear reference to the *Recherche*). The book opens with a Latin quotation ("*Infandum regina iubes renovare dolorem*")—the reference is to the scene in the *Aeneid* when Dido insists that Aeneas speaks about the Trojan War. From the very start Mazzantini therefore sets the tone of his account of the experiences of the soldiers of the RSI: epic heroes involved in a battle for their nation and whose deaths create within him the same "inexpressible pain" that Aeneas experienced. After this recondite allusion, the story proper begins at the narrator's house in Rome where news of Mussolini's removal from office has created confusion and disarray: "a world which had lost its centre and broken into fragments without links."[44] It soon emerges that the narrator's family are committed Fascists and that, of three brothers, two are members of the regular army while the third, Carlo (he is named at a later stage), is too young to fight. Despite, or perhaps because of his youth, Carlo along with a group of 20 friends, presents himself to a Captain Tannert of the Wehrmacht offering their services. Youth is indeed one of the key themes of the work and one that is central to its message—many of the volunteers for the RSI were young and, Mazzantini implies, they cannot be held fully responsible for their actions. Furthermore, the young men in question were not driven by the ideology of Fascism, but by vague concepts of "nation" and "honor." These are arguments that, as Germinario has demonstrated, have been a constant in the writings of former adherents of Salò.[45] And Mazzantini would also articulate them more explicitly and with considerably less subtlety in a later book, *I balilla andarono a Salò*, a work that helps to explain the ideology of *A cercar la bella morte*.[46] But what is special about Mazzantini's exculpatory strategy in this book is that, on the surface, it seems extraordinarily beguiling: the image of young men, not really aware of the import of their actions, politically uncommitted but patriotic, is a compelling one.

The whole of the fourth chapter is taken up with a minutely described and carefully crafted reconstruction of the executions of partisans in the main square of Borgosesia. At this point it is worth noting that the executions did, in fact take place in reality on December 22, 1943, and that they were carried out in response to the killings of two members of the GNR, namely Tartaglio and Landi who appear in the book. The episode does then have its origins in historical fact. But what Mazzantini does in his description of the scene is far from being an objective reconstruction, even assuming such a thing is possible. Carlo does not volunteer to be a member of the firing squad but is a spectator. What strikes him initially is the apparent complicity of the victims. Having accepted the ineluctable nature of their fate, none try to run away or resist—they simply walk "with their legs" to their place of execution. Try as he might, Carlo can no longer clearly see the reason for the executions: "I looked for images of the dead comrades: two young soldiers . . . their motives which up until then had seemed more than sufficient: betrayal, dishonor; but these counted for nothing, they had no use at all, they were brushed aside by that enormous reality . . . They had been stripped bare of all the rest, of all the reasons which had made them hate, all the reasons which had decided that fate, and now they were just men, men who were alive, that was all . . . and in a moment they would be nothing."[47]

Before death, therefore, Carlo becomes aware in this moment of epiphany that we all share a common humanity, regardless of political creeds or action. What is so powerful about this moment is how the narrative draws the reader into the anguished moral realm of Carlo. He imagines what goes through the mind of the volunteers as they load their rifles and aim at their targets: "his neck, just at that point where the hair is thinner and you can see their skin. You have to shoot him just there."[48] Soon afterward, the shots ring out and Carlo watches as they fall, with one exception. In a long passage of great intensity, Carlo describes how the survivor turned to look at him and his comrades "Still present, on this side, in the world where we were!" and he imagines what was going through his mind before the officer in charge of the squad ordered his men to fire again. As Hainsworth, who admits to being "disturbed by the strategic nullification of the issue of moral difference in Mazzantini" has acutely observed, "the whole strategy of the book is implicit in this execution section."[49] Mazzantini creates a picture in which all of the participants in the execution, including the executioners themselves, are depicted as human beings who live and breathe and suffer. And death, above all, whether it is the death of a Fascist soldier or a partisan, is far from beautiful.

The narrative proceeds through 1944 and from then up to April 1945 where Carlo finds himself in Milan, narrowly escaping death. As I have said before, the narrative is not straightforwardly linear, but is frequently punctuated by postwar encounters in which Carlo is both brought up to date with the fate of his comrades and relives certain episodes of his past. In addition to all those who died during the conflict, we learn that several took their own lives later. All, Carlo included, suffer from what could be described as a perpetual existential malaise. Instead of entering the history books as heroes they had "stayed there on a deleted page, without a voice, forever marked with infamy," victims of a "tangle of hatred and passions."[50] One of his former comrades, Giannetto Lettari, climbs on the equestrian statue of Marcus Aurelius and gives full vent to the idea that the former soldiers of the RSI are victims of history. The people who were on the other side, Lettari says, went back: "Life took them back again, their habits, their loves, work. Time passed: they grew, changed, changed in the light of what came after. For us that wasn't possible. For us it's as if we remained suspended in the air. Defeat has left us fixed down there in those barely sketched gestures, in those unfinished phrases: figures cut out in black, silhouettes, not men!"[51] Again, this and other episodes are compelling, and successfully draw the reader into the complex mental universe of the RSI faithful. As Ballinger has observed, Mazzantini manages to "humanize the vilified *ragazzi di Salò*" by endowing them with thoughts, feelings, and emotions.[52] *A cercar la bella morte* certainly confronts the issue of a civil war in a way that hitherto had not been described in a work of fiction, nor indeed in a work of history. Whether one agrees with the ideology of the work is another matter entirely.

Historiography

In terms of historiography, the 1980s saw a decrease in the overall number of works published. Nevertheless, there was still a lot of activity with key collections of documents relating to the *garibaldini* and the *giellisti* published in 1979 and 1985 respectively.[53] The editor of the GL documents, Giovanni De Luna, published his history of the PDA in 1982, a work that made a fundamental contribution to scholarship on a party second only to the PCI in terms of its contribution to the Resistance movement.[54]

For La Pietra the publishers that had been created to "house" the monumental *Enciclopedia dell'antifascismo e della Resistenza*, the 1980s was also a golden period. The last three volumes (of six) of the encyclopedia were published, as were an imposing number of autobiographical and biographical works, such as those by Isacco Nahoum and Remo Scappini, followed by Scappini's wife's memoir the year after.[55] But far and away the most important memoir of the period was Pajetta's *Il ragazzo rosso va alla guerra*, published in 1986, three years after the first installment (titled *Il ragazzo rosso*).[56] Pajetta's book was the subject of a review by Giampaolo Pansa in *La Repubblica*. In view of Pansa's increasingly clamorous writings in the new millennium, the sentiments expressed in this review, some 17 years before the sensational publication of *Il sangue dei vinti*, are worth looking at. Pansa highlighted the numerous occasions in the memoir in which Pajetta depicted Togliatti as, at best diffident, toward the Resistance movement and the idea of the wind from the North. What dramas occurred, Pansa asked, as Togliatti's PCI tried to convince other *ragazzi rossi* of the democratic line? What were the exact nature of relations between the partisans and the PCI leadership in the crucial, final phase of the war? Pajetta's memoir that appeared "always on the point of telling all" just stopped and so did not answer Pansa's questions. Only some doors of Pajetta's memory were opened. Many years later Pansa would make it his business to open these doors himself.[57]

Quite apart from his memoirs, Pajetta was particularly active in this period and he was present, and made a crucial *intervento* at a landmark conference held on the RSI at Brescia in 1985. The Brescia conference was sponsored by the Fondazione Luigi Micheletti, a former *garibaldino* who decided to spend considerable amounts of the vast fortune he had made as a businessman purchasing documents, propaganda, and all manner of materials relating to the RSI. Some of these materials found their way into the exhibition that accompanied the event.[58] The decision to have an exhibition was a shrewd move as it meant that the conference attracted a much wider audience than is usually the case at events of this nature—in addition to the hordes of academics and partisans there were also a large number of young people in attendance as well as many former RSI soldiers, one of whom asked to be allowed to make an *intervento*. After some discussion Mario Roda, a former member of the "Folgore" division was given two minutes. Leonardo Coen, the *La Repubblica* journalist who covered the event, reported the beginning of Roda's *intervento* as follows: "I'm one of those 700,000 who volunteered for the Republic of Salò, we thought we were saving Italy's honor. It is not right that you continue to call us '*repubblichini*' . . . it's more correct to say were 'social republicans,' I can tell you I only came across partisans after the war."[59]

There were some whistles and Pajetta retorted with a gratuitous insult. Despite the knock about, Roda's point about the use of the diminutive *repubblichino* had some validity. The use of this pejorative term had effectively reduced the significance of the RSI to little more than an appendage to the German forces occupying Italy, with Mussolini seen as a mere puppet. The aim of the conference was to take a fresh look at the RSI, to rethink it, but it was emphatically not a revisionist event, as Micheletti made clear in the conference proceedings published the following year. Micheletti explained that the original idea for the conference dated back to the late 1970s and that the subsequent "fall in ideological tension" of the 1980s had helped its course. The change in climate made the conference possible, but it also added to the risk of "exploitation" and "undue appropriation" by both "out and out nostalgics" as well as other forces in right-wing politics and culture who were engaged in a "vast operation on the fascist legacy." [60] What Micheletti wanted to organize was an academic conference, based on scrupulous archival research. As there were essentially two historical schools with widely different interpretations of Fascism, Micheletti decided to invite representatives from both currents. At an early stage, with the exception of Guido Quazza (who explained his objections at the end of the conference),[61] everyone from the two camps accepted the invitation to speak. But there were a number of last-minute defections, including Renzo De Felice who failed to show despite sending an abstract. And despite a series of promises, neither did he send his written contribution for the conference proceedings. Micheletti expressed his regret that the opportunity for a real debate between the two opposing sides had not taken place, but this had meant that more attention could be given to Claudio Pavone's paper on the "civil war" and to the "passionate and reasoned reply" by Pajetta.

Pavone's paper had all the characteristics that had marked out his previous contributions to the historiography of twentieth-century Italy including, above all, a wide range of sources. These sources included the usual archival documents, the last letters of RSI soldiers, memoirs as well as, perhaps for the first time, literary texts. Unsurprisingly, it was Fenoglio's short stories and *Il partigiano Johnny* that provided Pavone with a lot of useful material—the longest quotation in a study packed with examples is taken from the short story *Golia*, which describes the life of a well-liked German prisoner within a partisan formation. What Fenoglio's words (a discussion between two partisans as to why Fascists killed partisan prisoners and vice versa) demonstrated, according to Pavone, was one of the aspects of the "civil war," which caused most "worry": its fratricidal quality, its additional element of execration.[62] In addition to the numerous examples demonstrating that both sides were quite conscious of the nature of the conflict they were involved in, Pavone also commented interestingly on why for anti-Fascists the term "civil war" was used with great reticence in the postwar period while for former soldiers of the RSI, the term was widely and polemically used. In this first section of his study Pavone raised, although he did not use the term, many questions about the "public use of history." But the debate that followed did not address the relationship between interpretation and political context. Instead, discussion focused on one simple yes or no question: was it, or was it not a civil war? For Pajetta, it was emphatically not and he made this quite clear in his *intervento*. Pajetta stressed the mass, national character of the Resistance, as opposed to the limited, confined experience of the RSI. In a rather curious set of arguments, possibly predicated on the model of the Spanish civil war, Pajetta tried to suggest that after September 8, the nation had not split into two numerically equal camps, and that there had been no civil war in the liberated South. The period 1943–1945 was therefore a war of liberation.[63] Irrespective of the validity of the arguments, Pajetta was at least prepared to engage in discussion, unlike the journalist from *L'Unità* who wrote darkly of the "currents of thought" (Pavone is not even mentioned) who looked for signs of civil war in a conflict that ended in the "days full of sun and hopes of April 1945."[64] Pajetta's *intervento* was certainly not ignored by Pavone: his subsequent articulation of the idea of three simultaneous wars taking place in Italy would seem to owe something to the 1985 debate.

As was the case in previous periods, the 1980s also saw a lot of publishing activity on the Catholic contribution to the Resistance. Gioacchino Malavasi provided Giuseppe Acocella with a detailed interview on the history of the only Catholic anti-Fascist association, the Guelf Movement of Action. [65] But again the focus and organizer of most of this activity was none other than the senior Christian Democrat Paolo Emilio Taviani, and the journal he edited *Civitas*, which published a steady stream of articles throughout the period. The underlying purpose behind these many publications continued to be to offer an alternative as well as a corrective to what were euphemistically described as "unilateral opinions."[66] But as the decade proceeded, the need to reach out to youth also became an imperative, as was made clear in a collection of articles initially published in the journal and then put together in a volume published separately on several occasions during the period 1983–1988.[67] In an unsigned editorial, Taviani explained that the volume contained two general discussions of the partisan war, Taviani's "La guerra delle cento fonti," a piece that stresses the multifaceted nature of the Resistance, and Brizzolari's "Il contributo dei partigiani italiani." The rest of the pieces would concentrate on separate episodes. In this way, it was hoped that the "many young people" who recognized the "authentic values of the second Risorgimento" would also gain an understanding of the atmosphere and unique events of the Resistance. In actual fact the volume did not quite keep its word—the final piece is a lengthy and very scholarly piece by Taviani himself on the contribution of the Catholics to the Resistance (which repeats the second Risorgimento topos in its first sentence). But to be fair, the rest of the volume does pretty much correspond to the plan as outlined. There is, predictably, much familiar territory in *La guerra partigiana in Italia*: Vittorio Giuntella dedicates a long discussion to two Resistance martyrs, the town of Boves devastated by German flame throwers in the autumn of 1943, and the partisan leader Ignazio Vian, an exemplary Catholic who was executed in Turin in July 1944; the RAI journalist Giacomo De Antonellis provides a brief biography of Giancarlo Puecher "a typical martyr for the cause";[68] and, in a piece clearly aimed at the young, Gustavo Troiso offers brief, and largely plagiarized, sketches of the bravery of the Neapolitan *scugnizzi*.

Far and away the most interesting contributions in the collection are the brief sketches written by Taviani that punctuate the volume, such as "Il gozzo dalla vela nera: primo contatto con gli alleati in Corsica" and "Donne della Resistenza." In each

of these stories a footnote explains that they are "entirely taken from" the unpublished notes written by Taviani in May to June 1945. The pieces are all characterized
by a predominance of dialogue, a minimum of description, and by their paratactic
syntax. In other words, they appear to be the work of a neorealist author. These
narrative fragments were later published separately as *Pittaluga racconta*, which contains 47 of these short narratives.[69] *Pittaluga racconta* was republished in early 1989,
an indication that the text had had some success with the reading public. At the end
of the 1980s *Civitas* published more collections of articles, one of which included
an extract on partisan justice from Roberto Battaglia's 1945 memoir.[70] As we know
when he wrote his memoir, Battaglia was an actionist and not a communist, but
the appearance of an extract from the author of the notably communist *Storia della
Resistenza italiana* (the text is not, however, mentioned in a biographical footnote) is
a remarkable example of détente. A year later, *Civitas* published another Resistance
special and, on this occasion, took the bold step of actually indicating Battaglia's
history (along with Bocca's) as "a detailed and broad history."[71] Although the author
of the preface commented about both books "undervaluing" the contribution of the
Catholics and the Church to the Resistance movement, this was a unique moment
in the historiography of the Resistance and was a clear sign that things were changing. *Civitas* had come a long way since 1950 when it published articles with titles like
"School Teaching as an Instrument of Bolshevism."

La Bolognina

If things were changing at *Civitas* in the late 1980s, this was nothing as compared
to what was happening in the Soviet Union and, as a consequence, within the
PCI. Following the collapse of the Berlin Wall, Achille Occhetto made the decision
to reform and reshape the party he led. Returning from Brussels, where he had
met Neil Kinnock, he told journalists that an era had come to an end, as indeed
had the Second World War.[72] He then announced his intentions for the PCI, not
at a meeting of the party's central committee, nor indeed in a press release, but
at a meeting with partisans at a conference center in an area of Bologna called
"La Bolognina." The Bolognese partisans had, for many years, met to commemorate the battle of Porta Lame of November 7, 1944, at which many of their comrades had fallen. Ever since he had become party secretary, Occhetto had always
received an invitation to attend the event, but he had always been unable to make
it. They were, therefore, rather surprised by his presence. Kertzer even goes so far
as to say that the "excitement was palpable, the pleasure immense," which seems
to overstate matters a little. [73] Occhetto went through the usual ceremonial, lay-
ing a wreath in memory of the dead. In his speech, however, he referred to Gor-
bachev's recent meeting with World War Two veterans at which the Soviet leader
had underlined the necessity for change. From this, Occhetto went on: "we must
take up the challenge not to continue along old roads but to invent new ones so as
to bring together the forces of progress. Since the political imagination at the end
of '89 is galloping so swiftly, it is necessary to go forward in our actions with the
same courage which was demonstrated during the Resistance." This move forward

would involve, Occhetto continued, changing the party into something "bigger and more beautiful."[74] At the time, Occhetto was not entirely sure what the party would become, hence the subsequent use of the term "the thing" to describe what he planned for the party. But what is of more interest to us here is not "the thing," but the manner in which Occhetto decided to announce it. He did not, it goes without saying, casually decide to release his bombshell at a meeting of partisans. The choice was, above all, a symbolic one. The partisans represented the history of the party; their blood had been the cement of Togliatti's "new party." But at the end of 1989, things had changed. The "new roads" opened by the partisans had become the "old roads" Occhetto referred to in his speech. It was time for a "new" new party, and in order to take it forward it was necessary to abjure the past. As one former leader Alessandro Natta would reflect, it was "a kind of sacrificial ritual, a sort of *auto da fé*," a bonfire onto which were thrown the "name, the songs and symbols of the party."[75] The Bolognina has gone down in history as the moment that the PCI moved away from Marxism. But it was also the moment that it abandoned the Resistance, a movement about which it had, as this book has tried to show, consistently ambivalent feelings.

7

From the End of the First Republic to the *Cinquantennale*

1990–1995

The Bolognina was only the beginning of a complex process that saw the shattering of the paradigms of Italian politics.[1] In fact, the PCI's subsequent change of identity to the Democratic Party of the Left (PDS), and the associated creation of a splinter party (RC—*Rifondazione comunista*) that claimed to maintain the traditions of the old PCI, was mild compared to the fate of some parties.[2] Following the referendums of 1992, promoted by the dissident Christian Democrat Mario Segni, the corruption scandals of *tangentopoli* and much more besides, the PSI, the DC, the Republicans, and the Liberals, significantly all members of the CLN during the war, were wiped from the political planet, with their deputies either forced to abandon politics for good or associate themselves with one of any number of a bewildering array of organizations both large and small. To give but one highly relevant example of this complex diaspora, the former partisan, high-ranking member of the DC and close associate of Segni, Ermanno Gorrieri, formed the movement of the "*Cristiano sociali*" together with a former socialist. The movement swiftly allied itself to the PDS. For Gorrieri, one of the protagonists of the republic of Montefiorino, which saw communists and Catholics working together (albeit not without difficulties), it must have felt like a return to his youth.

When elections were called for 1994, it looked as if the PDS would sweep to victory. But the entrepreneur and media tycoon, Silvio Berlusconi, had different thoughts and formed the political movement Forza Italia! which, in partnership with what was now called *Alleanza nazionale* (National Alliance, the former MSI-DN), as well as the Northern Leagues, won a spectacular victory in the elections at the end of March. With the emergence of both new protagonists as well as old hands who had rebranded themselves during the so-called transition from the "first" to the "second" republic (the terminology is rightly contested) it was inevitable that Italy's past, including the Risorgimento, but above all the Resistance, would be the subject of much anguished discussion and soul searching. As Storchi has observed "with the . . . bipolar political system and the rise of the Right," the Resistance "returned to being one of the most prominent features of political controversy."[3]

The crisis of the 1990s was, therefore, as Focardi has argued, a crucial "push factor" in the process of rethinking the significance of the movement, a process that really began in the 1980s, as the previous chapter argued.[4] The questions asked were many. If the Resistance movement had led to the foundation of a flawed first Republic, what were the implications for the memory of the Resistance? What would happen to Italy's national identity, at best a fragile edifice, and now in a state of collapse? The political scientist Gian Enrico Rusconi summed it up in the apocalyptic title of his 1991 book, *Se cessiamo di essere una nazione* (If we cease to be a nation), which he would follow up with *Resistenza e postfascismo* in 1995, an influential and suggestive work that asked searching questions about the Resistance movement and its relationship to the problem of Italy's fractured national identity.[5] And Rusconi was not alone in tackling the issue—the influential Ernesto Galli Della Loggia went so far at to argue that with September 8, the nation died and emphatically did not rise again from the ashes of the Badoglio armistice in the shape of the Resistance movement.[6] Similarly, the status of another iconic date, the national holiday of April 25, became the subject of much soul searching.[7] Others asked whether it was still relevant to speak in terms of the oppositional formula: Fascism versus anti-Fascism.[8] The partisans themselves were consumed with disgust—in 1991, the ANPI's yearly "political document" baldly stated: "The Italy of today is not what the Resistance wanted."[9] Two years later, Vittorio Sgarbi, one of Italy's more unpleasant media figures, labeled Boldrini an "assassin." Enzo Lunari's cartoon (see Figure 7.1) published in *Cuore* in April 1993 captured the feelings of many—two little old men looked at a plaque commemorating a school friend killed years before by the Fascists. At the end of the cartoon the *vecchietti* reminisced that "everyone used to take the piss out of poor Barzanò" and the final image showed, in exquisite irony, the inscription on the plaque: "Here lived Ciro Barzanò—1911–1943—He sacrificed his life for a better Italy." Gundle's comment that "something in the Resistance tradition [had] broken down" put it rather mildly.[10]

As calls for a change to Italy's democratic system became more and more insistent, so too the constitution, a document that was the very embodiment of the Resistance and its values, came under heavy fire, with widespread calls made firstly by president Cossiga, whose *esternazioni* on all subjects became increasingly strange as time went on, and then by Berlusconi and many others, for a change to a "presidential" system. This was not, of course, a radically new development as it was Craxi who had initiated the attack on the constitution, firing off warning shots from the 1980s onward. In this highly charged climate it was clear that the "celebrations" (if this was the appropriate word) of the fiftieth anniversary of the Resistance movement would be especially significant, and this chapter devotes some space to them. Before discussing the Resistance debate in the *cinquantennale* period of 1993 to 1995, I would, however, like to devote some attention to the "triangle of death" (*triangolo della morte*) polemic from 1990 that raised very awkward questions about violence, democracy, and the activities of former partisans in the postwar period and constituted, in Storchi's words, "an outstanding example of the political use of history."[11]

Figure 7.1.   Enzo Lunari, "Vecchietti," originally published in *Cuore* (April 1993).

1990: The Triangle of Death

The local origins of the "triangle of death" controversy can be traced to two apparently separate polemics that were sparked in April and June 1990. The first of these was created by a letter sent by a Flavio Parmiggiani to the ANPI committee responsible for organizing the April 25 celebrations at Campagnola in Emilia. Parmiggiani's letter, which demanded the truth about postwar killings in the area and that was also distributed to every family in Campagnola, provoked a "vast polemic" in the pages of the local press, specifically the *Resto del Carlino*, the *Gazzetta di Reggio* and *L'Unità*, which continued well into May that year.[12] The second polemic began in June when a book, written by Liano Fanti (a former member of the PCI who joined the PSI in 1959) was published that accused a Stalinist PCI of a level of complicity in the executions of the Cervi brothers. The seven great communist martyrs, so the argument went, were killed by the party that did so much to champion them after the war.[13]

Both these episodes were essentially local matters and in normal circumstances would have remained local. However, the PCI was at this time going through an unprecedented period of transition and even apparently minor incidents had the potential to create much wider resonances. These wider resonances would become apparent at the end of August when the socialist Mauro Del Bue, a fervent and leading supporter of Craxi, issued an appeal through the pages of the *Carlino Reggio* asking Vaclav Havel to open the "secret archives of the Red Brigades." Del Bue linked this appeal to other related matters, as the *Carlino Reggio* made clear: "Del Bue asks for light to be shed on the 'desaparecidos' and terrorism" and "The proposal for a commemoration of Umberto Farri at Casalgrande. Skeletons from Reggio in Czechoslovakia." In other words, Del Bue was asking for clarification on a whole series of issues in the history of the PCI beginning with the killings of the Resistance period (the *desaparecidos* and the Socialist mayor Farri), followed by the flight to Czechoslovakia of the perpetrators of the killings and culminating with the training, by these very fugitives, of the Red Brigades in the 1970s. Above all, according to Del Bue, there were many question marks surrounding Togliatti's role in all of this.[14]

Otello Montanari, a senior figure in the Reggio PCI and, at the time, president of the Cervi Institute, responded to the challenge. Montanari penned a letter to the paper, but first sought clearance from Fausto Giovanelli, the young leader of the local party, which was given. Montanari's piece, published August 29, took as its starting point the forty-fifth anniversary of the killing of Arnaldo Vischi (August 31, 1945). Montanari briefly reconstructed the episode and singled out Arrigo Nizzoli and Didimo Ferrari for criticism, arguing that instead of referring the affair to the police they took matters into their own hands, hence failing to cut "from the very start, that cord which could have stopped further crimes." Further- more, and at this point Montanari referred specifically to Del Bue's accusations against Togliatti, the PCI leader had himself come personally to Reggio to issue a "very firm, repeated condemnation" of the postwar violence. [15] Montanari contin- ued asking why Eros fled to Czechoslovakia and what was his role there. In essence, the whole issue of Nizzoli and Ferrari's behavior in this period needed to be exam- ined as it was these two figures, he repeated, who followed a "double line" and were responsible for provoking "with a few acts, consequences and wounds which were very grave for democracy." There were, Montanari conceded, individuals such as Valdo Magnani who contested the position of Ferrari and Nizzoli, but there were other senior figures in the Reggio PCI who were not sufficiently "coherent and resolute."[16] The article finished with the now famous plea: "If you know something speak up, make a contribution, correct and even contest what I have written" (*Chi sa parli, dia un contributo, corregga e contesti anche questo mio scritto*).[17]

There were many genuinely felt sentiments behind Montanari's article, but there are also some rather questionable aspects to it. It is, for example, hard to believe that Montanari, who was in a hospital in Bologna at the time of the Vischi killing, but who became one of the most powerful and influential figures in the Reggio PCI, did not "know who knew." And it is equally difficult to believe that an individual of his status was entirely ignorant of Ferrari's role in Czechoslovakia. But in many ways these considerations are beside the point. Montanari was above all a politician and he wanted to initiate a debate that would have the effect of bringing out into the open "hidden aspects" of the history of the local PCI. Once out into the open, the party would be cleansed, the sins of the past washed away, the integrity of Togliatti (and Montanari) firmly established and, most impor- tantly, the local PCI would be in a position to contribute fully to Occhetto's *cosa*. These were Montanari's fairly restricted intentions. But what happened in Sep- tember 1990 went far beyond the level of open discussion within the local PCI.

The following day the first response to Montanari's plea came from Vincenzo Bertolini, up until recently the leader of the PCI in Reggio, who published an arti- cle in *Il Resto del Carlino* that spoke of the two souls within the PCI and also raised the case of Germano Nicolini, wrongly imprisoned for the Don Pessina murder and forced to live in an "impossible" relationship with a party who knew the real identity of the priest's killer. Within a few days, however, the "*Chi sa parli*" affair had reached national and even international levels, with the whole question of the PCI's role in the Resistance exposed to the merciless and unrelenting attention of the media. According to Glauco Bertani, the author of a detailed study of the affair, the month of September saw 1,321 articles relating to the "triangle of death" published in the national press, with a peak of 109 reached on September 7.[18] Numbers alone do not, of course reveal the whole story, but they are certainly an indication of the intensity of a debate that called into question, as Kertzer has written, "the historical image of the PCI."[19] One of the first reactions at a national level came from the respected *La Repubblica* journalist Miriam Mafai who, in a front page article, described Montanari's decision as an act that merited "great respect." Mafai added, however, that it was necessary to understand the nature of the period. In a moment of apparently unconscious irony she then went on to express the hope that "the search for historical truth . . . cannot be deviated by exploitation of a political nature." The assessment of these events, however severe it might be, should not modify "our judgment of the Resistance and its protagonists." In her concluding comments Mafai explicitly related the debate to the discussions within a PCI that was in the process of changing its skin and should serenely examine a period in its history which, in no way, affected its "essential political choices."[20]

The days that followed, however, were not characterized by the kind of measured calm that permeated Mafai's piece. Under pressure from journalists, the PCI veteran Gian Carlo Pajetta (and, intriguingly, Mafai's long-term partner) recklessly described Montanari as a madman whom he would oblige to see reason. As he shut his car door, he also suggested that Montanari should think twice about showing himself in public in Reggio. These were not the kind of reactions one might expect from a seasoned politician and Pajetta soon withdrew his comments and phoned Montanari to clear matters up. The PCI leadership soon realized that matters were taking a serious turn and asked one of its rising stars, Piero Fassino, to oversee developments in Reggio Emilia. Fassino met with Montanari, other senior figures within the Reggio federation, and Nicolini. Nicolini then published an article in *L'Unità* maintaining not only his innocence but also that of Ero Righi and Cesarino Catellani, who had denounced themselves in a letter to the trial judge in Perugia in the 1950s and fled to Yugoslavia. The real author of the crime was still alive and, so he claimed, his identity was known to the *carabinieri*.

The PCI, it was abundantly clear, was having considerable difficulties dealing with the situation. In a lucid examination of the situation Giorgio Bocca suggested, in an apt metaphor, that the PCI had lost its compass. This certainly seemed to be the case when Fassino, the "fixer" brought in to clear up the mess, gave an interview with *La Stampa* in which he was critical, from the perspective of morality, of Togliatti's role in allowing the existence of the exile route to Czechoslovakia. This did not go down well with some members of the party, who called for his resignation, and Fassino was forced to write a long explanatory piece in *L'Unità*, clarifying his role and the party's position. This was all rather ham-fisted, and it is evident that some senior figures in the old guard of the party were far from happy with the way that the new blood dealt with this particular crisis. What was also painfully evident about the Fassino interview in *La Stampa* was that the younger generation of PCI leaders still had much to learn about how to manage the media in Italy.

The triangle of death affair had its own legacy, and debate and discussion has rumbled on ever since, though nothing ever matched the intensity of September 1990. The many appeals for information about the whereabouts of individuals killed around Campagnola in April 1945 led, following a tip-off, to a location at a clay mine known as the "Cavon." There the remains of 18 people from Campagnola, Poviglio, and Castelnovo Sotto were discovered. Forensic examinations led by Francesco de Fazio, well known for his investigations into the "monster of Florence," suggested that the victims had been killed by a combination of gunshots and blows from both heavy and sharp instruments. Ten of the eighteen bodies were identified and, according to the *Corriere della Sera*, all were "good people" with no connections with Fascism nor the RSI. There were, according to the paper, 16 further "*desaparecidos*," whose remains had yet to be found.[21]

In a further twist in September 1991, a former partisan William Gaiti confessed that it was he who was responsible for the death of Don Pessina. It had, he claimed, been an accident with the gun going off while on a patrol with Righi and Catellani. Nicolini, he confirmed, had nothing to do with it. In December 1993 at the Court of Assizes in Perugia, Gaiti, Catellani, and Righi were found guilty of the crime, but the 1953 amnesty applied in each case. Germano Nicolini was cleared in 1994.[22] Why the PCI allowed Nicolini to spend 10 years in jail for a crime he did not commit has never been established.[23] Otello Montanari, whose "Chi sa parli" article set the whole ball rolling has remained a controversial and, in many ways, isolated and embittered figure.

As 1990 came toward its end, another singular incident took place that reminded the nation of just how bitter the Resistance struggle had been and how long-term were its effects. The incident had its distant origins in an episode dating back to November 1944: Giuseppe Bonfatti, a partisan in the area around Mantova, attempted to kill Omobono Fertonani, the leader of the *brigate nere*. However, he only managed to wound him and local *brigatisti* exacted revenge by burning down his house and beating up the inhabitants. In turn, Bonfatti swore revenge, but after the war he emigrated to Brazil. Nearly 46 years later, he returned to his home town, Viadana, and asked whether anyone knew the whereabouts of a certain Giuseppe Oppici (who had participated in the attack on his house). He walked into a bar, located Oppici, who was playing cards, and asked him to step outside. Inside a rolled up newspaper he carried an ice-pick that he repeatedly brought down on the head of his victim. He then walked into the square in the center of the town and gave himself up to the *carabinieri*. Initially, he was condemned to 16 years in jail, which at a second trial was reduced to 10. Because of his deteriorating health, he was freed and died in 1995.[24] The Cold War, arguably, was over, but the Italian civil war still raged on.

Pacification, *Parificazione*, and Post-Fascism

As we have seen, the PCI was going through a process of ostensibly moving forward during 1990, a process that involved the painful examination of some aspects of its past. Paradoxically, at exactly the same time, the party at the other end of the political spectrum, the MSI, appeared to be going backward. Suffering from ill health, the veteran leader Almirante had been replaced by the young dauphin Gianfranco Fini at the end of 1987, and it seemed that shouts of "Fascism is here" would no longer be heard at party congresses. But Fini was himself defeated at the sixteenth party congress in January 1990 and replaced by Pino Rauti, a former RSI soldier and one of the leading exponents of the theories of "socialization." Rauti was not an individual who would countenance the shedding of past glories. But after a disastrous election in July 1991 showed clearly that a return to "black" roots was not a viable strategy for the party, he was ousted and Fini was back, and this time he was determined not to lose his grip on a party at a time when new possibilities were clearly opening up. For the MSI-DN to occupy a new position in Italian politics, Fini was well aware that it would have to change, or at least appear to change. And in order for the party to gain support among the electorate, it would also have to be in a position to demonstrate stronger democratic credentials. While anti-Fascism had been one of the supporting pillars of the Republic, this was not going to be easy, but by the early 1990s the situation was changing fast. Fini, who was and still is an extremely able politician, soon realized that the ongoing discussions about the Resistance and the RSI, and above all the question of national reconciliation (the Italian term is *pacificazione*), could be turned to his party's advantage.

Fini chose to make his move on reconciliation in 1993, by which time the seismic effects of the *tangentopoli* affair meant that Italy was being led by the governor of the Bank of Italy, Carlo Azeglio Ciampi. The collapse of the DC center also meant that that there was a massive electoral constituency out there to be tapped. He decided to test the waters by putting himself forward as a candidate for the mayor of Rome. In the elections of December 1993, he lost out to the center-Left candidate, Francesco Rutelli, but it was a close affair with Fini polling 47 percent of the vote. The rhetoric of national reconciliation was a feature of MSI discourse at the time, but Fini also spoke of an "*Italia parificata*" as well, by which he meant that both sides in the struggle of 1943–1945 would be granted equal dignity and equal rights (to, for example, pensions). The fiftieth anniversary of September 8 offered an excellent opportunity to initiate a debate on a national level. On that day, which marked the official beginning of 20 months of intense commemorative activity, President Scalfaro was due to give a speech at Porta San Paolo, the site of one of the few effective military responses after the armistice declaration, and therefore one of the most potent symbols of the Resistance in Rome. Scalfaro had given a speech earlier on in the summer that had given signs of encouragement, referring to "all those who paid the highest price, even those who fought for ideals we do not share." Shortly before the Porta San Paolo event itself, Scalfaro received a joint declaration from Giulio Baghino, the president of the RSI veterans association, and General Luigi Poli, the president of the Associazione nazionale combattenti della guerra di Liberazione (and DC senator), asking for his help in the process of reconciliation and seeking a meeting at the Quirinal palace. In the event, Scalfaro disappointed the supporters of reconciliation. He showed his respect for "the dead of every front, of every battle" but made it clear that only "the loyal respect for the truth can be the secure base for a real pacification." The event thus offered no surprises and the speech Scalfaro made concentrated on liberty and the need to protect it, particularly when a nation passed through difficult times. It was clear that his preoccupations were with the present and that Poli and Baghino would have to wait for their invitation to the Quirinal. For the disappointed MSI deputy Tremaglia, the nation was "ahead of the institutions."[25] Tremaglia, also an RSI veteran, indicated that it was not only pacification that his party wanted but also *parificazione*.

With the victory of the Berlusconi-Fini-Bossi alliance in the elections of late March 1994, the question of the political legitimacy of the *Alleanza nazionale* (AN) became all the more pressing. How could a party, with its roots in Fascism, be part of the government of a nation whose roots were anti-Fascist? Just before April 25, 1994, Fini gave an interview to the *Corriere della Sera* expressing the hope that the anniversary could be the first day of a year of reconciliation for "the nation as a whole." His own gesture in this direction was to attend a Mass in Rome that honored the fallen on both sides. Fini arrived at the Basilica of Santa Maria degli Angeli at 10:30 where he told waiting journalists that he hoped April 25 could soon be considered the day the war finished and that all Italians might find "reasons to be reconciled and look towards the future" and cease to "hold aloft the stockades and hatred of the past." Not everyone within AN was happy with the idea, particularly Pino Rauti who attended the Mass, but spoke against the idea of reconciliation. Another veteran, Giuseppe Baratti, no doubt spoke for many of his comrades in the RSI: "I have always been a Fascist. I fought against the partisans and for me they are still the enemy." And the monarchist count Crispolti came up with the singular argument that in ancient Greece "any soldier who died for his ideals . . . was considered a hero." During the course of the Mass, at which Fini and the former DC politician D'Onofrio shook hands, the editor of the *Secolo d'Italia* hurled down a gauntlet: "From the Right we have made the first move, now it's up to the Left."[26]

In Milan, the symbolic capital of the Resistance, the response to Tremaglia, Fini, and Berlusconi was, it goes without saying, hostile. As is so frequently the case on April 25, it poured with rain. Nevertheless, some 300,000 people processed through the streets of Milan to Piazza Duomo. In order to cope with the extraordinary numbers, the authorities created two itineraries, one leaving from Corso Buenos Aires, the other from Piazza Medaglie d'oro. Both starting points were, of course symbolically significant—Piazzale Loreto is at the end of Corso Buenos Aires and many protestors gathered by the UPIM department store where 49 years before Mussolini and others had been held up for public execration.[27] For one veteran, Giovanni Pesce, the 1994 celebration was the "most beautiful": "'94 was the best of all from '45 to today . . . Above all the young people, this is the most beautiful thing about it. About 85% were young people! We remember these things! Who did the Resistance? It was the young."[28] Silvio Berlusconi did not attend, preferring to spend the *festa* at Arcore with his relatives from where, it was claimed, he would follow events on television. We do not know if he did watch, but he would have realized that he had made the right decision: the demonstration was both anti-Fascist and anti-Berlusconi. Umberto Bossi, on the other hand, joined the crowd, but was received with shouts of "Fascist, liar, betrayer." For his own safety Bossi was then given a police escort and explained the reasons for his attendance to a *Corriere della Sera* journalist. Apparently his party's struggle against "partyocracy" was a kind of "modern history of the war of Liberation."[29] This was just one in a long list of Bossi's eccentric interpretations of Italian history, both ancient and modern.

Bossi's was, of course, a rather singular interpretation, but it effectively highlights how the April 25 celebrations, whether in 1994 or for that matter any other year, were always about the political present rather than the historical past. But what was specific about April 25, 1994, was that, from then on, the whole question of Berlusconi's presence or absence would always be a topic of intense speculation.

Three days after the demonstration in Milan, Berlusconi was formally invited to form a government. A few days before Berlusconi was sworn in, a German officer, Erich Priebke, who had participated in the massacre at the Fosse Ardeatine, was tracked down by an American news team. The Priebke case would go on to provoke much anguished discussion in Italy in 1996 when a military court pronounced that his crime, a war crime rather than a crime against humanity, had expired. But before the Priebke trial, which for many observers really did mark the end of an era in Italy, there was still much happening within Italian politics.

Following the defeat in the 1994 elections, Achille Occhetto resigned as leader of the PDS. The favorite to succeed him was Walter Veltroni, the editor of *L'Unità*. In the event it was Massimo D'Alema who was elected to the post by the party's national council. D'Alema was of noted anti-Fascist stock: his father, Giuseppe, who died in November 1994, had been one of the organizers of the Resistance in Ravenna, along with Arrigo Boldrini. D'Alema had worked closely with Occhetto in 1989, and so was considered one of the architects of the transformation of the PCI to the PDS. Initially, at least, he made very few, if any interventions, about the Resistance, but in more recent years he has become more actively involved in discussions, declaring in 2005 that the execution of Mussolini was a mistake. Under D'Alema's leadership, the Resistance was largely placed on the PDS back-burner, almost as if the party's past sat uncomfortably with its future direction. "Rifondazione comunista," on the other hand, made a point of championing the Resistance cause. Emblematic of its stance was the decision to organize regular bus trips from Milan to Gattatico so the faithful could visit the Cervi house and museum.

For Fini's AN, however, the past was a significant obstacle to progress. For the party's conference at Fiuggi in January 1995, at which the party became officially "post-fascist," a long theoretical document was prepared. Opinion is divided on the interpretation of *Pensiamo l'Italia*, with some commentators arguing that it owes as much of a debt to Almirante's party as it does to Fini's. But whatever was the case, the Fiuggi declaration called for the end of all *fasci*, not just "Fascism" but also "anti-Fascism." Anti-Fascism, it was conceded, had been "historically essential for the return of democratic values compromised by Fascism," but it could not be considered a "value in itself" because it had been used in the postwar by the PCI in order to legitimize itself.[30] This was, again, a clever strategy by Fini and the AN, and the PDS struggled to find any kind of a response.

April 25, 1995

With the AN now avowedly post-Fascist, Italy approached the fiftieth anniversary of the Liberation, to be celebrated in a ceremony in Milan addressed by president Scalfaro. By then the Berlusconi coalition had dramatically collapsed, following the withdrawal of Bossi and the Leagues and Italy was being governed, temporarily, by Lamberto Dini. The event coincided with regional elections in Italy with the PDS doing particularly well, winning nine of the fifteen regions. Berlusconi told the press that there would be representatives from his party, Forza Italia!, in Milan, but that he would not be there in person. The reasons for his absence were, he claimed, linked to questions of his personal safety.[31]

With Berlusconi out of government, the event was much less charged than it had been the previous year. Nevertheless, the theme of reconciliation was again at the forefront of people's minds. The day before, Fini attended a ceremony at the tomb of the unknown soldier at which Edgardo Sogno and two adherents to the RSI, the author Carlo Mazzantini and Bartolo Gallitto, laid a wreath that bore the words "To our fallen brothers, from your reconciled brothers" (*Ai fratelli caduti, i fratelli riconciliati*). The youth wing of AN wrote a message to Scalfaro that spoke of the need of a "new national pact" that could not be based on the "oppositional value of anti-Fascism."[32] Would Scalfaro change from his, apparently steadfast, position of the previous year?

Before attempting to answer this tantalizing question, it is useful to give some details about the nature and dimensions of the celebrations of the period 1993–1995. To coordinate events, a national committee was set up under the presidency of senator Gerardo Agostini, who was also the president of the ANMIG (Associazione Nazionale Invalidi e Mutilati della Guerra—the national association for the war wounded). Boldrini was the vice president of the committee, and the secretariat included the socialist Aldo Aniasi (and FIAP president) as well as Paolo Emilio Taviani (president of FIVL). Luigi Poli, as we have seen, one of the prime movers for pacification, represented the Ministry of Defense. The organizing committee was thus a very broad church, with every possible current represented. But it was, above all, a state committee, and for this reason the celebrations gave particular emphasis to the role of the Italian armed forces in the period. This was a deliberate strategy that reinforced the idea that the war effort in 1943–1945 did not just involve the partisans, but Italy's regular forces, all fighting together for the sake of the nation. Ceremonies were held, for example, to commemorate the massacre at Cefalonia as well as the battle of Montelungo, where the Italian army regained some respectability after September 8. But in addition the *carabinieri*, traditionally a much-maligned organization, were thanked fulsomely for their sacrifices, such as that of Salvo D'Acquisto and of the *carabinieri* shot at Fiesole, just outside Florence. Even the finance police (the *guardia di finanza*) got in on the act.

The Italian state initially provided a very large sum to finance the *cinquantennale*, a cool 20 billion lira, but this was subsequently reduced to 16 billion and eight hundred million lira. Even with this reduction, this was still a lot of money. Of this, about 40 percent was spent on conferences, exhibitions, research projects, and the collection and archiving of documents. Just less than 30 percent was spent financing publications, competitions in schools, and theatrical productions. The rest, just less than 5 billion, was spent on commemorative events and celebrations of various types. According to the eight-hundred page official account of the *cinquentennale*, published by the state press, there were around five thousand commemorative events throughout Italy and abroad (there was even a ceremony in Adelaide), eight thousand school initiatives involving 2 million pupils and students, three hundred academic conferences, and 437 exhibitions.[33] The Minister of Education, Lombardi, called for schools to create "rigorous pathways of knowledge" to facilitate "independent thinking," so that children might internalize "positive values" and "refute violence in all its forms."[34] Although state funds did not offer subventions for everything, an official bibliography listed over two thousand titles published in the period 1943–1945. In short, the *cinquantennale* was arguably the largest politicocultural initiative in the history of the nation, bigger than all of the celebrations of the Risorgimento put together.

For president Scalfaro, the activities of April 25 began at the Altar to the Nation and at the Fosse Ardeatine. The lunchtime news on RAI Uno showed him at the Fosse Ardeatine, touching a huge laurel wreath with outstretched hands and pausing for a brief moment of reflection. He then flew to Milan where, at the *Arena civile*, he addressed the armed forces, an event shown live on RAI Uno, before attending the main event in the afternoon at Piazza Duomo. That morning, a Mass had been held in the cathedral with Cardinal Martini affirming that the "core values of the Resistance" were still intact and it was right to celebrate them. Compared to the previous year, the numbers were down with around 100,000 present in the center of the city. Still, not everyone could get into Piazza Duomo, one of the largest squares in Italy. The events in Milan on the afternoon of April 25 were broadcast to the nation by Rai Due. Coverage included a prerecorded interview with Giorgio Bocca, who insouciantly twirled his pen while railing against the pacification argument. In Piazza Duomo itself, an enthusiastic journalist interviewed senior ANPI officers, such as the Genoese Roberto Bonfiglioli, while the regulation speeches were made. The socialist Aniasi, who had blotted his copy book by being a supporter of Craxi, was greeted with boos and whistles by the local Milanese. The cameras then turned to Scalfaro whose speech was, largely, predictable. Toward the end, however, he turned his attentions to the soldiers of the RSI. Framing his comments with the need to respect historical truth, Scalfaro nevertheless recognized that, particularly the "young" of the RSI, had been convinced that they were serving the nation. This rhetoric marked a clear shift from his position at Porta San Paolo 20 months before, and the ideological distance Scalfaro had traveled was reinforced by a recondite allusion to the poet Carducci. With his arms outstretched in a beseeching gesture, Scalfaro intoned that "the poet" would invite us to remember: "Now O Lord, these men too have died, as we too died for Italy" (*ora o signor anch'essi sono morti, come noi morimmo, Dio, per l'Italia*). The quotation was a slight adjustment to lines from Carducci's patriotic ode "Piedmont" when it is Carlo Alberto ("he too died" [*anch'egli è morto*]) who had sacrificed himself for Italy. The poem itself ends with the impassioned plea to God: "O Lord, give back our country, give Italy back to the Italians" (*rendi la patria, Dio, rendi l'Italia a gl'italiani*). The reference to Carducci would, of course, have been way over the heads of many in the crowd, but the message that the young of the RSI had died fighting for their nation was clear enough, and indeed it was one of the aspects that the Rai Due journalist picked up on during his rapid summary of the speech. But rather surprisingly, in fact astonishingly, this very strong concession to the "national patriotic" RSI does not seem to have provoked any comment or discussion whatsoever. Perhaps Scalfaro's heavy cough proved a distraction, perhaps the recourse to a nineteenth century poet was too obscure, but the president had made a gesture that was as conciliatory as Violante's *ragazzi di Salò* speech a year later. But no one remembers Scalfaro's speech, whereas Violante's is seen as the quintessential watershed moment. In the evening, Scalfaro attended a Resistance concert at La Scala where, perhaps, he contemplated the press reaction to his speech which, in the event, never came. Meanwhile, RAI Due broadcast a special from Alba punctuated by a showing of a remastered print of Rossellini's *Roma, città aperta*, a film which, of course, emphasized the national-popular interpretation of the Resistance.

Historiography

During 1990 and 1991, the historian Claudio Pavone was busy correcting proofs of what was destined to become the most important work of scholarship on the Resistance movement. As we have seen, Pavone had first articulated the thesis of a civil war at the Brescia conference in the mid-1980s. Largely as a response to the debate created at Brescia, the Resistance Institute at Belluno organized, in October 1988, a conference titled "War, War of Liberation, Civil War." At this conference, Pavone gave a paper in which he developed the idea of three simultaneous and overlapping wars, hence the title "Le tre guerre: patriottica, civile e di classe" of his contribution. In his introduction to the conference proceedings, Quazza, the highly respected senior historian of the Resistance, scrupulously examined the semantics of the expression "civil war," proposing an alternative and less inflammatory interpretation of a "war of civilizations." The conference proceedings were published in 1990, before the triangle of death polemic emerged.[35] Pavone's book, on the other hand, came out barely a year after the polemic and its reception was heavily conditioned by this climate.[36] "Reception" is a deliberately chosen word, for Pavone's book is a work that has suffered the fate of being more talked about than read. There is a gulf between what is actually in Pavone's book and what is perceived to be in it. In part this gulf is related to the choice of title for the work. The book has the title *"Una guerra civile"* and the subtitle "A history of morality in the Resistance" (*Saggio storico sulla moralità nella Resistenza*). Naturally enough, it is the title with which everyone is familiar, and which has led to the unfortunately simplistic impression that *Una guerra civile*, a widely used short-form, is only and exclusively a work that argues the case for a civil war. In part this misconception is also deliberate and political in its origins. As we have seen, the idea of a civil war was used by the extreme Right for years in order to suggest that the war in Italy was an essentially patriotic affair with both sides fighting for their Nation. *Una guerra civile* was thus meat and drink to those very widespread forces in Italy who sought equal status, equal dignity, and equal memory for the soldiers of the MSI. As the historian Mario Isnenghi lamented in the pages of the *Corriere della Sera*, deliberately referring to the subtitle of the work: "Certainly there was no deliberate plan for the social use of the *Saggio storico della moralità nella Resistenza* by Claudio Pavone; but, since it came out in 1991 and since it had that title, this lofty and limpid analysis of a civil war has fallen headlong into the posthumous campaign aimed at the criminalization and the *damnatio memoriae* of the Communist Party and everything associated with it."[37]

So what, then, is in *Una guerra civile*? Pavone's book starts with a close analysis of the "choice," from both sides, although more attention is given to the "Resistance choice" than to the decision to join the RSI. The two chapters that follow examine the significance of the legacy of the Fascist war (chapter 2) and how the military paradigm of 1940–1943 fed into the organizational developments, but was also in part rejected by the forces of the Resistance (chapter 3). This third chapter, which devotes considerable space to the complicated question of the politicization of the Resistance forces is the only section of the book that analyzes the higher structures of the Resistance edifice: in other words, the CLN. As Pavone shows, there was a difference between the level of politicization desired by and exemplified by the CLN and the reality at ground level.[38] What Pavone is most interested in is, indeed, the rank-and-file partisans. What were their thoughts, feelings, fears, and emotions during the course of the war? What kind of war did they think they were fighting, and how did they cope with the moral issues that arose? Pavone explains in his preface that he wishes to avoid the French *histoire des mentalités* approach, but this is in many ways what he tries to do in the book. At the structural heart of the book are three chapters: "La guerra civile," "La guerra patriottica," and "La guerra di classe." The first of these is an expanded version of the famous Brescia conference paper, while the other two chapters discuss the other two overlapping and interlinked wars. As with the Brescia paper, Pavone employs a very wide range of sources, but memoirs and literary works are his texts of choice. In terms of memoirs, the diaries of Artom, Chiodi, Livio Bianco, Ada Gobetti, Pesce, and Revelli are the most frequently cited, while in terms of literary texts, Fenoglio is the most cited author, closely followed by Calvino. Vittorini and Pavese get a smattering of attention while Viganò, clearly not one of Pavone's predilections, is entirely absent from the text. Subsequent chapters address the question of violence from both sides (it is this chapter to which the subtitle is most directly applicable), and finally there is a return to politics and the aspirations of the Resistance for the future of Italy. A summary of this nature cannot possibly do justice to the breadth of the book, but it does show that it far exceeds in scope the mere articulation of the civil war thesis.

In 1992, Romolo Gobbi published a polemical book titled *Il mito della Resistenza*, which represents an important landmark in the entire debate over "revisionism." In terms of scale, Gobbi's book was the polar opposite of Pavone's: it is just over a hundred pages in length and is endowed with only a limited number of footnotes. But it caused quite a stir: the veteran trade unionist Vittorio Foa described it as "refuse . . . rubbish" and, when a history teacher at the famously anti-Fascist Liceo Massimo d'Azeglio in Turin made it into a set text for his course on "civic education" and the pupils asked Gobbi to address them, all hell broke loose. This was not, apparently, the same school that had seen the likes of Antonicelli, Bobbio, Leone Ginzburg, Augusto Monti, and Giancarlo Pajetta (to name but a few) grace its classrooms. In part, the impact of *Il mito della Resistenza* can be explained by the fact that Gobbi was far from being a right-wing historian—in his youth he had collaborated with Panzieri and the *Quaderni rossi*. But in the late 1960s, Gobbi developed a "workerist" position that set him against the PCI, a party that had apparently betrayed the working class and, as his 1973 book *Operai e resistenza* claimed, manipulated the history of the strikes of March 1943 and the party's role in the organization of them for political ends.

The strikes and Gobbi's 1973 book (that he quotes frequently) are also an important feature of *Il mito della Resistenza*, but the book examines a broad range of topics, such as the relationship between the peasants and the partisans and the insurrection, all of which, in his view, constitute elements of the Left's mis-appropriation of the Resistance. The specific targets of his analysis are some of the bastions of PCI historiography: Roberto Battaglia, Luigi Longo, and Giorgio Vaccarino, the director of the Resistance Institute in Turin where Gobbi had once worked. What is perhaps most interesting about Gobbi's book is that many of his sources are literary and include works by Fenoglio, Viganò, and Calvino. Gobbi's methodology consists in quoting or summarizing "mythical" views and compar-ing them with the "demythologizing" views that he finds in the literary texts. In fic-tion can be found the truth, but in history it is all politics. Gobbi's book is flawed in a number of ways—plainly it adopts a very simplistic approach to questions of historical and literary truth as well, indeed, as to the nature of myth, but it did raise some awkward questions.

Gobbi's book was cheap, readable, and designed for the mass market. It was a compelling formula and no doubt it had an impact on Renzo De Felice. By the 1990s, De Felice was working on the final volume of his large-scale biography of Mussolini, a volume that would bring the story up to the death of the *duce* in April 1945.[39] De Felice's final volume, titled *La guerra civile*, would be published incom-plete and posthumously in 1997, but to coincide with the fiftieth anniversary he decided to publish, on September 8, 1995 (the chosen date was not an accident), what might be termed a "digested" version, in the form of an interview with the *Panorama* journalist Pasquale Chessa. The book argued in trenchant terms that historiography had been dominated by a mythological "Resistance" vulgate (*vul-gata resistenziale*), which needed to be replaced without further delay by some-thing scientific and objective. Yet, for someone with such scientific pretensions, it was a pity De Felice dated Longo's 1947 *Un popolo alla macchia* to the 1960s, as one perceptive reviewer pointed out.[40] *Rosso e nero* was an instant publishing phenom-enon, generating countless responses from a range of commentators from Bobbio and Bocca at one end of the alphabet to Valdevit and Valiani at the other.[41] It ran to three editions by the end of 1995 and has been translated into Spanish and Por-tuguese. The approach De Felice adopted was similar to the one he had previously adopted with Michael Ledeen and the *Intervista sul fascismo* (republished in 1995), but there were differences as well. *Rosso e nero* is, in appearance at least, a "book interview" (*libro intervista*), which is framed by an introduction by De Felice and a rather perplexing *nota* by Chessa that is placed at the end. In this postface Chessa likens De Felice's historical method to that of Conrad, Proust, and Plato who, he says, wrote as if they were looking through a telescope. In De Felice's case, though, the telescope is turned the other way round. Strange though this optical meta-phor might be, what follows is rather more disquieting. Chessa goes on to explain how the text is not a reproduction of an interview or series of interviews. In the published text his leading questions to De Felice are placed at the beginning of each section, whereas in reality they punctuated the conversation. And De Felice's answers to his "questions" are the edited end-product of numerous conversa-tions, rather than a transcription. *Rosso e nero* would, therefore, appear not to be a "book-interview" at all, but a carefully crafted summary by someone who could write clear prose (Chessa) of the ideas of a historian who could not. One could, of course, raise a number of objections to this methodology, not the least of which is the fact that Chessa reveals the nature of his sorcery when the "interview" is, for the reader, effectively over. But more importantly, the Chessa-De Felice combination, which proved highly successful and persuasive (the book became a best-seller), raises a number of questions about the presentation of history to the Italian public at the end of the twentieth century. In order for complex ideas to be understood by anyone other than specialists, was it really the case that historians had to resort to journalists for help? Were Italian historians really so difficult to understand? Did one of the most complex and controversial periods in the history of modern Italy really have to be reduced to a series of easily digested chunks of between 10 and 15 pages, ideal for the daily commute? And were readers really so diminished as not to be able to tackle a book with footnotes and quotations from archives as well as other secondary sources? Italy, it seemed, was not just in a political morass, but the nation was floundering in an intellectual and cultural abyss.

Films

Two mainstream films were made during the period 1990–1995 that dealt with Resistance themes, *Il caso Martello* (1991) and *Gangsters* (1992). The first of these involved a very complex story line connected with an unclaimed insurance policy and contrasted the morality of the 1980s with that of the Resistance period. More significant than the film itself was its director, Guido Chiesa, who would go on to make a film version of *Il partigiano Johnny* at the end of the decade. Massimo Guglielmi's *Gangsters* took on a difficult subject and attempted to give a sympa-thetic portrayal of a group of Ligurian partisans who found themselves sucked into a murky world of postwar killings and common crime. But while the film may have started out as an attempt to examine the complex psychology of the partisans, the "triangle of death" controversy tended to push interpretation of the film into a simple condemnation of them. The film has since faded into obscurity.

By far the most influential "film" of the whole period was, ostensibly, not a fiction but a documentary film or series of documentary films that went under the title *Combat Film*. The films had been originally shot by specialist American cameramen and lain in the National Archives in Washington ever since. Roberto

Olla, who was responsible for the project and his copresenter, Leonardo Valente, explained to the press before the first "special" episode, scheduled for April 5, 1994 (shortly after the Berlusconi victory), that their role would be merely to present the material without intervention. All the films were silent, but no sound effects would be added, except for some special music composed by Ezio Rinaldi. Claims of nonintervention are always suspicious, particularly when it comes to television. The first program was due to be broadcast at 10:25 p.m. on April 5 and studio guests were to be Gianfranco Fini, Walter Veltroni, and Tina Anselmi. In the event, very little went to plan: Fini was replaced by Giano Accame, a former RSI soldier and editor of *Il secolo d'Italia*, and Veltroni substituted by Piero Fassino (the PDS's fixer during the triangle of death polemic). Anselmi turned up, but due to an over-run from earlier on in the evening, the program started at 11:50. The first program began with uncompromisingly shocking images: the corpses of both Mussolini and Petacci in a Milanese hospital. Mussolini's body, lying on a slab, bore the very clear marks of his recent autopsy, with large stitches down his torso. His head, sub-ject to the vagaries of the crowd, was horrifically swollen and misshapen. Petacci was in a coffin and an obliging medic lifted her head so the cameraman could get a better angle. This was the first of 10 sequences that showed, *inter alia*, the bodies of the *gerarchi* at Piazzale Loreto, the victims of the Fosse Ardeatine massacre, the execution of Fascist spies, the hunger of citizens of Lucca, the eruption of Vesuvius (the longest sequence) and, finally, Christmas Eve at an orphanage at Montecatini. As Simona Monticelli has shown in her brilliant analysis of this first episode there was nothing casual about this structure, nor in the way the program was presented to the Italian public.[42] *Combat Film* first strives to elicit audience sympathy for Mussolini and his lover: very few people will ever have to go through the haunt-ing experience of identifying a corpse in a mortuary, but all viewers of this epi-sode of *Combat Film* go through the ritual. Instinctively, one feels a sense of *pietas* before the almost unrecognizable images of Mussolini and his lover. But equally, the internalized pity of the spectator clashes with the smiling faces of the throng of unidentified individuals who crowd around the corpses. The equally pitiless gaze of the camera, obsessively filming every detail, contributes further to the troubling scene as a whole. By placing these images right at the start of the show, the pro-gram also problematizes the actual chronology of events leading up to the killings, and largely decontextualizes the reasons for the public vilification of the corpses.

The scenes were also accompanied by studio discussion as well as the present-ers' frequent assurances that what the audience was seeing was simply unaltered reality, as it happened. It was in one of these audience discussions that a young participant was discovered not to know who Badoglio was, provoking widespread panic about the failures of the Italian education system.[43] By the end of the first program, the underlying message of *Combat Film* was fairly explicit. Italy, the show suggested, had been through an appalling period of violence in which the whole nation had suffered, but none of this violence had apparently been carried out by the soldiers of the RSI. In contrast to the Italians, however, the American cameramen were part of an army which, though ostensibly liberating Italy, was effectively taking it over, with the all-pervasive lens a symbol of foreign masculine power and dominance. What was the purpose of the seven minutes and fifty-six

seconds of Vesuvius erupting? The answer was simple: violence was not historically or ideologically determined but elemental; it could explode at any time, but
then it would calm down. It came from the earth, and to the earth it returned.
Combat Film was an extraordinarily potent weapon in the pacification debate. It
could soon be purchased in VHS format, available on a fortnightly basis, with an
accompanying magazine. Evidently the Italian media had traveled a long way since
Love Story was sold bundled together with a box of *Baci* chocolates.

Literary Texts

In addition to the many works of history published on the Resistance, the period
under examination also saw the appearance of a large number of fictional works.
In terms of children's literature, one notable development was the publication of
Guido Petter's *Ci chiamavano banditi*, specifically aimed at the under-14 market.
Petter was, and still is, an interesting figure. He had participated, at a tender age,
in the Resistance in the Val D'Ossola and had made his debut in Resistance fiction
for children in the early 1950s before going on to become a professor of psychology at Padua University.[44] In his 1993 book *I giorni dell'ombra* he described, and
tried to understand, a vicious physical attack on him by youths belonging to an
organization called "organized proletarian communists."[45] He had been a target
precisely because of his Resistance past and was seen as the embodiment, at least
in the city of Padua, of the failure of the Resistance to remain truthful to its revolutionary spirit. In his 1995 book for children, Petter explained that it was a rewrite
of his 1978 *Che importa se ci chiaman banditi*. The changes involved a shift from
the third to the first person and a move from the past to the present tense. Apparently the younger readers of the original version had considered the book to be a
"novel" and so "in order to make more evident the full reality which characterized
the narrated facts and so eliminate all possibilities of misunderstanding" Petter
had undertaken the revision.[46] Unfortunately, we do not know how Petter's readers reacted to this ostensibly more truthful version, but this rather singular case
compellingly underlines just how difficult it could be to communicate to a young
audience. But Petter could not be faulted for trying.

The changes Petter made to his novel uncannily echoed the technical choices
made by Beppe Fenoglio in another first person text published in 1995. Written in
his father's notebooks Fenoglio had never published this diaristic account of his
partisan career from the recapture of Alba to the winter of 1944. But an apparently
chance discovery led to the unearthing of the manuscripts by Fenoglio that were
given the title *Appunti partigiani* by their editor, Lorenzo Mondo, who had been
responsible for the first edition of *Il partigiano Johnny* in the late 1960s. The *appunti*
contained episodes, written in the first person and in the present tense, which were
reworked in later manuscripts, and their existence seemed to definitively suggest
that *Il partigiano Johnny* was not, *pace* Corti and her associates, written immediately after the war. Apart from the philological implications, the *Appunti* contain
the type of narrative material that made Fenoglio posthumously famous, but it
generally lacks the intensity of *Il partigiano Johnny* and *Una questione privata*. The

enemy, though, are resolutely Italian, and the Germans remain, as they do in much of Fenoglio's work, offstage, emphasizing the civil war.[47]

Fenoglio's fellow *piemontese*, Nuto Revelli, published *Il disperso di Marburg* in 1994.[48] The book is an extraordinarily subtle and moving piece of detective work that crosses a number of genres by combining fiction with a historical and moral enquiry into the identity of a dead German soldier, the eponymous *disperso* of Marburg. Other books published in the period were more overtly *gialli* such as Lucarelli's *L'estate torbida*, as well as Angelino's *L'inverno dei Mongoli* and Gennari's *Le ragioni del sangue*.[49] These were all published by some of the biggest operations in Italy, notably Sellerio, Einaudi, and Garzanti. Whereas Lucarelli's detective is a professional, in the other two books, as is frequently the case in *gialli*, the detective figure is an amateur. In *L'inverno dei Mongoli*, the detective is an RSI soldier, Pietro Contini, who has to discover the identity of the assassin of a local Fascist within 36 hours; otherwise, the German soldiers stationed in a Ligurian village will carry out a brutal reprisal. There are, of course, conscious echoes here of the "Via Rasella" case. Using the traditional techniques of following and deciphering clues, Contini identifies the killer as a Jewish musician, Fantoni, and promptly hands him over to the Germans. The village has been saved, Contini has done his job, and the story would seem to reach a satisfactory conclusion. For both Contini and the readers of the book, there is a sense of relief. But the moral situation becomes decidedly uncomfortable for Contini when the Germans focus on Fantoni's status as a Jew when thanking the "detective" for his efforts. Both Contini and the inhabitants of the village become associated with the Shoah, whether they like it or not. The book thus exploits both the genre of the *giallo*, as well as contemporary debates about the RSI, to pose some very awkward questions about morality. The idea of a potential moral *parificazione* between the two sides involved in the civil war would, in Angelino's book, seem to be more problematic than was being claimed in the press and elsewhere. Gennari's *Le ragioni del sangue* does not, on the other hand, engage with the issue of RSI-Resistance pacification or *parificazione*, but it is nevertheless an interesting and complex text from the moral point of view. On this occasion, the detective-protagonist is the son of a partisan whose death at the beginning of the narrative leads to a twin search: on one level, the 40-year-old Giuseppe Marga seeks to understand his deceased father's character so he can understand himself, on the other, he seeks to understand his war-time activities so he can gain an understanding of the times his father lived in. The "reasons for blood" are thus personal (the blood running from father to son) and historical (the blood shed during and after the war).

Another text that presented itself as a *giallo* was *Ma l'amore no* by Giampaolo Pansa, the first of the Piedmontese journalist's explicitly fictional treatments of the Resistance period. The book was the first of a trilogy dealing with the Resistance and the postwar and has not received much attention, probably because it has been all but overshadowed by the more explicitly polemical works of the new millennium. This is a pity, as it is a text that contains much of interest. Before the novel itself begins, there are two pages of what literary critics term paratext: a quotation from the Nobel prize winner and Auschwitz survivor Elie Wiesel and a brief paragraph of thanks to Claudio Pavone, who had taught Pansa to use the expression "guerra civile" without fear, and to Beppe Fenoglio whose book, *Il partigiano Johnny*, had provided the author with "a number of words" and allowed him to discover the correct "state of mind" to write it. These thanks serve to establish a particular status for Pansa: there is an implicit suggestion that, along with the regulation act of homage to his masters, he is also trying to emulate Fenoglio and Pavone as well as write a work that is both historical and fictional, but above all, truthful. In an interview with Simonetta Fiori, Pansa offered some revealing insights into his motivations behind his first venture into fiction. After so many "dreadful and dull academic studies," Pansa told the *La Repubblica* journalist that he wanted to have a go at "narrative," so as to "give vent to everything" in conditions of "total creative freedom." Pansa compared himself to a painter and decorator, suddenly deciding he would become an artist.

Pansa, therefore, considered the shift from the *saggio* to the novel as an act of liberation. No more documents, no more newspaper articles, no more archives: creativity rather than drudgery. The shift to narrative certainly meant that Pansa has attracted a far wider reading public, and rendered Italy's past more easily accessible by writing in what Passerini has described as a "lively style."[50] For each person who has read the five hundred pages of Pansa's very scholarly *Guerra partigiana tra Genova e il Po*, there must be more than a hundred who have devoured *Ma l'amore no*.

Before the narrative of *Ma l'amore no* starts, there is a further prefatory text titled "The Prophesy" that introduces the protagonist Giovanni, a boy of seven-and-a-half years of age who lives with his mother, Giovanna, in a small Piedmontese city by the Po river. Though it is not named, it is clear that the city is none other than Casale Monferrato, Pansa's birthplace, and that Giovanni is an autobiographical figure. However, *Ma l'amore no* is not an autobiography but a work of fiction very loosely based on Pansa's own experiences as a boy in World War II. Along with Giovanni and his mother we are introduced to four other figures all of whom are female: a grandmother and three aunts. One of these aunts, Vanda, persuades Giovanna to have her fortune read by a tarot card reader who disquietingly predicts that a person she loves will take the life of another person she loves. The specific reference is to *Oedipus Rex* and so, it is clear from the start that Pansa is preparing us for a family tragedy of some sort. The novel begins in 1943 and is split into three major sections corresponding to the three years of the Resistance: 1943, 1944, and 1945. Each section is divided into a series of subsections that correspond to individual months. This chronological progression gives the impression of a diary that describes the events of the period in a simple, direct manner. Although the term "neorealist" has been much abused in both film and literary criticism, it does seem applicable here. Pansa is attempting to create the impression that what we are reading is unembellished reality. This impression is strengthened by the language and style of the work: short sentences, uncomplicated almost journalistic syntax (several sentences begin with the relative pronoun "che"), lots of dialogue, a smattering of Piedmontese dialect, and a restricted lexical palette.[51] In many ways, the language is not that of Fenoglio's *Il partigiano Johnny*, but of the short stories *I ventitré giorni della città di Alba*.

During the course of the novel, the child protagonist functions as a witness and as a focal point around which the narrative is organized. The obvious comparison is with Pin of Calvino's *Il sentiero dei nidi di ragno*, and it seems certain that Pansa invites his readers to make the connection. However, any similarities between Pin and Giovanni are limited to the absence of a father figure from both children's lives. Giovanni is not a street-wise urchin looking to enter the mysterious world of adulthood but a sensitive bourgeois who simply looks on, with some curiosity, at what goes on around him. The first section (1943) of the book is rather static. Giovanni learns of the arrest of Mussolini and his replacement by Badoglio while at a kind of summer camp, the Jews of the town are rounded up and sent to a concentration camp near Modena, and the mothers of the young men who do not respond to the RSI draft are imprisoned. In addition to the female characters who occupy an important part of the whole novel, we are also introduced to two partisans. One, Nino, joins a communist formation, while another, Galimberti, is a member of a communist formation that sees itself as to the Left of the PCI. It was this character who generated most interest among early reviewers.[52] Galimberti is, of course, a direct reference to Duccio Galimberti, but he is not to be confused with the *azionista*. There are other names as well that are drawn from reality such as Nuto, a reference to Nuto Revelli, and Artom. But in each case, the only similarity is in the name. Galimberti is, in fact, a fictional reconstruction of the real-life partisan Mario Acquaviva, who was executed in mysterious circumstances in July 1945 and who gets a brief mention in Pansa's much earlier "dull, academic study" *Guerra partigiana tra Genova e il Po*.[53] In the novel, Galimberti, who is strongly attracted to Giovanni's mother (the feelings are mutual), is murdered by PCI assassins guided to their target by Nino, whose role in the affair is revealed by the dogged investigations of Nuto, making the latter stages of the book into a kind of *giallo*. The prophesy at the beginning of the novel is thus realized and Giovanna mourns his death to the strains of the song "Ma, l'amore no." Pansa's book is, it is necessary to repeat, a fiction, but the boundaries between history and fiction are, as I have tried to suggest throughout this study, blurred, particularly when it comes to the Italian reading public. The attribution of the murder of a communist partisan to killers sent by the PCI is, to say the least, inflammatory, given that there is no evidence to suggest that any order to kill Acquaviva came from the top levels of the PCI. But this is the interpretation that Pansa proposes, without the documentary evidence that he had decided to eschew, as is made clear when he describes a triumphal journey through the town by Togliatti and Secchia "a guy with a head of scruffy hair, tiny glasses, and teeth which stuck out like a horse's." Giovanni's uncle explains Secchia's place in the party: "he's in charge of organisation" and then adds "Maybe he knows who shot Galimberti."[54] There is still much to be established in the Acquaviva case, but it seems more likely that the killing was the result of a localized feud among the left of Casale. That Secchia had any knowledge or involvement in the affair is most unlikely. Ironically then, Pansa, who would go on to argue that the interpretation of the Resistance has been consistently conditioned by the Left, allows himself to be guided by the equally politically motivated interpretations of the far Left.

The Galimberti *giallo* occupies the final section of the book, by which time the Resistance is over. But it is the pages dedicated to the Resistance period that are probably the most interesting and worthy of comment. On the Fascist side, the main character is a former pharmacist turned sadistic fanatic who rejoices in the unlikely

Latinate name of Evasio Deregibus. He is a monster who has "evaded" humanity, but in depicting him as such Pansa seems to be suggesting that, at the command level, Fascist violence was the product of warped, unhinged, and barely human individuals. Deregibus is plainly not one of the "ordinary" men made famous by Christopher Browning, but an extreme man, capable of inventing cruel and ghoulish types of torture, as evidenced by the instruments discovered after the liberation that are paraded around the streets of the town. Deregibus is, it could be argued, a fictional recreation of Mario Carità whose sadism, as described in postwar trials and newspaper reports, seemed to come from the Hammer House of Horror, rather than from specific historical circumstances. Of course, not all the followers of the RSI are as deranged as Deregibus, and Pansa takes the opportunity to try to give his readers a largely sympathetic picture of the RSI faithful in an episode that takes place in September 1944. A group of RSI soldiers and officials arrive in the town and one of the three officials, dressed in the blackest of black outfits, is identified by Giovanni's terrified grandmother as none other than Deregibus. Another official arrives astride a roaring Guzzi motorbike, and we are informed that he is a factory owner whose predilection for torturing captured partisans can be traced back to a single traumatic event: the gang rape of his wife by a group of partisans. Pansa is, of course, not seeking to excuse the official for his actions, but the story of the defiled wife adds to the picture of an obscure and chaotic moral universe where acts of cruelty were the generalized rule rather than the exception.

Pansa then moves to the rank-and-file soldiers and it is their comparative youth which, à la Mazzantini, is first highlighted. He then moves on to analyze their motives, apparently from the perspective of an external narrator, but at times it is almost as if, in a kind of free indirect discourse, the soldiers are "speaking": "They felt strong. And above all right. Yes, they and not the rebels were in the right. They had chosen not to hide like sick dogs. They had refused to go underground. And everyone convinced them that their choice to join Mussolini's republic was the noblest initiative of their young lives: they had chosen Italy, honor, loyalty, Fascism, against the power of the Allies, the dishonor of 8 September, the betrayal of Badoglio and the King, communism."

The passage is not placed within quotation marks, but expressions like "rebels," "sick dogs," "betrayal" and the emphatic "Yes" hint at a blending of voices between the narrator and the characters. This overlap invests other levels of the text, particularly when characters are endowed with a conveniently high level of prescience, but in this particular case, the technique enables Pansa to suggest that the young men of the RSI were not entirely to be blamed for their actions or beliefs: "Those amongst them who had read books added to the list of good reasons 'Europe' as well. European civilization needed to be saved. From the Russians, from the English, from the American negroes. Certainly, they were not aware of the inhuman evils of the Europe they wanted to defend. And those who survived the defeat would have learnt about them only afterwards. But for now this ignorance of theirs protected them and was sufficient for them."[55]

In the first part of the quotation, ending with "American negroes," the distasteful racism would clearly appear to be the thoughts of the soldiers, as described by Pansa. But in the three sentences that follow, beginning with "Certainly," there is a rather mysterious conflation of voices, arguments, and time frames. The soldiers did not know of the "inhuman evils" that were taking place in the death camps of Eastern Europe. Well, perhaps. But even if this was the case, how can this *post facto* knowledge in any way "protect" and "suffice" *at the time that the war was going on*? In what is a rather specious act of narrative and moral compression, Pansa seeks to absolve the RSI soldiers for "knowing not what they do." But his is the perspective of a man writing in the early 1990s, enjoying the considerable benefit of hindsight.

The RSI soldiers capture a partisan, and he is dragged into the town square to be executed. However, he has been so badly beaten that several soldiers, particularly those in the Decima Mas, protest to their commanders, with one of the youngest saying: "'we joined up to fight, not to be butchers.'"[56] Deregibus silences the protests by firing a round into the air, asks the partisan whether he wants a priest, and orders a sergeant to fire. In this way, the rank-and-file soldiers are partially acquitted, while Deregibus is depicted as the real villain. The attempt to "relativize" the moral responsibilities of this one killing is reinforced by the position in which the episode falls within the overall narrative structure of *Ma l'amore, no*. Prior to the episode, there is a substantial section describing the activities of a partisan band led by a certain Dik-Dik. His is an avowedly apolitical band, whose behavior is characterized by levity, callousness, and a woeful lack of preparation. Dik-Dik's partisans capture a young woman they believe to be a German spy, on the basis of some rather flimsy evidence, and promptly execute her. This leads to severe censure from the local partisan leader, Infuriato, who gives Dik-Dik a sound beating before ordering them to leave the town, which is then fully exposed to the wrath of the Germans. Sure enough, the Germans appear, almost immediately after the RSI soldiers carry out their execution of one partisan, and they execute ten men in the village, including the local priest. It is, of course, the Germans who carry out the brutal executions of these innocent people, but the partisans are shown to have had their role in the whole affair. *Ma l'amore no* thus deliberately creates three moral tiers, with the Germans clearly on the lowest tier, but with the partisans and the soldiers of the RSI occupying an ambiguous space somewhere between tiers two and three.

Songs

From the early 1990s onward, a number of Italian bands started to add Resistance songs to their repertoires. In most cases these were traditional songs given a contemporary twist, but there were examples of new songs as well. What this meant was that Resistance songs became a significant part of the youth culture of the 1990s. Of course, Resistance songs had been sung by young people before: at demonstrations as well as on school trips where "Bella ciao" was a standard feature, sung apparently by children all over Italy, regardless of political beliefs. But these songs acquired much greater credibility and more of a sense of a subversive charge when they were performed by Italian alternative bands. Of these, the group that would become most associated with this development were the "Modena City Ramblers." The Ramblers, as they are known, owed much of their style to traditional

Irish music and made a point of referring to Shane McGowan and the Pogues as well as the Waterboys in the sleeve notes to their first album *Riportando tutto a casa*. This 1994 CD contains a number of arrangements of Irish songs translated either into Italian or into Modenese dialect as well as a vigorous, and apparently drunken, version of the Boomtown Rats "The Great Song of Indifference," in which the line "I don't care at all" is rendered with the highly memorable "A m'in ceva un caz." The album also contained traditional Italian protest songs such as Paolo Pietrangeli's "Contessa," a homage to Berlinguer, as well as "Bella ciao." The Ramblers version of the song was the opposite of some of the dirge-like interpretations that had become widespread. Instead, their "Bella ciao" is fast and loud and clearly suggests that there was something akin to a new Resistance energy in the air.

In 1995, the Ramblers, as well as a host of other bands, participated in a free concert at Correggio on April 25, called "Materiale Resistente." The audience, largely made up of teenagers and Italians in their early twenties, drank beer and listened to 18 cover versions of Resistance songs, unconcerned by the dreadful weather that so frequently seems to arrive on April 25. At one point, Germano Nicolini, by then entirely cleared of any associations with the death of Don Pessina, took to the stage to the strains of "Bella ciao," wiped away a few tears and delivered a speech. Addressing the crowd, he thanked them for their "youthful enthusiasm" that took him back 50 years and that he felt was addressed to all the partisans of Italy. He was not an "expert in modern music" nor an "exegete" and so unable to understand it in all its profundity. When the shout went up of "Go on, sing us a song" he declined the offer, but recalled that he had sung throughout his 10 years of imprisonment at the Regina Coeli and the prisons of San Gimignano, Ancona, and Porto Longone in order to remind himself of the seventy thousand fallen partisans: "while I still had the gift of life and I'm here now speaking to you." He ended with a call for the fulfillment of Italian democracy. The crowd loved it. The Ramblers loved Germano Nicolini, and they wrote a song about him, in Modenese dialect, which was released the following year in their second album, *La grande famiglia*.

The concert also led to the production of a CD, a book, and a documentary film made by Guido Chiesa and Davide Ferrario. The documentary has at its core the various songs performed at the concert, but the music is interspersed with interviews of partisans and young people, and contains further material filmed in Turin and Rome. From the localized context of Correggio, the documentary thus extends to cover a wider geographical context. With the aid of some careful editing, the documentary thus continually juxtaposes and mixes the songs with the ideas and attitudes of the different generations. The "Materiale Resistente" concert, and the texts it generated, was an interesting moment in the history of Resistance culture. For the first time since the "boys in striped shirts" in the summer of 1960, there was a genuine feeling that the gap between the Resistance and a particular generation had been bridged.

The Resistance in the Years of the "Second Republic"

The fiftieth anniversary of the Resistance did not bring to an end the debate over the Resistance. On the contrary, in the years between 1995 and the present day, there have been many developments of great significance. These include the *ragazzi di Salò* episode, a landmark event if ever there was one, and the intense polemic provoked by the publications of Giampaolo Pansa. These have also been years characterized by great advances in historical studies. A number of important films have also been produced, although literary texts have been less prominent.[1] The Resistance debate continues and some Italians do still take to the streets on April 25 (see Figure 8.1).

Figure 8.1. Now and Forever Resistance. No to War, No to Violence. Milan 25 April 1999.

The *Ragazzi di Salò*

As we have seen, President Scalfaro's heartfelt appeal on April 25, 1995, to recognize the patriotic nature of the adherents of the RSI fell on deaf ears. For the
orphans of Salò to be welcomed into the democratic fold, it was clear that something more explicit was called for. This was not long in coming and took the form
of what has been called the *ragazzi di Salò* speech, made by Luciano Violante, in
1996. Violante was a senior member of the PDS, a distinguished jurist and expert
on organized crime and also, it is worth adding, a scholar of the Resistance. This
was not, then, a former Christian Democrat, or a member of Forza Italia!, but a
man who had for years been an important figure within the PCI, the party most
strongly associated with the Resistance tradition. But that party had changed identity in 1991, and for it to continue going forward, further changes were considered
to be necessary. On May 10, 1996, Violante made his inaugural speech in his capacity as President of the Chamber of Deputies (the equivalent of the UK speaker).
Led in by Ignazio La Russa, the acting President of the Chamber, Violante began
his speech by expressing his emotion and surprise at his election to this important
post. The speech contained little but the usual platitudes until he came to discuss
the question of national identity. Unlike other European countries, Violante suggested, Italy did not have "national values which are shared by all." The two signal
events in the history of the unified nation, the Risorgimento in the nineteenth
century and the Resistance in the twentieth, only affected a part of the country
and "a part of the political forces." In terms of the Risorgimento, Violante argued,
a combination of factors, involving both victors and defeated, had held back the
"innovative and national aspect" of the events themselves, creating a "false image"
(*immagine oleografica*), bereft of the values that had originally inspired it. The
Resistance ran the same risk as the Risorgimento and, furthermore, it had not
yet entered the collective memory of the Italian republic. Apostrophizing his colleagues, Violante asked "in all humility" what could be done to extend the values of
the Resistance to the nation as a whole so that Italy could exit positively from what
he termed, in a significant phrase, "the lacerations of the past." For this to happen,
he asked whether the Italy of 1996 should not start to reflect on the "defeated of
the past": "Not because they were right or because it is necessary to espouse, for
reasons of convenience which are not clear, a sort of unacceptable *parificazione*,
but because we have to try to understand, without false revisionisms, the reasons
why thousands of young men, and above all young women, when all was lost,
decided to fight for Salò and not for the side of rights and liberties [applause]. This
effort, half a century on, would help to understand the complexity of our country,
to make the Liberation a value of all Italians."[2]

The speech was certainly thought-provoking and, no doubt, well intentioned.
Violante was, and still is, a dignified politician and a man of deeply held convictions.
In the mid-1990s, Italy was suffering from lacerations, both past and present, and the
issue, not just of national identity, but of the nation as a whole, was extraordinarily
pressing. But Violante would have been acutely aware that his speech could well provoke strong reactions, particularly as he did not invite the *ragazzi di Salò* themselves
to reflect on their motives. This was a one-way gesture. To be sure, his language was

carefully chosen and designed to avoid, as far as possible, suggestions that he was in any way diminishing the significance of the Resistance movement and, as a consequence, valorizing the RSI. Nevertheless, this was precisely and not unexpectedly the reaction to the speech from some of those forces who strongly identified with the Resistance and with anti-Fascism generally. Rossana Rossanda, one of the founders of the dissident left-wing *Il Manifesto* newspaper, spoke for many when she referred to "Violante's distracted generation." But Rossanda did not offer any alternative. If the older generations to which she belonged were not "distracted," then it was surely up to them to recognize the fact that the values of the Resistance were not universally shared and do something about it. The political Right was, of course, in ecstasy following the speech, and felt that their day had finally come. In a transmission of *Porta a porta*, the RAI's flagship current affairs program, Mirko Tremaglia, a former *ragazzo di Salò* and leading member of AN, explained to the journalist Bruno Vespa that he and others who had joined the RSI had done so to "leave behind the twenty years of Fascism created by the party leaders and so construct socialization."[3] In other words, Tremaglia tried to suggest that the RSI was a fundamentally different concept ideologically, a break from the Fascism of the regime, and a return to the apparently "pure" early Fascism of 1919–1920. At a time of considerable political change, when the AN was trying to create a different image of the party, the *ragazzi di Salò* speech therefore offered it the opportunity to relaunch its history as a party that had inherited a forward-thinking social project. It is doubtful that such historically dubious reevaluations were part of Violante's original intentions, but by then he had set the ball rolling and was unable to stop it. By offering the neo-Fascists this democratic ticket, Violante also committed the strategic error of failing to ask for anything in return. But even if he had asked the *ragazzi di Salò* to make some kind of matching concessions there was, as Ellwood has commented, no "sign that the intended beneficiaries" of the speech "were grateful, or inclined to show the slightest reciprocal benevolence to the pro-Soviet past of the Italian Communists."[4]

It was, of course, appropriate that historians, too, participated in the debate. Giuseppe Vacca, the President of the Gramsci Institute, which houses the former communist party's extensive archives, located Violante's speech in the contemporary discussions on the potential dissolution of the country, which had been sparked by the political and electoral advances of the avowedly secessionist Northern Leagues, some of whose supporters would only a year later drive an armored car around Piazza San Marco in Venice and occupy the bell tower.[5] For Vacca, the use of political categories from 50 years earlier suggested to him that the battle had, in many ways, already been lost. This was an acute observation, clearly implying that the motives for the exhumation of the "pacification" debate were more contingent than anything else. Vacca also suggested that Violante saw the Leagues as representing a greater peril to the nation than the post-Fascist AN. By the mid-1990s, therefore, the emergence of new political forces was leading to a questioning of the paradigms (in Vacca's words "Fascism/anti-Fascism" and "communism/anticommunism") on which Italian political language, and Italian political life, was based. Vacca clearly implied that Violante's speech was just as much about finding a space for the "new" Left as it was for the "new" Right. This is an important point—the threat to the unity of the nation represented by the Leagues was, in the mid-1990s, a disquieting and most unwelcome development for a political class who were quite aware of the "Southern Question," but who had never considered the possibility of a federal Italy. Violante's speech is, therefore, at least in part, a reflection of the disorientation created by the emergence of Bossi and his movement. Enzo Collotti, one of Italy's most respected historians and a recognized authority on Nazi Germany, took a different line, and he began his comment on the speech by affirming that the topic of the motives of the *ragazzi di Salò* was not entirely foreign ground to historians (the landmark Brescia conference of 1985, at which Violante gave a paper, is a case in point). Collotti would not, it is worth adding, be the last historian to argue that a topic latched onto by politicians and the press had already received extended scholarly attention elsewhere. The problem was, however, that few people could be bothered to read the works concerned or simply ignored them—why this is so is not, unfortunately, an issue that many Italian historians have been prepared to address. Collotti, furthermore, was worried by the fact that a politician was making an "exploitative use" of the theme, "maybe out of the contingent necessity of an '*embrassons-nous*' with the other side." This largely echoed the point made by Vacca, but Collotti also went on to warn that Violante risked being "exploited himself," his "offering" ran the risk of slipping from his grasp and going "beyond his original intentions." On the other hand, Giorgio Rochat, a military historian and president of the national network of Resistance research institutes, congratulated Violante for publicly questioning the "official position" that the Resistance had involved the whole nation fighting together as one against the Germans. The Resistance had been a movement of a "great minority," he stated, and it had remained a minority value. Moreover, the Italy that the partisans had fought for had manifestly not been achieved. This was, in actual fact, a remarkably frank admission by Rochat and went much further than what Violante's speech had actually stated, indicating a willingness on Rochat's part to engage with the discussions and attempt to take them forward.[6]

Quite apart from what the likes of Vacca, Collotti, Rochat, and Nicola Tranfaglia stated to the *La Repubblica* journalist who summarized their views, the very fact that historians were called upon to pronounce in the pages of one of Italy's leading daily newspapers is itself worthy of comment. Ever since Jurgen Habermas published his famous essay "Concerning the Public Use of History" in 1988, Italian historians have been aware of what they call "the public use of history" (*l'uso pubblico della storia*) in which, as Pezzino has written "a historiographical discourse is construed to further the purposes of other orders of discourse (institutional, ideological, or party political)."[7] But the problem has been that, despite this awareness, they have sometimes struggled to contribute as effectively to "public" discussion and to the shaping of "public memory" as they would have hoped.[8] This is not necessarily for want of trying. *Combat Film*, discussed in the previous chapter, saw Claudio Pavone effectively involved in studio discussion, but in many ways the increasing "spectacularization" of history has proved a difficult challenge. Partly, this is because there is a feeling among historians that the public use of history is something that is inherently bad, involving media manipulation and an unprofessional and superficial approach to serious subjects. In the opening comments of his important essay, Santomassimo observes that "public memory is distinct from historiography. Historians only occasionally act in this arena, unlike political and institutional actors, the press and the mass media."[9] This may be so, but if in Italy serious history were to be made more accessible, more "public," things could change for the better. There are alternatives to the five hundred–page monograph, although with Berlusconi's control over television so pervasive it is difficult to envisage the kind of historical documentaries that have become a characteristic of British television in the last decade. The extent to which Italian historians have struggled to cope in a fast-moving and sometimes bewildering environment is graphically demonstrated by the Pansa affair.

The Pansa Affair and Historical Debate

If one name is associated with the recent discussions, or more precisely polemics, over the Resistance movement and the "public use of history," it is that of Giampaolo Pansa. His 1994 novel (see previous chapter) became the first volume of a trilogy published over a three-year period, of which the second and third volumes were *Siamo stati così felici* and *I nostri giorni proibiti*.[10] In these two books, Pansa moved into the postwar period, the polarized ideological climate of the 1948 elections (*Siamo stati così felici*), and the turmoil and disorientation in the Italy of 1956 (*I nostri giorni proibiti*). A common element to all three books was a tortured love story—in the case of the last book of the trilogy, this concerned the relationship between the son of a partisan and the daughter of a woman executed by partisans for being a Fascist spy. This last element was "based on a true story" from the late 1950s—the sensational case of Alfa Giubelli, who killed the partisan leader who had ordered the execution of her mother during the war.[11] The volumes were clearly fictional and presented to readers as such. While all of the books contained material that had the potential to provoke strong reactions, it is striking that the critical and popular reaction to them was anything but hostile. They were discreet successes for Pansa and one of them won a prestigious literary prize, the Premio Bancarella, beating off stiff competition from Luis Sepulveda.

Pansa offered some very revealing insights into his thinking toward the end of the millennium in a long interview with historian Roberto Botta, published in the 1998 reprint of his detailed and very scholarly study of the Resistance in Alessandria. Asked about his judgment on the recent historiography of the Resistance in the region, read by Pansa at the Resistance Institute in Alessandria, he replied positively, but expressed some rancor over the fact that his novels had not merited "a line of comment from qualified historians." Indeed, when he thought of "certain highly illustrious Professors," he confessed to smiling. He then suggested that Botta and his colleagues should write more provocative material, even at the risk of getting bad reviews. He counseled against spending much time over the partisan veterans (whose history Botta felt needed to be written) and suggested that the writing of history needed to be done by the young of different generations. As for subject matter, they would do well to "look into events and people who are not well known . . . even going beyond 1945."[12] By this, Pansa meant that the issue of killings that took place after the end of the war needed to be investigated. From this, and other comments made, above all in the final section of the interview, there is a clear sense that the person who was preparing to be more provocative was, in reality, Pansa himself.

Pansa continued to publish works of fiction until, in 2002, he adopted a different approach, in which, at least ostensibly, the balance between literature and history was altered. In *I figli dell'aquila*, Pansa created a fictional interlocutor, Alba, who tells the author the "real story" of the *ragazzi di Salò*, as personified by the central character and great love of her life, Bruno.[13] Of course, the dialogue between Alba and Pansa is fictional, and the knowledge that Alba has is really Pansa's, but this expedient enables the author to create a vehicle for a narrative that has all the appearances of historical authenticity. Indeed Pansa's *escamotage* was so successful that the book won a prize, the "Acqui storia," for a work of history, along with Walter Russell Mead's influential study of American foreign policy, *Special Providence*. In an interview with Pansa, the journalist Simonetta Fiori has neatly described the hybrid nature of the book: "fiction and history are mixed into a form of drama, which is not just an essay nor just a story, but both things at once." Fiori also commented that this operation, which very effectively moved the reader to sympathize with "those young people ready for a beautiful death to save the Nation's offended honor" also involved an element of risk. But it was a risk Pansa was happy to take: "They will call me a revisionist," he replied, but in one way or another he had always been a revisionist.[14] Nevertheless, despite the risks of writing a work that fits squarely in the context of discussions initiated by Violante, it still didn't really create much of a reaction. Pansa, no doubt, wondered what he had to do to really stir things up.

His next work, *Il sangue dei vinti* (the blood of the defeated), certainly did lead to a reaction that still reverberates today—a film version of the book, starring the popular actor Michele Placido, first met with a mixed critical reaction at the Rome film festival, and then from cinema audiences before it hit television screens in autumn 2009.[15] And in 2008, the historian Massimo Storchi published a book, a kind of counterattack to Pansa, titled *Il sangue dei vincitori* (the blood of the victors) that analyses, in extraordinarily graphic terms, the extent of RSI violence in Emilia Romagna during the period of the civil war.[16] The Resistance battle is clearly far from over, even as I write. Published in 2003, less than a year after *I figli dell'aquila*, *Il sangue dei vinti* uses the same technical formula but shifts attention to the postwar fate of the Fascists who had fought for and supported the RSI. Alba is substituted by Livia Bianchi, a younger and physically attractive character (Pansa rather disturbingly lingers over several details), who is a librarian at one of Italy's most revered repositories of knowledge, the National Library of Florence. The author and his interlocutor meet when he is not allowed to borrow a book on the postwar killings of Fascists first published in 1949. The librarian offers him a coffee, promises to photocopy the entire work for him (an unlikely scenario given the library's strict application of copyright regulations) and the rest, as Pansa would like his readers to believe, is history. From within the walls of her flat near Piazza della Signoria, Livia Bianchi and Pansa embark on a virtual journey and dialogue which, it is claimed in a message to the reader at the beginning of the book, will contribute to the unlocking of a door "barred for nearly 60 years" by anti-Fascist historiography.[17] The journey starts with three individual cases of Fascist deaths, the suicide of Giovanni Preziosi, and the executions of Carlo Borsani and Roberto Farinacci, all of whom represent different "degrees" of Fascism: the racist Preziosi, the one-eyed "dove" of Salò, Borsani, and the *ras* of Cremona, Farinacci. This last is shot in the back and dies with the words "Long Live Italy" on his lips. Different types of Fascist then, but they all met the same fate at the end of the war. From there we move to executions in Milan, Bergamo, the Valtellina, Vercelli, Novara, and Biella. This is just part one and corresponds to the first day of conversation between Pansa and Livia. On the second day, the story begins in Turin, followed by Cuneo, Imperia, Savona, and Genoa. At this point, they take a decision to hire a car and set out on a "real" journey that takes them to the Veneto, where they visit Oderzo, Schio and other locations, then south to Ravenna, across to Bologna, Modena, and Reggio Emilia, the city where the killings continued into 1946. The journey ends back in Florence with a discussion of the total number killed and, then, a twist in the tail. In an epilogue, Livia reveals during dinner that she is the daughter of one of the members of the *Volante Rossa* (Red Flying Squad), an organization of expartisans that continued to kill Fascists in Milan for several years after the end of the war.[18] The two part, Livia to her flat, Pansa to his hotel, but there is an element of sexual *frisson* in the taxi. Maybe they will see each other again, once he has finished the book that he, and we the readers, have now completed.

Il sangue dei vinti has the outward appearance of a study of postwar violence, but it is more of an atlas than a work of analysis, more geography than history. It also makes for easy reading. Pansa can tell a story with some panache, and the formula of the travelogue, combined with the sexual tension between the two interlocutors, as well as the complete absence of footnotes (although, in fairness to Pansa, many works are referred to in the narrative) is extraordinarily beguiling. To the horror of former partisans and the disgust of many academic historians, the book became a publishing phenomenon. It shot to first place in the best-seller list, displacing the fictional diary of a Sicilian adolescent, *Cento colpi di spazzola prima di andare a dormire* by Melissa P., and causing novels by Andrea Camilleri and Isabel Allende to slip down the table. By the end of October, the vicissitudes of the teenager from Catania made a return to the top, but *Il sangue dei vinti* would remain in the top 10 for some time, alongside other books such as *Harry Potter and the Order of the Phoenix* and the *Da Vinci Code*.

In some ways, Pansa needs to be congratulated for pulling off one of the biggest coups in the history of publishing in Italy. No book on the subject of the Resistance has ever sold as many copies nor, I suspect, will such a thing ever happen again. Having experimented with various formulae, Pansa had finally struck gold. *Il sangue dei vinti* is a deliberately, willfully, provocative work, designed to create apoplexy in some of his readers, and delight among the majority who finally got what they were apparently waiting for: the truth about the postwar killings, the reality of the horrors of the civil war, and a resounding kick in the teeth for the communist party. It didn't matter that the "anti-Fascist historians" he condemned (many of whom he refers to explicitly in the text) had already published many scholarly volumes on the postwar killings. It didn't matter that the whole issue of the postwar killings had already received a very public airing in the early 1990s and that the trials of expartisans throughout the 1940s and 1950s had for a long time kept the issue on the agenda. It didn't matter that Pansa quoted indiscriminately from Fascist sources (particularly Giorgio Pisanò), ignored some of the basic rules about the critical use of secondary materials, employed provocative chapter titles ("The Slaughter House of Milan," "Three Families for Killing," "The Gulag of Genoa," "Line Them Up Against the Wall," "A Prison Lynching"), framed his descriptions in deliberately loaded language, and took Livia's name from that of the partisan Dante Livio Bianco, who survived 20 months as a partisan commander only to be killed in a climbing accident in the 1950s. It didn't matter because when the book came out, Pansa's many readers, who were certainly not limited to neo-Fascists, did not, apparently, have the critical skills, knowledge, or desire, to realize the nature of the scam.

Il sangue dei vinti was not a one-off. Indeed, as Foot has tellingly observed, the "hostility to Pansa's work allowed him to claim that the left had tried to (and was still trying to) suppress knowledge about the *resa dei conti*, and this allegation in itself formed the basis for a long series of other books."[19] Pansa followed it up with *Sconosciuto 1945*, which adds more killings to the catalogue, then *La grande bugia*.[20] The latter book, which also topped the best-seller list, investigates the way that the Left have, it is claimed, dominated Italian historiography since the end of the war, creating a politically determined interpretation of the movement, a "big lie," which it is Pansa's avowed mission to expose. Pansa chose to present his book to the public in many venues throughout Italy including the Astoria Hotel in Reggio Emilia, but was interrupted by a young man with a shaven head, swiftly followed by a group of protestors from the "social centers" (*centri sociali*) of Rome and Reggio Emilia. Banners were unfurled and "Bella ciao" was sung. Scuffles broke out and even expartisans declared that they wanted to hear what Pansa had to say. The author, no doubt relishing the publicity that the episode would generate, refused to leave the hall, declaring that he was there to meet his readers from Reggio, and that he would not allow himself to be intimidated by a "group of intolerant individuals." The young men shouted "Long Live the Cervi Brothers," the seven Resistance martyrs executed at Reggio in 1943, and "Long Live Giorgio Bocca," the very much alive *L'Espresso* journalist and, apparently, one of the last bastions against the type of revisionism (a loaded term to which I will return) of which Pansa was the living embodiment.[21] The following day, senior politicians, including the president of the Republic, expressed their solidarity with Pansa who carried on undaunted. In the follow-up to *La grande bugia*, Pansa identified left-wing historians as *I gendarmi della memoria*, the gate-keepers who have for decades refused to let people in to see the truth.[22] In his next book, he returned to the novel form. *I tre inverni della paura* is a kind of Italian *Gone With the Wind*, mapping the effects of the civil war and in Emilia. Leaving aside the content, even the cover image that shows partisans walking up a hill is an act of provocation—it is none other than a pastiche of the logo of the Resistance Institute at Reggio Emilia.[23] At the end of 2010, Pansa returned to the formula of *Il sangue dei vinti* in his *I vinti non dimenticano* (The defeated do not forget), in which Livia makes a return, phoning Pansa to tell him there are still lots of gaps to fill in their map of violence. These gaps provide Pansa with in excess of four hundred pages of material, including one chapter dedicated to the topic of "antifascist rape." The book concludes, it is not clear why, with a dire warning that in the Italy of today "the blood may flow again."[24] This is not, I suspect, the last word from Pansa on these issues.

How do we explain the Pansa phenomenon? Storchi, the former director of the Resistance Institute at Reggio Emilia, rightly points out that Pansa, as a journalist, has a privileged access to the media that ordinary historians do not have. It is, in his words, "an unfair fight."[25] There is also, as I have suggested earlier, a problem with a readership which, in Luzzatto's words, "does not know how to distinguish between those who have scholarly credentials and those who don't, and for whom the act of purchasing a book is nothing more than a piece of extended channel-hopping with the remote control."[26] But there is more, and Italian historians, as well as the Italian publishing industry, need to accept some level of blame for having created a situation whereby the general readership feels greater confidence in the work of a talented journalist with an eye for publicity than a historian. Foot goes so far as to blame "forty years of public silence" for creating a "mass need for information and accounts of the *resa dei conti*."[27] The problem, as Foot also suggests, was not that the information was hidden, but it was not available in a format that was particularly user-friendly. Foot here refers to left-wing historians, but his comments can also be applied to historians of the political right. In 1990, Antonio Serena published a book that made the same claims to originality as Pansa did over a decade later.[28] Titled *I giorni di Caino* (the days of Cain) the work's subtitle was "the drama of the defeated in the crimes ignored by official history." The book's chapter titles are quite similar to Pansa's, and there are lots of photographs. But Serena uses lengthy quotations from trials and writes in a dense style. Serena's book no doubt had its fans, but Pansa has a way of telling a story that has made him the Dan Brown of Italian history.

Pansa's books are only the most popular example of a type frequently termed "revisionist"—a slippery term at the best of times. The situation is further complicated in that Pansa, and before him the academic (and very controversial) historian Renzo De Felice, profess to enjoying being referred to in this way. One of Pansa's recent books is, indeed, titled *Il revisionista*, and features a cover photo of its author putting his thumb to his nose and spreading out his fingers in a gesture, which in English is termed "cocking a snook," and in Italian *far marameo*.[29] It is, of course, tempting to ignore such posturing. As Bruno Bongiovanni, in an article that traces the history of the term from its first use in English, has commented, "Let's leave 'revisionism' to those who define themselves as 'revisionists.'"[30] But revisionism needs to be reckoned with and understood—Pansa is by no means a lone fanatic and his books are just the most commercially successful examples of a very significant trend that is now part of mainstream publishing. Pansa's books can be bought in bookshops, supermarkets, and airports. Gone are the days when the works of Pisanò (one of Pansa's preferred sources) circulated in an almost clandestine fashion, available by mail order from neo-Fascist bookshops in Rome and delivered to their purchasers in plain cover to anonymous post office boxes.

Pansa, as I have said, was far from alone and by no means the first. In 2000, Roberto Vivarelli, a historian of Fascism, a world authority on the anti-Fascist writer Gaetano Salvemini, a senior figure in the Florentine Resistance Institute, and the holder of one of Italy's most prestigious professorships of history, had created a huge stir when he published his memoir of his own experiences as a very young adherent to the RSI.[31] No one, it seemed, expected this, and the fact that Vivarelli also sought to justify the RSI only turned the knife in the wound. What also raised eyebrows in certain circles was the fact that the book was published by Il Mulino, a highly respected academic press based in Bologna. The publisher declared that it did not share Vivarelli's views. But more was to come from Il Mulino in the shape of a veritable "Bible of revisionism", in the words of the ever-perceptive Simonetta Fiori.[32] The work in question is the collective volume *Miti e storia dell'Italia unita*, which takes a dictionary style approach to what the editors call the mythography of the Italian republic.[33] In their list of "myths" are topics such as the *doppio stato* (the duplicity of the Italian state), as well as the "betrayal of the Resistance" and the "failure to enact the Constitution." These myths were, it is argued, largely the inventions of communist historians, with a big contribution also coming from the "actionist" tradition. The authors were not aware, or simply did not care, that the question of the betrayed Resistance was principally part of the debate *between* Actionists and Communists—with discussion focusing on the *svolta di Salerno* and Togliatti's "betrayal" of the political dimension of the movement. Throughout the history of the republic, the Christian Democrats were, it is argued, unable or unwilling to organize an alternative to the anti-Fascist paradigm, leaving the left the space available in which to establish a historiographical hegemony. Belardelli and his colleagues thus ignored, or simply were not aware of, the significant number of publications on the Catholic dimension of the Resistance that I have discussed in earlier chapters. And a string of more recent publications has added to what is now a very rich tradition.[34] They have, therefore, fallen victims of what Santomassimo has termed the "old phobia of the communist hegemony over the Resistance."[35] Leaving aside the "selective blindness" of these authors, the approach taken to the question of myth unconsciously highlights one of the wider problems of the enterprise, and that is an insufficiently nuanced articulation of the idea of myth or myths and their role in writing histories and constructing identities, which the editors wish to replace with something they believe to be the "truth." By myth, the editors appear to be implying a lie (like Pansa's "great lie"), rather than a narrative that allowed people to understand, make sense of, and organize their approach to the past within the framework of a search for a collective identity. But if we approach myth from this perspective, we can ask a number of questions that are, arguably, not just more interesting, but also more productive. Why and how did these myths form? Who organized them and how? When and why did they decline? For what reasons? These are not questions addressed in *Miti e storia dell'Italia unita*, and as a result, the volume is little more than a collection of connected rudimentary diatribes, redolent of the newspaper opinion pieces in which many of the ideas had been previously formulated.

Along very similar lines to *Miti e storia dell'Italia unita* is Sandro Fontana's *La grande menzogna*, published in 2001 by Marsilio of Venice, another big name in the Italian publishing industry, which attempts to expose the apparently mendacious historical strategies employed by the PCI and its successor party the PDS to gain political power (as it did in 1996).[36] In his preface, Fontana set the tone by saying that Italy was "perhaps the only case in the whole world" where the narration of history had been "bestowed" on a party that had lost the 1946, and every subsequent, general election (until 1996). Fontana, a professor of history at the University of Brescia, seemed unaware of the myriad contributions to the historiography of the Resistance made by anyone else other than communists. The "entirely Italian anomaly" described by Fontana is itself a myth—part of the process of discrediting the PDS and its more important ancestor, Togliatti's PCI.[37] The chapter on the Resistance is titled "The lie of the 'betrayed Resistance'" and advances the novel thesis that, in an act of "colossal censorship" and for reasons of political expediency, the PCI suppressed the memory of the peasant contribution to the Resistance.[38] Intriguingly, a much earlier "revisionist" book published by Romolo Gobbi, originally titled *Il mito della Resistenza*, but repackaged as *Una revisione della Resistenza* in 1999, also dedicates a lot of space to the peasants, arguing that the PCI had grossly *inflated* their contribution for reasons of political expediency.[39] Two different "revisionist" authors, therefore, argued that the PCI had abused the peasants, either by exaggerating their role or by diminishing it. The contradiction (largely attributable to Fontana's decision not to engage with the vast historiography on the peasant question) demonstrates one of the many complexities, if not frustrations, of the debate: there are, in too many cases, myths about myths as well as countermyths. And there are, what is worse, too many people who write about subjects they have insufficiently researched.

Fontana returned to the issue of the Left's perversion of the reality of the Resistance in a preface to Ugo Finetti's *La Resistenza cancellata*.[40] The book's cover provides a graphic illustration of the central thesis: a very famous photograph of Resistance leaders parading through the streets of Milan is cropped to highlight three key figures, the communist Luigi Longo, the independent Alfredo Pizzoni, and the Christian Democrat Enrico Mattei.[41] These last two figures are obliterated by red crosses while Longo looks on insouciantly. But it is not only Pizzoni and Mattei who the communists erased but also, as the book argues, the contributions of the orthodox Italian military forces, the massacre of Italian soldiers at Cefalonia, and much else besides. In this case we move to another key area of "revisionist" historiography: the claim that the historiographical tradition has suffered from selective blindness, discussing issues that were conducive and ignoring others that were problematic. Are the revisionist historians correct in their exposure of such selectivity, or is this just part of a rhetorical strategy that itself selectively ignores what has been discussed by historians? I have tried to address a number of these claims throughout this book and hope to have dispelled some of these myths about myths. As we have already seen, Pizzoni and Taviani were on the platform in Milan on April 25, 1955—if anything it was Longo who had been "cancelled." The much reviled Battaglia, for example, devotes ample space to these "cancelled" themes. Mattei would no doubt have become a central figure in the Catholic promotion of the Resistance in the 1960s and beyond, had he not been killed in a plane crash that was not, it is hardly necessary to add, a communist plot.

While the term "revisionist" does not necessarily help to understand and clarify the nature of contemporary debate, it is also necessary to use with caution terms such "anti-Fascist" historiography (a favorite of Pansa's), or the "historical vulgate" (*vulgata storica*)—a polemical expression employed by De Felice. Both terms suggest an organized bloc that did not exist in the past and certainly does not exist today, although naturally enough there are many works that in recent years have quite deliberately and consciously taken up positions in defense of the Resistance movement.[42] Giovanni De Luna has highlighted a wider problem. His justly praised history of the PDA, which was republished in 2006, is far from being an example of "the historical vulgate," but nevertheless the book is widely considered to be a "historiographical monument to the PDA." In reality, the book is a highly critical study that pulls no punches in terms of its analyses of the rifts and personality clashes that destroyed the party after the war. This misreading, or counterreading is, as De Luna comments in his new preface, an excellent example of the "split between the stereotypes which knock around in the public use of history and the actual results of academic research."[43] What, then, have the results been of this "academic research"?

The question of the postwar killings has, not surprisingly, received a lot of attention, both before and after Pansa's polemical intervention in 2003. Indeed, the very large number of books he refers to throughout *Il sangue dei vinti*, many written by "anti-Fascist" historians, would seem to pour water on his theory that the doors of history have been slammed shut and only opened by courageous individuals such as himself. Of these, the most important contributions are those by Storchi on Modena and Reggio Emilia and Mirco Dondi's wider-ranging discussion that concentrates on Emilia Romagna but also deals with the North of Italy generally, visiting many of the places Pansa and Livia Bianchi would later arrive at during their would-be path-breaking tryst in 2003. Storchi and Dondi have also turned their attention to episodes of conflict *between* partisans in works that have done a great deal to question the notion of the over-arching unity of the Resistance movement.[44]

In terms of general histories of the Resistance there has only been one really significant work, Santo Peli's synthesis first published by Einaudi in 2004.[45] The first part of the work is a critical analysis of the political and military aspects of the Resistance that also traces the complex history of the relationships between the various forces involved. In the second part, Peli examines a series of key issues that have attracted attention over the years including the idea of civil Resistance (and linked to this the question of women), the postwar killings and the 600,000 Italian soldiers who suffered internment in military camps when Italy pulled out of the Axis agreement in September 1943.[46] The two halves of the book complement each other but in an attempt to make Peli's work more widely accessible the first, more narrative, part has also subsequently been published separately.[47] In addition to Peli's texts, two reference-style works have been published, the multiauthored and two-volume Einaudi *Dizionario della Resistenza italiana* and an historical atlas of the Resistance, published by Bruno Mondadori.[48] The idea for the latter volume was first advanced as long ago as the late 1960s, but it was only in the early 1990s that the project, edited by Luca Baldissara, a historian with geographical and cartographical expertise, really got off the ground.

Since 1994, when a landmark conference was held in Arezzo on the Nazi massacres during World War II, a very impressive body of research has built up on the issue of the *stragi*.[49] The topic assumed even greater urgency when files relating to a never realized "Italian Nuremberg" were discovered in a "cupboard of shame" in a ministry in Rome. The scandal led to television denials by Giulio Andreotti, a parliamentary enquiry, and an extensive report was presented to the Chamber of Deputies on February 8, 2006.[50] The list of works published on the *stragi* before and after the parliamentary enquiry is long and has perhaps reached its culmination in *Il massacro*, jointly authored by Paolo Pezzino and Luca Baldissara. The massacre they study in the book, "the most important and consistent massacre of civilians in the Western theatre of operations during the Second World War," is commonly believed to have taken place at Marzabotto, whereas as the authors maintain from the very start, the actual location was Monte Sole.[51] For reasons connected to the processes of memory, the location crystallized into one single village, rather than a series spread out over quite a wide area. What this book and others demonstrate is that the mechanics of the Nazi massacres of civilians and partisans, particularly harsh during the summer of 1944, were complex and not, as was widely believed, simply related to reprisals for partisan attacks. Instead, it is argued that in Italy a model of occupation was employed that owed its ferocity to practices developed in Eastern Europe. Not then simply ad hoc responses to partisan activities, but a series of "eliminationist" massacres carried out according to a coherent plan.

One of the most innovative and challenging results of the early works dedicated to this theme was Giovanni Contini's study of the massacre, and the memory of the massacre, at Civitella in the Valdichiana.[52] Using oral testimonies as his main source, Contini brilliantly laid bare the complex processes that had led to a "divided memory" of the massacre, with many of the citizens of Civitella attributing more blame to the partisans operating in the area than to the German soldiers who carried out the killings. A very similar study of the mass executions at the Fosse Ardeatine in Rome, also using oral testimonies, has been published by one of Italy's best known oral historians, Alessandro Portelli.[53] Portelli's book demonstrates, among other things, how the idea that the partisans who carried out the killings that sparked the massacre could have prevented it by turning themselves in had no basis in fact, but belonged to the memory of the event. But it was a persistent memory and one that the extreme right continues to exploit, as graffiti spotted in the streets of Rome shows (see Figure 8.2).

Figure 8.2.   Partisan Cowards. Rome (2001).

The research on the massacres, as well as these books on memory, show how innovative approaches can cast new light on important topics. In an era in which revisionism has become part of the mainstream, it is significant, and almost paradoxical, that some of the best ever research on the Resistance has been published. All the Italian public now has to do is read it.

Resistance Cinema

The year 1997 saw the release of *Porzus* directed by Renzo Martinelli, a film that fits squarely within the revisionist tradition described earlier.[54] The title refers to a location in Friuli, near the border with Slovenia, where in February 1945 one of the most notorious events of the Resistance occurred. A group of communist partisans led by Mario Toffanin presented themselves at the winter quarters of another group of partisans known as the "Osoppo," named after a village in Friuli. The *osovani* were ostensibly politically neutral, but nevertheless held views about the future relationship between Friuli and Tito's Yugoslavia that were entirely antithetical to those of the communists, of which Toffanin's outfit was but one of many. In late 1944, the decision of some of the communist partisans to cross the Tagliamento river and ally themselves with Tito's IX Korpus only exacerbated the situation. In addition to the political tensions between the formations, which had surfaced on a number of occasions during the course of the Resistance, there were other factors that further problematized their already vexed relationship. The *osovani* had given shelter to a woman from Udine, who was reputed to be a Fascist spy, and there were suggestions and suspicions that some kind of negotiations had taken place between them and the RSI's Decima Mas, a crack outfit led by the so-called "black prince," the aristocrat Junio Valerio Borghese. That such parleying took place has, however, been consistently denied. Likewise, the status of the woman as a spy has always been contested. Toffanin's partisans made a decision or perhaps received orders from on high (but there is still controversy over this point) to kill the Osoppo leaders and the partisans at Porzus. These included the younger brother of one of Italy's most significant cultural figures, Pierpaolo Pasolini.

As I hope to have made clear, the dynamics of the Porzus killings were enormously complex, and there are still many matters that are unclear. As one might expect, the subject, which led to several trials for both murder and high treason, has always provoked controversy, resurfacing at times of political elections and other moments of crisis. The historical literature on the affair is extensive.[55] Porzus is clearly a topic, then, which required a sensitive and intelligent approach. Unfortunately, Martinelli's film, cowritten with the veteran Furio Scarpelli, lacks both these characteristics and much else besides. The film begins with dramatic and portentous music, involving drums and cello. A screen of text provides some historical context, accompanied by the ghoulish sounds of execution. As Marcia Landy has observed, the film has many of the characteristics of melodrama.[56] A group of young boys then finds bodies in the fresh snow before a flash-forward to 1980, when an old man gets out of a car in a town in Yugoslavia and asks the whereabouts of a Carlo Toffanin. We discover that the old man is none other than a former *osovano*, whose partisan name was "Storno," and who managed to escape the executions despite being wounded. He is a fictional character whose role in the film is that of grand inquisitor and, eventually, executioner of Toffanin, who did exist in reality, but whose first name was Mario, not Carlo, and who as a partisan was called Giacca, and not Geko (as he is in the film). The film moves backward and forward, from present to past and from past to present in a series of flashbacks and flash-forwards. At one point, early on in the film, there is a kind of "imagined flash-forward" when Storno executes Geko in Peckinpahesque slow motion, exploding blood capsules and all. Blood is, indeed, a major presence in the film— the ageing Toffanin suffers from an incurable illness that gives him both a very gravelly voice and a tendency to cough blood into a white handkerchief at regular intervals.

Martinelli was given historical advice by two experts and claimed he had read everything that had ever been written on the affair. Despite this, he opted to invent a scene, which takes place in the first flashback sequence, in which Toffanin's men are shot, by persons unknown, as they attempt to cross the Tagliamento in December 1944. There is, as far as I know, no evidence that Toffanin and his men tried to join the ninth Korpus at this time. Likewise, there is no evidence that a Yugoslavian partisan was part of Toffanin's group and carried out executions with cold brutality, nor that such an individual shot one of his own fellow communists when he protested about the killings. Nor did Toffanin (as he himself stated through his lawyers) ever suggest that the tricolor flag, together with the Savoy insignia, which belonged to the Osoppo, could be burnt because the communists had their own, very different one. The list could be extended to include Martinelli's depiction of the communists as long-haired and unshaven, while the *osovani* have smooth cheeks and choir-boy style hair. But simply pointing out these divergences is not necessarily a productive form of analysis. What is more interesting, I think, is to examine the techniques used in the film and what they reveal in terms of the implicit and explicit ideologies that characterize *Porzus*.

Porzus is characterized by frequent leaps between two time frames that involve the depiction of the past and the judgment of the past from the standpoint of the present. This "judgment" characteristic is underscored by the inquisitorial nature of the scenes in the present, with "Storno" functioning as the means by which the truth emerges. Toffanin's room is thus a courtroom and also, at the end of the film, an execution chamber. Toffanin is on a prosaic level the individual under investigation and the symbolic significance of his internal hemorrhages is clear enough—the blood he shed in the past has now come back to punish him. But it is clear the buck does not stop at Toffanin. Red is also the color of communism, and it is the Italian brand of this particular ideology that is really on trial in the film. And it is perhaps only in film, Martinelli seems to suggest, with its unique capacity to compress time by the use of flashback and flash-forward, which is the ideal vehicle for such a trial.[57] *Porzus* is then not only a film about an enormously controversial episode in Italian Resistance history but also a work that makes an implicit claim for the capacity of film itself to reveal verities buried in the past. It is only with film, Martinelli suggests, that truth will out. Finally, it is worth adding that the film's authenticity was given greater academic credibility when, in the

same year as its release, Sergio Gervasutti published his book *Il giorno nero di Porzus*, which contains an image of three very mean-looking communist partisans,
led by an unshaven Geko, looking directly out at the reader.[58]

The following year saw the release of *I piccoli maestri*, directed by Daniele
Luchetti. Unlike Porzus, *I piccoli maestri* is based on one text, the autobiographical
work by Luigi Meneghello first published in the mid-1960s. Meneghello's book is
not an autobiography, but neither is it a novel (although this is frequently the term
used to define it, and the one that appeared on the front cover when it was first
published).[59] What most clearly characterizes the book throughout is the use of
irony, which is very difficult to transfer to the screen. In the film version, Luchetti
substitutes the irony with comedy (reinforced by the ludic tones of the sound
track) and the end result is, as a consequence, rather flat. The film is faithful to
the novel in terms of narrative sequences, but Meneghello's subtlety is lost. But, of
course, one of the side-effects of a film version of an already existing literary text
is that it sometimes encourages viewers to go out and read the original. In this way
I piccoli maestri, a text which depicts the Resistance with irony, but not contempt,
was proposed to an entirely new generation of readers.

Like *I piccoli maestri*, Guido Chiesa's *Il partigiano Johnny* was also based on
an already existing literary source—the work of the same name written by the
Piedmontese author Beppe Fenoglio and first published posthumously in 1968.[60]
Fenoglio's work, or rather works, as it was made up of a series of different redactions, is widely considered to be one of the greatest achievements of twentieth-
century Italian literature. It is a complex text, written in a language that involves a
mixture of Italian and English lexis and syntax. One of the manuscripts is written
entirely in an English, which at times reads like a bad student translation from
Italian, and this section, known as the *Ur partigiano Johnny*, is only available in
a critical edition produced by a team of scholars and published in 1978.[61] Quite
apart from the language issues, which require potential readers to be able to think
in both Italian and English simultaneously, there has also been much discussion
about when the work was written—either at the beginning of Fenoglio's writing
career or at the height of his maturity in the mid-to-late 1950s. These are not
the idle issues of obsessive scholars but directly affect the interpretation of the
work. Chiesa was thus taking on board the kind of text that would put off all but
the bravest soul. For the film he stuck fairly closely to the 1968 version, but also
took some elements from other redactions, notably the female character Sonia. In
essence, this meant that the film provided viewers with an insight into an important section of Fenoglio's work that is only really known by those relatively few
people who have a familiarity with the critical edition. If only for this meticulously
philological approach to his source, Chiesa deserves congratulation. The film does
lose some of the elements that distinguish the written text—above all its complex
narrative technique that creates an interplay between the narrator and the perceptions of his protagonist. Much of the irony, something film seems to struggle with,
is also lost. In compensation, however, Chiesa manages to draw out and emphasize
some of the most compelling aspects of Fenoglio's masterpiece: the role of chance,
the depiction of violence, the interaction between partisans and nature, the obses-

sion with spies real or imagined (he turns out to be real), and emotions such as fear and loneliness.

Chiesa's film is not a deliberate attempt to counter revisionism but a very honest enterprise aimed at bringing Fenoglio's masterpiece to the screen. But unlike Martinelli, Chiesa has a skeptical attitude about the potential of film to simply reflect reality—an opening sequence of images of war and of Mussolini, taken from documentary films, dissolves as if the projector bulb has melted the celluloid. We are thus reminded that what we are about to see is, above all, a reel of plastic containing images and sounds and not a transparent window onto the historical truth of the Resistance.

Conclusion

Italy must be amongst the most historically sensitive countries in the world. The past matters here, sometimes very much.[1]

—Paul Ginsborg

As I write this conclusion, Italy is celebrating the one hundred fiftieth anniversary of the unification. In the city of Reggio Emilia, where the tricolor flag was invented, there are banners and posters everywhere inviting citizens to participate in the many forthcoming events. In Ravenna, Senator Sergio Zavoli, in a speech given in the presence of the Italian president, has just commemorated the exemplary contributions of Arrigo Boldrini and Benigno Zaccagnini to the democratic life of the Republic. Boldrini, the president of the ANPI for decades, was a communist, while Zaccagnini was himself a partisan, a leading figure in Christian Democracy, and the secretary of the DC at the time of the kidnap and murder of Aldo Moro. When he died in 1989, Boldrini gave his funeral oration. These two individuals are, the message is clear, symbolic of the unity of Italy. It could, of course, be objected that bringing together Zaccagnini and Boldrini in this way is, perhaps, a little forced. But that is not the point. Italy is currently going through another examination of its history, through the prism of a political situation that is characterised in some quarters by a desire for a federal state. History and politics are, as this book has tried to show, inextricably linked. And that is why Zaccagnini and Boldrini are themselves linked. The reason the past "matters" in Italy is that politics count—very much.

Italy was one of many participants in the Second World War. Under Fascism, Italy started the war fighting for the Axis, and under Badoglio and his successors, it finished it fighting for the Allies. But the change of sides in the summer of 1943 did not represent a clean break. It led to the formation of the RSI, to collaboration and, of course, to occupation and Resistance. But for all its differences from other countries in Western Europe, Italy is not unique and, *pace* the revisionists, it is not the only country that has taken an approach to its past that has been dominated by political contingencies. The Second World War has been remembered, celebrated, vilified, forgotten, and exploited in different ways and in different times by all the countries that participated in the conflict. This is not the time for an essay on the European memory of the Second World War, but it is necessary to recall that in Britain the Blitz, the Battle of Britain, and the Dunkirk spirit were narratives created to forge a sense of national identity.[2] In contrast, the citizens of postwar Germany could not recreate their own broken identity around their participation in the war, but they could attempt to differentiate between different sections of the Nazi war machine such as the "clean Wehrmacht." And after 1989, the citizens of unified Germany were given an opportunity to rethink their past in radical ways. In Spain, on the other hand, there was a failed attempt to bury the past of the Civil War after the death of Franco. But the "pact of forgetting" did not, and could not, last. So Italy is not alone when it comes to its vexed and complex relationship with its past, but the nature, duration, and intensity of discussions do suggest the past "matters" more there than in other countries.

The fractured nature of Italy's involvement in the Second World War has had an enduring effect on its legacy and this book has focused on one aspect of that involvement—the partisan Resistance. The Resistance movement has, as the book has demonstrated, had a profound influence on Italian society, politics, and culture. This influence has not, however, been linear, neither in time nor in space. The major articulations, with 1960 seen as the key turning point, are useful ways of organizing material, but they tend to simplify matters. The Tambroni affair and 1960 was an important moment, but it is clear that throughout the 1950s the keepers of the Resistance flame had not fallen silent. Instead, the different political parties, as well as former members of the PDA, all caught up in the Cold War atmosphere, all sought to claim what they felt was their rightful piece of Italy's near past. The PCI was very active in this process, but it was not alone. Moreover, the PCI was unable and also unwilling to throw everything into the postwar battle over the Resistance. Although it was politically expedient for a time for the DC to avoid the Resistance thematic, or use it as a way of fighting the PCI, this situation soon changed and really from the early 1950s there was an attempt by sections of the Catholic world to champion the "white Resistance." The very large number of publications on the white Resistance in certain areas of Italy, above all, but not exclusively in the Veneto, provide ample evidence that there was no PCI hegemony over the movement. In the 1960s the State, and the center-Left governments, had compelling reasons to "adopt" the Resistance in order to shore up what was a fragile coalition. With the violence of the 1970s, the idea of the Italy born of the Resistance was one weapon, among many, in the State's fight against terrorism. These processes of assumption and rejection from the parties, from the State, and from a broad spectrum of political actors have continued to this day. The idea, then, that the PCI "took out a mortgage on the Resistance" needs to be unpacked a little. To continue the metaphor, all the parties (including Bossi's Northern League) have borrowed against the Resistance and history, unfortunately, has no regulators— with the possible exception of historians who have, for various reasons, struggled to meet the challenge. The idea, therefore, of a single "Resistance myth" and even of an "anti-Fascist paradigm" does not stand up to analysis. There were a wide variety of different myths, as well as countermyths, myths about myths, and myths within myths. And whatever category these myths fall into they all have precise political origins and precise political explanations.

To speak of a red, or white, or even green Resistance myth also risks oversimplification. The Resistance as a second Risorgimento was a concept that was broadly supported across the political spectrum and, looking at the 1950s again, was an extraordinarily attractive vehicle for packaging lots of aspects of the movement in such a way as to support the nation-building aspirations of the times. The Resistance as a war of liberation from the Germans was a concept that had a wide appeal, but the problem was that it did not account for other aspects of the war: Italy's involvement with the Axis, collaboration and the RSI and, above all, the civil war. For the PCI to talk openly about the violence its partisans had embraced clashed with the democratic edifice it had tried to construct since the *svolta di Salerno* in 1944. The Resistance as understood and promoted by the PCI was not, therefore, a deepish red. In the late 1960s elements to the left of the PCI tried to reclaim the movement for what they felt it had been, but their interpretation exploited history as much as the elements they criticized.

The success of Pansa's publications on this issue of postwar violence graphically demonstrates that, whatever attempts had been made to confront the problem, they were not enough, and any attempts to create a common identity around the Resistance have met and always will encounter problems until such time as the question of violence can be adequately explained and conceptualized. But if the problem of violence could be adequately addressed and integrated into a shared narrative, then would it be possible to create a sense of national identity (if such a thing is desirable) around the Resistance? If *national* identity is too difficult to achieve, what about local or regional identity, particularly in view of the very regional nature of the Resistance legacy? What should the role of historians be, if anything, in this process? My own view, expressed in this book, is that Italian historians should take a more active role in explaining Italy's past, and that their explanations need to be made more accessible to a broader public than has been the case up until now. As Pavone has written in his *Prima lezione di storia contemporanea* the tasks of the historian are to "narrate, describe, understand and, if possible explain."[3] But, whether historians' views and explanations should be used to shape Italy's problematic identity into something more coherent raises many problems, the biggest of which is that such a process risks replacing one version of history for political ends with another. This is a risk, of course, but historians must surely have a civic role, and an awareness of the importance of the discipline beyond the academy.

Should the national holiday of April 25 be abandoned, as many have suggested? I sincerely hope not. By continuing to commemorate the liberation from Nazism and Fascism and its key role in rebuilding their country, Italians may yet come to understand the Resistance as a movement of a (mainly) virtuous minority that was full of contradictions and problems, but that made an important contribution to bringing to an end the most violent conflict of the modern era. Even 66 years on, that is still worth remembering, celebrating and, of course, discussing.

Notes

Introduction

1. On Berlusconi's first period in office see Ginsborg (2003, 294–99), Tranfaglia (2003, 51–53) and the essays in Katz and Ignazi (1996).
2. "Il premier: 'Via dalla Rai Santoro, Biagi e Luttazzi,'" *La Repubblica*, April 18, 2002. See also Philip Willan, "Berlusconi stokes new row on TV bias," *The Guardian*, April 20, 2002 and Jones (2003, 235–36). More generally on Berlusconi and the media see Ginsborg (2004).
3. On the immediate consequences for Santoro's relationship with RAI and with Saccà see Goffredo De Marchis, "Saccà richiama Santoro per la puntata di Sciuscià," *La Repubblica*, April 24, 2002, 13.
4. Concita De Gregorio, "Santoro canta Bella ciao . . . e litiga al telefono con Saccà," *La Repubblica*, April 20, 2002, 12. The footage is also freely available on YouTube, along with many other renditions of "Bella ciao," including the rice-pickers version sung by Milva in 1971 and one by the English band Chumbawamba.
5. On *canti partigiani*, the standard collection is Savona and Straniero (1985). For a stimulating discussion in English see Slowey (1991). In Italian see Pivato (2005, 170–88).
6. Rousso, (1991, 1).
7. For a general discussion in English of the French case, focusing on a variety of different periods see Gildea (1994). In Italian, see Troude-Chastenet (1999). For Rousso's contributions subsequent to *The Vichy Syndrome*, see Conan and Rousso (1994) and Rousso (2002).
8. For an insight into Bocca's recent views see, for example, his collection of articles (2006), as well as "La Resistenza cancellata," the new preface to his memoir (2005, 5–16). The memoir was itself first published in 1945.
9. For the "revisionist" view, see Serri (2002). Calabri (2007) is a vigorous and scholarly defense of Pintor. The whole case is discussed in Natoli, De Luna, and Santomassimo (2008).
10. Marco Revelli, "In montagna," *Il Manifesto*, April 25, 2009.
11. Santomassimo (2003, 137).
12. Rousso (1991, 11).
13. The Resistance museum in Turin, formerly an adjunct to the Unification museum, is now housed separately and is characterized by an imaginative multimedia approach, largely organized around oral testimonies. The Cervi museum in Gattatico has also seen many changes over the last decades, with greater emphasis now placed on the Resistance aspect of the museum. There have also been entirely new projects such as the excellent Museo Audiovisivo della Resistenza di Fosdinovo. However, many museums remain extraordinarily uninviting places, with little attempt at contextualization or at exhibiting

materials that might be of interest, particularly to young visitors. Others, such as the Resistance museum in the city of Lucca, are permanently closed.

14. Crainz and Gallerano (1987), Crainz (1996) and (2000).
15. Santomassimo's most extended contribution is the lengthy essay published in various locations (2003). But see also the collection of articles originally published in *Il manifesto* (2004). Focardi's book, significantly entitled *La guerra della memoria* (2005), combines a detailed discussion with a very useful anthology of texts (particularly newspaper articles and speeches by politicians). The Crainz study (1986), which also informs his general histories of postwar Italy, is published in a special number of *Problemi del socialismo* dedicated to Fascism and anti-Fascism in republican Italy (see also the contributions by Baldassare, Ganapini, and Gallerano). See also Quazza (1990); Bermani (1997); Lepre (1997); Gallerano, (1999a); Ballone (1997); Miller (1999); the essays in Miccoli, Neppi Modona, and Pombeni (2001); De Bernardi and Ferrari (2004); Luzzatto (2004); Rapini (2005); Craveri and Quaglierello (2006); Staron (2007); and Peli (2007).
16. Storchi (2007). Storchi has also contributed to an important essay on the role of the war in the construction of a "red" memory in Emilia Romagna (Bertucelli, Canovi, Silingardi, and Storchi, 1999).
17. Chiarini (2005); Cenci (1999) appears in a collection dedicated to the theme of memory (Paggi 1999).
18. Falaschi (1976); Re (1990); Cooke (2000a). Studies of French Resistance literature also tend to focus on a distinct period, sometimes with excellent results, such as Margaret Atack's book on 1940–1950 (1989). For a broad survey of literary responses to the Second World War (including Fenoglio) see Casadei (2000).
19. Ballone (1997).
20. Gundle (2000, 114). The article was previously published in a slightly different Italian version (1996).
21. Passerini (1999, 296).
22. Germinario (1999).
23. Contini (1997 and 1999), Foot (2009).
24. Storchi (2007, 241).
25. There are two quite recent works of synthesis: Peli (2004) and Behan (2009). See also P. Morgan (2007), which despite its misleading title (*The Fall of Mussolini*) is a clear and accessible overview of the whole war period in Italy.
26. The term "Mussolini's enemies" appears in the title of Charles Delzell's 1961 book, which remains the most comprehensive study in English of the Italian Resistance to Fascism.
27. Peli (2004). In the introduction to my anthology (Cooke 1997, 1–17) I delineate four phases, but I now prefer to follow Peli, which is the most authoritative short general account to have been published.
28. On the RSI the most comprehensive and accessible scholarly work is by Ganapini (1999, 2007). On the German occupation, the standard work is Klinkhammer (1993).
29. The "cinque lettere" episode is discussed in Gambino (1975, 20–25) and Quazza (1976, 299–308).
30. For the most recent discussion see Piffer (2010), which offers an overly positive interpretation of the Allies' strategy toward the partisans.
31. Gambino (1975, 28).
32. Dondi (1990, 219).

Chapter 1

1. Letter from PDA, October 1944, quoted in Galli (1958, 155).
2. "Dichiarazione sulla fucilazione di Mussolini e dei suoi complici," April 29, 1945, in Grassi (1977, 334–35). CLN documents are conserved in the Resistance institutes, and there are many editions (see, for example, *Documenti del CLN per la Liguria* [1968]).
3. Grassi (1977, 344, n1). On CLNAI social and economic policy, see Levi (1947). The standard history of the CLNAI is still Catalano (1956). See also Gaetano Grassi's authoritative introduction to the *Atti e documenti del CLNAI* (Grassi 1977, 9–91)
4. All quotations from "Verbale della riunione di CLNAI e CCLN del 7 maggio 1945" (Grassi 1977, 337–44).
5. Peli (2007, 168).
6. Quazza too (1966 and 1976, 317–63) sees the failure of the CLNs to impose themselves as crucial for the future direction of Italy but shifts the blame onto the tactics of parties of the Left. Even Giuseppe Mammarella, very much a champion of the PCI, concedes the party had "little commitment" to the CLNs, as well as other manifestations of direct democracy (Mammarella 1976, 61–62). The most recent discussion of the eclipse of the CLNs is Peli (2007, 167–71).
7. Ventrone (2008). This fine study, first published in 1996, stands apparently alone in arguing the novel, but sensible, thesis that both the DC and the PCI were genuinely committed to the reestablishment of democracy in postwar Italy.
8. Francovich (1961). *La nazione del popolo* began publication in August 1944 and ceased in July 1946. For a comprehensive selection of articles from the paper, see Ballini (2008).
9. On the Tuscan CLN, see Rogari (2006, 162–79), which is the most recent discussion of the topic.
10. Gambino (1975, 46).
11. There are two biographies of Parri: Aniasi (1991) and Polese Remaggi (2004).
12. "Comunicazione radio del presidente del CLNAI," May 15, 1945, in Grassi (1977, 351–52).
13. "Mozione per la costituzione del nuovo governo," May 18, 1945, in Grassi (1977, 353–54).
14. Grassi (1977, 363, n1).
15. The phrases are reported in Catalano (1966, 51), though no source is cited.
16. Gambino (1975, 52). Gambino also cites the relevant sections from the CLN document: (1975, 493, n81). De Luna (2006, 314) uses the term *affossamento* (burying) in connection with the Liberals' liquidation of the CLN.
17. "Ordine del giorno sulla soluzione della crisi di governo," June 1, 1945, in Grassi (1977, 362–63).
18. "Discorso tenuto alla radio del presidente del Comitato di liberazione nazionale Alta Italia," June 2, 1945, in Grassi (1977, 365–67).
19. On these points see De Luna (2006, 314–15), which represents the most reliable reconstruction of the process of Parri's selection. See also Valiani (1949), Giulio Andreotti's polemically entitled *Concerto a sei voci* (1945) and Colapietra (1969), which uses contemporary newspaper sources such as the CLN's *Italia libera*.
20. For Parri as a compromise candidate, see Pertini's report to the PSIUP of June 20, 1945. The report testifies to the dissatisfaction of the Socialists who reluctantly accepted him "for reasons of peace" ("per amore di concordia"; Gambino 1975, 55). See also the biographical notes to Parri (1976, 25) that describe his appointment as only apparently a

"homage to the moral leader of the Resistance," but in reality a "compromise between very different urgencies."

21. On the Parri government see, above all, Parri's own writings and parliamentary speeches, which can be found, respectively, in Parri (1976) and (1990). See also the relevant volumes in the critical edition of the *Verbali dei consigli dei ministri 1943–1948* (Ricci, 1994–1999); Catalano (1966); Colapietra (1969, 277–346 and 347–429), Colapietra (1998, 95–123); Piscitelli (1975), Gambino (1975, 55–92) and De Luna (2006, 311–16). The general histories of twentieth century Italy all dedicate space to the issue: Ginsborg (1990, 89–90), Lepre (1993, 61–70).

22. Nenni (1981, 124).

23. Bistarelli (2007, 234). Bistarelli's is the most recent study of the "returnees." See also Pavone (1985). For a detailed catalogue of the ministry's early legislation, see De Pascalis and Salemi (1946). On laws passed specifically for the benefit of partisans see Cozzolino (1971).

24. On the liberals' role in the crisis, see Orsina (2007).

25. Gundle (2000, 118).

26. De Luna (2006, 330). On the conference and its impact see De Luna (2006, 325–30).

27. Garosci (1953)

28. As quoted in Nenni's diaries (1981, 114).

29. Storchi (2007, 237). The literature on the postwar killings is now very extensive. On Reggio Emilia and the surrounding area, the most comprehensive work is Storchi (1998 and 2007). See also Alatri (1948); Alessandrini (1999); Crainz (1992, 1995, and 2007; Dondi (1999); Magnanini (1992); Oliva (1994); Pansa (2003); Pisanò and Pisanò (1992); Onofri (1994) and Storchi (1995).

30. On this highly controversial and contested event, Morgan (2000 and 2002) are the most serious studies by far. See also Villani (1999) and Serena (1990, 13–64).

31. The Govoni have recently had a square named after them at Cento: http://www .comune.cento.fe.it/ilcomune/sindacocomunica/pagina108.html.

32. See Pisanò and Pisanò (1992).

33. Onofri (1994, 99).

34. See Crainz (1992 and 2007, 110–11). The killings have also provided the subject matter for a novel by Carlo Lucarelli (1991).

35. Storchi initially suggests that it was a class killing (1998, 131), but then argues that the crime is almost certainly explained by Vischi's involvement with the deportation of Italian workers to Germany in 1944 (1998, 163). Dondi (1999, 170) is less convinced by this argument, attributing the crime to a clash within the "Reggiane" factory.

36. Storchi (2007, 241).

37. Storchi (1998, 131).

38. On *doppiezza*, the most important contribution is Di Loreto (1991). Much earlier, though nevertheless still valid, are the incisive comments made by Galli (1958, 241). For the thesis of the secret "Red Army" see, among others, Donno (2001).

39. Storchi (2007, 240).

40. Testimony of Scanio Fontanesi, quoted in Storchi (1998, 132).

41. Storchi (1998, 96).

42. Crainz (1992, 1994, 1995, 2007).

43. For the figures see Storchi (2007, 238).

44. Natta (1971, 57; emphasis added).

45. Partito comunista italiano (1963). On the PCI in this period see, above all, Martinelli (1995).

46. Flores and Gallerano (1992, 64). Flores and Gallerano go on to analyze the question of the "paternity" of the *svolta* (1992, 69–71), adducing evidence that Stalin, rather

than Togliatti, was the mastermind of the strategy. This issue continues to provoke intense and unproductive discussions among Italian historians, and even an article by a future president of Italy (Napolitano, 1994). For the most authoritative opposing views, see Aga Rossi and Zaslavsky (1997) and Gualtieri (1995). For an update of Gualtieri's views, see his comparative study of the PCI and the DC and their role in shaping Italian democracy (2006).

47. See Cooke (2006 and 2007c).

48. Morgan S. (2000, 148).

49. Martinelli and Righi (1992, 128). Later, at the same meeting, Secchia went on to repeat his comment, adding that there were many similarities between the violent behavior of the ill-disciplined *compagni* and the Fascists: "Another element which counts against us is that our comrades are still too much like partisans. I would even go as far as to say that they have a Fascist mentality" (135). The same comments were subsequently repeated at a meeting of the central committee at which Secchia also referred to "partisan systems" and "violent, turbulent comrades" (217).

50. Martinelli and Righi (1992, 145; emphasis added). Later, at the same meeting, Emilio Sereni contributed in the same vein, referring to the "prevalence of partisan methods" that had led to the use of summary "classist" methods within the *consigli di gestione*. Sereni rued the way certain *tecnici* were fired even if they had anti-Fascist pasts and had spent time in jail (165).

51. Martinelli and Righi (1992, 192).

52. Martinelli and Righi (1992, 192–93).

53. Speaking in a debate in the chamber of deputies in 1949, Togliatti explained that "The decree I presented, in two different drafts, ended up very different in its final approved form . . . and that was largely down . . . to the interventions of deputy Scelba, who will, I believe, not wish to deny the reality of these events." For the full text of the speech see Sircana (1977, 67). Franzinelli (2006) is a detailed reconstruction of the history and impact of the amnesty.

54. Dondi speaks of "major disagreements within the government" (1999, 61).

55. The text of the amnesty, as well as many other relevant documents, can be found in Franzinelli (2006).

56. A. Battaglia (1955, 348).

57. Storchi (2007, 242).

58. Storchi (2005, 174). Paolo Pezzino has also written compellingly on these questions from the perspective of a historian who has been asked to testify in court on historical matters (Pezzino 2010). On these issue see also Giannuli (2009, 98–139).

59. For Boldrini's own account of his experiences see Boldrini (1985), a book that features a young Denis Healey who at one point declares he is on the partisans' side (244).

60. On the FIVL there is one, essentially celebratory, study: (Fabris 1986).

61. Cecchini (1996, 69).

62. Secchia (1979, 203).

63. The episode is carefully reconstructed by Laurana Lajolo (1995). More generally, and more polemically, on partisan rebellions in Piedmont, see Gremmo (1995).

64. On Scelba's press conference of September 20, 1947, about the "plan K" see, for example, Pizzinelli (1982, 62). Though largely adulatory this biography is a cut above La Russa (2002), which can only be recommended for its moments of unintentional humor.

65. See Donno (2001), which reproduces copious numbers of documents but fails to contextualize them or approach them critically.

66. In his memoirs, which of course need to be interpreted, Emanuele Macaluso states that when he took over party organization he tried to "understand if this parallel structure had ever existed" but found "no trace." But he readily admitted that there

were partisans who kept their weapons waiting for a revolutionary opportunity (Macaluso 2003, 57–58).

67. Taviani (2002, 369–413). On these early Gladio-type operations, see Pacini (2008), which presents much documentation but tends to overestimate their scale.

68. Troilo (2005, 115).

69. See Troilo (2005), which is a detailed reconstruction but tends to dramatize and exaggerate. See also Mafai (1984), which takes a journalistic approach. Both works are also a little compromised by the direct relationships between the protagonists and authors—Troilo is the son of the prefect in question, and Mafai was Pajetta's long-term partner.

70. For a scholarly assessment of this movement see Mariuzzo (2010).

71. Gozzini (1998, 55) describes Longo and Secchia bending over their stricken leader to hear him whisper, "Stay calm. Don't do anything stupid." It is, of course, impossible to prove whether Togliatti said this to his deputy leaders, but it seems to fit in more with the rhetoric of Togliatti as the democratic leader of the PCI than to the reality of this dramatic event.

72. Teresa Noce in her autobiography (1974, 376) argues that the CGIL leader Giuseppe Di Vittorio saw the general strike as a way of channeling popular indignation and avoiding violence, but this seems an adventurous interpretation.

73. On the "plan K" see the excellent discussion by Marino (1995, 115–26).

74. Tobagi (1978, 22–23).

75. On this point see Marino (1991, 19–21). Marino's chapter (1991, 13–50) is the most authoritative discussion.

76. Tobagi (1978, 25–26).

77. Tobagi (1978, 61). The dead officer was Raniero Virgilio, who had actually been stabbed. For a more detailed account of the Abbadia San Salvatore episode, see Serafini (1981).

78. In Marino's analysis, the "judgment of the facts by the authorities was vitiated by the poisoned anti-communism of the times . . . made in almost adulatory support of Scelba's convictions about the existence of the so-called plan K" (Marino, 1991, 45).

79. Even Giorgio Bocca, who wrote of a "PCI military organisation now clamorously come to light" (*La Repubblica*, May 24, 1978), seems to have fallen for this fanciful interpretation.

80. On these debates, see Manacorda (1970, 3–27).

81. For more detailed discussions see Rosengarten (1968, 7–24), Tarizzo (1969), and Torcellan (1980).

82. Conti (1961).

83. Tarizzo (1969, 6).

84. Falaschi (1976, 16).

85. Santomassimo dates the invention of the second Risorgimento formula to the postwar, referring to an exhibition in Milan entitled "Exhibition of the First and Second Risorgimento" (Santomassimo, 2003, 141). He is certainly right in terms of "public memory," but my argument is that the concept's origins go back to the Resistance period itself.

86. Tarizzo (1969, 3).

87. Falaschi (1976, 16).

88. Bolis (1995), Gadola Beltrami (1979), Gracci (1995), Bocca (2005). The first two were originally published in 1946, while Gracci and Bocca's memoirs were published in 1945. For a study of texts commemorating fallen partisans see Perry (2001), which clearly illustrates their rhetorical characteristics.

89. Falaschi (1976, 28).

90. Valiani (1947).

91. Cadorna (1948). Longo (1947) was translated into Czech in 1949 and Russian in 1952.

92. According to Ajello (1997, 56) the book was written by a Guglielmo Peirce who received a signed copy from Longo for his efforts.
93. Passerini (1999, 295).
94. Milanini (1997, 173), Calvino (1949).
95. For the history of this institute (and for information on its many satellites throughout Italy), see Grassi (1993).
96. On Calvino's partisan activities, see Milanini (1997). On his stories, see Watson (1996).
97. Vittorini (1945).
98. The second volume was to have been titled *Quelli della Bisalta*, a reference to the partisan formations on Mount Bisalta. See Berrini (1945, 8).
99. Calvino (1949, 42).
100. *Scarpe rotte eppur bisogna andar* (1955), *L'Italia l' è malada* (1955).
101. Pedullà (2005).
102. Ferretti (1976, 332).
103. Gatto (1947), Meneghetti (1958).
104. McLaughlin (1998, 30). McLaughlin also identifies a number of other publications from the period in which Calvino manifested interest in the epic.
105. See McLaughlin (1998, 149–51).
106. The bibliography on Resistance cinema is extensive, although it is only very recently that there has been an attempt to study the phenomenon in its entirety: see Vercelli (2005) and Ghigi (2009). See also: *Dentro la storia, cinema, resistenza, pace* (1984), which contains a bibliography of articles and reviews of relevant films in cinema journals; *Cinema, storia, Resistenza, 1944–1985* (1987); and *La Resistenza nel cinema italiano 1945–1995* (1995), which contains a detailed filmography of 108 works.
107. Rousso (1991, 11).
108. Wagstaff (1996, 44).
109. The filmography in *Dentro la storia, cinema, resistenza, pace* (1984, 171) lists 10 documentaries produced from 1945 to 1948. *I giorni di gloria* is second on the list, but the first is a production by the Imperial War Museum. Other titles include *Aldo dice: 26 x 1*, *La Liberazione di Milano*, *Fascisti alla sbarra*, and *L'abbazia eroica*.
110. Domenico (1991, 93). On this episode see also Ranzato (1997).
111. De Santis, as quoted in Ghigi (2009, 79).
112. Sorlin (1987, 57; emphasis added).
113. Cereja (1987, 17).
114. Gundle (2000, 121).
115. Forgacs (2000).

Chapter 2

1. For the socialist leader Pietro Nenni, the wind had already stopped blowing as early as December 1945. See "L'anno che muore", *L'Avanti!*, December 30, 1945.
2. Ginsborg (1990, 120).
3. Peli (2007, 166).
4. On the period see Ginsborg (1990, 141–85 and 186–209) and Lepre (1993, 119–56).
5. Focardi (2000), Franzinelli (2002), Battini (2003). All three historians provide interviews on the subject in *Memoria e giustizia. Stragi, crimini di guerra, processi—Italia 1943–1945. Giorni di storia 8* (2003).
6. In France, for example, one well-known trial was that of Georges Guingouin, known as the "Limousin Tito," whose case was eventually dismissed in 1959. His defense lawyer

saw the attack on his client as an attempt at "a wholesale indictment of the *maquis* and of the Resistance." See Rousso (1991, 31–32).

7. The standard history of this movement by Setta, deals extensively with its attitude toward Parri (initially seen, in June 1945, as "one of us" [1975, 298]) but does not discuss the 1948 episode.

8. In the 1970s, the issue resurfaced and Parri published a more detailed account (Parri 1973) of his period of Nazi captivity.

9. See the letter from Calamandrei to Giorgio Agosti of November 7, 1951, in Calamandrei (1968, 297–98).

10. Cecchini (1996, 125). On the Parri trial itself, see Carli Ballola (1954) and Polese Remaggi (2004, 345–46).

11. The speech was published separately in Calamandrei (1954) and may also be found in the collection of speeches and other writings connected to the Resistance, first published in Calamandrei (1955). I quote from the 2006 edition of this work, edited by Sergio Luzzatto.

12. Calamandrei (2006, 35).

13. Calamandrei (2006, 3–35).

14. Cecchini (1996, 125–27).

15. Polese Remaggi (2004, 373).

16. Carli Ballola (1954, 29–30).

17. Polese Remaggi (2001, 247).

18. Santomassimo (2003, 148) argues that actionist culture was not confined to "one particular journal" but spread around a range of publications. There were, indeed, many other relevant publications, such as the Turin-based *Resistenza*, but *Il ponte* was far and away the most important.

19. Isnenghi (2007); Polese Remaggi (2001).

20. There is a very extensive bibliography on the *legge truffa*. For differing, but sympathetic, interpretations of the DC strategy, see Orlando (1989), Scoppola (1991, 263–74), Malgeri (1988–89). For a more critical approach see Rodotà (1992). For more recent studies see Piretti (2003) and the substantial collection of documents in Quaglierello (2003).

21. Calamandrei left the Social Democrats when Codignola (also a social democrat) was censured for speaking out against the *legge truffa* (see Polese Remaggi 2001, 396). The only monographic study of this short-lived organization is Mercuri (1978).

22. *Resistenza*, May 5, 1953. Parri was withering about the "open abdications" of the smaller parties who had allied themselves with the DC in exchange for an "uncertain booty." All quotations from Parri (1976, 221).

23. Indeed, the PCI only realized the importance of the Resistance and anti-Fascism once the electoral campaign was over. See Trombadori (1953).

24. *Il ponte*, Anno IX, no. 6 (June 1953), 741.

25. *Il ponte*, Anno IX, no. 6 (June 1953), 744.

26. De Luna (1985, 61).

27. Bianco (1954).

28. Calamandrei (1968, Vol. 2, 358–59).

29. Calamandrei (2006, 132).

30. Agosti (2005, 40).

31. Polese Remaggi (2001, 367).

32. The story in question was entitled "Assolto in istruttoria" and is published in the 1976 collection *Matrimonio in brigata* (Viganò, 1976).

33. For details of Viganò's correspondence with a wide variety of individuals, such as Cal-amandrei, and with the publishers Einaudi and Mondadori, see the "Epistolario" in Colombo (1995, 215–51).
34. Manacorda (1970, 42).
35. See Gatt-Rutter (1999, 531–557 [536]). On Viganò there is a useful biographical entry in Collotti, Sandri and Sessi (2006, 955–56).
36. Viganò (1955).
37. The most detailed discussion of the early reception of Fenoglio's short stories is Briganti (1984). On the short stories themselves, see Bufano (1999). The most authoritative stud-ies of Fenoglio's works by some margin are Bigazzi (1983 and 2011) and Saccone (1988).
38. The novel was drafted in 1949 and was turned down by Mondadori and Bompiani before being accepted, not without difficulties, by Einaudi. For Calvino's negative judgment on the typescript see Calvino (1991, 50–52). A second version with some extensive cuts was published by Einaudi in 1958. On the editorial history of the text see the detailed discussion by Andreini in Cassola (2007, 1769–86). The critical literature on Cassola is extensive. For the most up-to-date bibliography, see Andreini's compen-dious "Bibliografia della critica" in Cassola (2007, 1870–90). For specific analysis of *Fausto e Anna* see Asor Rosa (1988, 249–53); Ferretti (1964, 84–111); Macchioni Jodi, (1967, 79–86).
39. Asor Rosa (1988, 282) goes so far as to identify an "ideology of isolation" in Cassola's works that corresponded to the needs of the editorial market at the time. For more sympathetic assessments of Cassola's existential concerns see Moss (1977) and Pedroni (1985). Generally speaking, Cassola's works have had a better reception outside of Italy.
40. Giuliano Manacorda, *Rinascita*, March 1952, 186–87. For a brief discussion of this epi-sode, see Bertacchini, (1977, 12–14). Manacorda also later published a monographic study of Cassola that contains some cautious back-tracking over this spat. See Mana-corda (1973, 64–70).
41. The *postilla* was signed by "r.", an abbreviation of the pseudonym "Roderigo di Casti-glia" used by Togliatti (1952).
42. Malvezzi and Pirelli (1952). On Malvezzi, see the recent collection of essays edited by Solaro (2008).
43. There is a copy of the score at the National Library of Florence, *Lettere di condannati a morte della Resistenza italiana: per orchestra, voci recitanti e coro.* For a discussion of this piece and others inspired by the Resistance, see Pestalozza (1955).
44. *Lettere di condannati e morte della Resistenza*, read by Anna Proclemer and Arnaldo Foa.
45. Gundle (2000, 125).
46. The DC youth movement presented a special supplement of their journal *Impegno giovanile* at the DC conference of 1955 that contained the last letters of condemned Catholics. See Movimento giovanile della democrazia cristiana (1955).
47. Gatt-Rutter (1999, 537).
48. Information on this event is derived from Cecchini (1996, 103–4) and from the Gramsci Archive (329, 1293–94).
49. Calvino (2000, 275–76).
50. Battaglia (1953a).
51. Battaglia (1953b). The abridged version (Battaglia and Garritano 1955) is also avail-able in English translation.
52. The works of art history are mainly on the Roman Baroque (1942a, 1942b, 1943).
53. The documents are at Public Record Office: HS9/103/5.
54. Battaglia (1945). The most recent edition of this work is Battaglia (2004), with an informative preface by Ugo Berti.

55. See Battaglia (1947). On Battaglia's work in the field of postwar assistance see Istituto storico della Resistenza in Toscana, Fondo Battaglia Roberto, b. 3 (Battaglia Collection, File 3) that contains correspondence relating to the eight thousand men of the Pinerolo division who joined the Greek Resistance movement after September 8, 1943.
56. Battaglia (1949).
57. Togliatti's dearth of contributions on the Resistance is also noted by Ballone (1997, 421).
58. Togliatti (1953).
59. Sandro Pertini wrote a very critical article in *L'Avanti!*, February 24, 1955, 3.
60. Enriques Agnoletti (1954, 322).
61. For a broad survey of Italian historiography in the period, see Delzell (1956). Delzell detects a "decidedly Communist bias" (1956, 388) in Battaglia's work.
62. Secchia (1954a); Longo (1954). Both books were the subject of a lengthy review by Roberto Battaglia (1954).
63. De Micheli (1954).
64. Contini Bonacossi and Ragghianti Collobi (1954).
65. Contini Bonacossi and Ragghianti Collobi (1954, xii–xiii).
66. Ragghianti (1954).
67. Ragghianti (1954, 253–55). Ragghianti's book came in for hostile treatment by the PCI in the shape of a review by Luigi Longo (1955).
68. Ragghianti (1954, 41).
69. Salvadori (1955, 129).
70. Salvadori (1955, 87).
71. On the congress see Cecchini (1996, 95–99).
72. Cecchini (1996, 87).
73. Cecchini (1996, 64).
74. The painting was purchased by the Uffizi gallery in 2005 and a clear image of it is available at http://www.amicidegliuffizi.it/public/giornale/giornale_uffizi_33.pdf.
75. The first Resistance story for children was published by the Catholic writer and educationalist Enzo Petrini (1946). The field of children's Resistance literature is largely unexplored, but see Rotondo (1995).
76. Parca (1953, 18).
77. Sturani (1953, 39). Sturani was the daughter of the anti-Fascist Augusto Monti, who taught both Primo Levi and Emanuele Artom. She edited a Resistance anthology (1951) which is, as far as I know, the first volume of its kind.
78. Sturani (1953, 47).
79. Secchia (1954b).
80. The articles by Passerin d'Entreves, Pizzoni, and Marazza are reprinted in the *Civitas* anthology *Saggi sulla Resistenza* (1974, 1–7, 75–80, 173–88).
81. Santomassimo (2003, 153).
82. Marchetti and Tassinari (1955). The anthology was republished in 1975, minus Gronchi's preface.
83. The 1950s Catholic assault on the communist Resistance "monopoly" has been studied in considerable detail in Tedesco (2007).
84. Floreanini (1955).
85. Battaglia and Garritano (1955).
86. Cervi (1955), Pajetta (1955). On the Cervi brothers and their impact, see Cooke (2007a).
87. Milan and Vighi (1955).
88. Milan (1954). The book was published by the PCI's Editori Riuniti and centers on the experiences of an autobiographical protagonist, Marco.
89. Giorgi (1955).

90. Caleffi (1955). On the Edizioni Avanti!, see Mencarelli (2009).
91. *Il secondo risorgimento: nel decennale della Resistenza e del ritorno alla democrazia, 1945–1955* (1955).
92. Primieri (1955), ACS, PCM, minutes of meeting, January 29, 1955, cited in Tedesco (2007, 113).
93. Cadorna (1955, 261, 273).
94. Cadorna (1955, 288).
95. Battaglia, Calamandrei, Corbino, De Rosa, Lussu, Sansone and Valiani (1955).
96. See Amendola (1955). Amendola would continue to argue for decades against the thesis of a betrayed Resistance, taking on the proponents of the argument from within his own party. See Amendola (1994 [1976], 177).
97. Santomassimo (2003, 147).
98. Santomassimo (2003, 143).
99. Ballone (1997, 414).
100. *La democrazia cristiana resta fedele agli ideali della Resistenza* (1955).
101. Gundle (2000, 118).

Chapter 3

1. See Nenni (1981, 658–60) for an account of the election process and the socialist leader's key role in it. See also Santomassimo (2003, 154).
2. For example, in otherwise comprehensive studies both Santomassimo (2003) and Focardi (2005) do not cover this period, moving from Gronchi's speech of 1955 directly to 1960.
3. For a full list of the committee members, see Cecchini (1996, 157).
4. Cecchini (1996, 157).
5. Agosti (2005, 108).
6. Another commentator on the *raduno*, Lamberto Mercuri, described the speech as "without color" and wrote that it was interrupted by shouts of "Long live Parri" (Mercuri 1958, 603).
7. De Totto's gesture was greeted with glee by the *Meridiano d'Italia*, which published two articles on the event entitled "Il MSI ridicolizza la Resistenza" and "I giovani del MSI disinfettano l'Altare della Patria." For a full discussion, see Chiarini (2005, 57–58).
8. Agosti (2005, 118–20).
9. Agosti (2005, 152–53).
10. Barca (2005, 227–28).
11. See the *comunicato* of February 14, 1957, "Concetto Marchesi maestro di umanità, combattente per la libertà e il socialismo," in *Documenti politici e direttive del Partito comunista italiano dall'VIII al IX congresso* (1960, 25–27).
12. *Documenti politici e direttive del Partito comunista italiano dall'VIII al IX congresso* (1960, 26).
13. *Documenti politici e direttive del Partito comunista italiano dall'VIII al IX congresso* (1960, 526–27).
14. Commissione femminile dell'ANPI provinciale di Torino (1954).
15. Marchesini Gobetti (1956).
16. Massone Muratti (1959); Banfi Malaguzzi (1958).
17. *Donne cristiane nella Resistenza: testimonianze e documentazioni sul contributo femminile alla lotta partigiana in Lombardia* (1956).
18. On this monument, see Sega (2004).
19. ISTAT (1957).

20. Carli Ballola (1957).
21. Taviani (1956). All quotations are taken from the 1968 edition.
22. Taviani (1968, 10).
23. Taviani (1968, 11). In addition to the 1945 version in *Il ponte* and the 1956 publication, there have been numerous other editions of the text (in 1988 the eleventh edition was published), providing ample evidence of the importance of the work. The *Breve storia* also has the distinction of being translated into Spanish (published in 1974 by Le Monnier).
24. Taviani (1968, 13).
25. Taviani (1968, 30).
26. Zoli (1959); Barbieri (1958). Barbieri's book has run to five editions. Editori Riuniti published a number of popular books on the Resistance in this period such as De Jaco (1956), Nozzoli (1957), and Galassi (1957).
27. Francovich (1958a).
28. Zoli (1959, 13).
29. Secchia (1959).
30. Secchia and Moscatelli (1958, 11).
31. See the interview with Roberto Botta published in the 1998 edition of *Guerra partigiana tra Genova e il Po* (Pansa 1998, 527). Pansa also published an article on Resistance historiography in the same year (1959) that developed the ideas contained in his conference "intervention."
32. The article, "Le idee della Resistenza. Antifascisti e fascisti di fronte alla tradizione del Risorgimento" is now in Pavone (1995, 3–69).
33. Battaglia's reply, originally published in *Passato e presente* in 1959, is available in Battaglia (1964b, 21–32).
34. Paoluzi (1956, 11).
35. Paoluzi (1956, 37).
36. Paoluzi (1956, 37).
37. Paoluzi (1956, 39).
38. Paoluzi (1956, 43).
39. Paoluzi (1956, 65).
40. Paoluzi (1956, 70).
41. Paoluzi (1956, 72).
42. Calvino (1955).
43. Calvino (1957).
44. See Luciano Lucignani, "Attenti a quella sirena," in *La Repubblica*, August 3, 1988, p. 31.
45. The play is included in the 1959 edition of Squarzina's works.
46. Fenoglio (1959).
47. I would single out Nardo Dunchi's *Memorie partigiane* (1957) as the most significant actionist publication of the period. An extract first appeared in *Il ponte*, while the complete version was published in the "Quaderni del ponte" with a dedication "To the memory of Piero Calamandrei, apostle of the Resistance."

Chapter 4

1. For this period in the history of the DC, see Galli (1978), as well as the third volume of Malgeri (1988–1989).
2. Galli (1978, 175).
3. On the "New Resistance," and the anti-Fascism of the 1960s, the fundamental study is Rapini (2005). On the complex process of the formation of the center-Left see

Tamburrano (1990); Di Loreto (1992); Voulgaris (1998). On the Tambroni affair itself, see my own study (Cooke 2000b), which contains a number of extracts from contemporary accounts as well as full bibliographical details. For a fictional treatment, based on a wide array of materials, see Di Nori (2006).

4. Gorresio (1963, 114).

5. Vento (1981, 179).

6. The text of the speech can be found in Gandolfi (1960, 72–79); see also Cooke (2000b, 65–68).

7. In an interview from 1996, Primo Moroni described to Cesare Bermani how he saw a 120 mm cannon placed at a strategic point near the motorway exit to Genoa. See Bermani (1997, 179).

8. On Levi's articles in *ABC* see Cooke (2007a, 159–74).

9. Malvestiti (1960).

10. On this episode and its consequences, see Flores and Gallerano (1992, 188), and Barbagallo (2006, 72–80). More generally on developments within the PCI post-Togliatti see Vittoria (2006, 91–106). For Ingrao's own account see his autobiography (2006, 311–19).

11. Forgacs (1999, 186).

12. See Crainz (1986, 74–75).

13. See, for example, Repaci (1961).

14. Rossini's article is quoted in Santomassimo (2003, 157).

15. By the 1970s Taviani did, however, start to use references to the Resistance in his parliamentary speeches. See, for example, the speech following the Brescia killings of 1974 in Taviani (2005, 175–78).

16. Bendiscioli had contributed a chapter on the politics of the Resistance to the 1955 official volume that was reprinted in his *Antifascismo e Resistenza: impostazioni storiografiche* (1964) together with a number of other essays, the most significant of which were chapters 2 and 6. The former (1964, 114–27) offered a critical analysis of the limits of the term second Risorgimento, while the latter (1964, 211–40) laid the methodological foundations for a "critical reconstruction of the Resistance." Such a work was not subsequently published by the Catholic historian.

17. De Angelis (1966). Twelve of these texts were published between 1966 and 1968. Apart from Mattei, the other name that stands out is Teresio Olivelli, the author of a Resistance prayer that has had enduring popularity.

18. On Puecher see Bianchi (1965), which was published by one of Italy's leading publishing houses (Mondadori), and on Visentin, see Corletto (1965). More generally, on the Catholic Resistance in the Veneto see Mazzolari (1965) and Fantelli (1965).

19. For the text of Nenni's speech as published in *L'Avanti!* see Focardi (2005, 176–78).

20. According to Focardi (2005, 43) Moro used the word "Resistenza" no fewer than seven times, whereas at the commemoration of 1954 Taviani had only pronounced the word once. Focardi usefully provides the text of the speech in the anthological section of his book (2005, 178–83). The massacres at the Fosse Ardeatine were the subject of Robert Katz's book, published in Italian as *Morte a Roma* in 1968. The book had considerable impact, not least because it advanced the argument of Pius XII's nonintervention on behalf of the victims.

21. The state's financial help to the partisan associations was the result of a bill, no. 1896, originally introduced by Boldrini (ANPI), Riccardo Lombardi (FIAP), and Schiano (FIVL) on January 9, 1960.

22. *I dieci congressi nazionali dell'ANPI* (1991, 26).

23. Argenton's message read, "Twenty years ago a common enemy united us. Even though objectives and political methods separate us today we are brought together

by a patrimony of sacrifice and a certain reciprocal respect for the defense of the ideals of liberty." See *I dieci congress nazionali dell'ANPI* (1991, 26).

24. Cadorna published an article in *La Nazione* on April 25, 1965, stating that he had no intention of endorsing the communist monopoly on the Resistance. See Santomassimo (2003, 150).

25. Santomassimo (2003, 159).

26. For the full text see Cooke (2000b, 192).

27. Passerini (1988, 48).

28. See Monti and Sturani (1963). Sturani was Monti's grandson. His mother, Luisa Sturani, edited one of the first Resistance anthologies and also wrote one of the children's Resistance stories published by ANPI in the 1950s (see chapter 2). It is unclear whether Enrico Sturani actually penned the letter to his grandfather or if the exchange is a kind of fictional Socratic exchange. Monti himself died in 1966, with his former pupil Gian Carlo Pajetta penning his obituary in *Rinascita* (Pajetta, 1966).

29. For the text of Lepre's article and the replies by Secchia and Merli see Cooke (2000b, 198–203).

30. Gatto (1966).

31. Romano and Solza (1960).

32. The collection was published as *Vent'anni di Resistenza* and sold for the modest sum of 5,500 lire.

33. The conference in question was on the "Partiti politici nella Resistenza" held in Milan in November 1968. Papers were given by Ernesto Ragionieri (communists), Leo Valiani (actionists), Gianfranco Bianchi (Catholics), Eugenio Artom (liberals), and Arfé (socialists). The published volume, *Azionisti cattolici e comunisti nella Resistenza* (Bianchi, Ragionieri and Valiani, 1971) contained, as the title suggests, only the first three papers. The "socialist gap" in the historiography has now been filled by the works of Neri Serneri, such as the collection of documents (1988) and his detailed monograph (1995).

34. On this point, see also Santomassimo (2003, 148).

35. See *La camera dei deputati celebra il ventennale della Resistenza: 5 maggio 1965* (1965).

36. The speech was published: Saragat (1965). See Focardi (2005, 45) for an acute discussion of the speech.

37. There were many publications in the 1960s ranging from individual accounts, such as Zangrandi (1963), to the vast collection of documents edited by Etnasi (1966). On Zangrandi see the scholarly studies by Morris (1999 and 2000) and the informative website http://giovannazangrandi.com/.

38. Crainz and Gallerano (1987, 140).

39. On this episode and, for further critical reflection on RAI's programming during the period, see Cipriani (1965).

40. Morviducci (1995).

41. In April 1959, a conference on "La Resistenza e la Scuola" was held in Florence during which Roberto Battaglia issued a plea for the introduction of modern history as a response to the need to "give guidance to the young in the modern world." See Baldissara, Legnani, and Pedrolo (1993, 14).

42. Saitta (1961), Battaglia and Ramat (1961). For other volumes with similar aims published post-Tambroni see Armaroli (1961), Semi (1961), and Carocci (1963). The manuals produced for Italian schools have been analyzed in some detail in Orfei and Starita (1995) and De Bernardi, Gaballo, and Ziruolo (1995).

43. Bertoluzzi (1965).

44. For the text of the "Progetto per corsi di laurea in storia e in materie storiche" see Baldissara, Legnani, and Pedrolo (1993, 127–31).

45. For their impact, the most significant series of lectures was delivered in Turin in the spring of 1959 and published the following year: Permoli (1960). Eight "lessons" were given in all with contributions by the likes of Aldo Garosci, Ferruccio Parri, and Ugo La Malfa. The *Lezioni* were republished in 1962 and in 1999, on the latter occasion with a brief introduction by Marcello Flores.

46. Further evidence of the interest of Triestine Catholics in the Resistance is provided in Botteri (1960).

47. Cotta (1977, 1994).

48. Cotta (1962, 9).

49. Cotta (1962) 14.

50. Bocca (1963) and (1966).

51. Gorrieri (1966) is a detailed history, concentrating on the republic of Montefiorino and the wider context of the Emilian resistance; Bravo (1964) was, like Pansa (1967), originally a degree thesis written under the supervision of Guido Quazza. For an account of another important "zona libera," see Vuga (1961). By far the most important contribution to understanding the nature of the partisan republics was Legnani (1968), which argued that the politics of unity meant that the potential for social and economic innovation was severely circumscribed.

52. Gorrieri's book was highly critical of the communist partisans and provoked strong reactions. See Arturo Colombi's (1966) negative review in *Rinascita*.

53. Aurelio Lepre published a staunch defense of Togliatti's landmark initiative (1966).

54. The cover matter of the 1963 edition speaks of "the new Italy created by the second Risorgimento."

55. See Spriano (1966).

56. Battaglia (1964a).

57. Battaglia (1964b). Battaglia died in 1963.

58. Carli Ballola (1965), Francovich (1961), Franzini (1966), Piscitelli (1965).

59. Battaglia (1965), Lazagna (1966), Martini Mauri (1968). Chiodi's memoir (1946) was republished in 1961 with a brief preface in which the author explained that the new edition was aimed, above all, at the young.

60. Ronchi Della Rocca (1965).

61. Artom (1966) and (2008).

62. Secchia and Frassati (1962); Secchia (1963); Secchia and Frassati (1965). *Enciclopedia dell'antifascismo e della Resistenza* (1968–).

63. Only one of his speeches of the period has been published separately. See Secchia (1960).

64. On the issue of the parallel between the Risorgimento and the Resistance, see also the fine analysis in Rosengarten (1968, 147–68), which clearly illustrates how central the whole question was to 1960s discussions.

65. Longo (1965, 3). *Critica marxista* began publication in January 1963 and was initially edited by Longo and Alessandro Natta. It is worth noting that the *Rinascita* editorial for the twentieth anniversary edition continued to stress the connections with the Risorgimento. The editorial is attributable to Gian Carlo Pajetta (1965). On the other hand, *L'Unità* made the connection, and also saw links with Cuba, Algeria, and the Congo (Santomassimo 2003, 162). *L'Unità* would later publish a series of cartoons for children titled "I partigiani della giungla" (see, for example, June 28, 1968, 13).

66. In an early review, Giorgio Amendola expressed a certain guarded praise for the "unitary orientation" of the encyclopedia, but was critical of the "extension of the Resistance,

in time and space, to include the anti-imperialist and anti-colonial victories of the last twenty years." See Amendola (1969, 21).

67. For a more detailed comparative analysis than is possible here, see Ceva (1964).

68. *Associazione nazionale famiglie dei caduti e dispersi della RSI* (1960, 10).

69. *Associazione nazionale famiglie dei caduti e dispersi della RSI* (1960, 53).

70. Germinario (1999, 65).

71. Pisanò (1962 and 1965).

72. Germinario (1999, 101 and 122).

73. Pansa (1964).

74. Pansa (1965).

75. Pansa (1967).

76. Cassola (1960). *La ragazza di Bube* was one of the first novels to be published in Mondadori's "Oscar" series, which made books available in a cheap paperback format. The series was launched at the end of April 1965.

77. The story has been sympathetically reconstructed in Biagioni (2006).

78. The scene has been discussed by Aldo Viganò who suggests, rather too optimistically, that Risi was hoping to create the "premises for an ethically better society" (*La Resistenza nel cinema italiano 1945–1995*, 1995, 20).

79. See Brunetta (1998, 194). The comments are made in connection with a brief discussion of two war films, *Le quattro giornate* and Giuseppe De Santis' *Italiani brava gente* (on the retreat from Russia).

80. See Collotti (1963) and De Jaco (1962). De Jaco was himself the author of the canonical work on the topic (1956) published by the PCI's Editori Riuniti. For an interesting discussion of West German reaction to the film, see Staron (2007, 246–54).

81. See Cooke (2007b, 40–41), for a more extended discussion. See also Miccichè (1995, 125), and Brunetta (1998, 308). A documentary film Papà Cervi, directed by Franco Cigarini, was also made in 1968.

82. I discuss the film version in chapter 8. For an authoritative and recent discussion of Meneghello (and other works of the 1960s, seen as a period in which a new Resistance canon emerged) see Baldini (2008, 109–35).

83. Bertoli (1961). The book contains much polemical material concerning the Allies' discrimination against the communists, but also offers some remarkable descriptions of violence, including a scene describing the execution of a partisan guilty of a range of crimes. Antonicelli's play (1964), was performed by the Teatro Stabile of Bologna to apparently packed houses in Turin and elsewhere. The show entailed the reading of various "glorious anti-Fascist documents," which even a sympathetic reviewer admitted lacked "dramatic effect." See Scacherl (1965).

84. *Una questione privata* was first published in 1963, together with *Un giorno di fuoco* and a series of other short stories. Like *Il partigiano Johnny* it was unfinished at the time of the author's death and comprised a number of different redactions that are published in the critical edition (Fenoglio, 1978). The success of the book, as well as Calvino's praise in his preface to the 1964 edition of *Il sentiero*, have encouraged several filmmakers to produce their own versions, the first of these being Giorgio Trentin's 1966 film, followed by films for state television in 1982 and 1991, respectively.

85. Sacco (1964); Fossà (1964); Valdrè (1964); Bergamini (1964); Cannella (1964); Ariaudo, (1964); Ottolenghi Minerbi (1965); Seppia (1965); Spaziani (1965); and Patelli (1965). The books were published for a second time in the early 1970s. For some brief comments on these texts see Ballone (1997, 427–28).

86. Sturani (1966). The other works dedicated to the Resistance in the series were Francescotti (1966), Marianelli (1965), and Ugolini (1966). I am grateful to the staff of the children's library at the Sala Borsa in Bologna for their assistance in tracing these works.

87. Ugolini (1967). The supporting material was produced by Marisa Avigdor Malvano.

88. Picchio (1965) was translated as *Freedom Fighter* by Isabel Quigly (1980); Libenzi (1964).

89. Libenzi (1964, 172).

90. All information on this monument, and the quotations that follow, are taken from Comitato esecutivo per l'inaugurazione del monumento alla Resistenza di Udine (1970).

91. Taviani (2002, 267–68).

92. See, for example, the coverage in *Rinascita* 19 (May 7, 1966), 3–4. The most recent discussion of the death of Paolo Rosso is Panvini (2009, 10–17).

93. Parri's speech at the senate debate on the proposed dissolution of the MSI is reproduced in Parri (1976, 242–50). On the "Piano Solo," see Franzinelli (2010), which argues for a less dramatic reading of the mysterious events of 1964.

94. On this incident, see Nenni (1983, 178).

95. The expression is Franzinelli's (2001, 16) who includes the Florentine Angiolo Gracci in a list of former partisans who appealed to the younger generations. Gracci founded a social movement in the 1970s called "La Resistenza continua." For a history of this movement, see Cooke (2000c).

96. The first issue was published in March 1963, the last in June 1984. On this journal see Polese Remaggi (2004, 379–91).

97. A number of the *Resistenza* pieces can be found in the collection of Venturi's political writings (1996).

98. *L'Astrolabio*, VI.8 (February 1968), 15.

99. On Quazza as a figure of ridicule, see Passerini (1988, 109).

100. Amendola (1967).

101. The article is also reproduced in Focardi (2005, 198–205).

102. Del Carria (1966), Ganapini (1986, 100).

103. According to Barca (2005, 54) another partisan, Antonello Trombadori, had responsibility for looking after party leaders in Rome. This is the only information that I have found on PCI security measures for its leaders.

104. Pesce (1967, 136–45).

105. Ganapini (1986, 99).

106. Catanzaro and Manconi (1995).

107. Pesce (1967, 10).

108. Pezzino (2005, 397).

109. Santomassimo (2003, 164).

Chapter 5

1. On the 1970s see Ginsborg (1990, 348–404); Lepre (1993, 251–287); Clark (1996, 374–93).

2. Galmozzi (1986, 12).

3. Dogliani refers to the "moment of intensity" experienced while walking along the pathway of the "partigiane," which is punctuated by murals painted by local children and students (1995, 30).

4. For more details, see *Monumento ai 100 partigiani che furono fucilati a Sabbiuno nei giorni dal 14 al 23 dicembre 1944* (1975) and Preti (1994).

5. Gundle (2000, 129).
6. For more information on Zibecchi and Varalli see the site at http://www
.pernondimenticare.com.
7. The set contains Aldo De Jaco, *Le quattro giornate di Napoli*; Guido Nozzoli, *Quelli di Bulow*; Maurizio Milan, *Fuoco in pianura*; Mario De Micheli, *7a GAP*; Luciano Bergonzini, *Quelli che non si arresero*; Arturo Colombi, *Nelle mani del nemico*; Giuliano Pajetta, *Douce France*; and Robert Katz, *Morte a Roma*. With the exception of Katz's work, these were all books that had originally been published in the 1950s.
8. Longo (1973); Amendola (1973).
9. Cerchia (2004, 400) speaks briefly and vaguely of a "progressive and profound" act of "political rethinking" that led to a recovery of his "unitary vocation." For Amendola's own account, see Amendola (1973, 300–301).
10. Longo (1975).
11. Amendola (1994, 169–70).
12. Amendola (1994, 175).
13. Quazza (1976). For a perceptive discussion of this text see Delzell (1978).
14. See Ellwood (1975).
15. See, for example, *L'altra metà della Resistenza* (1978), which was originally a conference.
16. *La resistenza taciuta* (1976).
17. Guidetti Serra (1977).
18. Other works from the 1970s include: Papa (1975); Bortolotti (1978); *Donne e Resistenza in Toscana* (1978); *La donna nella Resistenza in Liguria* (1979). These were all, like *Compagne*, region specific. Other works recounted individual experiences: Giacobino (1978), Vinciguerra (1978). Ada Marchesini Gobetti's diary (1956), an established classic, was published in a special edition for schools, with an introduction and copious notes by Goffredo Fofi (1972). In the 1990s, three works were published that gave an overview of the whole question, but also acknowledged their debts to the pioneers of the 1970s: see Bravo and Bruzzone (1995); Slaughter (1997); and Addis Saba (1998). In the same period, the ANPI also published a comprehensive bibliography on the issue (Carrarini, 1994). More recently the most important work has been published by Gagliani (2000, 2006).
19. Of the literary texts the most significant was Dusi (1973). In terms of anthologies the most successful was Luti and Romagnoli (1975), which took an interdisciplinary approach. Marchetti and Tassinari also republished their 1955 anthology, minus the original preface by Giovanni Gronchi. For children's literature see, for example Tumiati (1976) and Frullini (1977). Tumiati's preface (1976, v-vii) is a frank and honest assessment of the difficulties of conveying the message of the Resistance to young people.
20. *La guerra civile in Italia* (1975).
21. The Secchia case is discussed in Dubla (1998). See also Mafai (1984). A large selection of Secchia's writings and speeches on the Resistance were published in the polemically titled *La Resistenza accusa* (1973).
22. There is precious little reliable information on these associations and on the proposed "*golpe bianco*" (white coup). For his last statements on this affair before his death, see Sogno and Cazzullo (2000). Sogno was also the author of *Guerra senza bandiera*, a popular memoir that has been frequently republished (Sogno 1995) and that gives full vent to his idea of an apolitical Resistance.
23. The original appears in an interview in *Gente* of August 1975. I quote from Silj (1977, 67).
24. Similarly, Martin Clark perceives the importance of the generational question: "their fathers had risked all in the struggle against fascism: now it was their turn" (Clark

1984, 386). Ginsborg widens the issue underlining the significance of the Tupamaros, but also states that the "other reference point was the Italian partisan movement of 1943–1945. The terrorists interpreted the Resistance as a striking example of a youthful minority using violent means for just ends" (Ginsborg 1990, 362).

25. A. Franceschini (1988, 4).
26. A. Franceschini (1988, 32).
27. *La mappa perduta* (1994).
28. Ronconi, one of the terrorists interviewed for Novelli and Tranfaglia's book, relates how his organization had the "pompous name of the Ferretto Brigade (the Resistance references are evident)." See Novelli and Tranfaglia (1988, 123).
29. Cecchini (1998, 231–32).
30. To be fair to the ANPI, it did have to defend itself against more than just misguided appropriation. Throughout the 1970s the ANPI, headquarters in Rome, as well as ANPI offices in many other cities were subject to frequent neo-Fascist attacks.
31. Soccorso Rosso, (1976, 91).
32. The "Volante rossa" also inspired the *sigle* of various organizations, including a minor formation of Prima Linea, in Rome the "Compagni organizzati in Volante Rossa" and, in Milan, a group within "Lotta continua."
33. Catanzaro and Manconi (1995, 8).
34. Catanzaro and Manconi (1995, 102).
35. The document Passerini refers to here is the statement read out at the GAP-BR trial in May 1979.
36. See, for example, the testimony of "Nitta," who describes how he would accompany his grandfather to the *osterie* of the Val di Susa where animated discussions on the Resistance would take place. From these discussions Nitta was left with a sense of a "betrayed Revolution" and "the sensation that all had been in vain and irrelevant" (Novelli and Tranfaglia 1988, 77). Similar sentiments are expressed by Roccazzella (Novelli and Tranfaglia 1988, 81), whose father had been a partisan leader decorated for his activities.
37. Ventura (1984, 84). For an example of the improvement in studies on Feltrinelli, see Grandi's biography (2000).
38. Mattioli (1972, 26).
39. Grandi (2000, 375).
40. See Progetto Memoria (1995, 38–39).
41. See Progetto Memoria (1995, 33–35).
42. Statement by Curcio, Augusto Viel, and others, cited in Grandi (2000, 440).
43. See Redazione materiali per una nuova sinistra (1988, 195).
44. For more details of this bizarre incident, see Willan (1991, 199).
45. One of the very few sources of information on Lazagna is Calegari and Costantino (1979).
46. On the circulation of the slogan, see Bermani (1997). Giorgio Bocca has argued, quite wrongly, that the idea of a "red" Resistance comes from the PCI propaganda machine (1978, 18).
47. The article is cited in Gundle (1996, 33). Nevertheless, it is difficult to agree with Archibugi's argument that the Resistance had enjoyed a revival in 1968, but that this had died out in the 1970s.
48. Fallani (*Note su quarant'anni di vita dell'ANPI provinciale di Firenze*, 88).
49. Fallani (*Note su quarant'anni di vita dell'ANPI provinciale di Firenze*, 99).
50. *I dieci congress nazionali dell'ANPI* (1991, 35).
51. *La Resistenza e la scuola* (1971, 5).

52. *La Resistenza e la scuola*, (1971, 117).
53. *La Resistenza e la scuola*, (1971, 118).
54. *La Resistenza e i giovani: trentennale della liberazione 1945–1975* (1975, 17).

Chapter 6

1. See Baldassare and Mezzanotte (1985, 220–27) for an account of this election. Ginsborg (1990, 142–43) writes that "Craxi had insisted that the next President be a Socialist" but that Pertini had not been his "first choice."
2. Despite his great significance, there is no full-length scholarly biography of Pertini. On Pertini's political career after the Resistance, but before his election to the presidency, see Scroccu (2008).
3. On the Resistance debate in the 1980s, see Focardi (2005, 56–61); Lupo (2004); Rapone (2000) and Gallerano (1986).
4. Ballone (1997, 417).
5. All quotations from *Camera dei deputati—Senato della Repubblica, VII Legislatura, Seduta comune di domenica 9 luglio 1978*, 1–3.
6. Cecchini (1998, 241).
7. Gianluca Scroccu, "In cella nasce l'amicizia tra Antonio e Pertini," in *L'Unione Sarda*, May 12, 2009.
8. Uboldi (1982, 105).
9. For a study of Valiani and his activities up to 1943, see Ricciardi (2007). There is, as yet, no detailed study of Valiani's wartime and postwar activities.
10. Valiani (1982). There is a very comprehensive bibliography of Valiani's publications (Busino 2000).
11. Valiani died in September 1999. In his commemoration, the president of the senate, Nicola Mancino, referred to him as "one of the highest figures of Italian Democracy," spoke of his "lesson of dignity and moral probity," and singled out his contribution to the "moral and civil resistance against the threat of armed subversion" (Valiani 2005, 293, 294).
12. On Pertini as an Italian who was "old and new at the same time," see Gervasoni (2010, 29).
13. Berlinguer's final speech is available on YouTube: http://www.youtube.com/watch?v=6udt2ZZinGI&feature=related.
14. For a detailed account of Craxi's leadership in the period 1976–1981, see Colarizi (2004). See also the volume jointly written by Colarizi and Gervasoni (2005, 76–113 and 114–50).
15. The article appeared in *L'Espresso* and can be read online at http://www.dorinopiras.it/ostrakon/politica.
16. Codignola (1978a).
17. "Parallels of this type lend themselves too easily to mystification, also because the moral force which inspired Rosselli, his concrete will and capacity for struggle and sacrifice, cannot be associated with the more mediocre reality of political maneuvering," Codignola (1978b).
18. Codignola (1981).
19. Codignola went on to form a "Lega dei socialisti," describing the project in an article published in *Il manifesto*. But he died on the same day as the article was published, December 12, 1981. In his last television appearance he gave, appropriately enough, an interview on Rosselli. For details and appreciations of Codignola's life, see Enriques

Agnoletti (1982), De Martino (1982) and, most usefully, Antonio Giolitti's commemorative speech a year after his death (1982). Codignola's political writings were subsequently published by La Nuova Italia, the publishing house he ran for many years (1987a). In the same year his writings on educational theory and the school system (1987b) were also published by La Nuova Italia.

20. The bibliography on Marzabotto is extraordinarily extensive with the most authoritative study being Baldissara and Pezzino, *Il massacro* (2009). See also Staron (2007), which deals at length with issue of memory, but which is flawed by its insistence on a two-dimensional "myth of the Resistance."

21. For the full text of the letter, see Giorgi (1991, 149–50).

22. Staron (2007, 316).

23. Sabbioni immediately received an invitation to appear on television alongside the mayor of Marzabotto, Dante Cruicchi. In her own account of these events (Sabbioni, 2002) she gave a nervous performance before the television cameras.

24. Giorgio Bocca, "Io sono a favore di Reder libero," *La Repubblica* (December 29, 1984), 6.

25. *La Repubblica* (January 25, 1985), 4.

26. *La Repubblica*, (January 30, 1985), 6.

27. Pecchioli (1985). The full text of the article is also reproduced in Focardi (2005, 242–45).

28. The debate over De Felice and the interpretation of Fascism is beyond the scope of this book. In terms of its connections with the "crisis of the anti-Fascist paradigm" see Gallerano (1986, 108–18).

29. Ostellino (1980).

30. Tranfaglia (1985); De Martino (1985); Arfé (1985). See also the editorial by Nicola Badaloni, (1985), which offers little more than formulaic appreciations of the wisdom of Gramsci and Togliatti.

31. Both pieces are reproduced in Focardi (2005, 249–51 and 246–49). Focardi acutely observes that, although Craxi participated in the official celebrations he was, in reality, the prime force behind the critical articles (Focardi 2005, 61). On Colletti and Guarini, see also Gallerano (1986, 127).

32. For an account in English of Colletti's varied career, see the *Guardian* obituary at http://www.guardian.co.uk/news/2001/nov/08/guardianobituaries.international educationnew.

33. Colletti and others would return to the attack on anti-Fascism at the end of 1987 in a period when Craxi again felt it necessary to create space for himself by undermining the so-called "constitutional arc." See De Luna and Revelli (1995, 3).

34. On *La notte di San Lorenzo* the most interesting analyses are by Marcus (1986) and Landy (2000). See also the detailed *scheda* in De Santi (1988, 115–23).

35. See Paoletti (2000) and, for the results of the official enquiry, Paggi (2004).

36. Foot (2009).

37. On developments in the Italian novel in this period, see the collection of essays edited by Baranski and Pertile (1993) and, above, all the introductory essay by Pertile (1–19).

38. Della Torre (1979).

39. Falaschi (1984).

40. Faggi (1981).

41. I therefore agree with Pamela Ballinger who argues that the text "helped prompt a more widespread appraisal of those adolescents" who fought for the RSI (2003, 118).

42. Bersellini (1998, 79). On Mazzantini's book, but also more generally on literary treatments of the Salò experience, see Liucci (1996).

43. Hainsworth (1999, 85). The book has also had a considerable impact in the English-speaking world, with the 1992 translation winning the Independent Foreign Fiction Award.
44. Mazzantini (1995, 20).
45. Germinario (1999).
46. One of the chapters of the book (Mazzantini, 1995b) is titled "The RSI is not a continuation of Fascism." On this text, see Bersellini's critical comments (1998, 79–82).
47. Mazzantini (1995, 81).
48. Mazzantini (1995, 82).
49. Hainsworth (1999, 86).
50. Mazzantini (1995, 138).
51. Mazzantini (1995, 202).
52. Ballinger (2003, 118).
53. Carocci, Grassi, Nistico, and Pavone (1979); De Luna (1985).
54. De Luna (1982).
55. Nahoum (1981); Scappini (1981); Chiarini Scappini (1982).
56. Pajetta (1986).
57. Giampaolo Pansa, "Perché Nullo non dice tutto?" *La Repubblica*, March 1, 1986, 27.
58. The conference proceedings, Poggio (1986), were published the following year and contain a wide variety of contributions as well as an introduction by William Deakin (Poggio 1986, 5–10), which focused on the lack of international recognition of the legitimacy of the RSI. It is worth mentioning in passing that Luciano Violante, who would several years later make the famous *ragazzi di Salò* speech, gave a paper on "L'amministrazione della giustizia" (Poggio 1986, 289–94).
59. *La Repubblica*, October 6, 1985, 5.
60. Luigi Micheletti, "Presentazione," in Poggio (1986, 5).
61. As Quazza explained (Poggio 1986, 447) his objection was not to the idea of the conference *per se*, but to the risk that by concentrating on the specific period of the RSI's history (November 1943 to April 1945) the phenomenon would be cut off from the long-term processes that led to its formation.
62. Claudio Pavone, "La guerra civile," in Poggio (1986, 409).
63. Giancarlo Pajetta, in Poggio (1986, 431–46).
64. *L'Unità*, October 5, 1985, 13.
65. Malavasi (1982).
66. *Civitas* 9 (1980), 3.
67. *La guerra partigiana in Italia* (1984).
68. De Antonellis published a full-length biography of Puecher in 1984.
69. Taviani (1988). Taviani would continue to publish on the Resistance, in separate articles (Taviani 1994, on women in the Resistance) as well as in his memoirs (2002).
70. *Episodi della guerra partigiana* (1988).
71. *Resistenza: un'ipotesi di lettura* (1989, 3).
72. *L'Unità*, November 11, 1989, 1.
73. Kertzer (1996, 1–3).
74. *L'Unità*, November 13, 1989, 8.
75. Natta (1999, 10).

Chapter 7

1. For a highly authoritative and trenchant analysis see Ginsborg (1996) and, in greater detail (2003, 249–84). See also Bufacchi and Burgess (2001).
2. On the transformation of the PCI, the best study in Italian is still Ignazi (1992). For an analysis of PDS strategy in the period 1992–1994, see Bull (1996). On "Rifondazione comunista" there is precious little secondary material with the exception of Foot (1996).
3. Storchi (2007, 237).
4. See Focardi (2005, 61–69, 61).
5. Rusconi (1993) and (1995).
6. See Galli della Loggia (1996).
7. For a vigorous defense of the *festa nazionale*, the key work is by the Catholic political scientist Pietro Scoppola (1995).
8. On this issue, see De Luna and Revelli (1995).
9. *Patria indipendente*, 1 (January 1993), 6..
10. Gundle (2000, 114).
11. Storchi (2007, 243).
12. Magnanini (1992, 11).
13. Fanti (1990).
14. *Carlino Reggio*, August 28, 1990, 3
15. Montanari (1998, 25).
16. Montanari (1998, 26).
17. Montanari (1998, 27).
18. Bertani (2002).
19. Kertzer (1996, 117).
20. Miriam Mafai, *La verità su quel triangolo rosso*, *La Repubblica*, August 31, 1990, 1.
21. Manfredi Luigi, "In archivio i delitti del '45," *Corriere della Sera*, March 3, 1992, 15.
22. Nicolini's suggestion that there had been a deliberately orchestrated plan against him led the *carabinieri* general Pasquale Vesce, who conducted the original investigations in 1947, to initiate defamation proceedings against him. Vesce died in February 1993. For his last statements on the whole affair, see Storchi (1990).
23. On the outcome of the Perugia retrial, see the *Corriere della Sera* of December 8, 1993. On Nicolini, the most balanced and comprehensive account is Sessi (2000). See Nicolini (1997) for his own account.
24. The episode is recounted in Bermani (1997, v).
25. *La Repubblica*, September 9, 1993, 11.
26. *La Repubblica*, April 26, 1994, 5.
27. Piazzale Loreto had, up until the end of the 1970s, been the traditional gathering place in Milan prior to the April 25 demonstrations, but there had subsequently been a switch to Porta Venezia at the other end of Corso Buenos Aires. As far as I know, the 1994 decision was exceptional.
28. Cenci (1999, 376).
29. Cenci (1999, 377).
30. *La Repubblica*, March 10, 1995, 36.
31. Paola Sacchi "25 Aprile di polemiche," *L'Unità*, April 25, 1995, 4.
32. Focardi (2005, 66). For a more extensive discussion of April 25, 1994, and 1995, the key article is Baldissara (2002).
33. *Comitato nazionale per le celebrazioni del cinquentennale della Resistenza e della guerra di liberazione* (1996), which is the source of the statistical information in these paragraphs.

34. Quoted in Colla (1995, 25).
35. Legnani, Pavone, and Vendramini (1995).
36. For a characteristically perceptive and scholarly discussion, including a long list of reviews, interviews, and opinion pieces, see Legnani (1992).
37. Mario Isnenghi, "C'è modo e modo di parlare di storia," *Corriere della Sera*, November 17, 1993, 39.
38. Pavone (1991, 160).
39. De Felice (1997).
40. Turi (1996).
41. De Felice (1995). On the reactions to this work, see the monumentally detailed "Bibliografia di e su Renzo De Felice," compiled by Fiorentino (2002). See also Bersellini (1998) and Pistillo (1998). For a general, and very critical, discussion of the entire Mussolini biography, see Mack Smith (2000).
42. See Monticelli (2000).
43. Research carried out around the same time that *Combat Film* was shown did, however, suggest that young Italians had a far better knowledge of, and sympathy for, the Resistance than was commonly believed to be the case. Of the young people surveyed, 56.8 percent knew that it was Badoglio who signed the armistice and 33.7 percent knew that Togliatti was the architect of the *svolta di Salerno*. The research was led by the sociologist Daniele Mezzana (1997). Further analysis of young people and their memory of the Resistance can be found in Baiesi and Guerra (1997).
44. The book for children, Petter (1953), was one of the series discussed in chapter 2.
45. Petter (1993).
46. Petter (1995, 4).
47. Fenoglio (1994). In the early 1990s, Fenoglio's writings were given the honor of publication in Einaudi's prestigious "Biblioteca della Pléiade" series (1992).
48. Revelli (1994).
49. Angelino (1995); Lucarelli (1991); Gennari (1995).
50. Passerini (1999, 294).
51. Simonetta Fiori speaks of "a kind of dialect pastiche which draws from the Piedmontese repertory," *La Repubblica*, October 15, 1994, 38.
52. See Dino Messina "La vita breve del partigiano Galimberti," in *Corriere della Sera*, October 15, 1994, 35, which publishes a long extract from the book.
53. See Pansa (1967, 6 n5).
54. Pansa (1994, 186).
55. Pansa (1994, 102).
56. Pansa (1994, 105).

Chapter 8

1. There have been a number of literary texts that have championed the RSI, such as the collection of short stories Accolla, Franzolin, Giorleo, and Grazioli (1998). Franzolin has also published his own collection of stories (1992) as well as a second edition of his novel *Il repubblichino* (1995), first published in 1985. For the partisans, on the other hand, see the novel by Giancarlo Governi (1998) about the partisan commander Alessandro Brucellaria, and Ravagli and Wu Ming (2000) that traces the vicissitudes of an Italian partisan who ends up fighting for the Resistance in Laos. Finally, and quite remarkably, the indefatigable Guido Petter published another narrative for children (2004), more than fifty years after his first attempt.

2. The full text of the speech can be accessed via Luciano Violante's website: http://www
   .lucianoviolante.it/.
3. "Salò, capire e superare," *La Repubblica*, May 16, 1996, 5.
4. Ellwood (2005, 391). Ellwood's piece is an introduction to a valuable special issue of
   the *Journal of Modern Italian Studies* on "The never-ending liberation."
5. On this incident see Ginsborg (2003, 307). Bossi would go on to establish a "Committee for the Liberation of Padania" in 1996, a conscious reference to the "Committee for
   National Liberation" of the period 1943–1945.
6. Michele Smargiassi, "Sui ragazzi di Salò idee da guerra fredda," *La Repubblica*, May 12,
   1996, 8.
7. Pezzino (2005, 397).
8. The late Nicola Gallerano was probably the Italian historian most passionately concerned with this theme. See Gallerano (1995) and (1999b). For a more recent and
   authoritative discussion, see Pivato (2007).
9. Santomassimo (2003, 137).
10. Pansa (1994, 1995, and 1996).
11. On the Giubelli case, see Bertoldi (1993, 205) as well as the more recent book by Cara-
    foli (2008).
12. Pansa (1998).
13. Pansa (2002).
14. Simonetta Fiori, "Storie dei ragazzi di Salò," *La Repubblica*, October 11, 2002, 46.
15. See Claudia Morgoglione, "Tutti gli orrori dei partigiani nel film più discusso del Festi-
    val," in *La Repubblica*, October 26, 2008. In the film the Pansa figure (recast as a detec-
    tive) is played by Michele Placido.
16. Storchi (2008).
17. Pansa (2003, ix).
18. On this organization, see Guerriero and Rondinelli (1996).
19. Foot (2009, 181).
20. Pansa (2005 and 2006).
21. "Contestato Pansa a Reggio Emilia" available at http://italy.indymedia.org/news/
    2006/10/1166655.php.
22. Pansa (2007).
23. Pansa (2008).
24. Pansa (2010, 462).
25. Storchi (2007, 244).
26. Luzzatto, quoted in Storchi (2007, 247).
27. Foot (2009, 182).
28. Serena (1990). He was by no means the first—see, for example, Giovannini (1975) that
    also makes copious works of photographic material and the works of Pisanò.
29. Pansa (2009).
30. Bongiovanni (2003).
31. Vivarelli (2000).
32. Simonetta Fiori, "La Bibbia dei revisionisti," *La Repubblica*, October 22, 1999.
33. Belardelli (1999).
34. See, for example Berti (2005), the Resistance diary of a Tuscan priest; Preziosi (2007), a
    collection of essays that publishes Teresio Olivelli's partisan prayer in an appendix and,
    most importantly, De Rosa (1997) that publishes the *atti* of a 1995 conference in Rome
    on "Cattolici, Chiesa. Resistenza" and is the first of a serious of no less than seven thick
    volumes on the subject.
35. Santomassimo (2004, 12).

36. Fontana (2001).
37. Fontana (2001, 9).
38. Fontana (2001, 50).
39. Gobbi (1992 and 1999).
40. Finetti (2004).
41. The Pizzoni case has been particularly controversial. His memoirs were first published by Einaudi in 1993, in an apparently small print run, and then by Il Mulino in 1995, with a preface by Renzo De Felice. His recent biographer, Piffer, also uses the word "cancelled" in the polemical title of his book (2005). The most even-handed discussion of Pizzoni is by Rusconi (1995, 131–36).
42. See, for example, Bersellini (1998). For a general survey of the historiographical debate provoked by "revisionism," see the collection of essays in Collotti (2000). See also Andrea Mammone's lucid article (Mammone 2006) and the excellent collection edited by Angelo Del Boca (2009), which has two chapters dedicated to the Resistance. Though less overtly reactions to revisionism, a discreet set of "popularizing texts" aimed at a younger market also fit into the category of works "in defense of the Resistance," for example: Anselmi (2003 and 2004); Cavaglion (2008).
43. De Luna (2006, xi).
44. Storchi (2005); Dondi (2004 and 2007).
45. Peli (2004). By Peli, see also *La Resistenza difficile* (1999), which examines a number of problematic issues related to the Resistance.
46. The rediscovery of the Internati Militari Italiani (IMI) has been a key issue in recent years. For two personal accounts (of the many that have been published) see the memoir by the former leader of the PCI Alessandro Natta (1997) and L. Collo (1995). The most detailed and exhaustive scholarly reconstruction is Hammermann (2004).
47. Peli (2006).
48. Collotti, Sandri, and Sessi (2000 and 2001); Baldissara (2000).
49. Paggi (1996) contains the proceedings of the conference. For a detailed overview of the research project that analyzed the massacres throughout Italy see Pezzino (2007); see also Klinkhammer (1997) and, more recently, Fulvetti (2009), which offers a comprehensive overview of the massacres in Tuscany. On individual *stragi* see Pezzino (1997 and 2008).
50. See, among others, Focardi (2000); Franzinelli (2002); Battini (2003).
51. Baldissara and Pezzino (2009).
52. Contini (1997).
53. Portelli (1999).
54. Martinelli would go on to direct a television version of Pansa's *La bambina dalle mani sporche* in 2005.
55. See Cesselli (1975), Gervasutti (1997), Padoan (1966 and 2000) and D. Franceschini (1998). Porzus has also inspired a novel by Carlo Sgorlon, *La malga di Sìr* (1997).
56. Marcia Landy, "History on trial: the case of Porzus," available at http://www.latrobe.edu.au/screeningthepast/firstrelease/fr0499/mlfr6c.htm.
57. The film scholar Zagarrio criticizes the film for its use of computer-generated special effects, such as the way the young Storno "morphs" into the old version, and the "recurrent flashbacks" (Zagarrio 1998, 109–10). But as I argue the films *deliberately* draws our attention to these aspects.
58. See Gervasutti (1997).
59. Meneghello (1964). On the genre of the book see Meneghello's preface to the 1976 Rizzoli edition: "The previous publisher called it a 'novel' and I don't doubt the new one will do the same; but I certainly hadn't set out to write a novel (nor, indeed, a

non-novel). Rather, I hoped that it could be read as a narrative, that it had a narrative construction" (1976, 9–10).

60. Fenoglio (1968).
61. Fenoglio (1978).

Conclusion

1. Ginsborg (2004, 153).
2. For a comparative study, see the various chapter in Evans and Lunn (1997) and, more recently, Macmillan (2009, 112–38).
3. Pavone (2007, 6).

References

The reference list contains all works cited in text, with the exception of newspaper articles, for which full references are given in the notes.

L'altra metà della Resistenza. 1978. Milan: Mazzotta.
La camera dei Deputati celebra il ventennale della Resistenza: 5 maggio 1965. 1965. Rome: Editoriale grafica.
Cinema, storia, Resistenza 1944–1985. 1987. Milan: Franco Angeli.
La Democrazia cristiana resta fedele agli ideali della Resistenza. 1955. Rome: Democrazia cristiana: Spes.
Dentro la storia: cinema, Resistenza, pace. 1984. Bologna: Patron.
I dieci congressi nazionali dell'ANPI. 1991. Rome: Arti Grafiche Jasillo.
Documenti del CLN per la Liguria. 1968. Rome: Sograro.
Documenti politici e direttive del Partito comunista italiano dall'VIII al IX congresso. 1960. Rome: Seti.
La donna nella Resistenza in Liguria. 1979. Florence: La Nuova Italia.
Donne cristiane nella Resistenza: Testimonianze e documentazioni sul contributo femminile alla lotta partigiana in Lombardia. 1956. Milan: Tip. A Molinari.
Donne e Resistenza in Toscana. 1978. Florence: Comitato femminile antifascista per il 30. della Resistenza e della liberazione in Toscana.
Enciclopedia dell'antifascismo e della Resistenza. Volumes 1–3. 1968, 1971, 1976. Milan: La Pietra.
Enciclopedia dell'antifascismo e della Resistenza. Volumes 4–6. 1984, 1987, 1989. Bergamo: Walk Over.
Episodi della guerra partigiana. 1988. Rome: Civitas.
La guerra civile in Italia: Racconti, testimonianze, ricordi. 1975. Milan: A. Mondadori.
La guerra partigiana in Italia. 1984. Rome: Civitas.
L'Italia l'è malada. 1955. Milan: Edizioni Avanti.
Memoria e giustizia. Stragi, crimini di guerra, processi—Italia 1943–1945. Giorni di storia 8. 2003. Rome: L'Unità.
Monumento ai 100 partigiani che furono fucilati a Sabbiuno nei giorni dal 14 al 23 dic. 1944. 1975. Bologna: Poligrafici L. Parma.
Progetto memoria. 1994. *La mappa perduta*. Rome: Sensibili alle foglie.
———. 1995. *Sguardi ritrovati*. Rome: Sensibili alle foglie.
La Resistenza e i giovani: Trentennale della liberazione 1945–1975. 1975. Parma: A. L. P. I.
La Resistenza e la scuola. 1971. Brescia: La scuola.
La Resistenza nel cinema italiano, 1945–1995. 1995. Genoa: Istituto storico della Resistenza in Liguria.
La Resistenza taciuta. 1976. Milan: La Pietra.
Resistenza: un'ipotesi di lettura. 1989. Rome: Civitas.
Saggi sulla Resistenza. 1974. Rome: Civitas.

Scarpe rotte eppur bisogna andar. 1955. Milan: Edizioni Avanti.

Il secondo risorgimento: Nel decennale della Resistenza e del ritorno alla democrazia, 1945–1955. 1955. Rome: Istituto Poligrafico dello Stato.

Accolla, F. E., U. Franzolin, A. Giorleo, and F. Grazioli. 1998. *Storie d'amore e di guerra.* Rome: Settimo Sigillo.

Addis Saba, M. 1998. *Partigiane. Tutte le donne della Resistenza.* Milan: Mursia.

Aga Rossi, E., and V. Zaslavsky. 1997. *Togliatti e Stalin: il PCI e la politica estera staliniana negli archivi di Mosca.* Bologna: Il Mulino.

Agosti, G. 2005. *Dopo il tempo del furore 1946–1988.* Edited by A. Agosti. Turin: Einaudi.

Ajello, N. 1997. *Il lungo addio. Intellettuali e PCI dal 1958 al 1991.* Rome: Laterza.

Alatri, P. 1948. *Triangoli della morte.* Rome: Tumminelli.

Alessandrini, L. 1999. "The Option of Violence—Partisan Activity in the Bologna Area 1945–1948." In *After the war. Violence, justice, continuity and renewal in Italian society,* 59–74, edited by J. Dunnage. Market Harborough: Troubador.

Amendola, G. 1955. "Dieci anni dopo." *Rinascita* (5): 329–35.

———. 1967. *Comunismo, antifascismo e resistenza.* Rome: Editori Riuniti.

———. 1969. "Antifascismo e Resistenza." *Rinascita* (4): 21.

———. 1973. *Lettere a Milano: Ricordi e documenti 1939–1945.* Rome: Editori Riuniti.

———. 1994. *Intervista sull'antifascismo.* Rome: Laterza.

Andreotti, G. 1945. *Concerto a sei voci: Storia segreta di una crisi.* Edizioni della Bussola.

Angelino, E. 1995. *L'inverno dei mongoli.* Turin: Einaudi.

Aniasi, A. 1991. *Parri: L'avventura umana militare e politica di Maurizio.* Rome: Nuova ERI.

Anselmi, T. 2003. *Zia, cos'è la Resistenza.* Manduria: Manni.

———. 2004. *Bella ciao. La Resistenza raccontata ai ragazzi.* Pordenone: Biblioteca dell'immagine.

Antonicelli, F. 1964. *Festa grande d'aprile: Rappresentazione popolare in due tempi.* Turin: Einaudi.

Arfè, G. 1985. "Da dove viene oggi l'insidia di destra." *Rinascita* (13): 8.

Ariaudo, R. 1964. *La barricata della Doganella: Romanzo per ragazzi.* Farigliano: N. Milano.

Armaroli, M. 1961. *Fascismo e Resistenza: Ad uso delle scuole medie superiori.* Milan: Principato.

Artom, E. 1966. *Diari. Gennaio 1940 febbraio 1944.* Edited by P. De Benedetti and E. Ravenna. Milan: Centro di documentazione ebraica contemporanea.

———. 2008. *Diari di un partigiano ebreo: Gennaio 1940–febbraio 1944.* Edited by G. Schwartz. Turin: Bollati Boringhieri.

Asor Rosa, A. 1988. *Scrittori e popolo: Il populismo nella letteratura italiana contemporanea.* Turin: Einaudi.

Associazione nazionale famiglie dei caduti e dispersi della RSI. 1960. *Lettere di caduti della Repubblica Sociale Italiana.* Rocca San Casciano: Arti Grafiche F. Cappelli.

Atack, M. 1989. *Literature and the French Resistance: Cultural Politics and Narrative Forms 1940–1950.* Manchester, England: Manchester University Press.

Badaloni, N. 1985. "Questo nostro 25 Aprile." *Rinascita* (15): 2–3.

Baiesi, N., and E. Guerra, eds. 1997. *Interpreti del loro tempo: Ragazzi e ragazze tra scena quotidiana e rappresentazione della storia.* Bologna: Clueb.

Baldassare, A. 1986. "La costruzione del paradigma antifascista e la Costituzione repubblicana." *Problemi del socialismo* (7): 11–33.

Baldassare, A., and C. Mezzanotte. 1985. *Gli uomini del Quirinale: Da De Nicola a Pertini.* Rome: Laterza.

Baldini, A. 2008. *Il comunista. Una storia letteraria dalla Resistenza agli anni settanta.* Turin: UTET.

Baldissara, L., ed. 2000. *Atlante storico della Resistenza italiana.* Milan: Bruno Mondadori.

————. 2002. "Auf dem Weg zu einer bipolaren Geschichtsschreiben? Der öffentliche Gebrauch der Resistenza in einer geschictslosen Gegenwart." *Quellen und Forshungen aus italienischen Archiven und Bibliotheken* (82): 599–604.

Baldissara, L., and P. Pezzino. 2009. *Il massacro. Guerra ai civili a Monte Sole.* Bologna: Il Mulino.

Baldissara, L., M. Legnani, and M. Pedrolo. 1993. *Storia contemporanea e università. Inchiesta sui corsi di laurea in storia.* Milan: Franco Angeli.

Ballinger, P. 2003. *History in Exile: Memory and Identity at the Borders of the Balkans.* Princeton, NJ: Princeton University Press.

Ballini, P., ed. 2008. *Un quotidiano della Resistenza. La Nazione del Popolo. Organo del Comitato toscano di liberazione nazionale, 11 agosto 1944–3 luglio 1946.* Florence: Polistampa.

Ballone, A. 1997. "La Resistenza." In *I luoghi della memoria,* 403–38, edited by M. Isnenghi. Rome: Laterza.

Banfi Malaguzzi, D. 1958. *A Milano nella Resistenza.* Rome: Editori Riuniti.

Barański, Z., and L. Pertile, eds. 1993. *The New Italian Novel.* Edinburgh, Scotland: Edinburgh University Press.

Barbagallo, F. 2006. *Enrico Berlinguer.* Rome: Carocci.

Barbieri, O. 1958. *Ponti sull'Arno: La Resistenza a Firenze.* Rome: Editori Riuniti.

Barca, L. 2005. *Cronache dall'interno del vertice del PCI.* Soveria Mannelli: Rubbettino.

Battaglia, A. 1955. "Giustizia e politica nell giurisprudenza." In *Dieci anni dopo: 1945–1955: saggi sulla vita democratica italiana,* 317–408, edited by A. Battaglia, P. Calamandrei, E. Corbino, G. De Rosa, E. Lussu, M. Sansone, and L. Valiani. Rome: Laterza.

Battaglia, A., P. Calamandrei, E. Corbino, G. De Rosa, E. Lussu, M. Sansone, and L. Valiani. 1955. *Dieci anni dopo: 1945–1955: Saggi sulla vita democratica italiana.* Bari: Laterza.

Battaglia, R. 1942a. *Crocifissi del Bernini in S. Pietro in Vaticano.* Rome: Reale istituto di studi romani.

————. 1942b. *L'Aventino nella rinascita e nel barocco attraverso i documenti iconografici: Con 16 illustrazioni e 6 tavole fuori testo.* Rome: Istituto di studi romani.

————. 1943. *Il palazzo di Nerone e la villa Barberini al Gianicolo.* Rome: Reale istituto di studi romani.

————. 1945. *Un uomo, un partigiano.* Rome: Edizioni U.

————. 1947. "Il riconoscimento dei partigiani." *Il ponte* (11–12): 1001–14.

————. 1949. "Come viene fatto il processo alla Resistenza." *Rinascita* (5): 203–10.

————. 1953a. *Storia della Resistenza italiana: (8 settembre 1943–25 aprile 1945).* Turin: Einaudi.

————. 1953b. *Storia della Resistenza italiana: 8 settembre 1943–25 aprile 1945.* Turin: Einaudi.

————. 1954. Review of Longo and Secchia (1954). *Rinascita* (5): 329–32.

————. 1964a. *Storia della Resistenza italiana.* Turin: Einaudi.

————. 1964b. *Risorgimento e Resistenza.* Rome: Riuniti.

————. 1965. *Un uomo, un partigiano.* Turin: Einaudi.

————. 2004. *Un uomo, un partigiano.* Bologna: Il Mulino.

Battaglia, R., and G. Garritano. 1955. *Breve storia della Resistenza italiana.* Turin: Einaudi.

Battaglia, R., and R. Ramat, eds. 1961. *Un popolo in lotta: testimonianze di vita italiana dall'unità al 1946.* Florence: La Nuova Italia.

Battini, M. 2003. *Peccati di memoria: La mancata Norimberga italiana.* Rome: Laterza.

Behan, T. 2009. *The Italian Resistance. Fascists, Guerrillas and the Allies.* London: Pluto.

Belardelli, G. 1999. *Miti e storia dell'Italia unita.* Bologna: Il Mulino.

Bendiscioli, M. 1964. *Antifascismo e Resistenza: Impostazioni storiografiche.* Rome: Studium.

Bergamini, R. 1964. *Il cuore della valle: Romanzo per ragazzi*. Farigliano: N. Milano.

Bermani, C. 1997. *Il nemico interno: Guerra civile e lotte di classe in Italia: 1943–1976*. Rome: Odradek.

Berrini, N. 1945. *Il villaggio messo a fuoco*. Borgo San Dalmazzo: Bertello.

Bersellini, G. 1998. *Il riscatto. 8 settembre–25 aprile. Le tesi di Renzo De Felice. Salò—La Resistenza. L'identità della Nazione*. Milan: Franco Angeli.

Bertacchini, R. 1977. *Carlo Cassola: Introduzione e guida allo studio dell'opera cassoliana: storia e antologia della critica*. Florence: Le Monnier.

Bertani, G. 2002. "La lente dei media. Settembre 1990: 'Operazione verità.' 'La Repubblica nata dalla Resistenza' tra storiografia, politica e mass media." *Ricerche storiche* (93): 11–50.

Berti, F. 2005. *Diario di un anno. Cattolici e Resistenza in Toscana*. Edited by P. L. Ballini. Florence: Edizioni Polistampa.

Bertoldi, S. 1993. *Dopoguerra*. Milan: Rizzoli.

Bertoli, U. 1961. *La quarantasettesima*. Parma: Guanda.

Bertoluzzi, C. 1965. "I nati dopo." *Il ponte* (3–4): 387–527.

Bertucelli, L., A. Canovi, C. Silingardi, and M. Storchi. 1999. "L'invenzione dell'Emilia rossa. La memoria della guerra e la costruzione di un'identità regionale (1943–1960)." In *Le memorie della repubblica*, 269–324, edited by L. Paggi. Florence: La Nuova Italia.

Biagioni, M. 2006. *Nada: La ragazza di Bube*. Florence: Polistampa.

Bianchi, G. 1965. *Giancarlo Puecher a vent'anni, per la libertà*. Milan: A. Mondadori.

Bianchi, G., E. Ragionieri, and L. Valiani. 1971. *Azionisti cattolici e comunisti nella Resistenza*. Milan: Angeli.

Bianco, D. L. 1954. *Guerra partigiana*. Edited by G. Agosti and F. Venturi. Turin: Einaudi.

Bigazzi, R. 1983. *Fenoglio: Personaggi e narratori*. Rome: Salerno.

———. 2011. *Fenoglio*. Rome: Salerno.

Bistarelli, A. 2007. *La storia del ritorno: I reduci italiani del secondo dopoguerra*. Turin: Bollati Boringhieri.

Bocca, G. 1963. *Una repubblica partigiana: Ossola, 10 settembre–23 ottobre 1944*. Milan: Il Saggiatore.

———. 1966. *Storia dell'Italia partigiana: Settembre 1943–maggio 1945*. Bari: Laterza.

———. 1978. *Il terrorismo italiano, 1970–1978*. Milan: Rizzoli.

———. 2005. *Partigiani della montagna*. Milan: Feltrinelli.

———. 2006. *Le mie montagne: Gli anni della neve e del fuoco*. Milan: Feltrinelli.

Boldrini, A. 1985. *Diario di Bulow*. Milan: Vangelista.

Bolis, L. 1995. *Il mio granello di sabbia*. Turin: Einaudi.

Bongiovanni, B. 2003. "'Revisionismo': storia e antistoria di una parola." *Passato e presente* (60): 17–28.

Bortolotti, F. P. 1978. *Le donne della Resistenza antifascista e la questione femminile in Emilia Romagna: 1943–1945*. Milan: Vangelista.

Botteri, G. 1960. *I cattolici triestini nella Resistenza*. Udine: Del Bianco.

Bravo, A. 1964. *La repubblica partigiana dell'alto Monferrato*. Turin: G. Giappichelli.

Bravo, A., and A. M. Bruzzone. 1995. *In guerra senza armi. Storie di donne. 1940–1945*. Rome: Laterza.

Briganti, P. 1984. "L'alba di Fenoglio. Cronache di un debutto letterario." *Studi e problemi di critica testuale* (29): 123–49.

Brunetta, G. P. 1998. *Storia del cinema italiano*. Rome: Riuniti.

Bufacchi, V., and S. Burgess. 2001. *Italy since 1989: Events and Interpretations*. Basingstoke, UK: Palgrave Macmillan.

Bufano, L. 1999. *Beppe Fenoglio e il racconto breve*. Ravenna: Longo.

Bull, M. 1996. "The Great Failure? The Democratic Party of the Left in Italy's Transition." In *The New Italian Republic: From the Fall of the Berlin Wall to Berlusconi*, 159–72, edited by S. Gundle and S. Parker. London: Routledge.

Busino, G., ed. 2000. *Tra storia e politica: Bibliografia degli scritti di Leo Valiani, 1926–1999*. Milan: Fondazione Giangiacomo Feltrinelli.

Cadorna, R. 1948. *La riscossa*. Milan: Rizzoli.

———. 1955. "La Resistenza: il Corpo Volontari della Libertà." In *Il secondo risorgimento: nel decennale della Resistenza e del ritorno alla democrazia, 1945–1955*, 263–90. Rome: Istituto Poligrafico dello Stato.

Calabri, M. C. 2007. *Il costante piacere di vivere. Vita di Giaime Pintor*. Turin: UTET.

Calamandrei, P. 1954. *Passato e avvenire della Resistenza: Discorso per il decennale, tenuto il 28 febbraio 1954 al Teatro Lirico di Milano alla presenza di Ferruccio Parri*. Milan: Grafica Milano.

———. 1955. *Uomini e città della Resistenza. Discorsi, scritti, epigrafi*. Bari: Laterza.

———. 1968. *Lettere 1915–1956*. Edited by G. Agosti and A. Galante Garrone. Florence: La Nuova Italia.

———. 2006. *Uomini e città della Resistenza*. Edited by S. Luzzatto. Bari: Laterza

Caleffi, P. 1955. *Si fa presto a dire fame*. Milan: Edizioni Avanti.

Calegari, M., and Costantini C., eds. 1979. *Antifascismo e partito armato. Intervista con G.B. Lazagna*. Genoa: Ghiron.

Calvino, I. 1947. *Il sentiero dei nidi di ragno*. Turin: Einaudi.

———. 1949. "La letteratura italiana sulla Resistenza." *Movimento di liberazione in Italia* (1): 40–46.

———. 1955. "Paese infido." *Il ponte* (4–5): 592–98.

———. 1957. *Il barone rampante*. Turin: Einaudi.

———. 1991. *I libri degli altri. Lettere 1947–1981*. Edited by G. Tesio. Turin: Einaudi.

———. 2000. *Lettere 1940–1985*. Edited by L. Baranelli. Milan: Mondadori.

Cannella, I. 1964. *Ciao, ragazzi: Racconti per ragazzi*. Farigliano: N. Milano.

Carafoli, D. 2008. *La bambina e il partigiano*. Milan: Mursia.

Carli-Ballola, R. 1954. *1953—Processo Parri*. Milan: Ceschina.

———. 1957. *Storia della Resistenza*. Milan: Edizioni Avanti.

———. 1965. *La Resistenza armata (1943–1945)*. Milan: Edizioni del Gallo.

Carocci, G. 1963. *La Resistenza italiana*. Milan: A. Garzanti.

Carocci, G., G. Grassi, G. Nistico, and C. Pavone, eds. 1979. *Le brigate garibaldi nella Resistenza: documenti*. Milan: Feltrinelli.

Carrarini, R., ed. 1994. *Le donne e la Resistenza. Rassegna bibliografica*. Rome: Arti Grafiche Jassillo.

Casadei, A. 2000. *Romanzi di Finisterre. Narrazione della guerra e problemi del realismo*. Rome: Carocci.

Cassola, C. 1952. *Fausto e Anna*. Turin: Einaudi.

———. 1960. *La ragazza di Bube*. Turin: Einaudi.

———. 2007. *Racconti e romanzi*. Edited by A. Andreini. Milan: Mondadori.

Catalano, F. 1956. *Storia del CLNAI*. Bari: Laterza.

Catalano, F. 1966. "La crisi del governo Parri." *Il ponte* (1): 51–71.

Catanzaro, R., and L. Manconi, eds. 1995. *Storie di lotta armata*. Bologna: Il Mulino.

Cavaglion, A. 2008. *La Resistenza spiegata a mia figlia*. Napoli: L'Ancora del Meditteraneo.

Cecchini, L. 1996. *Per la libertà d'Italia. Per l'Italia delle libertà. Profilo storico dell'Asssociazione Nazionale Partigiani d'Italia. Vol. I 1944–1960*. Rome: Arti Grafiche Jasillo.

———. 1998. *Per la libertà d'Italia. Per l'Italia delle libertà. Profilo storico dell'Asssociazione Nazionale Partigiani d'Italia. Vol. II 1961–1997*. Rome: Arti Grafiche Jasillo.

Cenci, C. 1999. "Rituale e memoria: le celebrazioni del 25 aprile." *Le memorie della repubblica*, 325–78, edited by L. Paggi. Florence: La Nuova Italia.

Cerchia, G. 2004. *Giorgio Amendola. Un comunista nazionale. Dall'infanzia alla guerra partigiana*. Soveria Mannelli: Rubbettino.

Cereja, F. 1987. "La cinematografia sulla Resistenza nella storia italiana." In *Cinema, storia, Resistenza 1944–1985*, 17–29. Milan: Franco Angeli.

Cervi, A. 1955. *I miei sette figli*. Edited by R. Nicolai. Rome: Edizioni di Cultura Sociale.

Cesselli, M. 1975. *Porzus due volti della Resistenza*. Milan: La Pietra.

Ceva, B. 1964. *Cinque anni di storia italiana 1940–1945 da lettere e diari dei caduti*. Milan: Edizioni di Comunità.

Chiarini, R. 2005. *25 aprile: La competizione politica sulla memoria*. Venice: Marsilio.

Chiarini Scappini, R. 1982. *La storia di Clara*. Milan: La Pietra.

Chiodi, P. 1946. *Banditi*. Alba: ANPI.

———. 1961. *Banditi*. Cuneo: Panfilo.

Cipriani, I. 1965. "La Resistenza secondo la TV." *Rinascita* (17): 23.

Clark, M. 1996. *Modern Italy 1871–1995*. London: Longman.

Codignola, T. 1978a. "Il garofano rosso." *Il ponte* (3–4): 300.

———. 1978b. "Questa famosa terza via." *Il ponte* (12): 1001.

———. 1981. "Una minoranza che non fa opposizione." *Il ponte* (1): 132–38.

———. 1987a. *Scritti politici, 1943–1981*. Edited by N. Tranfaglia and T. Borgogni. Florence: La Nuova Italia.

———. 1987b. *Per una scuola di libertà: Scritti di politica educativa, 1947–1981*. Edited by M. Corda Costa. Florence: La Nuova Italia.

Colapietra, R. 1969. *La lotta politica dalla liberazione di Roma alla costituente*. Bologna: Patron.

———. 1998. *Dai comitati di liberazione all'Assemblea Costituente*. Napoli: La Città del Sole.

Colarizi, S. 2004. "La trasformazione della leadership. Il PSI di Craxi." In *Gli anni ottanta come storia*, 31–64, edited by S. Colarizi, P. Craveri, S. Pons, and G. Quaglierello. Soveria Mannelli: Rubbettino.

Colarizi, S., and M. Gervasoni. 2005. *La cruna dell'ago. Craxi, il partito socialista e la crisi della Repubblica*. Rome: Laterza.

Colla, E. 1995. "Didattica e Resistenza nel panorama 'legislativo' del dopoguerra." *La Resistenza europea nella scuola*, 13–25, edited by A. Ventura. Manduria: Lacaita.

Collo, L. 1995. *La resistenza disarmata, la storia dei soldati italiani prigionieri nei lager tedeschi*. Venice: Marsilio.

Collotti, E. 1963. "I tedeschi e le 4 giornate." *Rinascita* (4): 32.

———, ed. 2000. *Fascismo e antifascismo: Rimozioni, revisioni, negazioni*. Rome: Laterza.

Collotti, E., R. Sandri, and F. Sessi, eds. 2000. *Dizionario della Resistenza. Vol. I. Storia e geografia della liberazione*. Turin: Einaudi.

———, eds. 2001. *Dizionario della Resistenza. Vol. 2: Luoghi formazioni, protagonisti*. Turin: Einaudi.

———, eds. 2006. *Dizionario della Resistenza*. Turin: Einaudi.

Colombi, A. 1966. "Montefiorino." *Rinascita* (48): 17.

Colombo, E., ed. 1995. *Matrimonio in brigata. Le opere e i giorni di Renata Viganò e Antonio Meluschi*. Bologna: Grafis.

Comitato esecutivo per l'inaugurazione del monumento alla Resistenza di Udine, ed. 1970. *Nel monumento di Udine la Resistenza in Friuli*. Udine: Del Bianco.

Comitato nazionale per le celebrazioni del cinquantennale della Resistenza e della guerra di liberazione. 1996. *Le radici e le ali: 1943/45–1993/95: memoria e storia delle celebrazioni del cinquentennale della Resistenza e della guerra di liberazione.* Rome: Istituto Poligrafico e Zecca dello Stato.

Commissione femminile dell'ANPI provinciale di Torino, ed. 1954. *Donne piemontesi nella Lotta di Liberazione.* 99 partigiane cadute, 185 deportate, 38 cadute civili. Turin: Tip. Impronta.

Conan, E., and H. Rousso. 1994. *Vichy: Un passé qui ne passe pas.* Paris: Gallimard.

Conti, L. 1961. *La Resistenza in Italia: 25 luglio 1943–25 aprile 1945: saggio bibliografico.* Milan: Feltrinelli.

Contini, G. 1997. *La memoria divisa.* Milan: Rizzoli.

Contini Bonacossi, S., and L. Ragghianti Collobi, eds. 1954. *Una lotta nel suo corso: lettere e documenti politici e militari della Resistenza e della Liberazione.* Venice: N. Pozza.

Contini, G. 1999. "La memoria dopo le stragi del 1944 in Toscana." *Le memorie della repubblica,* 191–220, edited by L. Paggi. Florence: La Nuova Italia.

Cooke, P., ed. 1997. *The Italian Resistance: An Anthology.* Manchester: Manchester University Press.

———. 2000a. *Fenoglio's Binoculars Johnny's Eyes: History, Language and Narrative Technique in Fenoglio's Il partigiano Johnny.* New York, Peter Lang.

———. 2000b. *Luglio 1960: Tambroni e la repressione fallita.* Milan: Teti.

———. 2000c. "The Resistance Continues: A Social Movement in the 1970s." *Modern Italy* 5 (2): 161–73.

———. 2006. "From Partisan to Party Cadre: The Education of Italian Political Emigrants in Czechoslovakia." *Italian Studies* 61 (1): 64–84.

———. 2007a. "Carlo Levi and the Tambroni Affair." In *The Voices of Carlo Levi,* 159–74, edited by J. Farrell. New York: Peter Lang.

———. 2007b. "What Does it Matter If You Die? The Seven Cervi Brothers." In *Assassinations and Murder in Modern Italy: Transformations in Society and Culture,* 33–44, edited by S. Gundle and L. Rinaldi. New York: Palgrave Macmillan.

———. 2007c. "Oggi in Italia: The Voice of Truth and Peace in Cold War Italy." *Modern Italy* 12 (2): 251–65.

Corletto, G. 1965. *Masaccio e la Resistenza tra il Brenta e il Piave.* Vicenza: Neri Pozza.

Cotta, S. 1962. *Interpretazioni della Resistenza.* Trieste: Tip. Adriatica.

———. 1977. *Quale Resistenza? Aspetti e problemi della guerra di liberazione in Italia.* Milan: Rusconi.

———. 1994. *La Resistenza: Come e perché.* Rome: Bonacci.

Cozzolino, I., ed. 1971. *Raccolta di leggi, norme e disposizioni per i combattenti della guerra partigiana.* Rome: Fondazione Corpo volontario della libertà.

Crainz, G. 1986. "La 'legittimazione' della Resistenza. Dalla crisi del centrismo alla vigilia del '68." *Problemi del socialismo* (7): 62–97.

———. 1992. "Il conflitto e la memoria. 'Guerra civile' e 'triangolo della morte.'" *Meridiana* (13): 17–55.

———. 1994. "La violenza postbellica in Emilia fra 'guerra civile' e conflitti antichi." In *Laboratorio di Storia. Studi in onore di Claudio Pavone,* 191–205, edited by P. Pezzino and G. R. Ranzato. Milan: Franco Angeli.

———. 1995. "Il dolore e la collera: quella lontana Italia del 1945." *Meridiana* (22–23): 9–47.

———, ed. 1996. *La Resistenza italiana nei programmi della RAI.* Rome: RAI-ERI.

———. 2000. "I programmi televisivi sul fascismo e la Resistenza." In *Fascismo e antifascismo: Rimozioni, revisioni, negazioni,* 463–92, edited by E. Collotti. Rome: Laterza.

———. 2007. *L'ombra della guerra. Il 1945, l'Italia.* Rome: Donzelli.

Crainz, G., and N. Gallerano. 1987. "I documentari televisivi dulla Resistenza." In *Cinema, storia, Resistenza 1944–1985*, 125–51. Milan: Franco Angeli

Craveri, P., and G. Quaglierello, eds. 2006. *La seconda guerra mondiale e la sua memoria.* Soveria Monnelli: Rubbettino.

De Angelis, S. 1966. *Enrico Mattei.* Rome: Edizioni Cinque Lune.

De Antonellis, G. 1984. *Il caso Puecher.* Milan: Rizzoli.

De Bernardi, A., and P. Ferrari, eds. 2004. *Antifascismo e identità europea.* Rome: Carocci.

De Bernardi, M. L., G. Gaballo, and L. Ziruolo. 1995. "Scuola, manuali, resistenza." In *La Resistenza europea nella scuola*, 49–72, edited by A. Ventura. Manduria: Lacaita.

De Felice, R. 1995. *Rosso e nero.* Edited by P. Chessa. Milan: Baldini & Castoldi.

———. 1997. *Mussolini l'alleato II. La guerra civile 1943–1945.* Turin: Einaudi.

De Jaco, A. 1956. *La città insorge: Le quattro giornate di Napoli.* Rome: Riuniti.

———. 1962. "Le 4 giornate di Napoli." *Rinascita* (29): 32.

Del Boca, A., ed. 2009. *La storia negata: Il revisionismo e il suo uso politico.* Vicenza: Neri Pozza.

Del Carria, R. 1966. *Proletari senza rivoluzione: Storia delle classi subalterne italiane dal 1860 al 1950.* Milan: Edizioni Oriente.

Della Torre, A. 1979. *Messaggio speciale.* Rome: Riuniti.

De Luna, G. 1982. *Storia del Partito d'azione, 1942–1947.* Milan: Feltrinelli.

———, ed. 1985. *Le formazioni GL nella Resistenza: Documenti settembre 1943–aprile 1945.* Milan: Franco Angeli.

———. 2006. *Storia del Partito d'azione, 1942–1947.* Turin: UTET.

De Luna, G., and M. Revelli. 1995. *Fascismo, antifascismo. Le idee, le identità.* Florence: La Nuova Italia.

Delzell, C. F. 1956. "Italian Historical Scholarship: A Decade of Recovery and Development, 1945–1955." *The Journal of Modern History* 28 (4): 374–88.

———. 1961. *Mussolini's Enemies: The Italian Anti-Fascist Resistance.* Princeton, NJ: Princeton University Press.

———. 1978. Review of Guido Quazza, *Resistenza e storia d'Italia. The Journal of Modern History* 50 (1): 160–62.

De Martino, F. 1982. "Un compagno e un amico." *Il ponte* (1–2): 10–13.

———. 1985. "Se la politica diventa solo lotta per il potere." *Rinascita* (13): 8.

De Micheli, M. 1954. *7a GAP.* Rome: Edizioni di Cultura Sociale.

De Pascalis, O., and G. Salemi. 1946. *Assistenza postbellica: Raccolta sistematica delle leggi e delle principali circolari concernenti provvidenze a favore dei reduci con note illustrative e commenti.* Rome: Lanciano.

De Rosa, G. 1997. *Cattolici, Chiesa, Resistenza.* Bologna: Il Mulino.

De Santi, P. M. 1988. *I film di Paolo e Vittorio Taviani.* Rome: Gremese.

Di Loreto, P. 1991. *Togliatti e la doppiezza: Il PCI tra democrazia e insurrezione, 1944–49.* Bologna: Il Mulino.

———. 1992. *La difficile transizione. Dalla fine del centrismo al centro-sinistra 1953–1960.* Bologna: Il Mulino.

Di Nori, P. 2006. *Noi la farem vendetta.* Milan: Feltrinelli.

Dogliani, P. 1995. "Monumenti alla Resistenza: Bologna e il suo territorio." In *La premiata Resistenza: Concorsi d'arte nel dopoguerra in Emilia-Romagna*, 21–36. Edited by Orlando Piraccini, Giovanni Serpe, and Alessandro Sibilia. Bologna: Grafis.

Domenico, R. P. 1991. *Italian Fascists on Trial 1943–1948.* Chapel Hill: University of North Carolina Press.

Dondi, M. 1990. "Piazzale Loreto 29 aprile: aspetti di una pubblica esposizione." *Rivista di storia contemporanea* (2): 219–48.

————. 1999. *La lunga liberazione: giustizia e violenza nel dopoguerra italiano*. Rome: Riuniti.

————. 2004. *La Resistenza tra unità e conflitto*. Milan: Bruno Mondadori.

————. 2007. "Division and Conflict in the Partisan Resistance." *Modern Italy* 12 (2): 225–36.

Donno, G. 2001. *La Gladio rossa del PCI, 1945–1967*. Soveria Mannelli: Rubbettino.

Dubla, F. 1998. *Secchia, il PCI e il movimento del '68*. Rome: Datanews.

Dunchi, N. 1957. *Memorie partigiane*. Florence: La Nuova Italia.

Dusi, G. 1973. *Gallo rosso*. Padova: Marsilio.

Ellwood, D. 1975. *L'alleato nemico*. Milan: Feltrinelli.

————. 2005. Introduction to "The Never-Ending Liberation." *Journal of Modern Italian Studies* 10 (4): 385–95.

Enriques Agnoletti, E. 1954. Review of Roberto Battaglia, *Storia della Resistenza italiana*. *Il ponte* 10 (2): 322–25.

————. 1982. "Un saluto e non un addio." *Il ponte* (1–2): 3–9.

Etnasi, F., ed. 1966. *Donne italiane della Resistenza*. Milan: Editrice Il Calendario.

Evans, M., and K. Lunn. 1997. *War and Memory in the Twentieth Century*. Oxford: Berg.

Fabris, G. 1986. *Storia della Federazione Italiana Volontari della Libertà*. Padova: FIVL.

Faggi, V. 1981. *Corno alle scale*. Milan: All'insegna del pesce d'oro.

Falaschi, G. 1976. *La resistenza armata nella narrativa italiana*. Turin: Einaudi.

————, ed. 1984. *La letteratura partigiana in Italia, 1943–1945*. Rome: Riuniti.

Fallani, A. 1985–1986. *Note su quarant'anni di vita dell'ANPI provinciale di Firenze*. Unpublished diary.

Fantelli, G. E. 1965. *La Resistenza dei cattolici nel padovano*. Padova: Federazione italiana volontari della libertà.

Fanti, L. 1990. *Una storia di campagna: Vita e morte dei fratelli Cervi*. Milan: Camunia.

Fenoglio, B. 1952. *I ventitré giorni della città di Alba*. Einaudi: Turin.

————. 1959. *Primavera di bellezza*. Milan: Garzanti.

————. 1963. *Una questione privata*. Milan: Garzanti.

————. 1968. *Il partigiano Johnny*. Turin: Einaudi.

————. 1978. *Opere*. Edited by M. Corti. Turin: Einaudi.

————. 1992. *Romanzi e racconti*. Edited by D. Isella. Turin: Einaudi.

————. 1994. *Appunti partigiani*. Turin: Einaudi.

Ferretti, G. C. 1964. *Letteratura e ideologia: Bassani, Cassola, Pasolini*. Rome: Riuniti.

————. 1976. "La letteratura della Resistenza." In *Enciclopedia dell'antifascismo e della Resistenza*, volume 3, 332–35. Milan: La Pietra.

Finetti, U. 2004. *La resistenza cancellata*. Milan: Ares.

Fiorentino, F. 2002. "Bibliografia di e su Renzo De Felice." In *Renzo De Felice. Studi e testimonianze*, 333–506, edited by L. Goglia and R. Moro. Rome: Edizioni di Storia e Letteratura.

Floreanini, G. 1955. "Una donna nel governo dell'Ossola." *Rinascita* (4): 267–68.

Flores, M., and N. Gallerano. 1992. *Sul PCI. Un'interpretazione storica*. Bologna: Il Mulino.

Focardi, F. 2000. "La questione della punizione dei criminali di guerra in Italia dopo la fine del secondo conflitto mondiale." *Quellen und Forschungen aus italienischen Archiven und Bibliotheken* (80): 543–78.

————. 2005. *La guerra della memoria. La Resistenza nel dibattito politico italiano dal 1945 a oggi*. Rome: Laterza.

Fontana, S. 2001. *La grande menzogna*. Venice: Marsilio.

Foot, J. 1996. "The 'Left Opposition' and the Crisis: Rifondazione Comunista and La Rete." In *The New Italian Republic: From the Fall of the Berlin Wall to Berlusconi*, 173–88, edited by S. Gundle and S. Parker. London: Routledge.

———. 2009. *Italy's Divided Memory*. New York: Palgrave Macmillan.

Forgacs, D. 1999. "Fascism and Anti-Fascism Reviewed: Generations, History and Film in Italy after 1968." In *European memories of World War II*, 185–99, edited by H. Peitsch, C. Burdett, and C. Gorrara. New York: Berghahn.

———. 2000. *Rome, Open City*. London: BFI.

Fossà, A. 1964. *L'assalto al forte di Monte Crocetta: Romanzo per ragazzi*. Farigliano: N. Milano.

Franceschini, A. 1988. *Mara, Renata e io. Storia dei fondatori delle BR*. Milan: Mondadori.

Franceschini, D. 1998. *Porzus: La Resistenza lacerata*. Trieste: Istituto regionale per la storia del movimento di liberazione nel Friuli-Venezia Giulia.

Francescotti, R. 1966. *Il battaglione Gherlenda*. Turin: Paravia.

Francovich, C. 1958. Review of Oreste Barbieri, *Ponti sull'Arno*. *Il ponte* 14 (10): 1471–76.

———. 1961. *La Resistenza a Firenze*. Florence: La Nuova Italia.

Franzinelli, M. 2001. "La Resistenza e le provocazioni del Sessantotto." *L'Impegno* 21 (2). Available at http://www.storia900bivc.it/pagine/editoria/franzinelli201.html. Accessed September 12, 2010.

———. 2002. *Le stragi nascoste. L'armadio della vergogna: impunità e rimozione dei crimini di guerra nazifascisti 1943–2001*. Milan: Mondadori.

———. 2006. *L'amnistia Togliatti. 22 giugno 1946. Colpo di spugna sui crimini fascisti*. Milan: Mondadori.

———. 2010. *Il piano solo. I servizi segreti, il centro sinistra e il 'golpe' del 1964*. Milan: Mondadori.

Franzini, G. 1966. *Storia della Resistenza reggiana*. Reggio Emilia: ANPI.

Franzolin, U. 1992. *Nostra gente*. Rome: Edizioni Settimo Sigillo.

———. 1995. *Il repubblichino: Romanzo*. Rome: Settimo Sigillo.

Frullini, G. 1977. *Il partigiano Rocambole: Racconti ai ragazzi di un ex-partigiano: con indicazioni bibliografiche per la ricerca e il lavoro di gruppo nella scuola dell'obbligo*. Pistoia: Centro documentazione.

Fulvetti, G. 2009. *Uccidere i civili. Le stragi naziste in Toscana (1943–1945)*. Naples: L'Ancora del meditteraneo.

Gadola Beltrami, G. 1979. *Il capitano*. Florence: La Nuova Italia.

Gagliani, D., ed. 2000. *Donne guerra politica: Esperienze e memorie della Resistenza*. Bologna: Clueb.

———, ed. 2006. *Guerra, Resistenza, Politica. Storia di donne*. Reggio Emilia: Aliberti

Galassi, M. 1957. *Resistenza e 36. Garibaldi*. Rome: Riuniti.

Gallerano, N. 1986. "Critica e crisi del paradigma antifascista." *Problemi del socialismo* (7): 106–33.

———, ed. 1995. *L'uso pubblico della storia*. Milan: Franco Angeli.

———, ed. 1999a. *La Resistenza tra storia e memoria*. Milan: Mursia.

———. 1999b. *La verità della storia. Scritti sull'uso pubblico del passato*. Rome: Manifestolibri.

Galli, G. 1958. *Storia del partito comunista italiano*. Milan: Schwarz.

———. 1978. *Storia della democrazia cristiana*. Rome: Laterza.

Galli Della Loggia, E. 1996. *La morte della patria: la crisi dell'idea di nazione tra Resistenza, antifascismo e Repubblica*. Rome: Laterza.

Galmozzi, L. 1986. *Monumenti alla libertà. Antifascismo Resistenza e pace nei monumenti italiani dal 1945 al 1985*. Milan: La Pietra.

Gambino, A. 1975. *Storia del dopoguerra dalla liberazione al potere DC*. Rome: Laterza.

Ganapini, L. 1986. "Antifascismo tricolore e antifascismo di classe." *Problemi del socialismo* (7): 98–105.

———. 1999. *La repubblica delle camicie nere*. Milan: Garzanti.

———. 2007. "The Dark Side of Italian History 1943–1945." *Modern Italy* 12 (2): 205–23.

Gandolfi, F. 1960. *A Genova non si passa*. Milan: Edizioni Avanti.

Garosci, A. 1953. *Storia dei fuorusciti*. Bari: Laterza.

Gatto, A. 1947. *Il capo sulla neve: Liriche della Resistenza*. Milan: Toffaloni.

———. 1966. *La storia delle vittime*. Milan: Mondadori.

Gatt-Rutter, J. 1999. "The Aftermath of the Second World War." In *The Cambridge History of Italian Literature*, 531–37, edited by P. Brand and L. Pertile. Cambridge: Cambridge University Press.

Gennari, A. 1995. *Le ragioni del sangue*. Milan: Garzanti.

Germinario, F. 1999. *L'altra memoria. L'Estrema destra, Salò e la Resistenza*. Turin: Bollati Boringhieri.

Gervasoni, M. 2010. *Storia d'Italia degli anni ottanta*. Venice: Marsilio

Gervasutti, S. 1997. *Il giorno nero di Porzus*. Venice: Marsilio.

Ghigi, G. 2009. *La memoria inquieta: Cinema e Resistenza*. Venice: Cafoscarina.

Giannuli, A. 2009. *L'abuso pubblico della storia*. Parma: Guanda.

Giacobino, T. 1978. *Sta bona, Tecla*. Susegana: Giacobino.

Gildea, R. 1994. *The Past in French History*. New Haven, CT: Yale University Press.

Ginsborg, P. 1990. *A History of Contemporary Italy: Society and Politics, 1943–1988*. London: Penguin.

———. 1996. "Explaining Italy's Crisis." In *The New Italian Republic: From the Fall of the Berlin Wall to Berlusconi*, 19–39, edited by S. Gundle and S. Parker. London: Routledge.

———. 2003. *Italy and Its Discontents 1980–2001*. London: Penguin.

———. 2004. *Silvio Berlusconi: Television, Power and Patrimony*. London: Verso.

Giolitti, A. 1982. "L'itinerario politico di Tristano Codignola." *Il ponte* (11–12): 1117–26.

Giorgi, R. 1955. *Marzabotto parla*. Milan: Edizioni Avanti.

———. 1991. *Marzabotto parla*. Venice: Marsilio.

Giovannini, A. 1975. *I giorni dell'odio. Italia 1945*. Rome: Ciarrapico Editore.

Gobbi, R. 1992. *Il mito della Resistenza*. Milan: Rizzoli.

———. 1999. *Una revisione della Resistenza*. Milan: Bompiani.

Gorresio, V. 1963. *L'Italia a sinistra*. Milan: Rizzoli.

Gorrieri, E. 1966. *La repubblica di Montefiorino: Per una storia della Resistenza in Emilia*. Bologna: Il Mulino.

Governi, G. 1998. *Hai visto passare un gatto nero*. Venice: Marsilio.

Gozzini, G. 1998. *Hanno sparato a Togliatti*. Milan: Il Saggiatore.

Gozzini, G., and R. Martinelli. 1998. *Storia del Partito Comunista Italiano. Vol. 7: Dall'attentato a Togliatti all'VIII congresso*. Turin: Einaudi.

Gracci (Gracco), A. 1995. *Brigata Sinigaglia*. Naples: Laboratorio politico.

Grandi, A. 2000. *Feltrinelli. La dinastia, il rivoluzionario*. Milan: Baldini & Castoldi.

Grassi, G., ed. 1977. *Verso il governo del popolo: Atti e documenti del CLNAI 1943/1946*. Milan: Feltrinelli.

———, ed. 1993. *Resistenza e storia d'Italia. Quarant'anni di vita dell'Istituto nazionale e degli Istituti associati 1949–1989*. Milan: Franco Angeli.

Gremmo, R. 1995. *L'ultima Resistenza. Le ribellioni partigiane in Piemonte dopo la nascita della Repubblica (1946–1947)*. Edizioni ELF: Biella.

Gualtieri, R. 1995. *Togliatti e la politica estera: Dalla Resistenza al trattato di pace, 1943–1947*. Rome: Riuniti.

———. 2006. *L'Italia dal 1943 al 1992. DC e PCI nella storia della Repubblica*. Rome: Carocci.

Guerriero, C., and F. Rondinelli. 1996. *La volante rossa*. Rome: Datanews.

Guidetti Serra, B. 1977. *Compagne*. Turin: Einaudi.

Gundle, S. 1996. "La 'religione civile della Resistenza.' Cultura di massa e identità politica nell'Italia del dopoguerra." In *L'immagine della Resistenza in Europa: 1945–1960*, 1–38, edited by L. Cigognetti, L. Servetti, and P. Sorlin. Bologna: Il Nove.

———. 2000. "The civic religion of the Italian Resistance." *Modern Italy* 5 (2): 113–32.

Hainsworth, P. 1999. "Imagining Losers in Bufalino's *Diceria dell'untore.*" *European Memories of World War II*, 78–86, edited by H. Peitsch, C. Burdett, and C. Gorrara. New York: Berghahn.

Hammermann, G. 2004. *Gli internati militari italiani in Germania*. Bologna: Il Mulino.

Ignazi, P. 1992. *Dal PCI al PDS*. Bologna: Il Mulino.

Ingrao, P. 2006. *Volevo la luna*. Turin: Einaudi.

Isnenghi, M. 2007. *Dalla Resistenza alla desistenza. L'Italia del "Ponte" (1945–1947)*. Bari; Rome: Laterza.

Istituto centrale di statistica. 1957. *Morti e dispersi per cause belliche negli anni 1940–1945*. Rome: Istituto centrale di statistica.

Jones, T. 2003. *The Dark Heart of Italy*. London: Faber and Faber.

Katz, R. 1968. *Morte a Roma: il massacro delle Fosse Ardeatine*. Rome: Riuniti.

Katz, R. S., and P. Ignazi, eds. 1996. *Italian Politics: The Year of the Tycoon*, Vol. 10. Italian Politics, a Review. Boulder: Westview Press.

Kertzer, D. I. 1996. *Politics and Symbols: The Italian Communist Party and the Fall of Communism*. New Haven, CT: Yale University Press.

Klinkhammer, L. 1993. *L'occupazione tedesca in Italia 1943–1945*. Turin: Bollati Boringhieri.

———. 1997. *Stragi naziste in Italia. La guerra contro i civili (1943–44)*. Rome: Donzelli.

Lajolo, L. 1995. *I ribelli di Santa Libera: Storia di un'insurrezione partigiana: agosto 1946*. Turin: Edizioni Gruppo Abele.

Landy, M. 2000. *Italian film*. Cambridge: Cambridge University Press.

La Russa, V. 2002. *Il ministro Scelba*. Soveria Mannelli: Rubbettino.

Lazagna, G. 1966. *Ponte rotto: Testimonianza di un partigiano della divisione garibaldina Pinan Cichero*. Alessandria: Quaderni de Il Novese.

Legnani, M. 1968. *Politica e amministrazione nelle repubbliche partigiane: Studio e documenti*. Milan: Istituto nazionale per la storia del movimento di liberazione.

———. 1992. "A proposito di storia, stampa e pubblico. Le accoglienze alla 'guerra civile' di Claudio Pavone." *Italia contemporanea* (186): 119–24.

Legnani, M., C. Pavone, and F. Vendramini, eds. 1990. *Guerra, guerra di liberazione, guerra civile*. Milan: Franco Angeli.

Lepre, A. 1966. *La svolta di Salerno*. Rome: Riuniti.

———. 1993. *Storia della prima Repubblica: L'Italia dal 1942 al 1992*. Bologna: Il Mulino.

———. 1997. *L'anticomunismo e l'antifascismo in Italia*. Bologna: Il Mulino.

Levi, R. 1947. "L'azione economica e sociale dei CLN dell'alta Italia." *Il ponte* (11–12): 994–1000.

Libenzi, E. 1964. *Ragazzi della Resistenza*. Milan: Mursia.

Liucci, R. 1996. "Scrivere e ricordare Salò. La Repubblica sociale italiana tra storia, memoria e letteratura." *Studi piacentini* (20): 35–70.

Longo, L. 1947. *Un popolo alla macchia*. Milan: Mondadori.

———. 1954. *Sulla via dell'insurrezione nazionale*. Rome: Edizioni di Cultura Sociale.

———. 1955. Review of C. L. Ragghianti, *Disegno della liberazione italiana*. *Rinascita* (3): 188–90.

———. 1965. Editoriale. *Critica marxista* 3 (2): 3–5.

———. 1973. *I centri dirigenti del PCI nella Resistenza*. Rome: Riuniti.

————. 1975. *Chi ha tradito la Resistenza*. Rome: Riuniti.

Lucarelli, C. 1991. *L'estate torbida*. Palermo: Sellerio.

Lupo, S. 2004. "Antifascismo, anticomunismo e anti-antifascismo nell'Italia repubblicana." In *Antifascismo e identità europea*, 365–78, edited by A. De Bernardi and P. Ferrari. Rome: Carocci.

Luti, G., and S. Romagnoli, eds. 1975. *L'Italia partigiana*. Milan: Longanesi.

Luzzatto, S. 2004. *La crisi dell'antifascismo*. Turin: Einaudi.

Macaluso, E. 2003. *Cinquant'anni nel PCI*. Soveria Mannelli: Rubbettino.

Macchioni Jodi, R. 1967. *Carlo Cassola*. Florence: La Nuova Italia.

Mack Smith, D. 2000. "Mussolini: Reservations about Renzo De Felice's Biography." *Modern Italy* 5 (2): 193–210.

Macmillan, M. 2009. *The Uses and Abuses of History*. London: Profile.

Mafai, M. 1984. *L'uomo che sognava la lotta armata*. Milan: Rizzoli.

Magnanini, G. 1992. *Dopo la liberazione: Reggio Emilia, aprile 1945–settembre 1946*. Bologna: Analisi.

Malavasi, G. 1982. *L'antifascismo cattolico. Il movimento guelfo d'azione*. Rome: Lavoro.

Malgeri, F. 1988–1989. *Storia della Democrazia cristiana*. Rome: Cinque Lune.

Malvestiti, P. 1960. *Achtung! Banditi: Saggio politico sulla resistenza: per nozze Gulminelli-Rodolfi*. Milan: M. Gastaldi.

Malvezzi, P., and G. Pirelli, eds. 1952. *Lettere di condannati a morte della Resistenza italiana: 8 settembre 1943–25 aprile 1945*. Turin: Einaudi.

Mammarella, G. 1976. *Il partito comunista italiano 1945/1975: dalla liberazione al compromesso storico*. Florence: Vallecchi.

Mammone, A. 2006. "A Daily Revision of the Past: Fascism, Anti-Fascism, and Memory in Contemporary Italy." *Modern Italy* 11 (2): 211–26.

Manacorda, G. 1970. *Storia della letteratura italiana contemporanea 1940–1965*. Rome: Riuniti.

————. 1973. *Invito alla lettura di Carlo Cassola*. Milan: Mursia.

Marchesini Gobetti, A. 1956. *Diario partigiano*. Turin: Einaudi.

————. 1972. *Diario partigiano*. Turin: G. Einaudi.

Marchetti, A., and G. Tassinari. 1955. *La Resistenza nella letteratura: antologia*. Milan: edito dall'Associazione partigiani A. Di Dio.

Marcus, M. 1986. *Italian film in the light of Neorealism*. Princeton: Princeton University Press.

Marianelli, S. 1965. *La mia Resistenza*. Turin: Paravia.

Marino, G. C. 1991. *Guerra fredda e conflitto sociale in Italia*. Caltanisetta: S. Sciascia.

————. 1995. *La repubblica della forza: Mario Scelba e le passioni del suo tempo*. Milan: Franco Angeli.

Mariuzzo, A. 2010. "Stalin and the dove: Left pacifist language and choices of expression between the Popular Front and the Korean War (1948–1953)." *Modern Italy* 15(1): 21–35.

Martinelli, R. 1995. *Il partito nuovo dalla liberazione al 18 aprile*. Turin: Einaudi.

Martinelli, R., and M. L. Righi, eds. 1992. *La politica del partito comunista italiano nel periodo costituente: I verbali della direzione tra il V e il VI Congresso 1946–1948*. Rome: Editori Riuniti

Martini Mauri, E. 1968. *Partigiani penne nere: Boves, Val Maudagna, Val Casotto, le Langhe*. Milan: A. Mondadori.

Massone Muratti, L. 1959. *Frammenti del diario di una partigiana*. Udine: Tip. A. Pellegrini.

Mattioli, N. 1972. *Feltrinelli, morte a Segrate*. Modena: Settedidenari.

Mazzantini, C. 1995a [1986]. *A cercar la bella morte*. Venice: Marsilio.

————.1995b. *I balilla andarono a Salò*. Venice: Marsilio.

Mazzolari, P. 1965. *La Resistenza dei cristiani*. Vicenza: La locusta.

McLaughlin, M. 1998. *Italo Calvino*. Edinburgh: Edinburgh University Press.

Mencarelli, Paolo. 2009. "I libri dell' 'altra Italia.' Le edizioni Avanti! di Gianni Bosio 1953–1964." Unpublished dottorato di ricerca. University of Siena.

Meneghello, L. 1964. *I piccoli maestri*. Milan: Feltrinelli.

————. 1976. *I piccoli maestri*. Milan: Rizzoli.

Meneghetti, E. 1958. *La partigiana nuda e altre cante*. Milan: Edizioni Avanti.

Mercuri, L. 1958. Governo e Resistenza. *Il ponte* 14 (4): 602–3.

————. 1978. *Il movimento di unità popolare*. Rome: Carecas.

Mezzana, D. 1997. *Memoria storica della Resistenza nelle nuove generazioni*. Milan: Mursia.

Miccichè, L. 1995. *Cinema italiano: Gli anni sessanta e oltre*. Venice: Marsilio.

Miccoli, G., G. Neppi Modona, and P. Pombeni, eds. 2001. *La grande cesura. La memoria della guerra e della resistenza nella vita europea del dopoguerra*. Bologna: Il Mulino.

Milan, M. 1954. *Fuoco in pianura*. Rome: Edizioni di Cultura Sociale.

Milan, M., and F. Vighi, eds. 1955. *La resistenza al fascismo*. Feltrinelli: Milan.

Milanini, C. 1997. "Calvino e la Resistenza: l'identità in gioco." *Letteratura e Resistenza*, 173–91, edited by A. Bianchini, and Lolli Francesco. Bologna: CLUEB.

Miller, J.E. 1999. "Who chopped down that cherry tree? The Italian Resistance in history and politics, 1945–1998." *Journal of Modern Italian Studies* 4 (1): 37–54.

Montanari, O. 1998. *Gli innocenti: Testi integrali delle sentenze con l'assoluzione di Germano Nicolini ed Egidio Baraldi*. Reggio Emilia: Tecnograf.

Monti, A., and E. Sturani. 1963. "Epistolary Exchange." *Belfagor* 18 (3): 353–59.

Monticelli, S. 2000. "National Identity and the Representation of Italy at War: The Case of *Combat Film*." *Modern Italy* 5 (2): 133–46.

Morgan, P. 2007. *The Fall of Mussolini*. Oxford: Oxford University Press.

Morgan, S. 2000. "The Schio Killings: A Case Study of Partisan Violence in Post-War Italy." *Modern Italy* 5 (2): 147–60.

————. 2002. *Rappresaglie dopo la Resistenza. L'eccidio di Schio tra guerra civile e guerra fredda*. Milan: Bruno Mondadori.

Morris, P. 1999. "A Woman's Perspective: Autobiography and History in Giovanna Zangrandi's Resistance Narratives". In *European Memories of the Second World War*, 35–43, edited by H. Peitsch, C. Burdett, and C. Gorrara. New York/Oxford: Berghahn Books.

————. 2000. *Giovanna Zangrandi. Una vita in romanzo*. Cierre: Sommacampagna.

Morviducci, M. 1995. "Oggetto: 25 aprile. Anniversario della Liberazione nelle circolari ministeriali e nell'esperienza di una scuola della Toscana." In *La Resistenza europea nella scuola*, 27–48, edited by A. Ventura. Manduria: Lacaita.

Moss, H. 1977. "The Existentialism of Carlo Cassola." *Italica* (54): 381–98.

Movimento giovanile della democrazia cristiana. 1955. *Valori morali della Resistenza italiana: Alcune lettere di condannati a morte*. Rome.

Nahoum, I. 1981. *Esperienze di un comandante partigiano*. Milan: La Pietra.

Napolitano, G. 1994. "La 'svolta di Salerno.'" *Critica marxista* (5): 66–71.

Natoli, C., G. De Luna, and G. Santomassimo. 2008. "Gli spazi bianchi di Giaime Pintor." *Passato e presente* (74): 15–28.

Natta, A. 1971. "La Resistenza e la formazione del 'partito nuovo.'" In *Problemi di storia del Partito comunista italiano*, 57–83. Rome: Riuniti.

————. 1997. *L'altra Resistenza. I militari italiani internati in Germania*. Turin: Einaudi.

————. 1999. "Eravamo già lontani dalle macerie." *Critica marxista* (5): 9–12.

Nenni, P. 1981. *Tempi di guerra fredda. Diari 1943–1956*. Milan: Sugarco.

————. 1983. *I conti con la storia. Diari 1967–1971*. Milan: Sugarco.

Neri Serneri, S., ed. 1988. *Il partito socialista nella Resistenza. I documenti e la stampa clandestina*. Pisa: Nistri-Lischi.

———. 1995. *Resistenza e democrazia dei partiti. I socialisti nell'Italia del 1943–1945*. Manduria: Lacaita.

Nicolini, G. 1997. *Nessuno vuole la verità*. Montecavolo: Dea Cagna.

Noce, T. 1974. *Rivoluzionaria professionale*. Milan: La Pietra.

Novelli, D., and N. Tranfaglia. 1988. *Vite sospese. Le generazioni del terrorismo*. Milan: Garzanti.

Nozzoli, G. 1957. *Quelli di Bulow: Cronache della 28. Brigata Garibaldi Roma*. Rome: Riuniti.

Oliva, G. 1994. *I vinti e i liberati: 8 settembre 1943–25 aprile 1945: Storia di due anni*. Milan: A. Mondadori.

Onofri, N. S. 1994. *Il triangolo rosso (1943–1947)*. Rome: Sapere.

Orfei, C., and C. Starita. 1995. "La Resistenza nei manuali di storia delle scuole medie, 1962–1971." In *La Resistenza europea nella scuola*, 73–112, edited by A. Ventura. Manduria: Lacaita.

Orlando, F. 1989. *Ma non fu una legge truffa*. Rome: Cinque Lune.

Orsina, G. 2007. *Translatio imperii*. "La crisi del governo Parri e i liberali." In *1945–1946. Le origini della Repubblica. Vol. II Questione istituzionale e costruzione del sistema politico democratico*, 210–56, edited by G. Monina. Soveria Mannelli: Rubbettino.

Ostellino, C. 1980. "Aldo dice 26 X 1." *Rinascita* (21): 2.

Ottolenghi Minerbi, M. 1965. *O partigiano portami via: Romanzo per ragazzi*. Farigliano: N. Milano.

Pacini, G. 2008. *Le organizzazioni paramilitari nell'Italia repubblicana (1945–1991)*. Rome: Prospettiva.

Padoan, G. 1966. *Abbiamo lottato insieme: Partigiani italiani e sloveni al confine orientale*. Udine: Del Bianco.

———. 2000. *Porzus: Strumentalizzazione e realtà storica*. Monfalcone: Edizioni della Laguna.

Paggi, L., ed. 1996. *Storia e memoria di un massacro ordinario*. Rome: Manifestolibri.

———, ed. 1999. *Le memorie della repubblica*. Florence: La Nuova Italia.

———, ed. 2004. *L'eccidio del duomo di San Miniato: La memoria e la ricerca storica, 1944–2004*. San Miniato: Comune.

Pajetta, G. C. 1955. Review of Alcide Cervi, *I miei sette figli. Rinascita* (10): 652–54.

———. 1965. Editoriale. *Rinascita* (17): 1.

———. 1966. Obituary of Augusto Monti. *Rinascita* (29): 16.

———. 1986. *Il ragazzo rosso va alla guerra*. Milan: Mondadori.

Pansa, G. 1959. "Vecchio e nuovo nella storiografia della Resistenza." *Rivista storica del socialismo* (7–8): 710–22.

———. 1964. *Viva l'Italia libera: Storia e documenti del primo Comitato militare del CLN regionale piemontese*. Turin: Istituto per la Storia della Resistenza in Piemonte.

———. 1965. *La Resistenza in Piemonte: Guida bibliografica 1943–1963*. Turin: G. Giappichelli.

———. 1967. *Guerra partigiana tra Genova e il Po: La Resistenza in provincia di Alessandria*. Bari: Laterza.

———. 1994. *Ma l'amore no*. Milan: Sperling & Kupfer.

———. 1995. *Siamo stati così felici*. Milan: Sperling & Kupfer.

———. 1996. *I nostri giorni proibiti*. Milan: Sperling & Kupfer.

———. 1998. "Intervista con l'autore a cura di Roberto Botta." In *Guerra partigiana tra Genova e il Po: La Resistenza in provincia di Alessandria*, 511–567. Bari: Laterza.

———. 2002. *I figli dell'aquila*. Milan: Sperling & Kupfer.

———. 2003. *Il sangue dei vinti*. Milan: Sperling & Kupfer.

———. 2005. *Sconosciuto 1945*. Sperling & Kupfer.

———. 2006. *La grande bugia*. Milan: Sperling & Kupfer.

————. 2007. *I gendarmi della memoria*. Milan: Sperling & Kupfer.

————. 2008. *I tre inverni della paura*. Milan: Rizzoli.

————. 2009. *Il revisionista*. Milan: Rizzoli.

————. 2010. *I vinti non dimenticano*. Milan: Rizzoli.

Panvini, G. 2009. *Ordine nero, guerriglia rossa: la violenza politica nell'Italia degli anni Sessanta e Settanta, 1966–1975*. Turin: Einaudi.

Paoletti, P. 2000. *San Miniato. Tutta la verità sulla strage*. Milan: Mursia.

Paoluzi, A. 1956. *La letteratura della Resistenza*. Rome: Edizioni 5 Lune.

Papa, C., ed. 1975. *La dimensione donna nella Resistenza umbra: primi risultati di una ricerca condotta nella provincia di Perugia*. 1975. Perugia: Tip. Guerra.

Parca, G. 1953. *Il piccolo ribelle*. Rome: Edizioni ANPI.

Parisella, A. 2005. *Cultura cattolica e resistenza nell'Italia repubblicana*. Rome: AVE.

Parri, F. 1973. *Due mesi con i nazisti*. Rome: Carecas.

————. 1976. *Scritti 1915–1975*. Milan: Feltrinelli.

————. 1990. *Discorsi parlamentari*. Rome: Senato della Repubblica.

Partito comunista italiano. 1963. *Il comunismo italiano nella seconda guerra mondiale: Relazione e documenti presentati dalla direzione del partito al 5. Congresso del Partito comunista italiano*. Rome: Riuniti.

Passerini, L. 1988. *Autoritratto di gruppo*. Florence: Giunti.

————. 1999. "Memories of Resistance, Resistances of Memory." In *European memories of World War II*, 288–96, edited by H. Peitsch, C. Burdett, and C. Gorrara. New York: Berghahn.

Patelli, C. 1965. *Pattuglia eroica: Romanzo per ragazzi*. Farigliano: N. Milano.

Pavone, C. 1985. "Appunti sul problema dei reduci." In *L'altro dopoguerra. Roma e il sud 1943–1945*, 89–106, edited by N. Gallerano. Milan: Franco Angeli.

————. 1991. *Una guerra civile: Saggio storico sulla moralità nella Resistenza*. Turin: Bollati Boringhieri.

————. 1995. *Alle origini della repubblica: Scritti su fascismo, antifascismo e continuità dello stato*. Turin: Bollati Boringhieri.

————. 2007. *Prima lezione di storia contemporanea*. Rome: Laterza.

Pecchioli, U. 1985. "Perché si è riaperto il dibattito su fascismo e antifascismo." *Rinascita* (8): 8–9.

Pedroni, P. N. 1985. *Existence as Theme in Carlo Cassolà's Fiction*. New York: Peter Lang.

Pedullà, G., ed. 2005. *Racconti della Resistenza*. Turin: Einaudi.

Peli, S. 1999. *La Resistenza difficile*. Milan: Franco Angeli.

————. 2004. *La Resistenza in Italia. Storia e critica*. Turin: Einaudi.

————. 2006. *Storia della Resistenza in Italia*. Turin: Einaudi.

————. 2007. "L'eredità della Resistenza." In *1945–1946. Le origini della Repubblica*, 165–88, edited by G. Monina. Soveria Mannelli: Rubbettino.

Permoli, P., ed. 1960. *Lezioni sull'antifascismo*. Bari: Laterza.

Perry, A. 2001. *Il santo partigiano martire: la retorica del sacrificio nelle biografie commemorative*. Ravenna: Longo.

Pesce, G. 1967. *Senza tregua: La guerra dei GAP*. Milan: Feltrinelli.

Pestalozza, L. 1955. "Musica ispirata dalla Resistenza." *Il ponte* 11 (4–5): 687–95.

Petrini, E. 1946. *Piccole fiamme verdi*. Brescia: La scuola.

Petter, G. 1953. *La valle impenetrabile*. Rome: ANPI.

————. 1993. *I giorni dell'ombra*. Milan: Garzanti.

————. 1995. *Ci chiamavano banditi*. Florence: Giunti.

————. 2004. *Una banda senza nome*. Florence: Giunti.

Pezzino, P. 1997. *Anatomia di un massacro. Controversia sopra una strage tedesca*. Bologna: Il Mulino.

————. 2005. "The Italian Resistance between History and Memory." *Journal of Modern Italian Studies* 10 (4): 396–412.

————. 2007. "The German Military Occupation of Italy and the War against Civilians." *Modern Italy* 12 (2): 173–88.

————. 2008. *Sant'Anna di Stazzema. Storia di una strage.* Bologna: Il Mulino.

————. 2010. "'Experts in truth.' The politics of retribution in Italy and the role of historians." *Modern Italy* 15(3): 349–63.

Picchio, C. 1965. *Scarola.* Florence: Marzocco.

————. 1980. *Freedom Fighter.* Oxford: Oxford University Press.

Piffer, T. 2005. *Il banchiere della Resistenza. Alfredo Pizzoni, il protagonista cancellato dalla guerra di liberazione.* Milan: Mondadori.

————. 2010. *Gli alleati e la Resistenza italiana.* Bologna: Il Mulino.

Piretti, M. S. 2003. *La legge truffa: Il fallimento dell'ingegneria politica.* Bologna: Il Mulino.

Pisanò, G. 1962. *Sangue chiama sangue.* Milan: Ediz. Pidola.

————. 1965. *Storia della guerra civile in Italia.* Milan: FPE.

Pisanò, G., and P. Pisanò. 1992. *Il triangolo della morte.* Mursia: Milan.

Piscitelli, E. 1965. *Storia della resistenza romana.* Bari: Laterza.

————. 1975. *Da Parri a De Gasperi: Storia del dopoguerra, 1945–1948.* Milan: Feltrinelli.

Pistillo, M. 1998. *Fascismo—Antifascismo—Resistenza. Mussolini—Gramsci. "La guerra civile 1943–1945" di Renzo De Felice.* Manduria: Lacaita.

Pivato, S. 2005. *Bella ciao. Canto e politica nella storia d'Italia.* Rome: Laterza.

————. 2007. *Vuoti di memoria. Usi e abusi della storia nella vita pubblica italiana.* Rome: Laterza.

Pizzinelli, C. 1982. *Scelba.* Milan: Longanesi.

Pizzoni, A. 1993. *Alla guida del CLNAI: Memorie per i figli.* Turin: G. Einaudi.

————. 1995. *Alla guida del CLNAI: Memorie per i figli.* Bologna: Il Mulino.

Poggio, P. P., ed. 1986. *La Repubblica sociale italiana, 1943–45: atti del convegno, Brescia 4–5 ottobre 1985.* Brescia: Fondazione Luigi Micheletti.

Polese Remaggi, L. 2001. *Il ponte di Calamandrei, 1945–1956.* Florence: L. S. Olschki.

————. 2004. *La nazione perduta: Ferruccio Parri nel Novecento italiano.* Bologna: Il Mulino.

Portelli, A. 1999. *L'ordine è già stato eseguito.* Rome: Donzelli.

Preti, A. 1994. *Sabbiuno di Paderno. Dicembre 1944.* Bologna: University Press Bologna.

Preziosi, E., ed. 2007. *Ribelli per l'amore. I cattolici e la Resistenza.* Soveria Mannelli: Rubbettino.

Primieri, C. 1955. "La Resistenza: Il contributo delle Forze Armate alla Guerra di Liberazione." In *Il secondo risorgimento: nel decennale della Resistenza e del ritorno alla democrazia, 1945–1955*, 181–261. Rome: Istituto Poligrafico dello Stato.

Quaglierello, G. 2003. *La legge elettorale del 1953.* Bologna: Il Mulino.

Quazza, G. 1966. "Il problema storico." In *Il governo del C.L.N. Atti del Convegno dei Comitati di liberazione nazionale*, 3–72, edited by. G. Quazza, L. Valiani, and E. Volterra. Turin: Giappichelli.

————. 1976. *Resistenza e storia d'Italia: Problemi e ipotesi di ricerca.* Milan: Feltrinelli.

————. 1990. "L'antifascismo nella storia italiana del Novecento." *Italia contemporanea* (178): 5–16.

Ragghianti, C. L. 1954. *Disegno della liberazione italiana.* Pisa: Nistri-Lischi.

Ranzato, G. 1997. *Il linciaggio di Carretta: Roma 1944.* Milan: Il Saggiatore.

Rapini, A. 2005. *Antifascismo e cittadinanza. Giovani, identità e memorie nell'Italia repubblicana.* Bologna: Bononia University Press.

Rapone, L. 2000. "Antifascismo e storia d'Italia." In *Fascismo e antifascismo: Rimozioni, revisioni, negazioni*, 219–40, edited by E. Collotti. Rome: Laterza.

Ravagli, V., and Wu Ming. 2000. *Asce di guerra.* Milan: Marco Tropea.

Re, L. 1990. *Calvino and the Age of Neorealism: Fables of Estrangement*. Stanford: Stanford University Press.

Redazione materiali per una nuova sinistra, ed. 1988. *Il Sessantotto: la stagione dei movimenti, 1960–1979*. Rome: Edizioni Associate.

Repaci, A. 1961. *Dio e popolo: antologia del Risorgimento e della Resistenza*. Turin: Bottega d'Erasmo.

Revelli, N. 1994. *Il disperso di Marburg*. Turin: Einaudi.

Ricci, A. G., ed. 1994–1999. *Verbali del consiglio dei ministri: Luglio 1943-maggio 1948*. Rome: Presidenza del consiglio dei ministri.

Ricciardi, A. 2007. *Leo Valiani. Gli anni della formazione. Tra socialismo, comunismo e rivoluzione democratica*. Milan: Franco Angeli.

Rodotà, C. 1992. *Storia della legge truffa*. Rome: Edizioni Associate.

Rogari, S. 2006. *Antifascismo, Resistenza, Costituzione*. Milan: Franco Angeli.

Romano, T., and G. Solza, eds. 1960. *Canti della Resistenza italiana*. Milan: Edizioni Avanti.

Ronchi Della Rocca, I. 1965. *Ricordi di un partigiano: La Resistenza nel Braidese*. Turin: I.R.D.R.

Rosengarten, F. 1968. *The Italian Anti-Fascist Press (1919–1945): From the Legal Opposition Press to the Underground Newspapers of World War II*. Cleveland: Press of Case Western Reserve University.

Rotondo, F. 1995. "Da Pin a Rosa Bianca con occhi di bambini." *Sfoglialibro* 8 (3–4): 10–16.

Rousso, H. 1991. *The Vichy Syndrome: History and Memory in France since 1944*. Cambridge MA: Harvard University Press.

———. 2002. *The Haunting Past: History, Memory and Justice in Contemporary France*. Philadelphia: University of Pennsylvania Press.

Rusconi, G. E. 1993. *Se cessiamo di essere una nazione*. Il Mulino: Bologna.

———. 1995. *Resistenza e postfascismo*. Bologna: Il Mulino.

Sabbioni, L. 2002. *Marzabotto, diario del perdono e della rabbia*. Bologna: Lupo.

Sacco, E. 1964. *Il partigiano Marco: Racconto per ragazzi*. Farigliano: N. Milano.

Saccone, E. 1988. *Fenoglio: I testi, l'opera*. Turin: Einaudi.

Saitta, A. 1961. *Dal fascismo alla Resistenza. Profilo storico e documenti*. Florence: La Nuova Italia.

Salvadori, M. 1955. *Storia della Resistenza italiana*. Venice: N. Pozza.

Santomassimo, G. 2003. "La memoria pubblica dell'antifascismo." In *L'Italia repubblicana nella crisi degli anni settanta*, 137–71, edited by F. Lussana and G. Marramao. Soveria Mannelli: Rubbettino.

———. 2004. *Antifascismo e dintorni*. Rome: Manifestolibri.

Saragat, G. 1965. *Messaggio del Capo dello Stato agli italiani: Milano, 9 maggio 1965*. Rome: Litostampa Nomentana.

Savona, A. V., and M. L. Straniero, eds. 1985. *Canti della Resistenza italiana*. Milan: Rizzoli.

Scacherl, B. 1965. "Tutta Torino alla festa d'aprile." *Rinascita* (4): 28.

Scappini, R. 1981. *Da Empoli a Genova: 1945*. Milan: La Pietra.

Scoppola, P. 1991. *La repubblica dei partiti: Profilo storico della democrazia in Italia, 1945–1990*. Bologna: Il Mulino.

———. 1995. *25 aprile: liberazione*. Turin: Einaudi.

Scroccu, G. 2008. *La passione di un socialista: Sandro Pertini e il Psi dalla Liberazione agli anni del centro-sinistra*. Manduria: Lacaita.

Secchia, P. 1954a. *I comunisti e l'insurrezione: 1943–1945*. Rome: Edizioni di Cultura Sociale.

———. 1954b. *Il programma della Resistenza ed il governo Scelba, 23 Feb. 1954*. Rome: Bardi.

———. 1959. *Resistenza e risorgimento*. Biella: ANPI.

————. 1960. *La Resistenza e la grande svolta: Nel 15. anniversario della liberazione di Ravenna.* Rome: Tip. NAVA.

————. 1963. *Aldo dice: 26 X 1: cronistoria del 25 aprile 1945.* Milan: G. Feltrinelli.

————. 1973. *La Resistenza accusa: 1945–1973.* Milan: G. Mazzotta.

————. 1979. *Fondazione Giangiacomo Feltrinelli. Annali. Archivio Pietro Secchia 1945– 1973.* Milan: Feltrinelli.

Secchia, P., and F. Frassati. 1962. *La Resistenza e gli alleati.* Milan: Feltrinelli.

————. 1965. *Storia della Resistenza italiana: La guerra di liberazione in Italia 1943–1945.* Rome: Riuniti.

Secchia, P., and C. Moscatelli. 1958. *Il Monte Rosa è sceso a Milano: La Resistenza nel Biellese, nella Valsesia e nella Valdossola.* Turin: Einaudi.

Sega, M. T., ed. 2004. *La partigiana veneta. Arte e memoria della Resistenza.* Portogruaro: Nuova dimensione.

Semi, F. 1961. *La Resistenza italiana: Breve sintesi storica ad uso dei licei e degli istituti magistrali e tecnici.* Turin: SEI.

Seppia, E. 1965. *Il ragazzo rana: Romanzo per ragazzi.* Farigliano: N. Milano.

Serafini, G. 1981. *I ribelli della montagna Amiata 1948: Anatomia di una rivolta.* Montepulciano: Editori del Grifo.

Serena, A. 1990. *I giorni di Caino: Il dramma dei vinti nei crimini ignorati dalla storia ufficiale.* Padova: Panda.

Serri, M. 2002. *Il breve viaggio. Giaime Pintor nella Weimar nazista.* Venice: Marsilio.

Sessi, F. 2000. *Nome di battaglia: Diavolo. L'omicidio di Don Pessina e la persecuzione giudiziaria contro il partigiano Germano Nicolini.* Venice: Marsilio.

Setta, S. 1975. *L'Uomo qualunque 1944–1948.* Rome: Laterza.

Sgorlon, C. 1997. *La malga di Sir.* Milan: Mondadori.

Silj, A. 1977. *"Mai più senza fucile!" alle origini dei NAP e delle BR.* Florence: Vallecchi.

Sircana, G. 1977. *Momenti dell' "anti-Resistenza" (un dibattito parlamentare).* Rome: Tip. Proietti.

Slaughter, J. 1997. *Women and the Italian Resistance, 1943–1945.* Denver: Arden Press.

Slowey, G. 1991. "Songs of the partisans." *Tuttitalia* (3): 2–9.

Soccorso Rosso. 1976. *Brigate Rosse. Che cosa hanno fatto, che cosa hanno detto, che cosa se ne è detto.* Milan: Feltrinelli.

Sogno, E. 1995. *Guerra senza bandiera.* Bologna: Il Mulino.

Sogno, E., and A. Cazzullo. 2000. *Testamento di un anticomunista: dalla Resistenza al golpe bianco.* Milan: Mondadori.

Solaro, G., ed. 2008. *Il mondo di Piero. Un ritratto a più voci.* Milan: Franco Angeli.

Sorlin, P. 1987. "Di qua e di là delle Alpi: com'è stata rappresentata la Resistenza." In *Cinema, storia, Resistenza 1944–1985,* 57–73. Milan: Franco Angeli.

Spaziani, O. 1965. *Il messaggio.* Farigliano: N. Milano.

Spriano, P. 1966. "L'Italia partigiana." *Rinascita* (31): 21.

Squarzina, L. 1959. *Teatro.* Bari: Laterza.

Staron, J. 2007. *Fosse Ardeatine e Marzabotto. Storia e memoria di due stragi tedesche.* Bologna: Il Mulino.

Storchi, M. 1995. *Uscire dalla guerra. Ordine pubblico e forze politiche Modena 1945–1946.* Milan: Franco Angeli.

————. 1998. *Combattere si può vincere bisogna: La scelta della violenza fra Resistenza e dopoguerra (Reggio Emilia 1943–1946).* Venice: Marsilio.

————. 2005. *Sangue al bosco del Lupo. Partigiani che uccidono partigiani. La storia di "Azor."* Reggio Emilia: Aliberti.

————. 2007. "Post-War Violence in Italy: A Struggle for Memory." *Modern Italy* 12 (2): 237–50.

————. 2008. *Il sangue dei vincitori: Saggio sui crimini fascisti e i processi del dopoguerra, 1945–46*. Reggio Emilia: Aliberti.

Sturani, L., ed. 1951. *Antologia della Resistenza*. Turin: Centro del Libro Popolare.

————. 1953. *Una storia vera*. Rome: Edizioni ANPI.

————. 1966. *I partigiani della ciar*. Turin: Paravia.

Tamburrano, G. 1990. *Storia e cronaca del centro-sinistra*. Milan: Rizzoli.

Tarizzo, D. 1969. *Come scriveva la Resistenza: Filologia della stampa clandestina 1943–1945*. Florence: La Nuova Italia.

Taviani, P. E. 1956. *Breve storia dell'insurrezione di Genova*. Rome: AGI.

————. 1968. *Breve storia dell'insurrezione di Genova*. Rome: OPI.

————. 1988. *Pittaluga racconta: Romanzo di fatti veri 1943–45*. Genoa: ECIG.

————. 1994. *Donne nella Resistenza*. Rome: Civitas.

————. 2002. *Politica e memoria d'uomo*. Bologna: Il Mulino.

————. 2005. *Discorsi parlamentari*. Bologna: Il Mulino.

Tedesco, L. 2007. *La Resistenza ritrovata. Interpretazione etico-religiosa, guerra dei simboli e uso pubblico della storia*. Rome: Aracne.

Tobagi, W. 1978. *La rivoluzione impossibile*. Milan: Il Saggiatore.

Togliatti, P. 1952. "Postilla." *Rinascita* (4): 249–50.

————. 1953. "Una storia della Resistenza italiana." *Rinascita* (12): 678–80.

Torcellan, N. 1980. "La Resistenza." In *La stampa italiana dalla Resistenza agli anni settanta*, 91–167, edited by G. De Luna, N. Torcellan, and P. Murialdi. Rome: Laterza.

Tranfaglia, N. 1985. "L'antifascismo non è alle nostre spalle." *Rinascita* (11): 8–9.

————. 2003. *La transizione italiana. Storia di un decennio*. Milan: Garzanti.

Troilo, C. 2005. *La guerra di Troilo. Novembre 1947: l'occupazione della prefettura di Milano, ultima trincea della Resistenza*. Soveria Mannelli: Rubbettino.

Trombadori, A. 1953. "L'unità della Resistenza e il voto del 7 giugno." *Rinascita* (6): 345–47.

Troude-Chastenet, P. 1999. "La Francia e Vichy: Un passato che non vuole passare." *Critica marxista* (1–2): 68–73.

Tumiati, L. 1976. *Racconti della Resistenza europea*. Florence: La Nuova Italia.

Turi, G. 1996. "Rosso e nero, rien ne va plus." *Passato e presente* (37): 129–34.

Uboldi, R. 1982. *Il cittadino Sandro Pertini*. Milan: Rizzoli.

Ugolini, L. 1966. *Il romanzo della mia terra*. Turin: Paravia.

————. 1967. *Quei giorni*. Milan: Bietti.

Valdrè, L. 1964. *La banda di Ringo: Racconto per ragazzi*. Farigliano: N. Milano.

Valiani, L. 1947. *Tutte le strade conducono a Roma: Diario di un uomo nella guerra di un popolo*. Florence: La Nuova Italia.

————. 1949. *L'avvento di De Gasperi: Tre anni di politica italiana*. Turin: De Silva.

————. 1982. *L'Italia di De Gasperi (1945–1954)*. Florence: Le Monnier.

————. 2005. *Discorsi parlamentari*. Bologna: Il Mulino.

Vento, S. 1981. "Gli anni Sessanta a Genova." *Classe* (19): 176–187.

Ventrone, A. 2008. *La cittadinanza repubblicana: Come cattolici e comunisti hanno costruito la democrazia italiana, 1943–1948*. Bologna: Il Mulino.

Ventura, A. 1984. "Il problema delle origini del terrorismo di sinistra." In *Terrorismi in Italia*, 73–149, edited by D. Della Porta. Bologna: Il Mulino.

Venturi, F. 1996. *La lotta per la libertà. Scritti politici*. Edited by L. Casalino. Turin: Einaudi.

Vercelli, C. 2005. "Cinema resistente: Uno sguardo d'insieme sulla raffigurazione della Resistenza dal dopoguerra ad oggi." *Asti contemporanea* (11): 303–88.

Viganò, R. 1949. *L'Agnese va a morire*. Turin: Einaudi.

————. 1955. *Donne della Resistenza*. Bologna: STEB.

————. 1976. *Matrimonio in brigata*. Milan: Vangelista.

Villani, S. 1999. *L'eccidio di Schio: Luglio 1945: Una strage inutile*. Mursia: Milan.

Vinciguerra, R. 1978. *Elisa: La partigiana di Monza ed i suoi compagni*. Monza: Tipo-litografia Provelli.

Vittoria, A. 2006. *Storia del PCI 1921–1991*. Rome: Carocci.

Vittorini, E. 1945. *Uomini e no: Romanzo*. Milan: Bompiani.

Vivarelli, R. 2000. *La fine di una stagione 1943–1945*. Bologna: Il Mulino.

Voulgaris, Y. 1998. *L'Italia del centro-sinistra: 1960–1968*. Rome: Carocci.

Vuga, F. 1961. *La zona libera di Carnia e l'occupazione cosacca (luglio-ottobre 1944)*. Udine: Del Bianco.

Wagstaff, C. 1996. "Il cinema europeo e la Resistenza." In *L'immagine della Resistenza in Europa: 1945–1960*, 39–61, edited by L. Cigognetti, L. Servetti, and P. Sorlin. Bologna: Il Nove.

Watson, D. 1996. "The Representation of Reality in Italo Calvino's *racconti partigiani*." *Canadian Journal of Italian Studies* (19): 1–18.

Willan, P. 1991. *Puppet Masters. The Political Use of Terrorism in Italy*. London: Constable.

Zagarrio, V. 1998. *Cinema italiano anni novanta*. Venice: Marsilio.

Zangrandi, G. 1963. *I giorni veri*. Milan: Mondadori.

Zoli, A. 1959. *Acqua limacciosa sotto "Ponti sull'Arno."* Florence: Industria tipografica fiorentina.

Index